Pierrot and his world

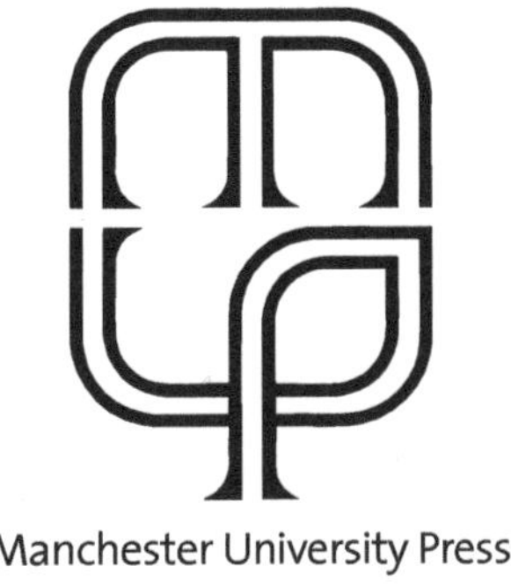

Manchester University Press

Pierrot and his world

Art, theatricality, and the marketplace in France, 1697–1945

Marika Takanishi Knowles

Manchester University Press

Published by Manchester University Press
Oxford Road, Manchester M13 9PL

www.manchesteruniversitypress.co.uk

British Library Cataloguing-in-Publication Data
A catalogue record for this book is available from the British Library

ISBN 978 1 5261 7409 3 hardback
ISBN 978 1 5261 9471 8 paperback

First published 2024
Paperback published 2026

The publisher has no responsibility for the persistence or accuracy of URLs for
any external or third-party internet websites referred to in this book, and does not
guarantee that any content on such websites is, or will remain, accurate or appropriate.

EU authorised representative for GPSR:
Easy Access System Europe – Mustamäe tee 50, 10621 Tallinn, Estonia
gpsr.requests@easproject.com

Typeset in 10/12 Apolline Std by
Cheshire Typesetting Ltd, Cuddington, Cheshire

Contents

Plates

14 Nadar and Adrien Tournachon, *Pierrot the photographer*, 1854–55. Salted paper print, 27.3 × 20.1 cm. Musée Carnavalet, Paris.
15 Magic lantern slide with two levers, *Pierrot says bonsoir*, late nineteenth century. Painted glass, 28.1 × 15.3 cm. Cinémathèque française, Paris.
16 Jules Chéret, *Pantomimes lumineuses, théâtre optique de E. Reynaud*, 1892. Coloured lithograph, 88 × 124.6 cm. Rijksmuseum, Amsterdam.

Figures

Introduction

The first time Pierrot appeared on the French stage, he longed for ribbons. This was in 1665, when the playwright Molière introduced a bumbling peasant named Pierrot into his re-telling of the tale of Don Juan, a suave and aristocratic womaniser. In a lengthy monologue – strikingly long for a character whose primary function is comic relief – Pierrot describes watching Don Juan get dressed in a lacy chemise, be-ribboned silk stockings and high-heeled shoes, and garments shot through with gold thread. Pierrot pretends to be indignant, but he protests too much. In fact, he is awestruck. While Pierrot continues to ponder Don Juan's extraordinary attire, the Don seduces his girlfriend.

The history of Pierrot, a theatrical stock character who also enjoyed an enduring life in visual representation, has tended to focus on the second part of this story – Pierrot as a foolish cuckold who always ends up alone and who becomes a source of melancholy identification for artists, poets, and loners. In this book, I want to focus on the first part of the story, when Pierrot discovers the miracle of ribbons. As his career as a stock character progressed, Pierrot tended to turn up in the places where ribbons and articles of dress were sold. He appeared on the stages of the eighteenth-century Parisian fairgrounds, seasonal markets featuring boutiques selling fabric and trimming. As a valet in the eighteenth-century theatre, Pierrot begs his master for cast-offs. In the nineteenth-century pantomime, Pierrot steals the garment of a nobleman from an old-clothes seller (*marchand d'habits*), whose ghost returns to terrorise Pierrot. This scenario is restaged in the film *Children of Paradise* (1945), when the actor who plays Pierrot clashes, both on- and offstage, with an old-clothes seller.

This is not a book about dress or fashion, however, but a book about the relationship between the representation of a theatrical character and social life as imagined through the marketplace. At the origins of this account is Antoine Watteau's large painting of Pierrot at life size and full length (see Plate I). This painting depicts Pierrot as Watteau encountered him on the stage of the Parisian fairs (*foires*), in particular the Foire Saint Germain, which was originally a wholesale fabric market. At the fair, the presence of both theatre and retail shaped forms of sociability. The result is marketplace theatricality as a form of social address. It is this address that Pierrot performs in Watteau's large painting. This account focuses on Pierrot, but one of the many remarkable things about Pierrot is the way that representations of the character, as created by a series of talented artists, enable reflection upon the larger category of images to which they belong. For this reason, as well as many others that will become clear over the course of this study, Pierrot is a 'front man'. He is both emblematic of a form of address – marketplace theatricality – which increasingly characterises the representation of human figures, as well as, literally, in front of things. He stands in front of the theatre that he advertises. He is imagined as standing or hanging outside shop fronts. In Watteau's painting, Pierrot's frontality draws attention to the two-dimensionality of the image, to the costume he wears as a front behind which there is nothing but bare canvas (*toile nu*), which is in fact already what Pierrot's garment is intended to allude to – linen (*toile*) underclothes. Clothing is thus significant to this account, but less for its fashionability than for its character as a front, a surface that both constitutes the figure and addresses the marketplace.

After capturing the imagination of Watteau, Pierrot would go on to feature in key works by French artists attentive to both theatricality and the marketplace. Over the course of this study, which spans the eighteenth and nineteenth centuries as well as a brief moment in the mid-twentieth century, Pierrot's theatres and Pierrot's character undergo important changes, which I shall trace. The marketplace changes as well, from the wooden stalls of merchants at the eighteenth-century fair to the soaring glass ceiling of the Universal Exposition. Different people play Pierrot, from the eighteenth-century actors about whom relatively little is known, to the celebrity mime Baptiste Deburau in the early nineteenth century, to a member of the Comédie-Française who was also a mime and a movie star, Jean-Louis Barrault. This book traces Pierrot's progress from the rococo to the post-Revolutionary marketplace and the painting of Édouard Manet, to the photographic practice of Nadar and on into early cinema. Intersections of theatre, the marketplace, and visual art would continue to characterise Parisian consumption throughout the eighteenth and nineteenth centuries, and indeed, so would Pierrot.

The marketplace and social appearance

Through Pierrot, I follow a history of the marketplace as a real and as an imagined forum for social life. It is necessary to distinguish here between the art market as an object of study and the marketplace as a social phenomenon. I am interested in places where paintings were sold: the Parisian fairs, the boutiques of merchant mercers and second-hand shops. Yet rather than a history of pricing and fluctuating value or changing inventories, I offer a consideration of the way that being in the marketplace affects the way that the artwork, or a figure in the artwork, addresses the viewer in an appeal to be seen. This appeal represents the fundamentally social character of the marketplace. Mikhail Bakhtin was one of the most influential critics to treat the marketplace as a social phenomenon, in his famous *Rabelais and his World*.[1] Bakhtin considers Rabelais's representation of the late-mediaeval festive marketplace as an opportunity for the ecstatic dissolution of physical boundaries. During carnival, bodies ingest, merge with, and expel one another through feasting, drinking, copulating, and purging. In some respects, the transactional character of the marketplace underlies the exchange of bodily fluids (semen, vomit, excrement), but Bakhtin is far less concerned with the specific nature of marketplace transactions than with the market as a place where bodies meet. The present account starts, to some extent, where Rabelais left off, when the marketplace ceases to be represented as an embodied experience and is cast instead as a matter of fronts, surfaces, and apparitions. The post-Rabelaisian marketplace, which Bakhtin found joyless and sterile, is not so much represented (as Pieter Bruegel represented the mediaeval marketplace) as representational, in that it produces and retails the media with which its participants represent themselves.

During Watteau's lifetime, European cities held daily, weekly, and annual markets as well as fairs, which lasted from several days to several months and could take place within the walls of the city or on its outskirts. The marketplace had specific physical borders: the buildings that surrounded a town square where the weekly market was held, or the walls of a monastery that hosted an annual fair on the name day of its patron saint. The marketplace was activated when it was inhabited, by vendors hawking their wares, by cooks looking for their masters' dinners, by townspeople curious about both the goods and other people. Desire of various sorts flowed between the inhabitants of the marketplace, from the rumblings of an empty belly to the furtive glances of a kitchen maid at a masked noblewoman.[2] Bakhtin argues that during the late-mediaeval period the festive marketplace allowed differences in rank to dissolve, fleetingly, in a world turned upside down, as peasants and lords stewed together in a sea of bodily fluids.[3] Yet by the early eighteenth century, when Watteau frequented the fair, exchanges between inhabitants of the marketplace were characterised differently, as more distant, ocular and spectacular rather than tactile. This was in part due to the influence of retail and forms of marketplace architecture, the emergence of which began to distinguish between the participants in the marketplace. In Watteau's era, the shop counter arose to distinguish between those who bought and those who sold. The counter now stood as a barrier; coins or credit were needed to breach it. The experience of the marketplace became one of difference and distinction. The theatrical offerings of the fairgrounds also reflected these changes. As the fairground theatres grew in size and in ambition, occupying purpose-built structures rather than simple trestles in the open air, the actor and the stage picture were increasingly presented as distinct, framed by a proscenium that marked the boundary between stage and hall (*salle*).[4]

The marketplace was a traditional location for performance both theatrical and social. Stages set up in the marketplace were used for executions and corporal punishments, for the reading of royal decrees.[5] Mediaeval mystery plays took place on trestle stages erected in the marketplace. Retailers also erected stages and populated them with clowns, whose antics and cries attracted customers to their booths or shops. Quack doctors (*charlatans*) selling ointments, oils, and syrups teamed up with comic actors and travelled the country to set up their trestles (*tréteaux*) at seasonal markets. Occasionally, the charlatan's fame would be eclipsed by that of the actor, whose monologues or skits could be collected and published. By at least the sixteenth century critics and moralists had begun to remark upon the similarity between the behaviour of professional performers and actors in the marketplace. At the base of these concerns was the issue of misrepresentation: that sellers were not truthful about the qualities of the wares they advertised, that agents played a role to secure a better deal. The theatre responded by staging plays about the marketplace and its shenanigans, perpetuating the equivalence between what happened on stage and what happened in the marketplace.

In a remarkable study, Jean-Christophe Agnew has explored the way that the contemporary English theatre supplied the terms with which sixteenth-century critics were able to condemn the marketplace.[6] As suspicion towards the marketplace grew, sellers were described as 'masked'; a 'cunning craftsman' became a 'cunning actor'.[7] The idea of acting itself as the disguising of a 'true' self became a way to characterise the presentation of goods in the marketplace, the actual character of which was concealed from prospective customers. More important, seemingly, than the question of the market itself was what happened to human identity when subjected to the conditions of the marketplace. The very idea that a person's appearance could be duplicitous, in life as on the stage, was attributable, at least in part, to the intensification of marketplace activities. Renaissance theorists like Castiglione had taken for granted the theatrical presentation of the self in a courtly society, because in this context to perform was to fulfil one's birthright.[8] In a market society, however, without fixed estates, performance was aspirational rather than self-fulfilling. This is where visual art, and my account of it, enters the fray as a purveyor of human costumes and guises.

The era this book covers is widely identified as a key moment in the transformation of the marketplace and consumption.[9] In addition to Agnew's study, I am indebted to several accounts that have drawn attention to marketplace intersections between art, social life, and theatre. In literary and cultural studies, Ann Rosalind Jones and Peter Stallybrass's work is particularly valuable for its insistence upon the early modern marketplace as a site where commerce and festivity intertwined.[10] In addition, a crucial book by the same two authors, *Renaissance Clothing and the Materials of Memory*, establishes significant connections between the sartorial practices of actors and the marketplace for second-hand clothes.[11] In the field of art history, Elizabeth Honig's exemplary study, *Painting and the Market in Early Modern Antwerp* has helped me think through the relationship between art and the marketplace as a social phenomenon.[12] Honig emphasises the way that works of art were 'engaged in *constructing* new systems of understanding in a world where perception was being reshaped by the values generated by the market in its broadest sense' (italics original).[13] As she shows, participants in the marketplace – and increasingly this was everyone, particularly in towns and cities – began to look at other people in terms of their potential as 'partners in exchange'.[14] Honig is primarily concerned with representations of marketplaces that include a view of the town square, backed by the church or the town hall, packed with vendors and their wagons of fruit, vegetables, joints of meat, and barrels of wine. I am interested, instead, in representations that condense the activities of the marketplace into the presentation of a single human figure.

For critics of the market, to 'market' an object was to misrepresent it, the model for which misrepresentation was found in the theatre and the profession of the actor, who pretended to be other than they were. Agnew focuses on parallels between the market and the theatre, but I want to add visual art as a third term and, in particular, the visual representation of social appearance, a project that was intimately intertwined with both theatre and marketing. By social appearance, I mean to distinguish between portraiture, which depicts an individual, and the depiction of a person through the rubric of a national, ethnic, professional, or theatrical type. While Watteau's large painting of Pierrot may in fact depict a particular actor, it is far more powerful as a projection of a human type, the features of which are vested in a distinctive appearance consisting of costume and pose. Social appearance is apparitional – a front – in the sense that it does not promise that something lies beneath the surface or that the surface is an accurate reflection of what does lie beneath. The superficial aspect of social appearance is one of the dangers harped upon by critics of the marketplace, yet it is also a condition of possibility. Indeed, social appearance is the threshold across which the market is entered. Pierrot must don his costume – however silly and infantilising it is – to appear on the market. Furthermore, as a stock theatrical character whose identity is entirely dependent upon costume, for Pierrot, the only way to be is to appear. It is for this reason that 'costume prints' play a key role in this study. A capacious genre, subsets of which will be discussed in detail, costume prints date to the mid- to late sixteenth century. As a visual medium, costume prints project social identity through a figure's surface appearance as composed by garments – hence 'costume'.

In comparisons of the theatre and the market, it was not the question of the true value of goods that preoccupied critics, but rather the face value of social appearances. Pierrot is a cipher for such concerns, a figure who is simultaneously utterly transparent and completely masked. Each of this book's first four chapters describes a specific historic marketplace or set of marketplace practices: the fair, rococo retail, bric-à-brac, the Universal Exposition. Yet it bears repeating that I am concerned primarily with the way these marketplaces were represented in critical and visual discourse as models of exchange with bearing upon the nature of social life and the encounters between persons. Interpersonal (and increasingly *impersonal*) relationships are at the heart of Georg Simmel's account of the marketplace in *The Philosophy of Money*, in which he describes the emergence of personality as a 'counterpart and correlate' that performs objective difference.[15] Persons adopt personalities, Simmel argues, because personality objectifies by consolidating a person's difference into a set of expressed characteristics. The objectifying function of personality is necessary when social life has adopted the form of exchange: 'the relations between the objects are really relations between people'.[16] A theatrical stock character like Pierrot is a model for this understanding of personality as a kind of objecthood. As I will insist in this account, Pierrot cannot exist except through external expressions, which take the form of clothing, of facial expression, of gesture (or lack thereof). In this model, personality is not a supplement – the way a particular person behaves or acts as distinct from their fundamental existence as a person – personality is personhood, which is also objecthood. Pierrot-hood is the expression of this convergence. I situate Pierrot in the marketplace in the sense of situating him in a social world imagined as a meeting place of strangers, each of whom offers, for assessment, the objective guise of personality. It sounds dystopian, but Pierrot, despite his pathos, is also full of hope.

Theatricality

In my use of 'theatricality' to describe marketplace behaviours, I am concerned with the theatrical disposition as outward facing, openly directed towards an audience.[17] As Erika Fischer-Lichte suggests, in dialogue with the early twentieth-century critic Nikolaj Evreinov, theatricality can be understood as 'the specific *mise-en-scène* of bodies with regard to a particular form of perception'.[18] Marketing and the theatre are both forms of *mise-en-scène* in the sense of setting things on a stage to be perceived. The 'particular form of perception' that characterises the market is that of judgement and assessment. For Fischer-Lichte, theatricality enables humans to 'compose an image of themselves as another, which they can then reflect on through the eyes of another or see reflected in the eyes of another'.[19] As Josette Féral points out, theatricality is a crucial element of forms of modern performance, which takes as its subject the relationships that unfold between the body of the actor as it presents itself and the audience.[20] Because of the frankness of its address, theatricality as a mode of exhibitionism has often been the target of what Jonas Barish has compellingly described as the 'anti-theatrical prejudice'. This sentiment has arisen even amongst practitioners of theatre, who argue that not all theatre has to be explicitly theatrical.[21] The early twentieth-century Russian impresario Konstantin Stanislavski, for example, required that his performers do their best to ignore the existence of the audience and focus only on the relationships taking place on their own side of the proscenium.[22]

Sociology and affect theory have also offered theories of performance, theatricality, and social encounter.[23] In a continuation of the questions explored in my book *Realism and Role-Play: The Human Figure in French Art from Callot to the Brothers Le Nain*, I am in dialogue with Erving Goffman's classic account of social life as a series of encounters between performing persons.[24] For Goffman and other 'role theorists', social roles are staged and performed with the help of costumes, makeup, props, and scenery (furniture, pets, vehicles, real estate). An individual adopts numerous roles over the course of a lifetime or even in the span of a single day. Most importantly, roles are directed, primarily, at others, as a bid for intelligibility within the conventions of the social repertoire. It is Goffman who has provided an extended discussion of 'front' as an element of social performance.[25] For Goffman, the front is an 'expressive equipment of a standard kind', which can take the form of a costume or a décor, and which can also manifest through posture, speech, expression, appearance, and manner.[26] Fronts can be changed and re-used; they are not integral to their bearer. Goffman's indication of the front as 'of a standard kind' indicates that a given front is available to multiple users, an availability enabled by the circulation of fronts through cultural repertoires like those offered by literature and visual art.

Historians of theatre and performance, most notably Richard Schechner and Victor Turner, have studied role-playing across different cultures.[27] They note the distinction between staged drama and role-playing. While the former is confined to specific architectural spaces, the latter can take place 'offstage', in social life and through cultural rituals. For Elizabeth Burns, whose work is little known to art historians but considered essential by theatre historians, theatricality consists precisely in this 'double relationship between the theatre and social life',[28] as if theatricality becomes palpable because of its migration offstage into social life. Read differently, the double relationship between theatre and social life exists because of what could be described as the inherent sociability of the theatrical, the way that the disposition of the stage – whether or not the actors turn their backs to the audience – acknowledges the presence of the viewer and is in fact always for a viewer.[29] For Schechner, glossed by Turner, 'the paradigmatic theatrical situation is a group of performers soliciting an audience who may or may not respond by attending'.[30] Solicitation is both social and, in certain contexts, transactional.[31] I will take the opportunity to say now that what Schechner describes as the paradigmatic theatrical situation is also Pierrot's paradigmatic situation, as he is represented by Watteau. Pierrot solicits an audience 'who may or may not respond by attending'. In the 'may or may not' lies most of Pierrot's pathos. He is forever awaiting a judgement.

As a disposition of display and outwardness, which enables performative encounters to unfold between figures and viewers, theatricality can be thematised explicitly in works of art.[32] Portraits are an obvious example, as well as any composition that includes a human figure who addresses the viewer. Michael Fried's work has shown that in the French tradition theatricality in the visual arts was often contested and suspect.[33] Beginning in the eighteenth century in the work of Denis Diderot, Fried identifies a tendency to decry any element of a painting that seems to address a viewer.[34] For Diderot, it was perfectly possible for a work to be theatrical even if none of its figures acknowledged the viewer. For example, a figure whose pantomime and facial expression Diderot judged to be excessively histrionic was theatrical, because this behaviour attested to consciousness of being looked at. The rococo style itself often merited complaints about theatricality, because the highly decorative nature of the style seemed to want too much to please the viewer by presenting pretty and expensive things. Diderot's rants against the inclusion of silk cushions in Boucher's pastorals targeted both frivolity itself – shepherds do not need silk cushions – and the way that the cushion addresses itself to the viewer as a tempting object that the viewer might like to acquire.[35] For Jean-Jacques Rousseau, another important 'anti-theatrical' voice in eighteenth-century France, theatre mimicked the social world in its desire to gain the approval of others by showing off.[36] Displays of luxury were key to this project, both on stage and in social life. Both Rousseau and Diderot were aware, in other words, of the relationship between theatricality and the marketplace. Their dislike of theatrical painting had as much to do with a desire for moral seriousness as an aversion to painting as an instrument of marketing. Tracing the relationship between theatricality and the marketplace will be one of the objects of this study.

Pierrot *parade*

To some extent, 'marketplace theatricality' is a redundant term. As this account will suggest, theatricality and the marketplace are difficult to disentwine. One form in which the two phenomena are vividly and demonstrably linked is the *parade*, a brief skit that took place outside a theatre in order to entice viewers to pay to enter the theatre. Performed on trestle stages or balconies affixed to the fronts (*façades*) of theatres, *parades* were used widely at the fairgrounds where Watteau first encountered Pierrot. As Thomas Crow has argued, in a foundational account of Watteau's relationship to theatre, the painter's *oeuvre* attests to a fascination with the *parades*, which he would have seen performed at the fairs.[37] The *parade* continued to be an iconic feature of Parisian culture through the nineteenth century, until it was largely replaced by the advertising poster, a medium in which Pierrot also played an important role. The *parade* was a theatrical appeal to the marketplace, explicitly so because it asked onlookers to become paying customers.

As one of the theatre's clowns, Pierrot was an indispensable player in the physical antics of the *parade:* he is distinctly visible on the *façade* of a fair theatre in at least one period print (see Figures 0.1 and 0.2). In a crucial early scene in the French film *Children of Paradise* (1945), the actor who will assume the role of Pierrot appears in his theatre's *parade*, where he performs a brilliant pantomime, thereby attracting the admiration of the film's heroine and creating the film's 'hook' (Figure 0.3). The *parade*, as a pitch for a theatre made through the medium of a figure performing on an empty stage, enacts the outward, appealing disposition of figures on the market. Positioned outside the theatre, with the actors placed against a relatively plain or bare décor, the *parade* models the desirable mobility of goods. As a form, the *parade* also underlies the visual logic of the costume print. Many of the social types in the repertoire of the costume prints are ambulatory and itinerant – old-clothes sellers, ragpickers, travelling musicians, and actors – without a stable residence or place of business, except

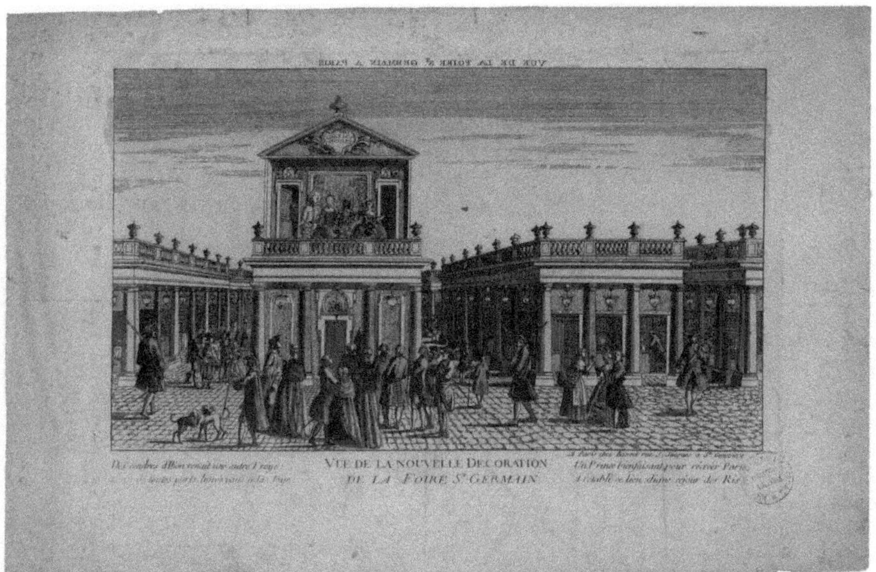

0.1 *View of the New Decoration of the Saint Germain Fair*, ca. 1760. Hand-colored etching. Source: Bibliothèque Nationale de France, Paris. EST SALLES OPERA-COMIQUE ©BNF.

the baskets and boxes they carry with them. These types lend themselves to the preferred format of the costume print, which tends to present a figure without an environment depicted, against a plain or bare ground. This format both expresses the figure's nomadism and contributes to their marketplace pitch: like the goods they sell, they are ready to move. Pierrot's groundlessness is one of the motifs of this study, which follows Pierrot as he recurs in numerous different environments and against numerous different grounds, without ever establishing a necessary relationship to a single one. By 'necessary relationship', I mean a relationship that would render his figure unintelligible or uninteresting if it were to recur without that ground. I argue that this groundlessness is part of Pierrot's appeal as well as a key technique of marketplace theatricality. To market a figure is to suggest it could be re-used in a variety of contexts, as well as the figure's readiness to travel, to accompany its purchaser wherever they wish to go.

Together with Christopher Wood, I have suggested *parade* as a way of thinking about a particular category of works of art, in which figural existence, recurrence, and survival are prioritised over the 'aesthetic text' in the sense of composition and narrative story-telling internal to the work.[38] *Parade* describes works of art whose primary interest is the human figure's expression of itself – its standing, its disposition towards the world – as opposed to its expression of emotions related to story-telling. In French art from the seventeenth century onwards, the figures of *parade* coexist alongside the human figures of history

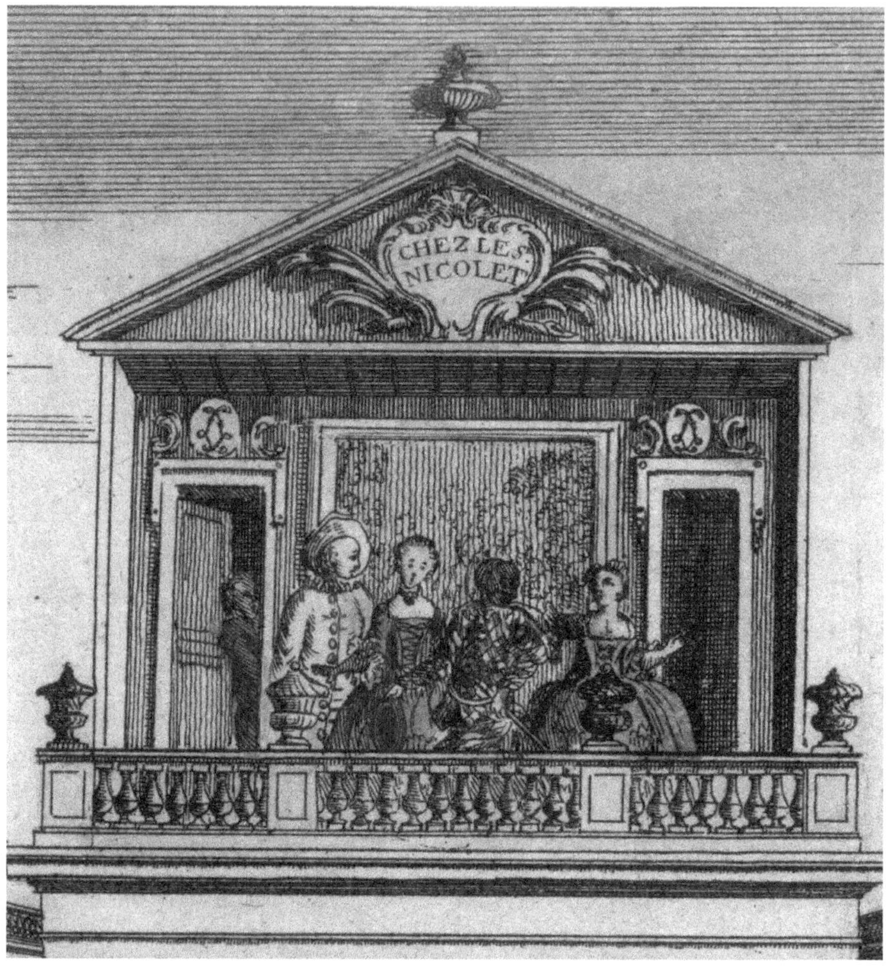

0.2   Detail of Figure 0.1.

painting and genre painting. My first book, *Realism and Role-Play: The Human Figure in French Art from Callot to the Brothers Le Nain*, was concerned with establishing the origins of the theatrical figure in early seventeenth-century print culture and decorative painting. Emmelyn Butterfield-Rosen has recently provided a crucial account of the endgame of the 'beaux-arts figure', which she convincingly describes as the human figure instrumentalised by narrative expressed through physical torsion.[39] Yet for much of the period covered by these books, these two figural practices coexist, with frequent exchanges taking place between the two modes. For example, Pierrot, as photographed by Nadar and his brother Adrien Tournachon, was borrowed by Jean-Léon Gérôme for a novel experiment in history painting, *Duel After the Masked Ball* (1857).[40] In this painting, a reveller dressed as Pierrot is slain in a duel by

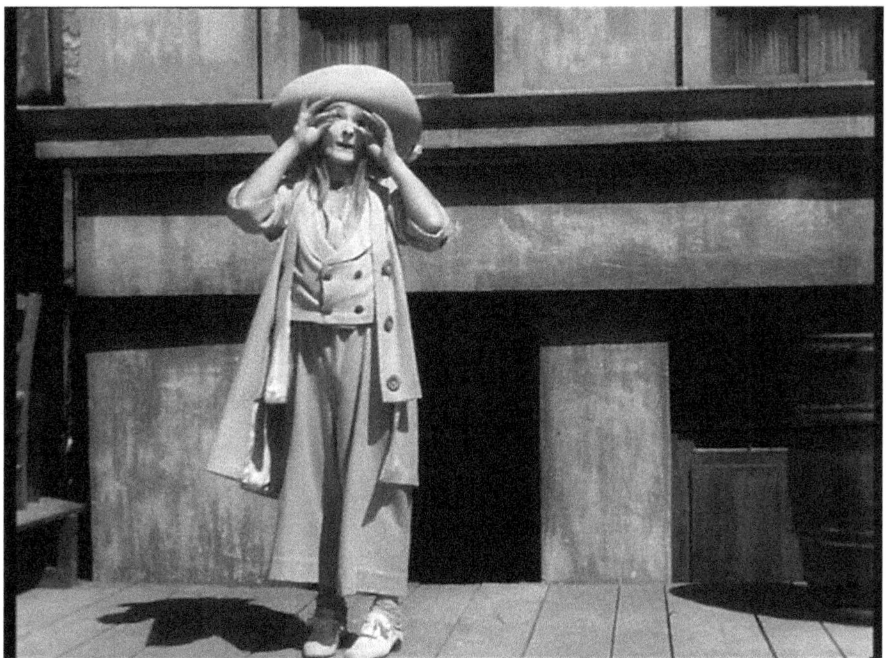

0.3   Marcel Carné (dir.), Jean-Louis Barrault as Baptiste Deburau in *Children of Paradise*, 1945. Source: Pathé.

another masked figure. Gérôme's Pierrot is prevented from addressing the viewer by the requirements of the pantomime, which demand that he swoon onto the snow-covered ground. Despite the tremendous commercial success of Pierrot's cameo in Gérôme's popular painting, which was reproduced widely as a print, Pierrot's activities as a paradigmatic figure of marketplace theatricality continued unabated, leading him into the fairground aesthetics of early cinema.

In this account of Pierrot, I situate *parade* more explicitly in terms of theatricality and the marketplace. In the volume I co-edited with Wood,[41] there were few considerations of retail and marketing, with the partial exception of Christiane Hille's essay on tailoring and the cutting out of the human figure.[42] Indeed, the question of costume and dress is essential to an understanding of Pierrot and his key place within the larger project of figuring the marketplace through the human figure. The theatricality of the figure in the costume print lay in its address, but it was in no small sense the figure's dress that performed the address. It is no surprise then, to find that vendors in the garment and cosmetic trades recur throughout the figural repertoires of the marketplace. In Watteau's large painting of Pierrot, the costume subsumes the body behind it, the articulation of which holds little interest for Watteau. If the limbs – tendon, muscle, skin – of the human figure were the expressive medium of history painting, dress is the expressive medium of marketplace theatricality. Dress is the front, the *parade* for the person, the obligatory threshold for an identity that positions itself in terms of the social world.

Repertoire

To follow Pierrot in visual art is necessarily to follow him through an array of other media and spaces, including theatre and marketplaces. Nor is it simply a question of identifying plays in which Pierrot appeared. In largely unscripted genres, seeking the content of performances leads to other media: frontispieces to collections of published scenarios, advertising materials including posters, the accounts of government censors who attended performances, and guides for tourists. In the nineteenth century, when Pierrot was the hero of the popular pantomime theatre, representations of the character circulated in both tony literary journals and inexpensive pamphlets as well as popular caricatures. To describe this collection of cultural representations, forged between word, image, and performance, I use a term that has been enriched by scholarship in theatre studies – repertoire. For Tracy Davis, repertoire is a way of describing the body of shared knowledge produced over time through the interactions between performances, performers, and audiences.[43] The media of existence in repertoire are heterogeneous, encompassing visual art, but also theatre posters and programmes, caricatures, newspaper accounts, even diaries, oral histories, and audience memories. Repertoire is both 'transmedial', in the sense that its figures move between media, and 'intermedial' in that a figure like Pierrot is known as the result of his cumulative representations across media.[44] Jacky Bratton has referred to this approach to theatre history as 'intertheatricality', in which the object of study consists of a 'mesh of connections' between theatre texts, stage décor, genre, theatrical ephemera, and the recounted experiences of actors and viewers.[45] This concept is particularly helpful in accounting for the creation and survival of popular theatrical types, like Pierrot. Pierrot thrives in unscripted genres; his emergence as a well-loved type cannot be traced to a single theatrical text or a single performance.

Davis sees repertoire as a mechanism, a process by which knowledge can be shared among communities of performers and users. Yet repertoire is also a collection, a range, a set of representations. When I refer to a figural repertoire, I mean a collection of figures, usually human figures, which have been made available and which circulate in theatre, literature, and art. Figural repertoires are defined by multiplicity, by the recurrence of a figural type over time and in different media. Recurrence and multiplicity in the repertoire as collection help to engender cultural memories as well as textual reception, building up a type's complexity, resilience, and sheer recognisability. Pierrot remains intelligible and recognisable over time because his existence takes place between theatrical instantiations, visual and textual images, and the memory of audiences. Repertoire is characterised by 'reiteration, revision, citation and incorporation', and of course 'recombination', all of which are practices that emphasise re-use and second-hand-ness, rather than absolute novelty.[46] Re-use and recombination are also practices used by numerous marketplace actors, including artists and retailers. Chapter 5 in this book, however, discusses a moment when the marketplace as a repertoire was virulently rejected, requiring Pierrot to take on a new role.

Chapter summaries

Pierrot's story can be told in many ways. It has taken me a long time to write this book, in part because it has taken me a long time to find out which of these stories I want to foreground. In one telling, Pierrot is a favoured vehicle for French avant-garde practitioners – Watteau, Nadar, and Manet – whose careers broadly conform to the trope of the exceptional artist who breaks with tradition and shuns financial success in pursuit of an elusive ideal. This is the story that I told in my dissertation (2013).[47] Over the years, Pierrot has attracted the attention of a handful of scholars, primarily historians of theatre and literature. In the field of literary studies, Robert Storey has written two excellent books about Pierrot, the first a comprehensive theatrical history and the second a finer-grained exploration of Pierrot, pantomime, and poetry in the nineteenth century.[48] The art historian Judy Sund has written a substantial article-length study on Watteau's Pierrots and their afterlives.[49] However, Sund's scrupulous iconographic account still leaves room for my account of Pierrot's relationship to the marketplace and social life. The French critic Jean de Palacio has written a study of Pierrot in the *fin-de-siècle*, a period when the character tends towards the macabre and mournful, while also becoming more physically violent: in a famous late nineteenth-century pantomime, Pierrot tickles his wife to death.[50] I am grateful for Palacio's account, because my work does not attempt to delve into this thicket and its complex cultural politics. Really, my account ends with Nadar and Manet, at the cusp of the 1860s, while including instances of the survival of Nadar's Pierrot in the work of Jules Chéret and Émile Reynaud. The final chapter, on *Children of Paradise*, presents the film as retrospective in nature, a meditation on the cultural politics of the marketplace in the light of the Nazi occupation.

Each of the book's chapters studies the relationship between visual art and a different marketplace. The first chapter considers Watteau's creation of a distinctive figure for Pierrot and the monumental representation of this figure in the large painting, *Pierrot*. I locate Watteau's encounter with Pierrot at the Parisian fairs, where Pierrot's troupe, the Comédie Italienne, had migrated following its expulsion from Paris in 1697. The fair theatre, which was based on the repertoire of the Comédie Italienne, fixated on the relationship between costume and social identity, a relationship that is vital for understanding Pierrot's identity as entirely reliant upon his costume or mask. Departing from previous emphases on the fair as a melting pot for social class, I stress instead the fair as an opportunity for visual scrutiny in which differences were manifested through social appearances. In light of the significant differences between this painting and the smaller *fêtes galantes* for which Watteau was known, I suggest a more appropriate category, the *fête marchande*. I do so in part by establishing the relationship between the composition of the large painting, the disposition of its central figure, and the repertoire of printed images known as *costumes* or *modes* or *habillemens*. In addition, this chapter explores forms of fairground architecture, the stall (*loge*) and the counter (*comptoir*), which structured social encounters at the fair according to a theatrical model.

The second chapter considers the repertoire of rococo ornament and decorative arts, in which Pierrot plays a starring role. Watteau's Pierrot was liberally copied by rococo artists and designers, from sought-after decorative artists like Jacques Lajoue to lowly painters of inexpensive faience. Rococo artists relied upon repertoires in order to build decorative ensembles, in which motifs were borrowed and reassembled in a mode of 'scrapbooking'.[51] The repertoire of objects and motifs would become a foundation of rococo retail strategies, from the merchant mercers to female fashion merchants to dealers in paintings. A related kind of marketing was initiated by the amateur and collector Jean de Jullienne, who commissioned four volumes of etchings after Watteau's *oeuvre*, including two volumes reproducing Watteau's drawings. Pierrot appeared six times in these two volumes. As a collection that addresses both the marketplace and the 'disinterested amateur', *The Figures of Different Characters* can be understood as a tool both for remembrance and for marketing.

The third chapter moves to the second-hand marketplaces of post-Revolutionary Paris, in the midst of which Watteau's large *Pierrot* appeared in the collection of Dominique Vivant Denon, a connoisseur who was also Napoléon's Director of the Arts, in charge of what would become the Musée du Louvre. Moving between Denon's discovery and Édouard Manet's breakthrough painting, *The Old Musician* (1861–2), this chapter argues that Manet's painting depicts a range of types with meaningful relationships to the marketplace for old things. This chapter also explores a new theatrical milieu *cum* marketplace, the Boulevard du Temple, where the character of Pierrot had been re-invented by Baptiste Deburau at the Théâtre des Funambules.

The fourth chapter locates Pierrot at the Exposition Universelle of 1855, where Nadar and his brother Adrien Tournachon exhibited a series of photographs of Deburau's son Charles in the costume of Pierrot. The photographic repertoire of this period was inhabited by actors and actresses, political celebrities, and the literati. The Exposition Universelle became the stage for this glittering performance of the photographic medium as a star-maker. Intended as publicity materials for Adrien Tournachon's studio, the photographs launched Pierrot as a distinctive silhouette, whose appearance shared features with the figures of magic lantern slides. During the *fin-de-siècle*, Pierrot becomes increasingly weightless as well as groundless, a condition that favours his role in those optical technologies like animation and projection, as well as photography, the meeting of which would lead to the invention of cinema.

In the backstage drama *Children of Paradise* (1945), written by Jacques Prévert and directed by Marcel Carné, Nadar's Pierrot is re-embedded in a fantastically detailed historical environment, the nineteenth-century Boulevard du Temple and the Théâtre des Funambules. The film depicts the offstage life of the actor who played Pierrot in the nineteenth-century theatre, Baptiste Deburau. Played in the film by Jean-Louis Barrault, Deburau regards the role of Pierrot not as a mask, but as a projection of his (Deburau's) soul. From this uncompromisingly serious attitude arises many of Deburau's problems, as he seeks to navigate the backstage world of actors, courtesans, criminals, and old-clothes sellers. I argue that the film registers elements of a conservative cultural backlash against the relationship between the marketplace and creative artistry. Beginning in the late nineteenth century, Pierrot had become increasingly politicised, a mascot for conservative and reactionary figures like the artist Adolphe Willette and the mime Séverin. An aesthetic of whiteness, luminosity, and clarity was cast as distinctly 'French', as opposed to a piecemeal culture of the second-hand, which anti-Semitic critics cast as the fruits of 'Jewishness'. In the film, the latter is represented by the old-clothes seller Jericho, Deburau's nemesis. Part of the point of this juxtaposition, I argue, is to recast Pierrot as an emblem of aesthetic purity.

At the fairground where Pierrot attracted Watteau's attention, fabrics, linens, ribbons, and ready-made clothing were bought, sold, and paraded through the shop-lined avenues. Delight was taken in the fronts it was possible to construct and adorn, the miracle of which Pierrot ponders when he watches Don Juan get dressed. Some of this joy is expressed in a wonderful painting, which I do not discuss at length: Fragonard's *Pierrot*, a confection of ribbons, trim, rouge, and flowers, which serves a Pierrot whose cheeks are made of the colour of the flowers on his garment, whose eyes are the same blue as his ribbons, and whose flossy hair is the same cream as his silk jacket (see Plate 2). In Fragonard's meringue of a painting, figure and sartorial front have merged entirely; this is Pierrot as sheer froth. By the end of this account, however, Pierrot's delight in clothing will become suspect. During the Nazi occupation of France, anti-Semitic ideologues will compare contemporary theatre and cinema to old clothes patched to look new; second-hand clothing becomes a metaphor for the condition of art when subjected to the pressures of the marketplace.

This book's subject is both Pierrot and his world: the world of theatre, costume, the marketplace, and of visual art as a form of costume. In Pierrot's world, visual art is an agent of marketplace sociability, which takes the form of theatricality – of a call to the street made by an actor from the balcony affixed to the façade of a theatre. Pierrot is at home in this world because he is a theatrical character whose identity is nowhere but in a costume. The historical protagonists who feature in this book – artists, collectors, editors, and authors – thrived in Pierrot's world, the superficial aspects of which they took as opportunities. The spaces and the media of this world changed over time, from painting to print to photography, from luxury retail to flea markets, from spoken theatre to pantomime. Its personalities, however, remain relatively constant, favouring theatrical performers and ambulatory dealers in second-hand goods and garments. Among these personalities, some artists find models for their own vocation, as dealers in old myths, as givers of surfaces. Pierrot of the marketplace, like a shiny silk ribbon stretched taut, is all front. The front of the shop, the front of house, the front man – at long last, in this book, Pierrot comes first.

Notes

1 Mikhail Bakhtin, *Rabelais and His World*, trans. Helene Iswolsky (Bloomington: Indiana University Press, 1984).

2 Accounts of the marketplace have been crucial in narrating the history of modern cultural life. Jürgen Habermas identified the marketplace as a foundation of the bourgeois public sphere as well as the origin of culture as a commodity. For Habermas, the circulation of goods in a market society necessitates the circulation of information, which encourages the press and other communicative, 'private' enterprises that both address and represent the public. This also leads to the creation of culture as a good to be consumed and exchanged. Jürgen Habermas, *The Structural Transformation of the Public Sphere: An Inquiry into a Category of Bourgeois Society*, trans. Thomas Burger and Frederick Lawrence (1962; Cambridge, MA: MIT Press, 1991), pp. 14–17, pp. 36–7.

3 Although he described Rabelais watching 'marketplace spectacles' on 'theatre scaffoldings' erected in the square (Bakhtin, *Rabelais and his World*, p. 155), Bakhtin believed that these performances were able to dissolve the separation between the performers and the crowd.

4 For an exemplary account of theatrical architecture and its conceptual underpinnings, see Pannill Camp, *The First Frame: Theatre Space in Enlightenment France* (Cambridge: Cambridge University Press, 2014).

5 On punishment in the early modern English marketplace, see Dave Postles, 'The market place as space in early modern England', *Social History* 29:2 (2004), 41–58.

6 Jean-Christophe Agnew, *Worlds Apart: The Market and the Theatre in Anglo-American Thought, 1550–1750* (Cambridge: Cambridge University Press, 1986).

7 Agnew, *Worlds Apart*, p. 76.

8 Agnew, *Worlds Apart*, p. 75. See also Jonas Barish, *The Antitheatrical Prejudice* (Berkeley: University of California Press, 1981), pp. 168–72.

9 See Daniel Roche, *The People of Paris: An Essay in Popular Culture in the 18th Century*, trans. Marie Evans and Gwynne Lewis (New York: Berg, 1987), pp. 127–59; Daniel Roche, *France in the Enlightenment*, trans. Arthur Goldhammer (Cambridge, MA: Harvard University Press, 1998), pp. 548–77. On the commodities that began to inhabit Parisian interiors in the eighteenth century, see Annik Pardailhé-Galabrun, *La naissance de l'intime: 3000 foyers Parisiens XVIIe–XVIIIe siècles* (Paris: Presses Universitaires de France, 1988). On fashion and the consumer revolution in France, see Jennifer M. Jones, *Sexing 'La Mode': Gender, Fashion and Commercial Culture in Old Regime France* (Oxford: Berg, 2004). A classic essay on the trickling down of consumer goods in eighteenth-century France is Cissie Fairchilds, 'The production and marketing of populuxe goods in eighteenth-century Paris', in John Brewer and Roy Porter (eds), *Consumption and the World of Goods* (London: Routledge, 1993), pp. 228–48. Also of note, particularly on the perception that appearances had become unreliable in the age of the consumer revolution, is John Shovlin, 'The cultural politics of luxury in eighteenth-century France', *French Historical Studies*

23:4 (2000), 577–606. For a survey of theoretical literature on the history of consumption, see Don Slater, *Consumer Culture and Modernity* (Cambridge: Polity Press, 1997). See also Mike Featherstone, 'Perspectives on consumer culture', *Sociology* 24:1 (1990), 5–22.

10 Ann Rosalind Jones and Peter Stallybrass, *The Politics and Poetics of Transgression* (Ithaca, NY: Cornell University Press, 1986), pp. 27–43.

11 Ann Rosalind Jones and Peter Stallybrass, *Renaissance Clothing and the Materials of Memory* (Cambridge: Cambridge University Press, 2000), pp. 175–206.

12 Elizabeth Alice Honig, *Painting and the Market in Early Modern Antwerp* (New Haven, CT: Yale University Press, 1998).

13 Honig, *Painting and the Market*, p. 2.

14 Honig, *Painting and the Market*, p. 10.

15 Georg Simmel, *The Philosophy of Money*, ed. David Frisby and trans. Tom Bottomore, David Frisby and Kaethe Mengelberg (New York: Routledge, 1990), p. 302.

16 Simmel, *The Philosophy of Money*, p. 176.

17 Theatricality is of course a feature of the *theatrum mundi* (theatre of the world), yet it refers more specifically to ways of being and behaving within this theatre. On the 'Theatrum Mundi' see Erika Fischer-Lichte, 'From *theatrum mundi* to theatricality', in Elena Penskaya and Joachim Küpper (eds), *Theater as Metaphor* (Berlin: De Gruyter, 2019), pp. 253–63, here pp. 254–6.

18 Fischer-Lichte, 'From *theatrum mundi* to theatricality', p. 262. On Evreinov and theatricality, see also Tony Pearson, 'Evreinov and Pirandello: twin apostles of theatricality', *Theatre Research International* 12:2 (1987), 147–67, here pp. 153–64.

19 Fischer-Lichte, 'From *theatrum mundi* to theatricality', p. 262. See also Erika Fischer-Lichte, 'Introduction: theatricality: a key concept in theatre and cultural studies', *Theatre Research International* 20:2 (1995), 85–9.

20 Josette Féral, 'Performance and theatricality: the subject demystified', trans. Terese Lyons, *Modern Drama* 25:1 (1982), 170–81.

21 Jonas Barish, 'Exhibitionism and the antitheatrical prejudice', *English Literary History* 36:1 (1969), 1–29.

22 Barish, *The Antitheatrical Prejudice*, pp. 156–7, 344–5.

23 For a particularly useful survey of the literature on using performance as a tool of historical and cultural analysis, see Peter Burke, 'Performing history: the importance of occasions', *Rethinking History* 9:1 (2005), 35–52.

24 Erving Goffman, *The Presentation of the Self in Everyday Life*, reprint (Edinburgh: University of Edinburgh Press, 1958). Performance theorists have productively engaged with Goffman's assertion that perceptions of social 'reality' are both made through performances and palpable within them: Richard Schechner, *Performance Theory*, rev. edn (New York: Routledge, 1988), p. 90; Victor Turner and Edith Turner, 'Performing ethnography', *Drama Review* 26:2 (1982), 33–50, here p. 34.

25 Goffman, *The Presentation of the Self*, pp. 13–19.

26 Goffman, *The Presentation of the Self*, p. 13.

27 Their findings suggest that the suspicion towards role-playing tends to be particular to Western cultures. Victor Turner, *From Ritual to Theater: The Human Seriousness of Play* (New York: Performing Arts Journal Publications, 1982), pp. 102–23. Turner's accounts, in particular, often essentialise, describing 'simpler preindustrial societies' as more receptive to masking and role-playing (p. 115).

28 Elizabeth Burns, *Theatricality: A Study of Convention in the Theatre and in Social Life* (London: Longman, 1972), pp. 122–43 on role theory, p. 3.

29 While I cannot speak to the complexity of the theatrical address in the twentieth and twenty-first centuries, during the eighteenth and nineteenth centuries the conception of the theatre as addressed to an audience remained consistent. Even Diderot could not eliminate the presence of the spectator, although he might reduce that spectator to a single person, a member of the extended family who happened, as if by accident, to come upon a 'scene' enacted between two of his familiars.

30 Turner, *From Ritual to Theater*, p. 112.

31 Stanislavski's theatre is in this sense rather anti-social, although the other side of the argument is that a superior and genuine form of sociability exists between the actors once they disregard the audience.

32 Among the more interesting discussions and contestations of Fried's account, see Patricia Smyth, 'Theatricality, Michael Fried and nineteenth-century art and theatre', *Performance Research* 24:4 (2019), 5–9; Marvin Carlson, 'The resistance to theatricality', *SubStance* 31:2–3 (2002), 238–50; Michael Quinn, 'Concepts of theatricality in contemporary art history', *Theatre Research International* 20:2 (1995), 106–13.

33 Fried has made this argument in a trilogy of books, of which two are particularly relevant to my account: Michael Fried, *Absorption and Theatricality: Painting and Beholder in the Age of Diderot* (Chicago: University of Chicago Press, 1980); Michael Fried, *Manet's Modernism, or The Face of Painting in the 1860s* (Chicago: University of Chicago Press, 1996).

34 Michael Fried, 'Art and objecthood', *Artforum* 5:10 (1967), 12–23. In early essays, like 'Art and objecthood', Fried used this understanding of theatricality to develop an argument about abstraction, suggesting that an artwork that addresses the viewer too stridently cannot seriously engage with its own form. To incorporate a theatrical disposition is to borrow from an alien medium – it is a cheap trick, which is how Fried famously saw Minimalist sculpture. Fried backtracked from this argument in later work, which offers a more considered approach to different kinds of theatrical address in artworks.

35 For Diderot's entertaining condemnations of Boucher, see *Diderot: Salons*, ed. Michel Delon (Paris: Gallimard, 2008), pp. 48–9, 73–5, 106–12. In 1765, Diderot becomes consumed with outrage because Boucher includes a silk cushion in his painting of Angélique and Médor in the forest (p. 109).

36 Barish, *The Antitheatrical Prejudice*, p. 256.

37 Thomas Crow, *Painters and Public Life in Eighteenth-Century Paris* (New Haven, CT: Yale University Press, 1985), pp. 45–74.

38 Marika Takanishi Knowles and Christopher Wood, 'Editorial: *La parade*', *RES: Anthropology and Aesthetics* 73/74:1 (2020), 1–9.

39 Emmelyn Butterfield-Rosen, *Modern Art & the Remaking of Human Disposition* (Chicago: University of Chicago Press, 2021). She traces the stillness and inexpression of *fin-de-siècle* figures to new theories of human psychic life.

40 On this painting, which Çakmak shows to be no ordinary history painting but rather a complex *mélange* of genre-painting and satire as well as a tribute to Jacques-Louis David's *Death of Marat*, see Gülru Çakmak, 'Jean-Léon Gérôme: the innovative years (1851–1859)', PhD dissertation, Johns Hopkins University, 2010, pp. 12–74.

41 *RES: Anthropology and Aesthetics* 73/74:1 (2020).

42 Christiane Hille, 'Albrecht Dürer and the tailoring of the human form', *RES: Anthropology and Aesthetics* 73/74:1 (2020), 10–22.

43 Tracy C. Davis, 'Nineteenth-century repertoire', *Nineteenth Century Theatre and Film* 36:2 (2009), 6–28.

44 I use the definitions of transmedial and intermedial offered in Éricka Wicky and Kathrin Yacavone, 'Introduction: *portraitomanie* and intermediality in nineteenth-century France', *L'Esprit Créateur* 59:1 (2019), 1–11, here p. 6.

45 Jacky Bratton, *New Readings in Theatre History* (Cambridge: Cambridge University Press, 2003), pp. 37–8.

46 Davis, 'Nineteenth-century repertoire', 7.

47 Marika Takanishi Knowles, 'Pierrot's costume: theatre, curiosity, and the subject of art in France, 1665–1860', PhD dissertation, Yale University, 2013.

48 Robert Storey, *Pierrot: A Critical History of a Mask* (Princeton, NJ: Princeton University Press, 1978); Robert Storey, *Pierrots on the Stage of Desire: Nineteenth-Century French Literary Artists and the Comic Pantomime* (Princeton, NJ: Princeton University Press, 1985). In this vein, see also Louisa E. Jones, *Sad Clowns and Pale Pierrots: Literature and the Popular Comic Arts in 19th-century France* (Lexington, KY: French Forum Press, 1984).

49 Judy Sund, 'Why so sad? Watteau's Pierrots', *Art Bulletin* 98:3 (2016), 321–47.

50 Jean de Palacio, *Pierrot fin-de-siècle: ou, les métamorphoses d'un masque* (Paris: Séguier, 1990).

51 For this phrase see Katie Scott, *The Rococo Interior: Decoration and Social Spaces in Early Eighteenth-Century Paris* (New Haven, CT: Yale University Press, 1995), p. 133.

∛ I ∛

Antoine Watteau and the *fête marchande*

The chief argument of this chapter is that Watteau's large painting *Pierrot* (formerly and erroneously called *Gilles*) owes its compositional singularity and its affective power to the genre of the 'costume' or 'costume print' (see Plate 1). This is a complex and multi-faceted genre, several aspects of which will be explored below. A classic, early example of the costume print is the 'English Merchant', one of the hundreds of woodcuts that illustrated Cesare Vecellio's famous book *Habiti antichi, et moderni di tutto il mondo* (1598) (see Figure 1.8). This woodcut, made by Christoph Krieger after a model provided by Vecellio, exemplifies the essential features of the genre: a single human figure, fully clothed, presented at full length against a largely empty background. This boilerplate format would rapidly evolve, drawing into its remit the construction of national, ethnic, professional, and theatrical human types. I say 'construction', because these images should not be understood as documents but as performances and projections, the aim of which was often disciplinary, slotting human experience into a repertoire of fixed human types. With regards to *Pierrot*, Watteau's debt to the costume print has been noted, yet there is still more to be said about the way this genre constructs an essential relationship between social life and the marketplace.

As I show in the first part of this chapter, the situation of the Italian theatre within the grounds of the Parisian fairs would have accentuated the parallels between what happened on stage and the activities of the marketplace. This was particularly true at the Saint Germain fair, which specialised in the sale of fabric, linens, and trimming (*mercerie*), as well as northern genre paintings. As the clientele of the fair selected and donned new fabric surfaces, the Italian actors did the same. Social disguise through costume was one of the favoured motifs of this theatre, which was already premised upon a repertoire of stock characters identified by fixed garments and masks. Watteau's depictions of the fair theatre should be understood within this context of a marketplace for appearances, which also hosted a theatre whose comedy was based on the exchangeability of appearances. In addition, the theatre and the marketplace offered parallel forms of address. While Watteau depicts the Italian troupe encountering their audience across the theatrical proscenium, retailers at the fair faced their prospective clients across counters. These kinds of encounter are key to understanding both the structure of social relationships in the marketplace and the way that visual art subsumed the representation of the marketplace into the address of the human figure.

Watteau's *Pierrot* has not previously been considered in relationship to the marketplace. In his larger *oeuvre*, Watteau was known for his creation of a genre called the *fête galante*, in which courtiers and theatrical types mingled in dewy parks, listening to music, sitting on the sun-dappled grass beside fountains, whispering things to one another behind their fans.[1] These paintings depicted elite social life as an eternal, ironic masquerade. When he appears in Watteau's *fêtes galantes*, Pierrot stands out for his stiffness and his frontality, his inability to mould his body into the elegant, torqued poses adopted by Watteau's other figures. While Watteau strings men, women, and children together in delicate chains of outstretched hands, arched necks, and *profils perdus*, Pierrot sits or stands lumpishly in the middle of a group, disengaged from his companions. Disengagement is one of the more striking and disturbing features of the large painting, because Pierrot is both isolated in his inaction and imposing in size. Meeting the viewer's gaze, yet for no apparent reason, Pierrot is a disconcerting presence. What Marianne Roland Michel describes as the 'psychological intensity' of Pierrot's gaze is unexpected in Watteau's work, in which emotions are expressed through nuances of environment, through small movements of the head and the hands.[2] Pierrot makes the viewer uncomfortably aware of the expectation that when a person brings themselves to the notice of another, they have something to 'show for themselves', some pressing reason or special status, which their exhibition of themselves will make clear.

Scholars have offered different readings of this painting. Mid-twentieth-century accounts of the painting tended to perceive melancholy and mourning, an existential disappointment in the condition of humanity. For critics as eminent as Jean Starobinski and Erwin Panofsky, Pierrot was a kind of proto-Bartleby, a figure whose refusal to engage expressed a deep scepticism about the value of human effort.[3] For Panofsky, who sees Pierrot as Watteau's 'self-revelation', if not self-portrait, the character faces the void that answers all human action – death. More recent scholarship has positioned Pierrot within histories of the body and its expressive norms. Sarah Cohen sees the painting as the 'inquiring underside' of the 'artful body' of elite life.[4] Mary Vidal argues that Pierrot represents Watteau's vision of the artist-as-aristocrat, who refuses to sing for his supper.[5] Christian Michel, who does not believe the painting is by Watteau, for reasons that will be discussed later, suggests that Pierrot is 'the place of all projections' regarding Watteau's melancholy poetics and abbreviated life.[6] Refusal, failure, melancholy – what many of these accounts share is a recognition that Pierrot offers a commentary on Watteau's larger *oeuvre*, a commentary that would be less acute if it were not for the existence of the large painting, which magnifies Pierrot's peculiar status.

I want to focus here on Pierrot's relationship to the Parisian fairs. Watteau arrived in Paris in the middle of the first decade of the eighteenth century. Having obtained some training as a painter in Valenciennes, a French town near the border with Belgium, Watteau found work churning out inexpensive devotional panels at a picture merchant (*marchand de tableaux*) on or near the Pont Nôtre Dame. He drew furiously in his spare time, filling notebooks with studies of human figures. Perhaps in search of new models, the artist began to frequent the fair, where all manner of goods and people could be seen and studied. It was likely at the fair that Watteau met his first teacher, Claude Gillot. Thomas Crow has offered a crucial account of the way that the fair as a distinctive public space – a *fête publique* – shaped the *fête galante*.[7] One of the (few) elements left out of Crow's discussion, however, is the character of the fair as a place of retail and commerce, a *fête marchande*. In a consideration of the fair as a *fête marchande*, Watteau's Pierrot emerges as representative of the theatrical address of the marketplace. In the first part of this chapter, I describe the theatrical, material, and social commerce that took place at the fair. I also identify the special relationship between the theatre in which Pierrot emerged as a stock type and the performance of the social role as a masquerade. In the second part, I explore the relationship between Pierrot, the costume print, the curtain call, and the shop counter.

The fair and its theatre

There were two major fairs in eighteenth-century Paris. On the left bank of the Seine, the Foire Saint Germain was a fabric market that had expanded into a ritzy venue for shopping, entertainment, and the promenade. The fair hosted vendors of luxury and imported goods, including Flemish paintings and Asian 'curiosities', as well as a lively nightlife frequented by the dandies of the court.[8] The Foire Saint-Laurent, to the north-east of the city centre, was known for its plainer household goods: merchants sold woven baskets, wooden barrels, copper pots, rice, and beer.[9] There were also vendors selling dolls, as well as gloves and *mercerie* (ribbons, buttons, and trimming). A third, smaller fair, the Foire Saint-Ovide, was held in late August in what is now the Place Vendôme. The larger fairs were open for three to six weeks a year (the Foire Saint-Laurent opened in late July and closed in early September, the Foire Saint Germain was open in February and March).[10] The fairs were entered through gates, opening onto covered wooden halls, divided into stalls (*loges*). Cafés and bars fuelled shoppers who browsed late into the night, taking advantage of the fact that the boutiques stayed open until 10 or 11 pm. In the evening, the beautiful people of Paris came to the fair to see and be seen, promenading through the streets, eyeing the displays of fans and jewellery. Pickpockets, cardsharps, and bands of rowdy lackeys roved the corridors of the market and hunted for victims in the crowds.

Since at least the mid-seventeenth century, the fairs had featured live performances by human 'curiosities' and troupes of acrobats (*danseurs de corde*).

By the late-seventeenth century, other actors, popping up for a song or a spot of comic dialogue, had begun to supplement the activities of the tightrope walkers and dancing dogs. A major influx of new performers occurred in 1697, when Louis XIV rescinded the privileges of the Comédie Italienne, the Parisian iteration of the *commedia dell'arte*. This was Pierrot's troupe, which had been performing regularly in Paris since the 1650s, under the protection of the king. Having been officially expelled from Paris, the Italian performers quickly began to reappear at the fair theatres, where they joined existing troupes or formed new ones. Much of the repertoire of the old troupe, which had been published in 1701, was appropriated and re-used by the fair performers.[11] The Comédie-Française, bastion of French tragedy, was not pleased with the re-appearance of the Italians. A series of legal battles unfolded between representatives of the fair theatres, who claimed to be protected by the privileges that governed duty-free commerce at the fairs, and the Comédie-Française, which claimed its exclusive right to the *comédie* defined as staged, spoken theatre.[12]

When Watteau arrived in Paris and began frequenting the fairs, these disputes were in full swing. While awaiting a favourable judgement, the fair troupes adapted their repertoires. Dialogue (speech between two or more actors) was off-limits, but clever workarounds were invented, like having the actor's lines written on a scroll above the stage and spoken or sung by the audience. Pantomime and physical comedy, in which the Italians already specialised, was also a natural fit. Interestingly, Pierrot acquired greater importance in the fair theatre. In several plays, he was even presented as the personification of the fair.[13] Eventually, the fair theatres would be granted their own remit as the Opéra Comique, which after 1716 would go on to coexist with the re-established Comédie Italienne.[14] The fair theatres worked hard to attract audiences, appealing to fairgoers and competing against one another through the *parade*, a brief pantomimic skit performed by actors on the balcony on the theatre's façade or on a trestle stage (*tréteaux*) set up in the street. As period prints show, fair theatres had balconies on their first storeys from which performers could regale the passerby, offering what was in effect a preview or a live advertisement for the offerings inside the theatre. Bernard Picart's frontispiece for the publication of a Dutch edition of *Le théâtre de la foire* in 1731 shows a stage decorated with a set representing the exterior of one of the fair theatres (see Figure 1.1).[15] (Somewhat confusingly, it was common for plays performed at the fair to be set at the fair, a *mise-en-abyme* that I will discuss further below.) The muses of comedy, poetry, music, and dance stand towards the front of the stage, which is hung with a painted backdrop (*toile de fond*) showing the façade of a fair theatre. A crowd gathers beneath a balcony on the theatre's façade, on which eight of the actors have gathered, including Pierrot at the far left (stage-right). Two doors on either side of the façade allow for entrances and exits. Arlequin strikes his characteristic, hip-cocked, leg-raised pose, which he directs to the crowd, while Scaramouche, in the centre of the balcony, points to the large canvas hung above the balcony, on which a nearly life-sized tightrope walker is depicted.

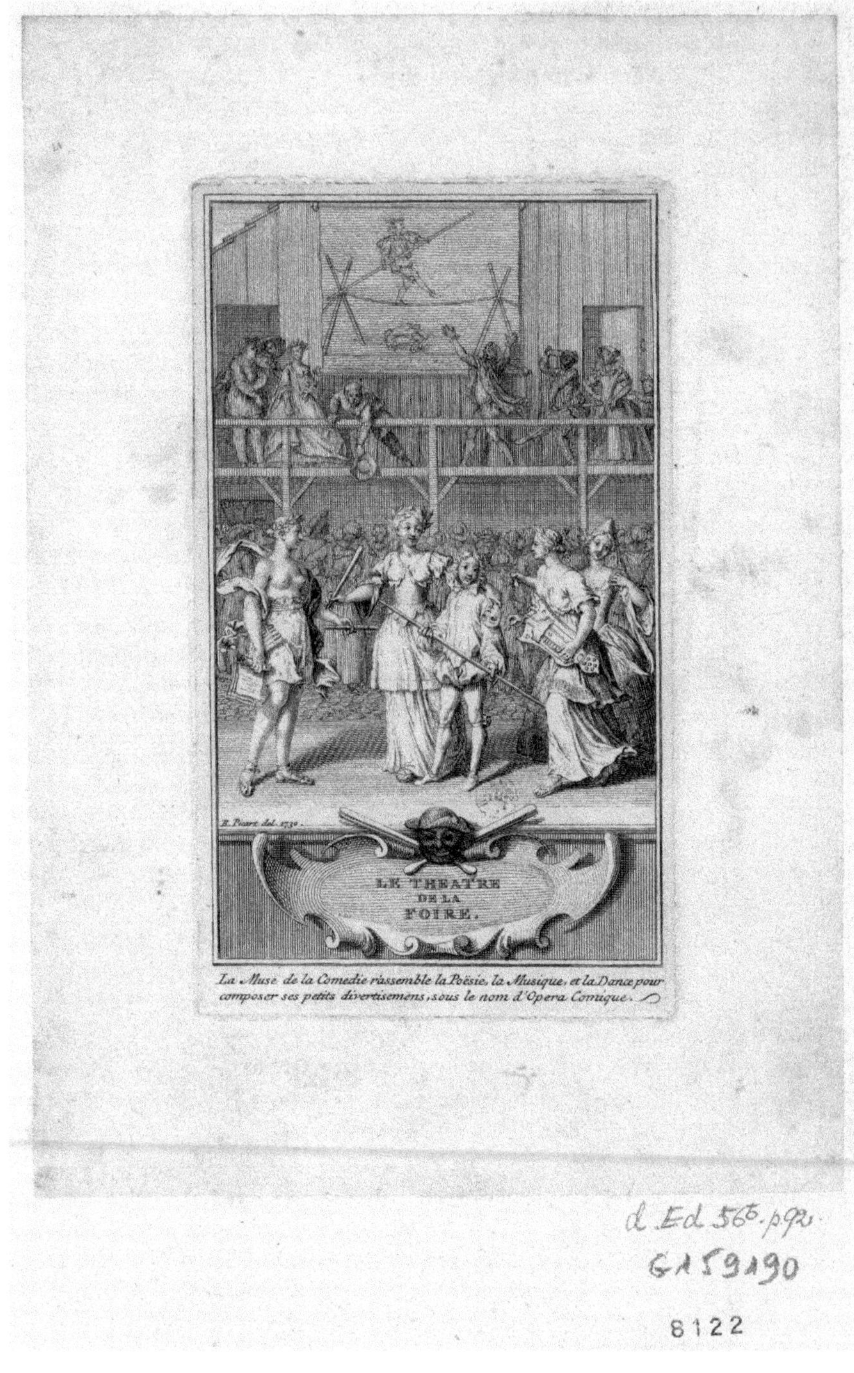

1.1   Bernard Picart, Frontispiece for *Le théâtre de la foire*, 1730. Etching. Source: Bibliothèque Nationale de France. RESERVE QB-201 (93)-FOL ©BNF.

In its placement outside the theatre, the *parade* participated in a long tradition of street theatre: performances that occurred in the open air, the audience for which was mobile and shifting, composed of passersby. Street theatre had long been a vibrant tradition in France and was particularly tied to open-air urban marketplaces, where charlatans and their clowns held sway.[16] Brief skits and bawdy dialogues helped to gather a crowd of potential purchasers. These skits and their tactics were at the origins of the fairground *parades*. To attract the attention of the passerby, the antics of the *parade* pushed the envelope of both physical humour and propriety.[17] Pierrot was a regular in the *parades*, where he received his usual share of kicks and punches. The *parade* was different enough from the theatre proper to resort to a different character, closely related to Pierrot, as the butt of jokes in the *parade*. Called 'Gilles' or 'a Gilles', this character was a bumbling naïve who wore a tunic and trousers of rough white linen.[18] Gilles was the Pierrot of the *parades*, which is one of the reasons why Watteau's painting has long had two names: *Pierrot, called Gilles*. Compared to the performance that went on inside the theatre, which was also addressed to the paying audience, the *parade* exaggerated and made explicit the address of the marketplace: the way that the performance was both for and directed at the consumer.

The fair and its marketplace

The fair was set apart from the city, entered through gates. The ground of the Saint Germain fair was a few feet lower than the surrounding streets, which furthered the sense of distinction. The fair concentrated the activities that would eventually come to be associated with Paris as a capital of consumption: shopping, promenading, people-watching, the last of which took place both in the streets of the fair and in the fair theatres. Beautiful women worked as vendors at many of the fair's stalls, advertising their own charms alongside those of their merchandise.[19] Throughout the eighteenth century, the merchants operating at the fair both complained about the distractions posed by the theatre and fought vigorously to ensure that the theatres did not move elsewhere.[20] After watching a performance that ended at seven or eight in the evening, the audience would spill out into the fair. Gentlemen would buy baubles or drinks for their female companions; gambling was also a popular activity. The theatres both attracted customers and prepared the audience for further pleasure. The eating, drinking, and listening to music that happened on stage could be replicated in the fairground outside the theatre. In fact, plays were frequently set at the fair itself, which meant that the appearance of the fair was recreated on the stage of the fair theatres, further encouraging viewers to conceptualise the fair as a stage.[21] The plays established a normative repertoire of fair activities and a cast of typical fair denizens: young lovers and their guardians, worldly-wise ladies' maids seeking additional income as money lenders, barkers whose services were available for a price. When a performance of *Pierrot Roland* ended with Pierrot celebrating drunkenly in a bar, the play modelled a form of behaviour that would have been possible only a few metres away from the stage, in one of the many cafés.

Much has been made of the class mixing produced at the fair, which was attended by the entire range of the social spectrum. Following Bakhtin's discussion of the mediaeval carnival, these accounts characterise the fair as a place of hybridity and 'contamination', where classical order is dissolved in the crush of the crowd.[22] Different social types are thrown together, a baker's apprentice against a duchess, a thief against a magistrate, and so on. The density of the crowd could become deadly – at least a hundred people were killed during a stampede at the Foire Saint-Ovide in 1770.[23] Yet the fair was also a place where social distinctions were performed and enumerated. Authors of guides to Paris tended to list the different kinds of people who came to the fair; for example, Nemeitz in 1727: 'all is pell-mell, masters with valets and lackeys, pickpockets with honest persons. The most refined courtiers, the prettiest girls, the most cunning thieves, are as enlaced together.'[24] While this description presents a diversity of types, thrown together at the fair, and even 'enlaced', the listing of the types works against the idea of a homogeneous mass, in which social distinctions dissolved. In other words, the very fact that Nemeitz is able to list distinct social categories indicates that differences had not been utterly lost.[25] I would suggest that what was operative was not dissolution of difference but rather proximity to difference. At the fair, there would have still been opportunity for a particular kind of measured, calculated, 'misanthropic' looking, which took for granted that all roles were merely appearances.[26] This kind of looking did not attempt to discover the truth behind the appearance, but merely to evaluate the result of appearances constituted through costume and performance. Moreover, retail activity accentuated differences, not only because not everyone could buy everything, but because retail itself established a separation between those who sold and those who bought, a gap occupied by gazes of desire, of assessment, of speculation. In this environment, difference inspired the desire to consume as a means of closing the gap between oneself and what was desired.

By creating a space for shopping, socialising, theatre, and performance, the fair crystallised the emerging terms of a relationship between urbanity, commercial culture, and the theatre.[27] In this relationship, the fair was understood as a stage where individuals performed the social identities to which they aspired, to the extent that their purses could afford. The idea that social identity lay in outer manifestations, in expressions like clothing, jewellery, as well as an entourage of liveried servants or guards, had long been an accepted bulwark of the state and the privileges of the elite.[28] The performance of status bolstered the political system; the 'theatre state' of Louis XIV performed noble exceptionalism through pomp and ceremony.[29] Yet industrial and demographic changes in the eighteenth century – the concentration of salaried workers in cities, the importing and production of cheap, semi-disposable commodities – enabled a greater portion of the public to access the costumes, props, and settings of the theatre state. Freshly costumed and in search of a stage, the new masqueraders would find an outlet at the fair. Performing identity was not new, but the number of performers increased, as did the density of performances. What had also changed was the nature of the stage. Instead of performing the courtly rituals of the hunt or the tournament, fairgoers took to the stage of retail. In Watteau's era, this transformation was in its infancy. However, the fair and its theatres would provide a guiding light, a space for rehearsing the changes to come.

Selling cloth surfaces

Originally a wholesale textile market, by the early eighteenth century the Foire Saint Germain hosted numerous retail boutiques selling directly to consumers (*commerce en détail*). The shops were called *loges*, which was also the term for a private box at the theatre as well as for the actor's dressing room. Indeed, the shops functioned as places from which to observe the spectacle of the fair. Nemeitz indicates that idle fairgoers would 'post themselves in a boutique, from which they would watch the passersby'.[30] Period illustrations suggest several possible arrangements for the shops. In one, the shop was entirely open on one side; counters lined the remaining three sides of the booth. Further merchandise could be stored in an attic room above the shop, which also featured a window. Vendors stood behind the counters. In another arrangement, the client could not enter the shop but only transact across a counter flush with the shop's façade.[31] Those walking through the fair could easily observe the activities of those inside the shops, where consumption was performed as gallantry and leisure. In common parlance, gallantry was closely associated with sartorial bits and bobs, such as gloves, fans, ribbons, and lace, which were offered by suitors and friends as tokens of admiration. These favours were referred to as 'gallantries' and sold at *boutiques de galanterie*, which were thick on the ground at the fair.[32] In addition to the traditional media of conversation and music, gallantry was now enacted through shopping, a phenomenon symptomatic of 'the commercialization of social life in urban France'.[33]

Paintings were also on display and for sale at the fair. This may have been one of the reasons that Watteau was initially attracted to the fair, where he would have been able to study a range of artworks. Prior to 1737, when Salons became a regular event, the fair was the most significant space for viewing easel painting in Paris. Dealers sold landscapes, still lifes, and genre scenes. These Flemish and Dutch specialties were popular decorations for the home.[34] It is unlikely that Watteau's own paintings were sold at the fair. Watteau worked on commission or with dealers who had shops in Paris, outside the fairs.[35] Yet he would certainly have seen the booths of the painting sellers, which meant that he would have seen paintings displayed for sale, as opposed to a painting on an easel in an artist's studio or in a collector's cabinet. Alongside barkers of curiosities, actors in the *parade*, bolts of fabrics, and imported ceramics, paintings pitched themselves at fairgoers, doing their best to be noticed and to be looked at.

Cloth, ribbons, sartorial 'gallantry', and paintings – these were the media through which the surface of appearance was constructed and performed. Alongside bodies clad in cloth surfaces, the fair booths also offered the sight of uninhabited surfaces: bolts of cloth, collars and trim, and linens. Linens – stockings, petticoats, chemises – were some of the earliest garments to be sold ready-to-wear, as opposed to made-to-order. There were enough sellers of linens (*lingères*) at the Foire Saint-Laurent for an entire street to be named Rue de la Lingerie.[36] Linen garments were hung and pinned on boards as a mode of display (*étalage*). These empty garments, advertising their availability, populated the fair's visual spectacle. Paintings were another of the surfaces offered by the fair, including the paintings of performers that hung outside the theatres, the paintings for sale in the booths, and the portraits of actors and nobility that were used as shop signs by individual booths. Both paintings and garments were cloth surfaces, which made them suspect for critics of the marketplace or of the theatre, whose concerns centred around the superficial character of appearances. Pierrot's theatre, the Comédie Italienne, offered satirical insight into the exchangeability of garments and paintings.

The Comédie Italienne and the culture of appearances

The *commedia dell'arte*, which originated in early sixteenth-century Italy, presented the antics and the romances of a set of 'masks' or stock characters.[37] A particular costume was associated with each character; this garment constituted the character's mask. Each mask was visually and behaviorally distinct and represented a different age, class, and temperament.[38] The standard repertoire of masks included the young lovers, the lecherous and greedy old men (*vecchi*), and the clowns (*zanni*) who doubled as household servants. Pierrot was one of these clown servants. The performances were unscripted, but not entirely improvised. A scenario or *canevas* would be provided and the actors would fill in the gaps with set speeches that illustrated their comic characteristics, and physical gags. Young lovers wished to unite; old men got in their way; servants schemed against their masters; vainglorious military types bragged of their courage and ran away at the first hint of conflict.

The Medici consorts of French kings were responsible for introducing the Italian theatre to France.[39] By the mid-seventeenth century, Paris had its own troupe of Italian comedians, the Comédie Italienne, which performed at the Palais Royal and enjoyed the benefits of royal protection.[40] It was in France that Pierrot emerged as a stock type in the Italian troupe.[41] His character was a naïve valet from the countryside; he was earthy and literal, a familiar of farm animals and flour mills, an emissary of nature at its least refined. In reflection of his rural origins, Pierrot wore a simple costume of tunic and trousers made of white canvas (*toile*), which led Arlequin in one play to refer to Pierrot as a human windmill (windmills, during the period, were covered in unpainted canvas).[42] Pierrot is illiterate, although sometimes he indicates that he can write by copying the shapes of letters. He is lazy; he loves to eat and drink.

Pierrot generally works as an upper-level household servant, a 'body servant' or valet to his masters. He runs errands, delivering letters or picking up medicine; he acts as a confidant to his master; he fetches articles of dress and cosmetics for his mistresses.[43]

The Italian comedies fixated upon a particular set of social issues that had arisen around the body servant's relationship to class. Because body servants were responsible for maintaining their masters' wardrobes, brushing and mending clothes, laying out the linens that had been bleached and laundered by other, lower categories of servant, they often received old clothes from their masters as a tip. Living in close proximity with their masters, servants learned the behaviours and speech patterns of the upper classes. In several instances, having borrowed their master's clothes or received them as a gift, servants were able to pass themselves off as their masters or as members of the upper classes.[44] These instances, however, were few and far between. Stories of a servant's successful counterfeiting fascinated and terrorised in inverse proportion to the actual feasibility of such events. Most servants were obliged to wear clothing chosen for them by their masters. Upon entering a new household, a servant received a set of clothes and, often, a new name.[45] The furnishing of clothes, as well as food, to servants, was referred to as 'livery'. A servant's own clothing – the garments worn on arrival, which very often constituted the individual's entire stock of clothing – could be held, as a form of security, by the master.[46] A servant who wanted to leave employment would have to beg their master or mistress for their old clothes.

In the repertoire of the Comédie Italienne, clothing is the favourite medium for trickery, comic disguise, and social climbing. In a self-conscious doubling of masks, masked characters don further layers of disguise, creating hybrid identities like 'Arlequin-marquis'. As this name would suggest, the Comédie Italienne used costume to fixate on a particular aspect of the luxury debate – the possibility that non-nobles, including servants, could use costume to disguise themselves as nobles. In one play, Pierrot pesters his master, the Doctor, for the gift of an old suit of clothes. He informs his master that once he has put on this suit, he will become 'just as much a Doctor as you'.[47] His master rebuffs him for his foolishness, yet Pierrot's comment cuts to the heart of the matter. In sixteenth- and seventeenth-century France, the expense of cloth and tailoring meant that people only owned a few garments. As a result, clothes were highly meaningful and generally accurate indices of social position; indeed, clothes not only expressed status, clothes constituted status, 'investing' a person with a role or a duty.[48] The preoccupations of the Comédie Italienne describe a changing situation, in which appearances have become less reliable as well as less permanent. In *The Culture of Appearances*, Daniel Roche suggests that over the course of the eighteenth century it did indeed become increasingly easy to counterfeit sartorial identities.[49] There were more clothes and they circulated more widely through shops, fairs, and informal networks. In this context, theatre became an important model for the creation of identity through clothing, an argument that has been made by Ann Rosalind Jones and Peter Stallybrass in their work on clothing in the Renaissance.[50] Theatres bought, stocked, and traded inventories of second-hand clothes so that actors could create roles by physically inhabiting costumes, thus modelling the possibilities for consumers. These practices are treated quite literally in the Comédie Italienne, with characters demanding the gifts of second-hand clothes so as to change their social role.

On stage, Pierrot frequently expressed dissatisfaction with the plainness of his costume. He blames his 'suit of canvas' (*habit de toile*) for his inability to attract women.[51] *Toile* was a catch-all term for woven fabric, yet the word was most widely used to designate fabric woven of linen or hemp, both of which were fibres widely cultivated in France, particularly in northern regions close to the sea.[52] Linen was incredibly versatile; its products ranged from very coarse and heavy fabrics, which could be used as ship sails or as wrappers for merchandise in transit, to the finer textiles used for undergarments like shirts, shifts, and underskirts. *Toile de lin* was also used for household textiles like tablecloths, napkins, and sheets. At the Foire Saint Germain, canvas sellers (*toilliers*) and linen merchants (*marchands lingers*) sold linen in bulk. Linen *en détail*, sewn into household linens and undergarments (*lingerie*), was also sold at both fairs. Two further, highly significant uses of *toile* include the surface (the canvas) used by painters and the stage curtain in theatres.

In the Comédie Italienne, painting serves as a tool of social masquerade. Arlequin, when he wants to disguise himself as a marquis or a magistrate, has his portrait painted. When other characters try to wear this portrait, they perform the capacity of painting to serve as a disguising surface. In *Colombine Lawyer, For and Against*, Arlequin, masquerading as a gentleman, commissions a portrait of himself wearing the attire of his new social class. He is painted at full length. Later in the play, Arlequin's angry ex-girlfriend Colombine sticks her head through the painting of Arlequin as a gentleman, thereby wearing Arlequin's surface herself and literalising the equation between painting and costume. The same play also includes a remarkable instance of a painter mistaking Pierrot for a blank canvas and daubing paint on his face. Pierrot protests, crying, 'hey, mister, I'm not the *tableau*'.[53] To someone who could hardly see, Pierrot in his suit (of *toile*) might indeed resemble a large, blank canvas. Furthermore, Pierrot *is* a blank canvas to the extent that dress itself was a form of canvas to be further embellished with the addition of ribbons, lace, and gold trim.

In fact, in a moment often cited as the birth of the Pierrot type, Pierrot envies another man's ribbons and trimmings.[54] Between 1660 and 1673, the Comédie Italienne shared a stage, the Palais Royal, with Molière's troupe. In 1665, Molière created a poorly mannered peasant, Pierrot, to appear in *Dom Juan, ou le festin de pierre*, a retelling of the Don Juan tale.[55] To save Don Juan from drowning, Pierrot interrupts a game in which he throws fistfuls of dirt at a friend. Pierrot's good deed does not prevent the Don from going on to cuckold him with Charlotte, his girlfriend. Before this can happen, however, Pierrot is treated to the sight of Don Juan and his entourage getting dressed. In the first scene of the second act, Pierrot delivers a long monologue in which he describes in awestruck tones the quantity of ribbons, lace, layered undergarments, chemises, wigs, and jackets that compose a gentleman's *toilette*.[56] He has never seen 'so many ribbons, so many ribbons', the quantity of which cannot compare to the single strip of ribbon he occasionally buys for Charlotte from a passing mercer.[57] With his two appearances on stage, Pierrot stole the show. A few years later, the Comédie Italienne would stage a satire of Molière's play, marking the first time that the actor Gératon would appear as Pierrot (although no comic monologue is offered).[58] While I cannot directly follow this longing into the Pierrot that Watteau painted, Molière's Pierrot is a testament to the comic theatre's obsession with clothing and impersonation. Pierrot is born of a desire for *galanterie* in the form of ribbons. He believes that Don Juan must be a 'great, great Monsieur, because he had gold on his suit from the bottom to the top and those who serve him are Monsieurs themselves'.[59] This naïve equation was sure to elicit laughter, or at the very least a few nervous titters. In his simplicity, Pierrot cuts to the heart of the problem: Don Juan is noble, but he is not a gentleman. His cloth mask, therefore, is opaque rather than transparent, a barrier to truth and a surface of deception.

The Comédie Italienne was an antic genre, in which social surfaces were tossed on and off with glee, cast aside like an old chemise, picked up by the next passerby, with hilarious consequences. Painting and clothing were both represented as agents of false appearance, yet the desire to don such disguises burns in the hearts of the characters playing the role of servants and clowns. The fair was the ideal locale for this theatrical genre, as Regnard's play *La Foire Saint Germain* (1695) suggests. A print, which both advertised the play and commemorated its performance, shows the stage made up as an aisle at the fair (see Figure 1.2). The print offers fascinating information about the possible appearance of the fair booths, which are separated from the aisles of the covered hall by counters. Wooden shutters, closed at night, are flipped up above the booths, which contain further counters, behind which young women busy themselves. Merchandise is arranged on shelves. Several stalls are marked by signs painted with human figures at three-quarter length. The frontispiece represents the play's opening scene, which begins with the cries of the merchants advertising their wares. Arlequin, taking a stroll through the booths, meets Mezzetin dressed as a *garçon pâtissier*, carrying a tray of cakes (*ratons*). Mezzetin sings a ditty spoofing the cries of the merchants: 'oranges from china, oranges, ribbons, hair ribbons'.[60] Tempted by the goods on offer, Arlequin tries on a chemise and a dressing gown, foreshadowing the numerous disguises he will go on to assume over the course of the play. In the print, these cloth surfaces are offered to him by attentive vendors. Comically, a further vendor approaches bearing a large wheel of parmesan cheese.

At the fair, cloth disguises were readily available. Just as an actor slipped into his *loge* to change costume, at the fair clients entered the shops (*loges*) to procure new surfaces and new identities. In *La Foire Saint Germain*, a young woman, Angélique, conceals herself at the fair to avoid the advances of her lecherous guardian. Upon meeting her old servant Colombine, who has become a money lender at the fair, Angélique says she wants 'to lose herself

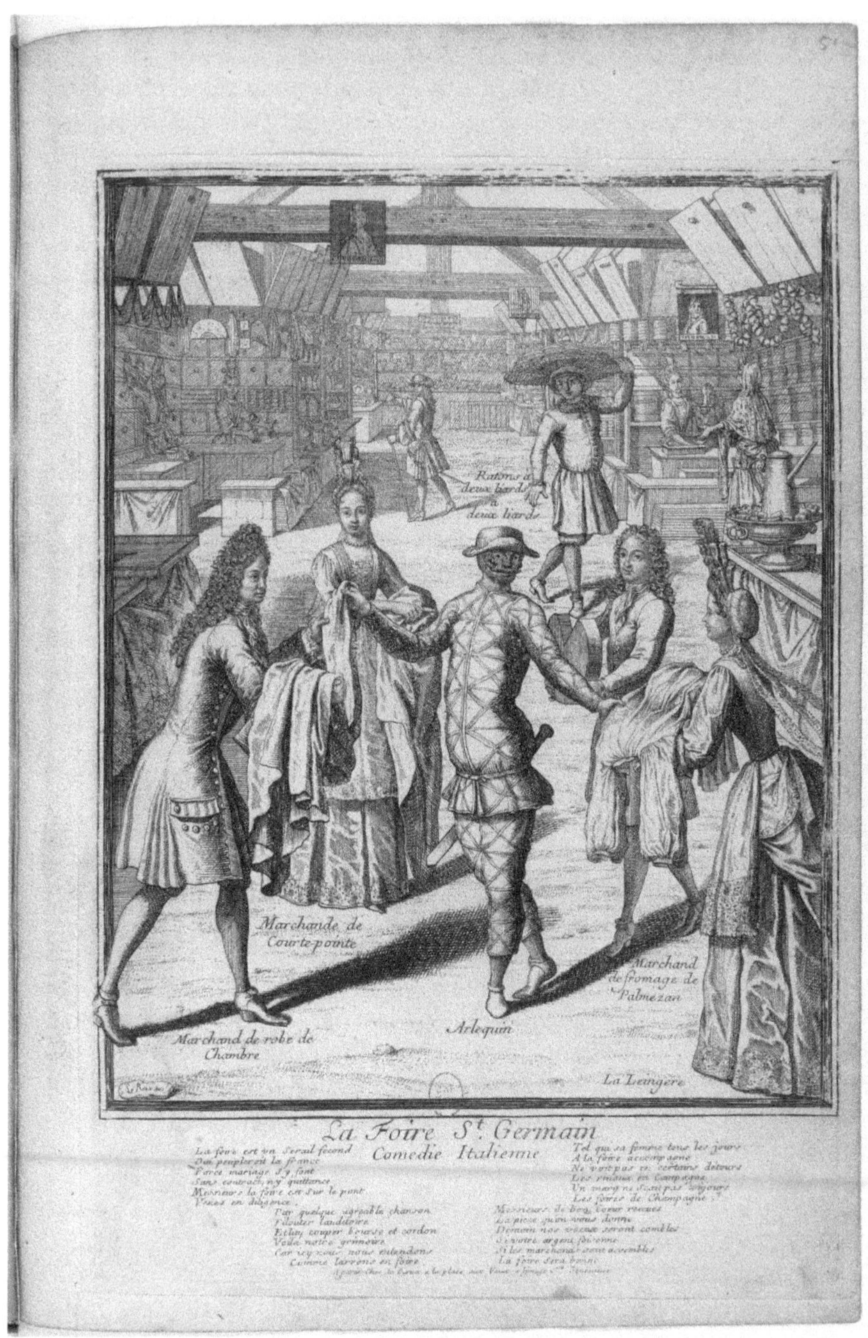

1.2　A. Le Roux (publisher), *La Foire Saint Germain*, late seventeenth century. Etching, approx. 36.5 × 25 cm. Source: Bibliothèque Nationale de France. Bibliothèque-musée de l'opéra, RES 926 (4) ©BNF.

at the Fair'.[61] To this Colombine responds that it is difficult to lose oneself in a 'public place'.[62] Yet Colombine mistakes the public place for a space of transparency, when in fact the public marketplace offered ample opportunities to procure masks with which to obscure one's identity. While Regnard's play was originally performed at the Hôtel de Bourgogne, prior to the troupe's expulsion, its setting and themes anticipated the troupe's future home. The fair provided the means, the opportunity, and the stage for the marketing of human persona as surfaces both painted and worn. Marketing emerged as an activity that was indebted to theatrical presentations of the human body, especially those that occurred in the *parade*. Social exchanges, in both fair theatres and fair shops, became a particular kind of encounter – ocular assessment across a threshold.

Picturing the fair

In the sixteenth and seventeenth centuries, northern artists had represented their marketplaces, open spaces bordered by stately architecture, teeming with people and vendors. In northern Europe, the market scene was popular enough to become a setting for the *ecce homo* motif, in which Pilate exhibits Christ to a teeming marketplace of vendors and customers.[63] Jacques Callot, whose work would have been well known to Watteau, offered a crucial and widely disseminated representation of the rural fair, including its trestle-stage performers, in his etching *The Fair of Impruneta* (c. 1617).[64] Yet very few artists attempted similar representations of early eighteenth-century Parisian fairs. Watteau, despite the time he spent at the fairs, never attempted a composition in the style of Callot. There are several prints of the period which offer highly informative representations of the fair, for example the well-known aerial view of the Foire Saint Germain, which includes the 'field of spectacles' in the foreground, where performances take place in the open air (see Figure 1.3). In the left-hand corner, the print shows a trestle stage above which is hung a large canvas depicting rope walkers and other actors, presumably members of the troupe (see Figure 1.4). If the marketplace as an architectural environment populated with figures was of minimal interest to eighteenth-century French artists, the act of *marketing*, represented through the human figure's theatrical presentation of itself, proved a subject of enduring interest.

In what follows, I explore Watteau's representations of the fair theatre and the shop counter in order to argue, ultimately, that Watteau's Pierrot can be understood to incorporate, by way of the costume print, the social dynamics of both theatre and counter. Watteau's representations of the curtain call explore the relationship between theatre and marketing, while his interest in the shop counter reveals sensitivity to the thresholds that structure social encounters. In the many costume prints that do not depict the character's surroundings, the theatrical proscenium and the shop counter survive in the figure's mode of address. In the guise of a personification of both proscenium and counter, Watteau's Pierrot represents not the market

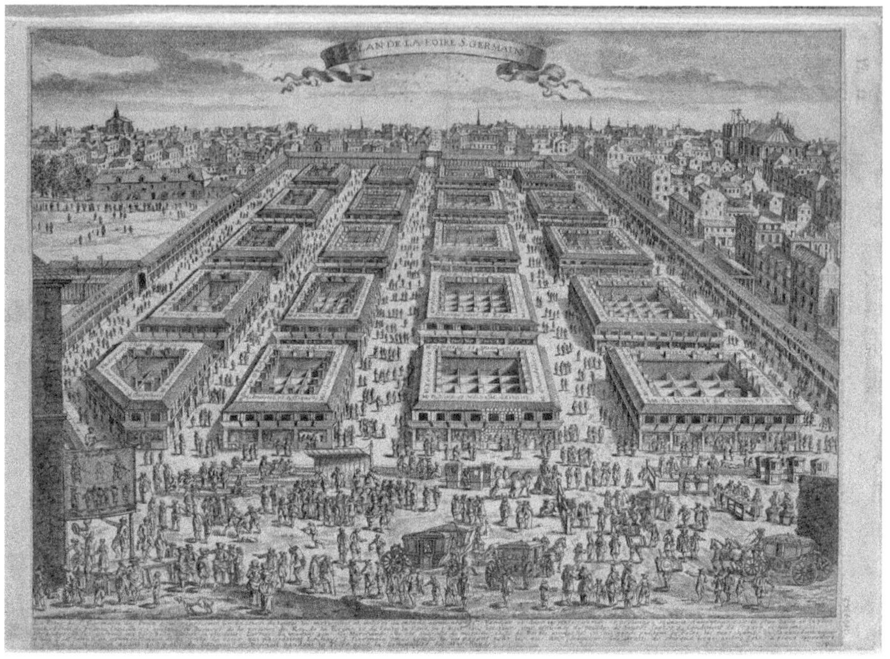

1.3 *Plan of the Saint Germain Fair*, eighteenth century. Etching. Source: Bibliothèque Nationale de France. VA-267 (D)-FOL H047362 ©BNF.

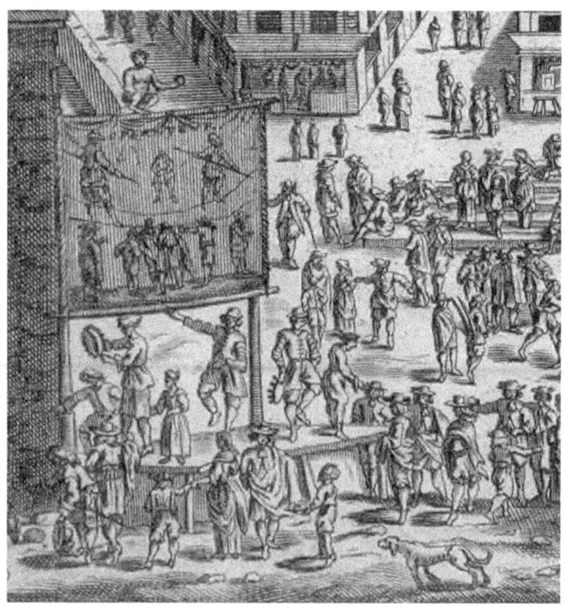

1.4 Detail of Figure 1.3.

itself, but the way that the marketplace embeds itself within the fabric of the social encounter.

Curtain call

The distinctive figure that Watteau created for Pierrot appears to have evolved out of a series of drawings of curtain calls, the moment at the end of the performance when the actors assemble to receive applause.[65] Watteau drew the curtain call a number of times, always putting Pierrot at the centre of the group of actors lining up on the edge of the stage.[66] In the drawing at the National Gallery, Washington, Pierrot bends forward in a half-bow (see Plate 3). He has removed his hat, which he has turned over and which he presents to the audience, in the hope that a few happy spectators will toss in a handful of coins. The décor of the stage presents the shallow playing space flanked by two wings, one of which is decorated with a statue enclosed in a pediment. At the back of the stage is a *toile de fond* painted with a perspective décor, which continues the recession begun by the two wings. To indicate the proscenium, Watteau uses a handful of curving strokes to draw a curtain across the stage. The stage décor remains visible through the strokes delineating the curtain, which suggests that Watteau added the curtain atop the décor he had already drawn, to clearly mark the threshold of the stage, just beyond which Pierrot and the other players stand.

Watteau gradually reworked this motif, drawing Pierrot and the curtain into closer alignment, by pulling Pierrot back and by suppressing his bow. This is the case in one of the rare autograph etchings by Watteau, *The Costumes are Italian*, in which Pierrot appears immediately adjacent to the curtain, which falls along the same, single plane as his tunic, now that he is no longer bending forward in a bow. In this composition, Watteau contrasts Pierrot's tense stiffness with the exquisite ease of the two female figures showing off beside him (see Plate 4). In Watteau's only extant painting to depict a curtain call, *The Italian Comedians*, Pierrot forms the pale summit of a pyramid of gesticulating Italian masks (see Plate 5). The actors stand before a curved stone wall, punctuated by a doorway, which Pierrot's figure blocks. Pierrot stands further from the red curtain draped over the the right-hand corner of the stage, but the surface of his costume is still aligned with it. Behind the troupe, through the doorway, lies a garden typical of Watteau's *fêtes galantes*. The garden is where Watteau's Italian masks habitually perform; the composition suggests that the troupe has stepped out of the performance to take their bows.

The Italian Comedians amplifies the contrast between Pierrot's stillness and straightness and the physical behaviour of the other Italian characters. Arlequin shows off in his signature, hip-cocked posture, partially concealed by a guitar-player who sways to the sound of his music, while Colombine, one of the young lovers, coquettishly glances at the viewer, her swan-like neck displayed to full effect. In the relative simplicity of his pose, Pierrot anchors the composition. The other characters have snapped into action, as if trying to diffuse the tension of the moment. Yet Pierrot, characteristically literal, gets straight to the point of the curtain call: he presents himself and awaits the audience's verdict. The curtain call is both a presentational and a transactional moment that makes explicit the fact that the performance, all along, was intended for the audience, who either has paid or will pay for their pleasure. The curtain call articulates the theatrical address of the performance: the way that the play solicits the audience. As Marie-Claude Groshens has argued, in a brief but fascinating account, the character of theatrical performance as solicitation is amplified in the context of fairs, which are underlain by an 'order of exchange' (*ordre marchand*).[67] She characterises the fair as a 'merchant festivity' (*fête marchande*), an evocative juxtaposition to the Royal Academy's description of Watteau's work as 'gallant festivities' (*fêtes galantes*). Against the backdrop of the *fête marchande*, theatrical 'presentations and counter presentations' take on an 'agonistic' character, pitting audience against actors.[68] For Bakhtin, this is why eighteenth- and nineteenth-century marketplaces represent a fallen, un-festive world, because pleasure has been monetised. This monetisation is represented, structurally, by the proscenium, which enunciates the distinction between actors and audience. There will be no more delightful merging of bodies, but rather scrutiny and projection across the proscenium.[69] To borrow a term from Richard Sennett, the curtain call, as a 'bridge' between theatre and marketplace, enables behavioural conventions to move between the two spaces.[70] Behaviour learned in the theatre re-appears in the marketplace and vice versa.

Watteau's figure for Pierrot condenses the curtain call into a single figure. Stage curtains, in this period, were not always used. Yet in his representations of the curtain call, Watteau almost always includes a curtain, which he uses to mark the proscenium, the edge or threshold of the stage. Increasingly, Pierrot becomes coincident with this curtain, as in *The Costumes are Italian*, where the surface of his body is aligned with that of the curtain, were it to be drawn across the picture. In addition, because Pierrot faces the viewer frontally, the symmetrical contours of his figure echo those of the proscenium, the arch or frame that faces the viewer 'head on'. With his relatively unadorned costume hanging on the 'frame' of his body like a large piece of fabric, Pierrot is even somewhat suggestive of a proscenium hung with a curtain. In *The Costumes are Italian*, were the curtain itself to be removed, he would remain as the personification of the proscenium's disposition. The first Parisian theatre to feature a fixed proscenium arch as well as a curtain was the theatre at the Palais Royal, purpose-built by Cardinal Richelieu and opened in 1641. It was this same theatre, which Molière's troupe shared with the Comédie Italienne, which saw the appearance of Pierrot in *Dom Juan*, followed by the Italian troupe's adoption of the type. During Watteau's lifetime, the theatre at the Palais Royal housed the Opéra. While Watteau would not have seen Pierrot tread the boards of the Palais Royal, he would have known the celebrated etchings by Stefano della Bella, which depicted the performance of the opera *Mirame* in 1641 and included the neo-classical proscenium arch framing the stage picture. Indeed, the series' frontispiece shows the arch hung with a curtain, on which is written an advertisement for the opening of the theatre as well as the play's name.

This resemblance between Pierrot and a stage curtain can only be suggestive, of course, yet it helps to ascribe a meaningful action to a figure who appears, at first, to be simply inactive. Instead of doing nothing, Pierrot is holding the stage – literally – by maintaining the position of the stage in relation to the audience. This pose also begins to explain Watteau's elevation of Pierrot to the focal point of so many of his compositions. Watteau loads Pierrot with all the stakes of the theatrical encounter, which is at the same time, given the context of the fair, the marketplace encounter. In an account that has not been given its due, Dora Panofsky has compared the composition of *The Italian Comedians* to two etchings by Rembrandt, including his *Ecce Homo*, which shares with Watteau's painting an emphasis on 'the action of presentation as such' (see Figure 1.5).[71] In both compositions, a group of figures appears on a raised platform in front of an arched doorway. Pilate raises his arm and points at Christ, a gesture echoed by the figure in gold taffeta in *The Italian Comedians*. Rembrandt has Pilate show Christ outside a

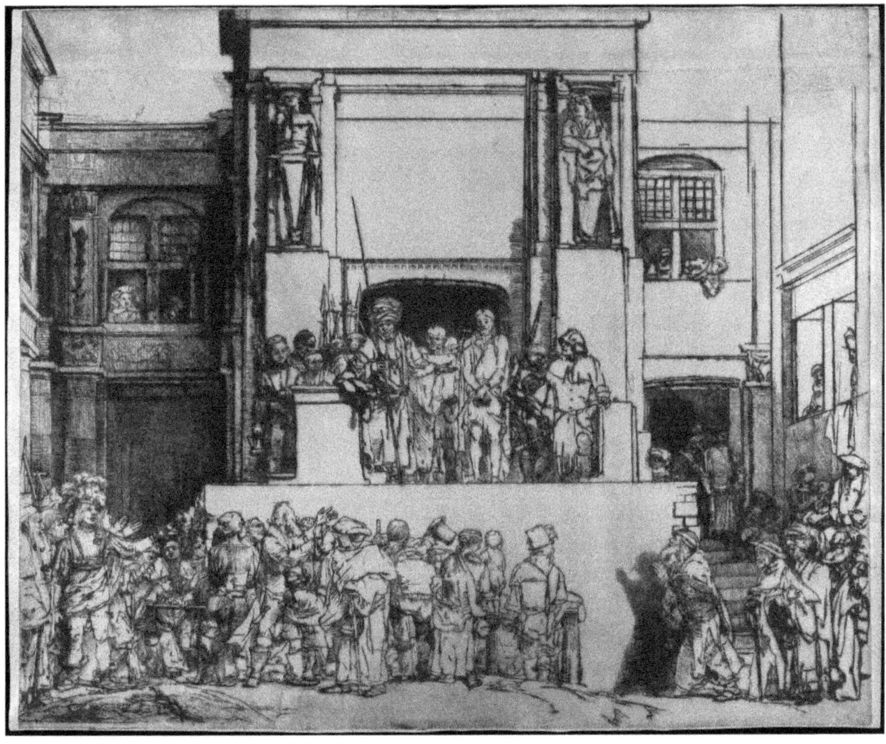

1.5   Rembrandt van Rijn, *Christ Presented to the People*, 1655. Drypoint on japan paper; second stage of eight, 38.4 × 44.9 cm. Source: Metropolitan Museum of Art, New York. 41.1.34 ©metmuseum.org.

typical Dutch town hall, which fronted the market square. Pilate, Christ, and other officers stand on an elevated stone platform, framed by an archway that is suggestive of a theatrical proscenium. This mode of presentation also suggests the *parade*, when it took place on the balcony of the theatre. As noted above, Rembrandt's Dutch and Flemish contemporaries often painted Pilate's showing of Christ in the marketplace. Honig's account of this tradition has emphasised the marketplace as a site of commerce, theatre, and justice or judgment, where what is displayed is weighed, measured, and assessed on both economic and moral grounds.[72] Christ's display, in this context, represents what is at stake for Christian participants in the market, who must make fair and honest judgements when buying and selling goods. Rather than assert a definitive connection between Rembrandt's etching and Watteau's way of presenting Pierrot, I would suggest that both these compositions reflect a curiosity about the dynamics that accompany the setting forth of a figure to be judged. Both Christ in the marketplace and Pierrot in the curtain call are marketed, in the sense of being set forth and subjected to evaluation. The crowd is asked whether it will spare Christ; the audience is asked whether it will throw Pierrot a coin.

Counter

> Immediately he slips from her and through a by-way, that remains visible only for half a moment, with great address entrenches himself behind the counter: here facing her, with a profound reverence and modish phrase he begs her favour of knowing her commands.
>
> Bernard Mandeville, *Fable of the Bees,* cited in Wolfgang Fritz Haug,
> *Critique of Commodity Aesthetics*, trans. Robert Bock [1971;
> Cambridge: Polity Press, 1986], p. 57

As period prints suggest, including the aerial view of the Saint Germain fair as well as the print advertising Regnard's play, counters were an essential feature of fairground architecture, delineating the separation between the vendor and the client, as well as the shop and the street. Even more so than the proscenium, the counter articulated the meeting of two persons as a transactional event. Because eighteenth-century boutiques did not display large amounts of merchandise, the vendor played a starring role in the revelation and the display of goods.[73] The environment foregrounded the interpersonal characteristics of retail, with the body of the vendor standing in for (and sometimes doubling as) the goods for sale.[74] In his comments on the new culture of consumerism, cited in Wolfgang Fritz Haug's analysis of commodity aesthetics, Bernard Mandeville attended to the moment when the salesman, who has been waiting outside the shop, assumes his position behind the counter. In a movement that is nearly imperceptible, the salesman transforms himself from gallant chevalier, who has escorted the woman from her carriage into the shop, into antagonist, who nevertheless retains the mask of the courtier. For Haug, the seller's 'character-mask' combines servility, flattery, and flirtation.[75]

The counter provides the threshold across which this performance takes place, as well as the stage on which sellers present their wares.

Counters have long been a defining element of retail architecture. In French, *comptoir* can refer metonymically to an entire shop or to a trading enterprise more generally. The simplest boutiques in Renaissance Italy were closed by two shutters; to open the boutique the top shutter folded upwards to create an awning and the lower shutter downwards to create a counter.[76] In shop settings, counters are practical, creating a place to put the cash box and packaging. In certain forms of shop design, including those that were commonly used at the fair, the counter created a barrier between the customer and the merchandise, which the vendor brought out from boxes, shelves, and storerooms, and displayed on the counter.[77] The counter announced distance and formalised the interaction that took place across it. The counter provided a kind of set or stage, a prop for the vendor's assumption of their role – hence the change that takes place when Mandeville's salesperson moves behind the counter. Goods move across the counter, while the encounter is animated by the uncertainty of the direction in which the goods will move, whether outwards towards the customer or back to the vendor.

Watteau represented several shop counters.[78] In one drawing, he depicts a draper's shop, a significant choice given that the original purpose of the Foire Saint Germain was the trade in fabric (see Plate 6). An elegant dandy stands at the centre of the shop, leaning casually against the counter, on the other side of which sits a female shop assistant. The woman offers something, perhaps a bunch of ribbons, which the client examines negligently. He declines to fully face the shop assistant, turning only his head. He has yet to fully commit to this encounter, which is part of the game, of course. The stage-like arrangement of the shop, which is missing a 'fourth' wall (the 'third' wall is implied, although not visible), reflects the architecture of the fair booths, which were often open on one side. Watteau pursues the merging of shop and stage in his most significant representation of a shop, *Gersaint's Shop Sign*, which very loosely depicted the interior of his friend Gersaint's boutique on the Pont Neuf (see Figure 1.6). In fact, the façade of Gersaint's shop was enclosed as well as narrow, but Watteau depicts a wide space open to the street.[79] He places an L-shaped counter on the right-hand side of the painting. A young female vendor sits behind the counter, on which is placed a red lacquer box, perhaps the container for a *nécessaire*. The prospective client is a woman dressed in magnificent white satin striped with pink. Like the gentleman in the draper's shop, this woman also hesitates at the threshold, turning only her head towards the merchandise, as well as the mirror that the shop assistant props up.

The counter both represents and enforces the increasingly bilateral underpinnings of market exchange, in which persons are set against (counter) one another. The counter enforced a distance across which the parties in an exchange looked at each other. In this respect, countering can be understood as a particular form of image-making. In previous work, I have discussed the relationship between making images and 'countering'.[80] (In French, it must be noted, the

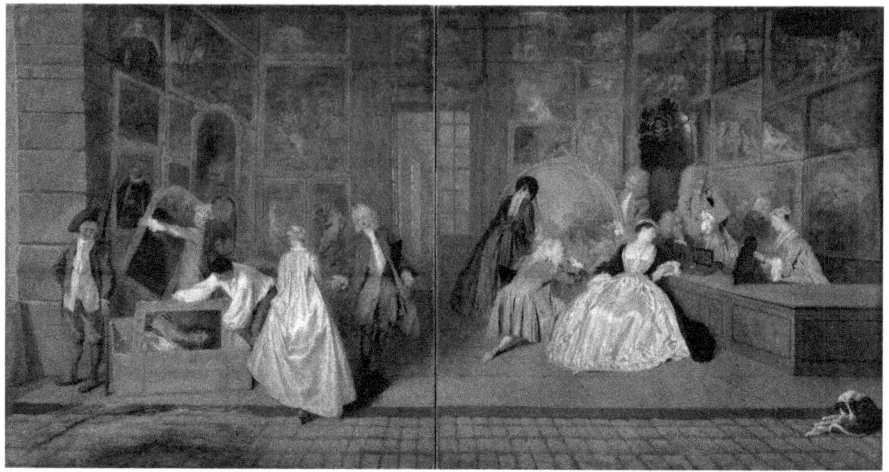

1.6   Antoine Watteau, *Gersaint's shop sign*, 1721. Oil on canvas, 166 × 306 cm.
Source: Stiftung Preussische Schlösser und Gärten, Schloss Charlottenburg, Berlin.
F0016962; GKI1200/1201 ©BPK, Berlin, Dist. RMN-Grand Palais/Jörg P. Anders.

object [counter, *comptoir*] and the verb [to encounter, *rencontrer*] do not share the
same root.) During the sixteenth and seventeenth centuries, visual representations made 'after life' were often referred to as *contrefait*, which translates literally
as 'made against'.[81] In *Gersaint's Shop Sign*, the vendor who positions the mirror
for her client enacts a form of counterfeiting, in making an image of her client.
In the mirror, the customer would have glimpsed her head and bust, alongside the objects she contemplated buying. The counter on which the mirror is
placed stands between the prospective buyer and this image of herself as she
might appear were she to buy the lacquered *nécessaire*. The vendor counters
her client with a flattering mirror of possibility. In one of Gillot's depictions of
the Italian theatre, Pierrot holds a freshly painted portrait of Arlequin in the
costume of a *procureur* (see Figure 1.7). Scaramouche has also lent a hand, but
Pierrot bears most of the weight of the oval, bust-length portrait, which has
concealed the majority of his torso. Arlequin peers curiously at the portrait as if
to assess its likeness. In this exchange, Pierrot assumes the role of the assistant
in *Gersaint's Shop Sign*: he counters Arlequin with a freshly painted mirror. This
incident draws attention to a further understanding of *contrefait* as counterfeit.
Arlequin may look like a *procureur* in the portrait, but he is not one. Concerns
of counterfeiting lined many marketplace exchanges. Buyers could counterfeit
currency or letters of credit; sellers could offer counterfeit goods. Most worrying,
however, was the counterfeiting of social identity that occurred in and through
the marketplace.

At the fair, spaces were designed to be looked across: across the counter,
across the proscenium.[82] Bodies were encountered visually rather than physically, in mirrors held up as counters. One side offers; the other side evaluates

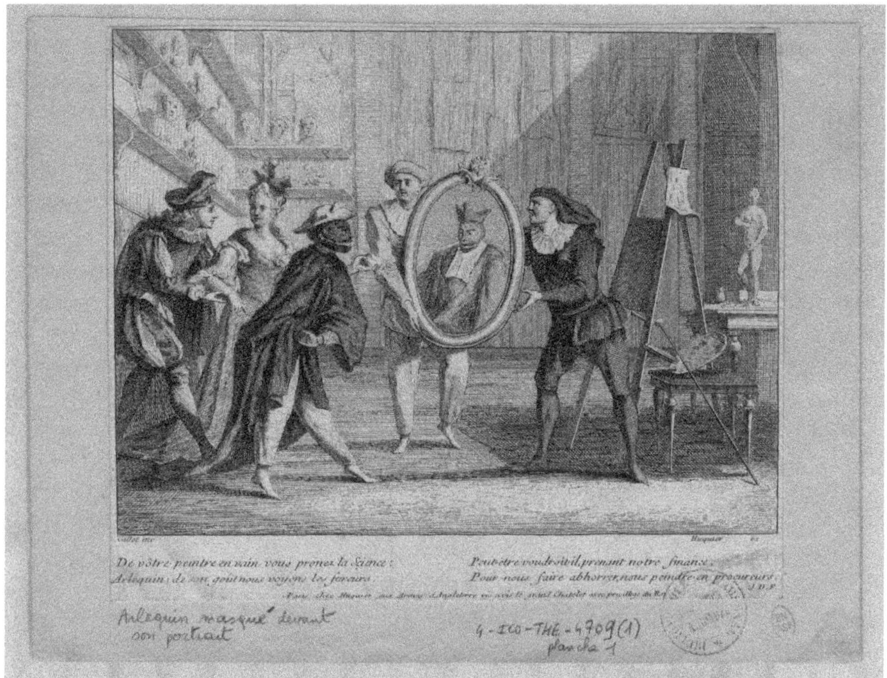

1.7   Gabriel Huquier after Claude Gillot, *The Portrait of the Procureur*, 1729–32. Etching, 26 × 20 cm. Source: Bibliothèque Nationale de France. 4-ICO THE-4709 ©BNF.

the offering. It is this kind of looking that Watteau invites in his representations of Pierrot, but most particularly in the large painting. To create this striking composition, however, the painter depicted neither a stage nor a shop counter (although the setting of the large painting is stage-like, there is neither curtain nor boards – the stage has been utterly naturalised). Instead, he borrowed the setting, and the threshold, of the costume print.

Costume

The costume print presents a single human figure at full length, occupying the height of the sheet. The figure is often accompanied by text identifying it and categorising it according to profession, nationality or race, class, or theatrical role.[83] From the late sixteenth century, these prints circulated widely at modest prices, disseminating the types to a large audience.[84] The first of these prints were early sixteenth-century German and Swiss mercenary prints, in which virtuoso print-makers revelled in the opportunity to represent the outlandish, textured dress of nomadic mercenary soldiers (*Landsknechten*).[85] Other types of secular, single-figure prints illustrating contemporary social identities soon followed, including the *cris de Paris*, series of prints showing itinerant vendors and tradespeople, like knife-grinders, a figure that Watteau would later draw.[86] The late sixteenth century saw the emergence of the 'costume book', a bound collection of prints representing full-length human figures in the guise of generic regional and social types, like the 'English Merchant' (Figure 1.8) or the Italian 'Doctor of Law' from Vecellio's *Habiti antichi, et moderni di tutto il mondo* (1598) (Figure 1.9).[87] The lawyer, incidentally, wears the same kind of richly brocaded robe that Arlequin is shown donning, in order to disguise himself, in another frontispiece to Regnard's play (see Figure 1.10). As the title of the genre indicates, the representation of garments was key to this project, so much so that figures could be represented with their backs turned, as was the 'Doctor of Law'. The garment itself was the 'front' of the figure, even when seen from the back. Costume books catered to readers whose curiosity had been aroused by the expansion of trade and empire. While visualising encounters with strangers from other nations, costume books insisted upon clothing as a surface for the performance of national and social identity.[88]

Theatrical costumes also belonged to the repertoire of the costume print. Theatrical costume or character prints represented stock theatrical types clothed in the character's typical costume or 'mask'. Often, a particular actor was identified as the wearer of the costume. Theatrical character prints could function as marketing tools, publicising the appearance of an actor or a type and mentioning the theatre where they could be seen. The earliest known costume print showing Pierrot is based on a drawing by Bernard Picart, who shows Pierrot standing on a stage of planks, carrying a hunting rifle, with a brace of dead game hung at his waist in a rather suggestive position (see Figure 1.11). Gillot would also depict Pierrot with a rifle, which suggests that hunting was one manifestation of Pierrot's rusticity and his association with nature.[89] Watteau, however, would entirely exclude this aggressive accessory from his depictions of Pierrot. Picart's print, along with depictions of eleven other masks from the Italian theatre, was published by Jean Mariette in 1696. The series' title, *12 Fashions of the Italian Theatre* (*12 Modes du Théâtre Italien*) is indicative of the closeness between representations of theatre and fashionable types. In the same year, Mariette published another suite by Picart, *31 French Fashions* (*31 Modes françaises*), which offered a range of fashionable and 'typical' figures, from the elegant noblewoman to the rustic spinner. As the titles suggest, a theatrical mask was, like any choice of garment, a fashion (*mode*) of appearing.

Mariette's *31 French Fashions* were, in essence, fashion plates, a genre that dated to the early seventeenth century.[90] Rather than the armchair tourism provided by the costume books, fashion prints advertised a lifestyle and created models for social emulation. They were often produced in bulk alongside *cris de Paris*, which continued to be produced throughout the seventeenth century. Two important series of criers, by Abraham Bosse and Pierre Brébiette, were published in Paris around 1640. In the late seventeenth century, the Bonnart brothers were known for series of criers, as well as fashion prints, theatrical character prints, and a new genre called *portraits en mode*, in which figures in

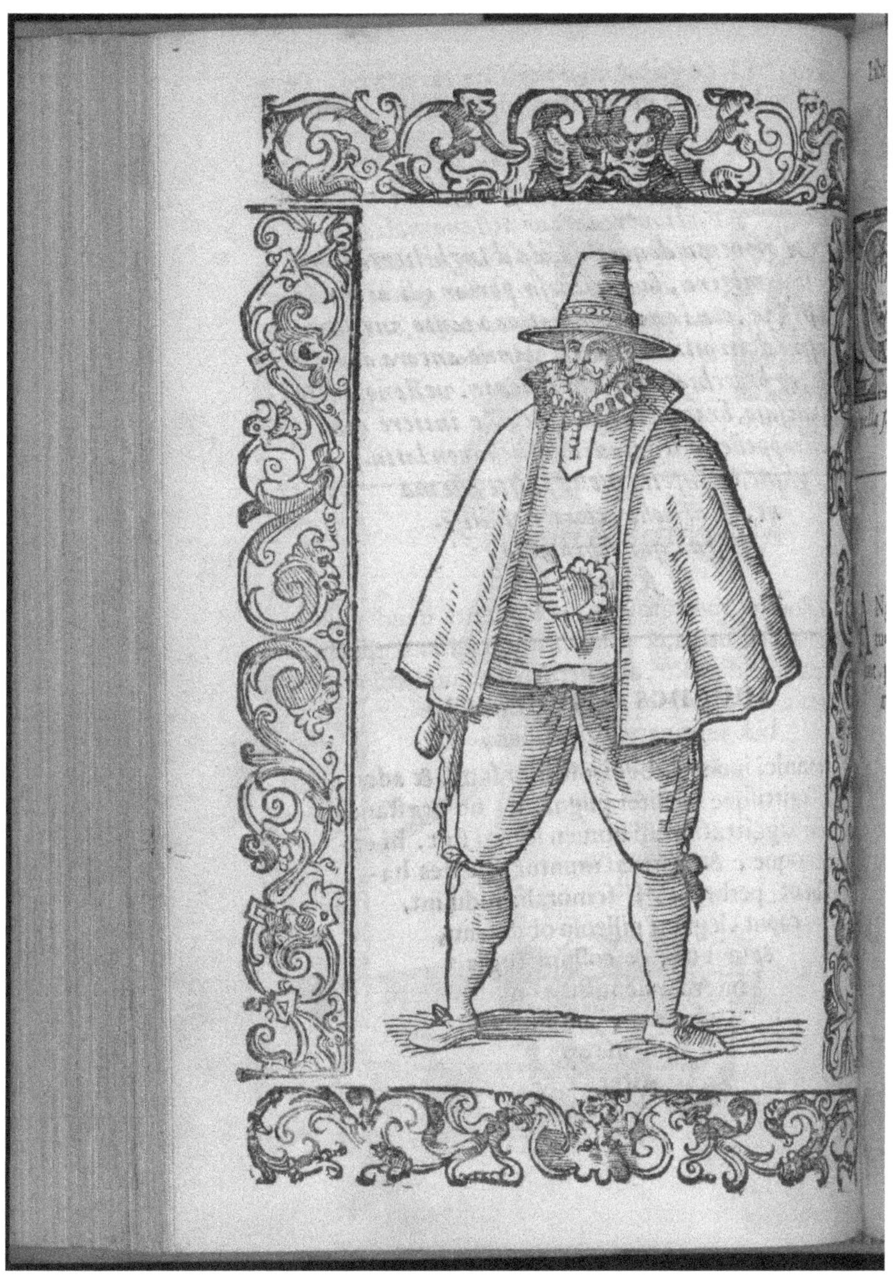

1.8   Christoph Krieger after Cesare Vecellio, *English Merchant*, from *Habiti antichi et moderni di tutto il mondo*, 1598. Woodcut, 15.5 × 9 cm. Source: Rijksmuseum, Amsterdam. BI-1938–0066–278 ©Rijksmuseum.

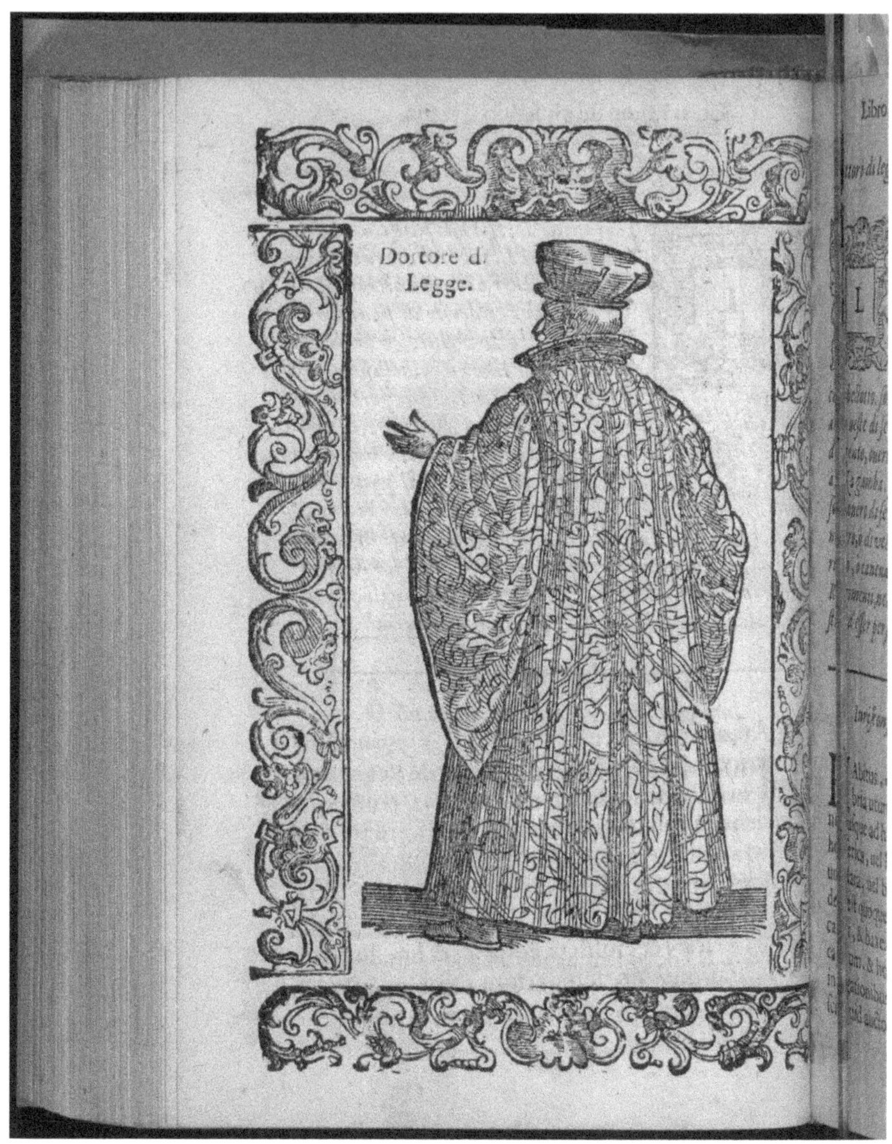

1.9   Christoph Krieger after Cesare Vecellio, *Doctor of Law*, from *Habiti antichi et moderni di tutto il mondo*, 1598. Woodcut, 15.5 × 9 cm. Source: Rijksmuseum, Amsterdam. BI-1938–0066–121 ©Rijksmuseum.

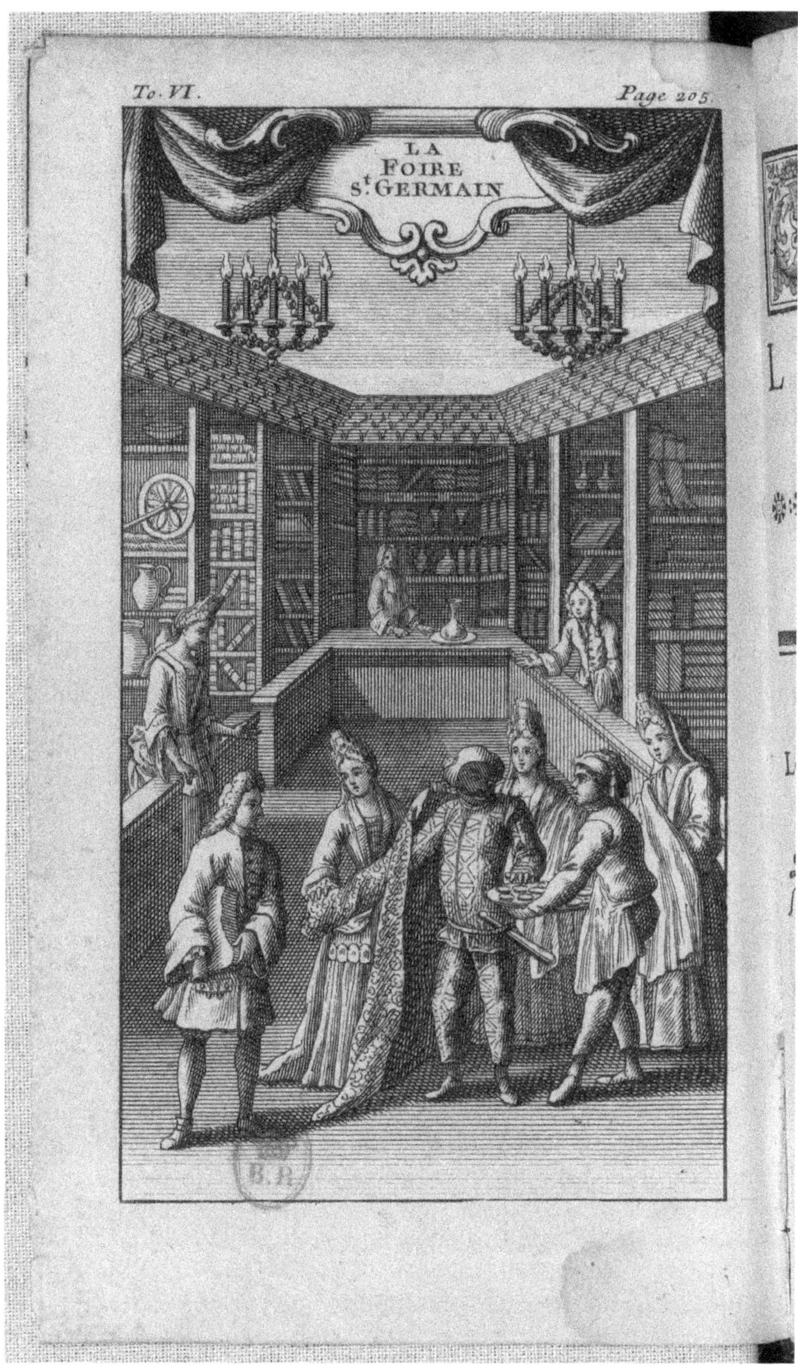

1.10   *La Foire Saint-Germain* from *Le Théâtre Italien*, vol. 6, folio 175, 1701. Source: Bibliothèque Nationale de France. YF-5784 © BNF.

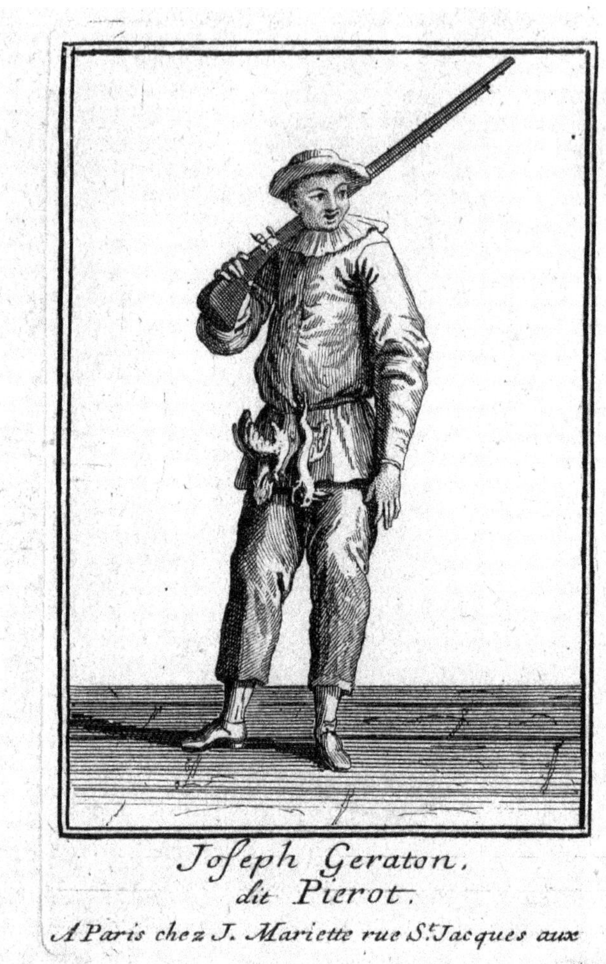

1.11 Bernard Picart, *Joseph Geraton, called Pierrot*, 1696. Etching, 11.6 × 19.7 cm (whole plate). Source: Bibliothèque Nationale de France, Paris ©BNF.

generic fashion prints were named as members of the court. As Pascale Cugy has shown, the multi-generational business enterprise of the Bonnart brothers and their offspring played an instrumental role in the 'considerable enlargement of the notion of the *image de mode*', the frontiers of which were 'already porous and unstable'.[91] For Cugy, the Bonnarts' *oeuvre* created an influential repertoire, 'a vast ensemble' in which 'elegant avatars of all the echelons of society intermingle', alongside characters from myth and history.[92]

Costume prints asked that the figure be evaluated in terms of its dress. As Bronwen Wilson has put it, costume prints allowed viewers to experience their garments as the threshold, 'skin', or 'screen', through which they took their places in the social world.[93] What is more, Cohen suggests that the figures themselves, 'through their seamless frontal display', 'evince' the theatrical proscenium.[94] Cohen, whose comments on these types of print are invaluable, also points out the way that these repertoires thematise masquerade through their standardised, serial format, in which very similar human figures appear constantly in new costumes.[95] A viewer accustomed to perusing such repertoires would be schooled in an equivalence between changing one's costume and changing one's role. Consumers of prints even 'dressed' the prints with hand-painting and scraps of fabric, a practice suggestive of the way the standardised figure performed itself as a template for any costume whatsoever.[96] Such bits of fabric could have been bought at the fair, where the media of masquerade were sold.

As subset of the costume print, the *cris de Paris* stage the social encounter across a threshold of retail. The Bonnarts' *Mercer*, for example, shows the crier wearing a wooden display case around his neck, the shelves of which are stocked with reading glasses, packets of ribbons, and bottles of ointment (Figure 1.12). This is the kind of itinerant mercer who trod the pavements of Paris and trekked into the countryside, where they sold ribbons to peasants. Molière's Pierrot, when he complains that Charlotte does not love him, reminds her that he has always bought her 'without reproach, ribbons from all the mercers who pass by'.[97] In addition to trimming, this mercer also carries a stack of printed images draped over the bottom edge of his case. These could be inexpensive devotional prints, yet given that fashion merchants were also known, on occasion, to sell costume prints, it is not impossible that the ambulatory mercer sells the type of image in which he himself appears.[98] This clever print confuses evaluating the mercer with evaluating his goods for sale. One of the ways it does so is by subsuming the mercer's body with his goods. His fingers are replaced by the tines of the combs he holds. His torso has become a display case, as well as another human face; a pair of eyeglasses is strategically positioned on the top shelf of the case.

Scholars have tended to group together these different categories – costume, fashion, theatrical character, and crier prints – and rightly so. Artists did the same, creating fascinating fusions. Nicolas I and Nicolas II de Larmessin, for example, combined costume and crier prints in the *costumes grotesques*, an extensive series of eighty to ninety prints, which show human figures whose garments are constituted of the materials of their trade.[99] In the Larmessins' *Lingère*, for example, the linen-seller wears a 'skirt' that is in fact a counter, on the front of which are pinned chemises, stockings, sleeves, and other undergarments (Figure 1.13).[100] Her torso consists of a set of drawers, each one of which holds a different item of linen. The *lingère* wears both her merchandise and her boutique in the form of the furnishings with which she organises and displays her merchandise. The Larmessins' series, which featured luxury retailers rather than itinerant urban trades, may have been inspired by Jean Lepautre's prints after costumes designed by Jean Bérain for a recreation of the Foire Saint Germain in the apartments of Madame de Montespan, a mistress of Louis XIV.[101] This courtly festivity, organised in 1682, seized upon the fair

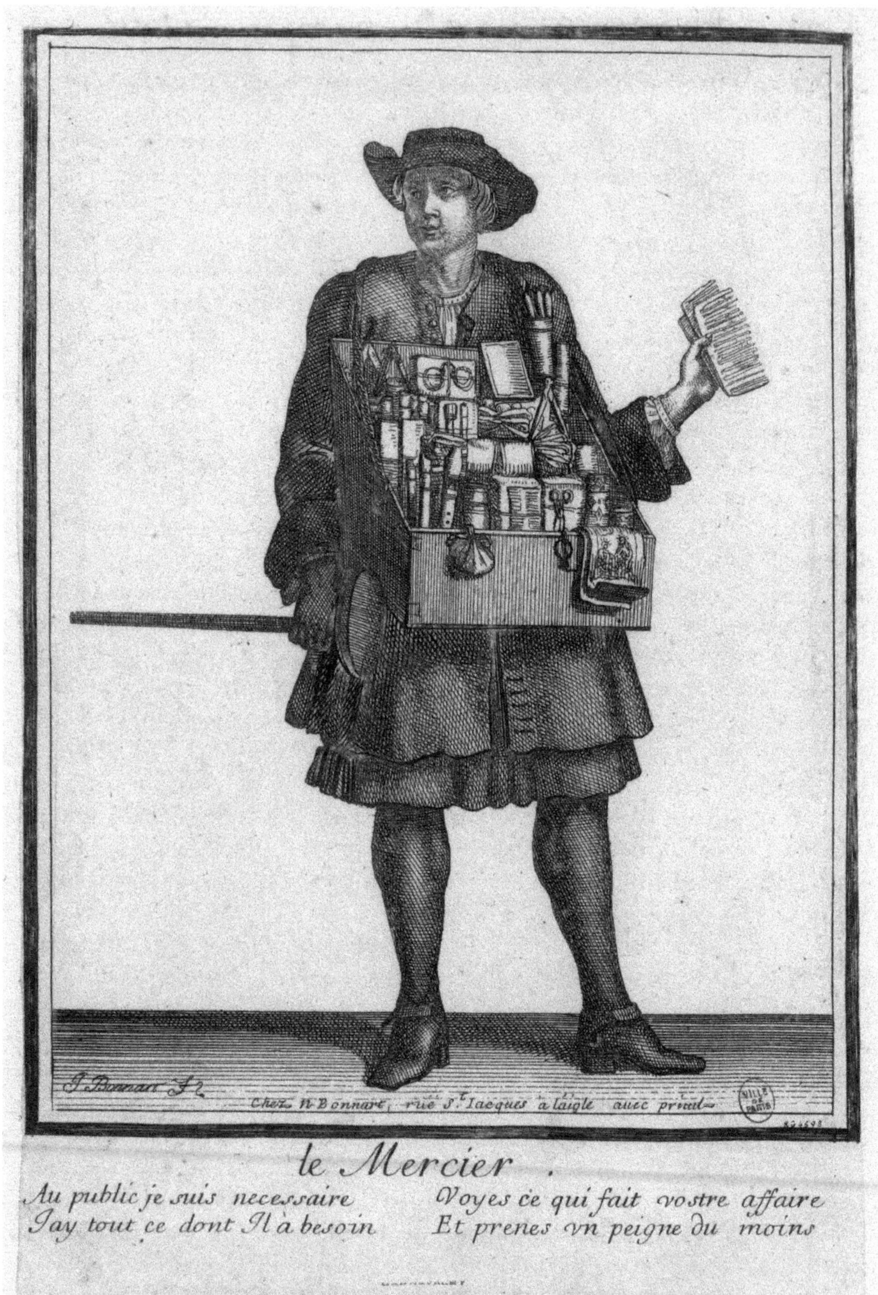

1.12   Jean-Baptiste Bonnart, *The Mercer*, 1680s. Etching, 26.9 × 17.6 cm. Source: Musée Carnavalet, Paris. G.4698 ©Musées de la ville de Paris.

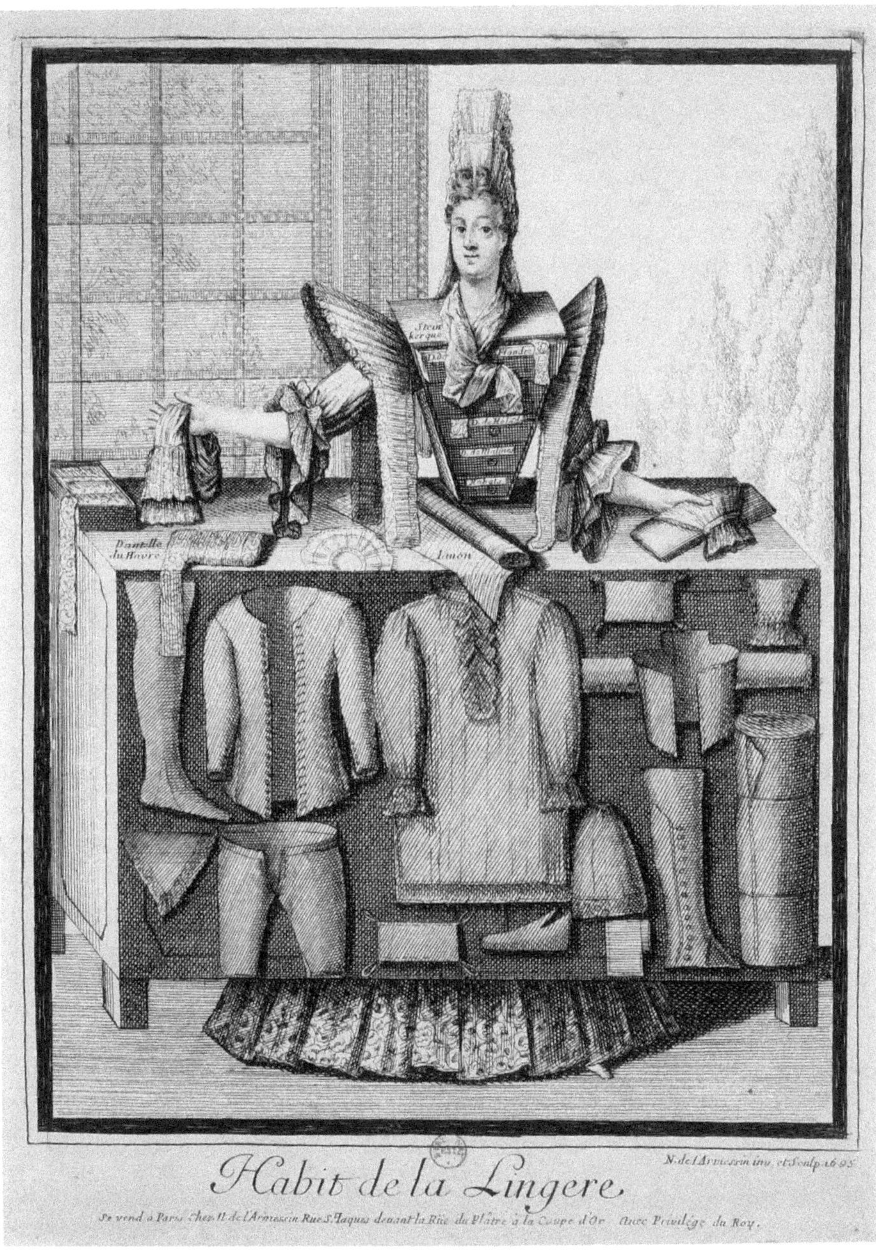

1.13   Nicolas I and Nicolas II de Larmessin, *Habit de la lingère*, ca. 1695. Etching, approx. 28.5 × 20 cm. Source: Bibliothèque Nationale de France. OA-60-PET FOL ©BNF.

as a theatrical space, the performative possibilities of which lay, at least in part, in the role of the retailer. For courtiers accustomed to selling their grace and naïveté in the marketplace of courtly favour, it may have been a relief to pretend to sell buttons and petticoats.

The Larmessins' linen-seller provides a vivid example of the way that costume can function as both a theatrical threshold and a marketplace threshold. The figure's shop counter doubles as her skirt, which she wears strapped to her waist like an apron. Further garments, including a chemise with a ruffled placket and cuffs, are hung on the front of her counter-skirt. To put on her costume is to put on a counter: the 'seller-mask' is nothing other than the shop itself, transformed into a garment. If the print did in fact serve as inspiration for a masquerade costume, the garment would have simultaneously functioned as a costume-mask and a proscenium. At a masquerade, in which participants mingle with one another without the boundary of a stage, the costume serves as the threshold of the theatrical performance. Finally, the linen-seller sells garments, which makes her into one of the *ur*-figures of the costume print as a genre, alongside sellers of old clothes and hats, sellers of ribbons, and sellers of trimming, all of whom appear in the repertoires of the *cris de Paris* or in the Larmessins' *costumes grotesques*. This category of vendor, who we will encounter frequently in the following chapters, sells the very media of marketplace theatricality.

Not all costume prints represent theatrical performers or costumes, just as not all costume prints represent vendors. All costume prints, however, address the marketplace theatrically in the sense that every costumed figure is set forth to be assessed according to criteria of beauty or ridiculousness, likeability and credibility. Presented alone, without scenic or figurative accessories, the figure of the costume print has no alibi except its address to the viewer. The costume prints theatricalise the human figure in order to market it, staging appearance as an object of exchange, to be assessed by the viewer as a form of merchandise viewed across a counter. Thanks to the costume print, the visual world was inhabited by thousands of figures hailing from across classes and the globe. This was a kind of virtual carnival, in a sense, although Bakhtin would have been saddened by the fact that the format of the prints kept the figures apart from one another. Indeed, it is easy to ascribe melancholy to these figures, whose generally wooden expressions can lead a sympathetic viewer to believe that the mercer, for example, is not happy with his lot. More realistically, the blank expressions of these figures suggest that the criteria of personhood had become utterly intertwined with surface, social appearance. How viewers, let alone the subjects of the prints, may have felt about this is much more difficult to say.

Pierrot's costume

By stripping the composition of the large painting, *Pierrot*, of literal references to the theatre, Watteau engenders a strong resemblance between his painting and the costume print. As in a costume print, a single figure shown at full length fills the height of the frame. As in a costume print, Pierrot addresses the viewer through his frontality and through his lack of engagement with other figures. The painting is distinct both in Watteau's *oeuvre* and in the artistic output of his time. As a full-length, nearly life-size representation of a figure, the painting can be compared to state portraits, or historical portraits commissioned for galleries, large rooms displaying suites of portraits depicting a specific category of associated individuals, like Cardinal Richelieu's gallery of 'Illustrious Frenchmen'. Yet there are no galleries known to have featured Italian masks or even costumed actors. Contemporary elites did commission portraits of themselves disguised as gods and theatrical characters, but these were usually half-length formats.[102] In addition, the Italian characters do not appear to have been popular masks for these types of portrait. There has been much speculation regarding the original purpose of the painting, of which there exists no trace (yet discovered) in the historical record of Watteau's life or even the entire eighteenth century (this curious silence will be discussed in Chapter 3). Several possible purposes for the painting have been suggested and dismissed. I would like to return to some of these dismissed suggestions, not necessarily to affirm them as true, but to explore what they say about the painting's relationship to the marketplace.

One of the actors known for his performance of Pierrot at the fair was called Belloni. The Parfaict brothers, eighteenth-century historians of theatre, indicated that Belloni had hung a portrait of himself as Pierrot outside his café in the Rue Quincampoix.[103] In 1977, Hélène Adhémar suggested that Watteau's painting was this very sign.[104] Her argument was based, in part, on the existence of *Gersaint's Shop Sign*, although Gersaint, recognising the painting's quality, did not allow it to be exhibited outside for very long. However, while Gersaint's shop sign was mentioned in numerous accounts of Watteau's life, written by people who knew him, these accounts name neither a shop sign for Belloni nor an unusually large painting of Pierrot.[105] In the streets of Paris, signs were evident, and often disruptive performers in the marketplace.[106] Unusually shaped, garishly painted, and large enough to block the paths of carriages, signs, like actors in the *parade*, competed with one another to attract customers to their shops. Many signs represented human figures, like the paintings of half-length figures hung above the booths in the etching of the set for Regnard's *La Foire Saint Germain*. In a famous passage, Louis-Sébastien Mercier imagined the crusty old monarchs on discarded signs arguing with one another, a reflection of the fact that signs were in fact quite noisy, creating a ruckus as they swung on their metal brackets (*potences* – also the name for gallows).[107] Although sign painting was scoffed at by the Royal Academy, ambitious painters, including Jean-Siméon Chardin and François Le Moyne, may have executed signs for shops as a vehicle of self-promotion.[108] For these painters, the presentation of a sign acted as a *parade* for their own studio.

In an earlier account, Adhémar suggested that the large painting was 'a sign for a fair theatre'.[109] Period imagery suggests that signs used by fair troupes were unstretched canvases hung on the façade of the theatre itself. Picart's depiction of a fair theatre sign shows an acrobatic performance that resembles the one taking place on the balcony immediately below the sign, which suggests that signs could perform the *parade* when actors were not present (Figure 1.1). A similar sign is hung above the trestle stage in the print representing the field of spectacles at the Saint Germain fair (Figure 1.4). It may have been the case that life-size paintings of performers were also exhibited as signs outside theatres. This was certainly the case in the nineteenth century, as a lithograph by Henri Monnier indicates.[110] A fascinating seventeenth-century painting by Karl Dujardin shows a charlatan's troupe of actors, who have set up their trestles on a country road (see Plate 7).[111] At the back of the stage hangs a painting of a nearly life-size figure, probably representing the charlatan himself, holding a glass of the potion for sale. As far as can be made out, the composition of this painting within a painting resembles the format of the costume print, offering a single full-length figure who occupies the height of the support. While the pictured charlatan is nowhere to be seen, his actors have taken to the stage to entertain the crowd. An Arlequin type plays a guitar; a sad Scaramouche stands on tiptoe, facing the small crowd that has gathered, including a pack horse and a donkey. A woman in a blue jacket counts out coins in the palm of her hand. Either she is paying for the charlatan's medicines, visible in an open box set on the stage, or she is rewarding the performers. At the left-hand side of the composition, a baker's boy approaches, bearing his cakes (*ratons*) on a wooden tray. Out of the barest elements – a crier, performers, a trestle stage, and an audience – a tiny marketplace has arisen. Yet there is little jolliness. Dujardin's composition cannot be described as a festive marketplace. The woman takes her time counting the coins while Scaramouche appears to wait, resigned, for the judgement that the coins will offer. Perpetually on tiptoe, eternally waiting for a verdict, Dujardin's Scaramouche represents the mundane humiliations of the actor in the marketplace.

Watteau had played with a similar transformation of the street into a fair in a painting now known as a print, *The Departure of the Italian Comedians* (Figure 1.14). The composition imagines the scene outside the Hôtel de Bourgogne upon the expulsion of the Italian troupe in 1697. The masks express their despair (Pierrot is curled into a ball at the door of the theatre). People have gathered in the windows overlooking the street, signalling that while the performances inside the theatre have ceased, the street will serve as a new stage, which also foretells the transition to the fair theatres.[112] The street has also become a marketplace. A standard figure from the repertoire of criers, a baker's boy with a tray of cakes, has arrived 'stage left', anticipating the gathering of a crowd. At the very moment when the architectural threshold of the theatre is lost, the mobile counter fills its place. A retrospective, 'historical' recreation of an event that occurred two decades prior to his depiction, *The Departure of the Italian Comedians* shows Watteau's recurrent interest in the relationship between theatre and the marketplace.

Denuded of an architectural threshold, the large painting of Pierrot poses Pierrot's costume as threshold and counter. With his costume, Pierrot counters the viewer, soliciting an assessment. Just as the mercer has donned

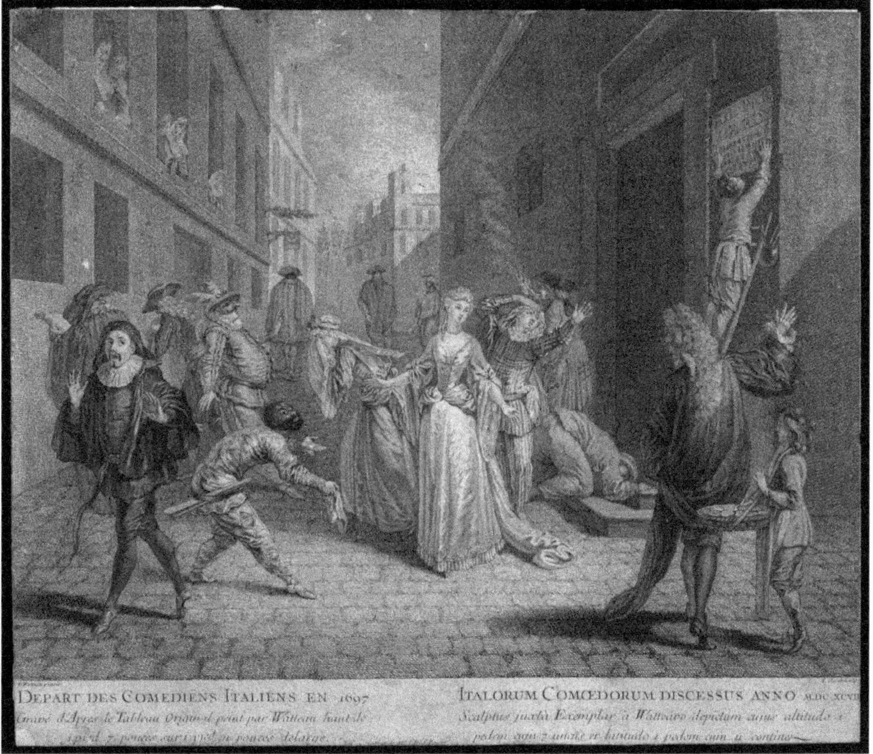

1.14   Louis Jacob after Antoine Watteau, *Departure of the Italian Comedians in 1697*, 1729. Etching, 37 × 42.7 cm. Source: Victoria & Albert Museum, London. S.3774–2009 ©Victoria & Albert Museum, London.

his case of merchandise, which he offers to those he meets, Pierrot has donned his costume, through which he appears to the viewer as a rustic, childish servant. What remains elusive is the nature of Pierrot's offering. The mercer sells ribbons, prints, eyeglasses, combs. Theatrical character prints sold the extraordinary qualities of the performer or the grotesqueness of the character. Because Pierrot makes so little effort to sell himself, he strips the costume print of its distractions. Failing to present himself in a sophisticated manner was of course one of the points of Pierrot's naïve, rustic character. Yet when made large in Watteau's painting, this failure registers more poignantly. Viewers were used to seeing costume prints, which they encountered casually, pinned up in a bar or a bedroom, collected in an album, in the window of the print shops on the Rue Saint Jacques. Watteau's painting cannot be encountered casually. It arrests the viewer, demanding consideration, even producing discomfort, because the confrontation staged between Pierrot and the viewer is so insistent. The viewer cannot flip by this painting as if leafing through a collection of criers.

Because of its size, the painting monumentalises and slows the disposition of the costume print, drawing attention to the social stakes of this genre. In the attention that Watteau lavishes on the painting of Pierrot's costume – from each pearly button to the serpentine wrinkles in the sleeves – the painter compels the viewer to consider what it is that is being offered. Through Pierrot's figure, the scaffolding of the costume print is exposed, as well as the scaffolding of the encounter in the marketplace. Were a person to walk into a shop and find Pierrot, as he stands in Watteau's painting, it would be deeply disconcerting. (Represented in a comic skit, it would also be quite funny.) The same would be true if Watteau's Pierrot were to appear on the stage, particularly if there were no other actors to provide a contrast. Yet in both scenarios, Pierrot would be doing nothing other than mimicking the underlying structure of the encounter. Mandeville's salesman tries to conceal the movement with which he arrives behind the counter. Pierrot is always, already, the counter. Behind him stands a herm – half-man half-pillar – a boundary-marker used in contemporary garden design. In the ancient world, herms presided over crossroads and marketplaces as ambassadors of Hermes, the protector of traders and messengers. The herm, nearly hidden in the trees, is the old marketplace. Pierrot is the new.

It was at the fair that Watteau experienced the encounters staged by both theatre and retail. Rather than paint the fair itself, Watteau wove social phenomena found at the fair into his depiction of other subjects. In his *fêtes galantes*, Watteau explored elite sociability in garden settings pointedly removed from the streets of the fair. Yet as Crow has shown, the fair infiltrated the *fêtes galantes* in the form of the Italian characters, whose presence signalled both the artifice of sociability and the nobility's refusal to support the elevated genres patronised by the crown. *Pierrot* figures the fair to be *fête marchande* – a marketplace for human personality, where counterfeiting was increasingly common. In his simplicity and his literalness, Pierrot performs the most basic act of the marketplace, which is to put himself forward. In one *parade*, Gilles (Pierrot's street-theatre counterpart), is told to guard the door of his master's house so that the womenfolk do not run away to meet their lovers. While Gilles stands at the door (another threshold), the women slip out of the window. When his master returns, Gilles insists that he only did what he was told. It is as if, in Watteau's painting, Pierrot has been told to put himself on the market, which he does. Yet he fails to mask the underlying dynamics of the encounter. In a performance of sophisticated disinterest, the gentleman in Watteau's drawing of a draper's shop refuses to face the shop assistant. Pierrot faces the viewer, which enables him to show the viewer the entirety of his costume, this remarkable painted surface, which Watteau has made both as an offering to the viewer and as a shield for the naïveté of this character, who would go hang himself if he were told to.

Finally, and what is more important than the discovery that theatre and the marketplace are boon companions, is the effect that this companionship is shown to exercise upon the visualisation of the human figure. The costume print, which Watteau's *Pierrot* makes sure we will never forget, attests to a world in which to appear is to theatricalise, to theatricalise is to market, and to market is to counterfeit. The fairground provided a perfect environment in which to test a 'theatrical theory of personality'[113], which is just the kind of personality that Pierrot, as portrayed by Watteau, sets forth. Fair theatre offered lessons in disguise and social masking; fair boutiques sold the media of sartorial transformation. Watteau depicts Pierrot as nothing other than a costume, which is also a surface, the surface of the painting. Pierrot is not a named historical subject like the subject of a portrait, but a personality, in that he bears the features of a person as an objective expression that takes the form of a painted surface. This is what Pierrot markets – the surface of a person in the guise of Pierrot. Costume could act as a kind of prison; there is no Pierrot without the costume, it is his obligatory, if infantilising, threshold. Yet such practices could be liberating. A culture of appearances was a field of opportunity for those with the means or the guile to procure the surfaces they wished to wear. In Molière's play, Pierrot wanted ribbons. In the large painting, Pierrot has been given two ribbons: these beautiful pink bows on his white shoes. He has also received a jacket made of a silky fabric that appears to be much finer than a plain canvas (*toile*). He has been given dozens of expensive, fabric-covered buttons. This painting is Pierrot's reward, offered by Watteau, who may have been moved by this character's regard for surfaces as a medium for being. No other character would be so grateful; only Pierrot would accept his surface with such seriousness, even if it was not as adorned as he wished it to be. Nevertheless, having received his ribbons, Pierrot is on his way to becoming a *gros monsieur*. Indeed, he is *gros* in this painting, because he has grown up into a life-size figure, the same size of painting that Arlequin commissioned, and that Colombine then 'wore' when she stuck her head through the back of it. Pierrot is ready, now, to try his luck in the marketplace.

Notes

1 On the *fête galante* and those themes important to this book, namely theatre and social performance, see Marianne Roland Michel, *Watteau: An Artist of the Eighteenth Century*, trans. Richard Wrigley (London: Trefoil Books, 1984), pp. 171–91; Mary Vidal, *Watteau's Painted Conversations, Art, Literature, and Talk in Seventeenth and Eighteenth Century France* (New Haven, CT: Yale University Press, 1992); Sarah R. Cohen, *Art, Dance, and the Body in French Culture of the Ancien Régime* (Cambridge: Cambridge University Press, 2000); Aaron Wile, 'Watteau, reverie, and selfhood', *Art Bulletin* 96:3 (2014), 319–37; Thomas Crow, *Painters and Public Life in Eighteenth-Century Paris* (New Haven, CT: Yale University Press, 1985); Julie Ann Plax, *Watteau and the Cultural Politics of Eighteenth-Century France* (Cambridge: Cambridge University Press, 2000), pp. 108–53; Suzanne R. Pucci, 'Watteau and theater: movable fetes', in Mary Sheriff (ed.), *Antoine Watteau: Perspectives on the Artist and the Culture of His Time* (Newark, DE: University of Delaware Press, 2006), pp. 106–22; Katherine Baetjer, *Watteau, Music, and Theater* (New York: Metropolitan Museum of Art, 2009).
2 Roland Michel, *Watteau*, p. 175.

3 Jean Starobinski, *L'Invention de la liberté 1700–1789* (Geneva: Albert Skira, 1964), p. 88; Erwin Panofsky, '*Et in arcadia ego*: on the conception of transience in Poussin and Watteau', in R. Klibansky and H.J. Paton (eds), *Philosophy and History: The Ernst Cassirer Festschrift* (New York: Harper & Row, 1936), pp. 223–54, here p. 251.

4 Cohen, *Art, Dance, and the Body*, pp. 262–70, here p. 270. For an account of the painting in relationship to seventeenth-century norms of heroic composition, see Thomas Kirchner, *Le héros épique: Peinture d'histoire et politique artistique dans la France du XVIIe siècle*, trans. Aude Virey-Wallon and Jean-Léon Muller (Paris: Éditions de la Maison des sciences de l'homme, 2008), 387–92. Also, Sund sees the painting as marking a rupture with 'the artifice of both the theatrical production and the painting that represents it', as the moment when the actor removes his mask and adopts a 'casual demeanor': Judy Sund, 'Why so sad? Watteau's Pierrots', *Art Bulletin* 98:3 (2016), 321–47, here p. 332.

5 Vidal, *Watteau's Painted Conversations*, pp. 144–8.

6 Christian Michel, *Le 'célèbre' Watteau* (Geneva: Droz, 2008), p. 269: 'lieu de toutes les projections'.

7 Crow, *Painters and Public Life*, pp. 45–74.

8 For a detailed history of the Foire Saint Germain in the late sixteenth and early seventeenth century, see Léon Roulland, 'La Foire Saint Germain sous les règnes de Charles IX, de Henri III et de Henri IV', *Mémoires de la société de l'histoire de Paris et de l'Ile-de-France*, 3 (1877), 192–218. The fair was particularly unruly during this period; Henri III and his *mignons* enjoyed stirring up a ruckus, harassing and insulting the public at the fair. The turmoil caused by the religious wars also led to frequent cancellations of the fair.

9 For a list of merchants at the Foire Saint-Laurent during the eighteenth century, see Arthur Heulhard, *La Foire Saint-Laurent: Son Histoire et Ses Spectacles* (Paris: Alphonse Lemerre, 1878), pp. 33–52.

10 Period descriptions of the fairs provide useful documents, both for reconstructing the fair and for understanding how it was viewed by contemporaries. In addition to those cited below, see the very early text from 1643 by Paul Scarron, 'La Foire Saint Germain', in *La ville de Paris en vers burlesques* (Troyes: Jean Oudot, 1705), pp. 86–99. See also the description of that fair prior to its destruction by fire in 1762 (it was then rebuilt), *L'incendie de la Foire Saint Germain et sa nouvelle reconstruction, poëme en quatre chants* (Paris: Langlois, 1764), pp. 10–13.

11 Evariste Gherardi, *Le théâtre italien de Gherardi ou le recueil général de toutes les comédies et scènes françoises jouées par les comédiens italiens du roi, pendant tout le temps qu'ils ont été au service de sa Majesté*, 6 vols (Amsterdam: Chez Adrian Braakman, 1701). This was an amplified version of the first edition, which was a single volume, published in Paris in 1694.

12 On the battles between the *forain* troupes and the Comédie-Française, see Heulhard, *La Foire Saint-Laurent*, pp. 187–229.

13 François Moureau, *Le goût italien dans la France rocaille: théâtre, musique, peinture* (Paris: Presses de l'université Paris-Sorbonne, 2011), p. 77.

14 On the re-establishment of the Comédie Italienne – which, at its inception, had no Pierrot – see Nicolas Boindin, *Lettres historiques à Mr D*** sur la nouvelle Comédie italienne, 3eme lettre* (Paris: The Author, 1717).

15 This was a multi-volume collection of plays and comic operas performed at the fair. Alain-René Lesage and Jacques Philippe d'Orneval, *Le théâtre de la foire, ou l'opéra comique*, 9 vols (Paris, 1721–37). Picart's print is clearly dated as made in 1730;

however, it was published as the frontispiece to a Dutch edition of Volume 6 in 1731 (Amsterdam: Z. Chatelain, 1731).

16 Victor Fournel, *Les spectacles populaires et les artistes des rues* (Paris: E. Dentu, 1863). See in particular Chapters VII, 'Opérateurs et charlatans' and VIII, 'Les arracheurs de dents'.

17 Elite audiences were particularly drawn to the *parade* as a performance of unstudied 'nature'. Crow has commented extensively on this phenomenon and its relationship to Watteau's work: Crow, *Painters and Public Life*, pp. 54–5. A fad arose for staging *parades* at aristocratic country homes, a practice that extracted the *parade* from an explicitly transactional context. The self-proclaimed progenitor of this trend was Thomas-Simon Gueullette, a wealthy magistrate. Gueullette and his friends formed an unofficial troupe and put on *parades* in their own homes and country houses, a social milieu that included courtiers, wealthy lawyers, judges, and bureaucrats, many of whom were ennobled. See J.-E. Gueullette, *Thomas-Simon Gueullette: un magistrat du 18e Siècle, ami des lettres, du théâtre et des plaisirs* (Paris: Librairie E. Droz, 1938). Gueullette also published his *parades*: Thomas Simon Gueullette, *Théâtre des boulevards, ou recueil des parades*, 3 vols (Paris: A. Mahon de l'imprimerie de Gilles Langlois, 1756).

18 On this confusion, see Dora Panofsky, '*Gilles* or Pierrot? Iconographic notes on Watteau', *Gazette des Beaux-Arts* 39 (1952), 319–40, here pp. 324–5.

19 See, for example, the *Folie du jour, ou la promenade à la Foire Saint Germain* (Paris: Valade, 1770), pp. 7–8. See also the discussion in Jennifer Michelle Jones, *Sexing 'La Mode': Gender, Fashion and Commercial Culture in Old Regime France* (Oxford: Berg, 2004), pp. 155–60.

20 Véronique Laporte, 'Dans les coulisses de la séduction. Les divertissements à la foire Saint Germain-des-Prés, Paris, 18e siècle', MA thesis, Université de Sherbrooke, 2005, pp. 49–54.

21 For example, Marc-Antoine Legrand, *La Foire Saint-Laurent* (Paris: P. Ribou, 1709), in which the fair is the setting for an attempt to kidnap a young woman who does not want to marry her fiancé. Legrand was a *comédian du roi*, which meant that the play may have been performed at the Comédie-Française; but fair troupes frequently adapted the 'official' repertoires. Gherardi's repertoire includes an important play by Jean-François Regnard, *La Foire Saint Germain*, which premiered in Paris at the Hôtel de Bourgogne on 26 December 1695: see Gherardi, *Le théâtre italien*, 6:175–268. Written for the Italian troupe in 1695, this play was performed at the Foire Saint-Laurent, where Gillot drew the performance. Regnard's one-act play, *Les momies d'egypte* (Gherardi, *Le théâtre italien*, 6:271–96), is also set at the Foire Saint Germain, in a boutique that shows Egyptian 'curiosities'. See also 'La Querelle des Théâtres, Prologue', in Lesage and d'Orneval, *Le théâtre de la foire*, 3:39–59. This play is a parody in which the Italian characters dress as personifications of the Parisian theatres, several of which have come to the fair to see the Opéra Comique in action. Pierrot plays the Fair. There are several other, similar plays in the same volume.

22 Daniel Vaillancourt, 'Le spectacle du lieu public: éléments d'esthétique urbaine', in Marie-France Wagner and Claire Le Brun-Gouanvic (eds), *Les arts du spectacle dans la ville (1404–1721)*, pp. 205–36, here p. 224. Vaillancourt relies particularly upon Scarron's poem of 1643. See also Robert M. Isherwood, 'Entertainment in the Parisian fairs in eighteenth-century Paris', *The Journal of Modern History* 53:1 (1981), 24–48, here pp. 27–8.

23 Sophie Descat, 'La boutique magnifiée: commerce de détail et embellissement à Paris et à Londres dans la seconde moitié du XVIIIe siècle', *Histoire urbaine* 2:6 (2002), 69–86, here p. 74.

24 J.C. Nemeitz, *Séjour de Paris, c'est à dire, instructions fidèles pour les voyageurs de condition*, 2 vols (Leyden: Jean van Abcoude, 1727), 1:171: 'tout y est pêle-mêle, les maîtres avec les valets et laquais, les filoux avec les honêtes gens. Les courtisans les plus raffinez, les plus jolies filles, les filoux les plus subtils, sont comme entrelacez ensemble.'

25 *Cf.* the later account by Rétif de la Brétonne of the Foire Saint-Laurent: Rétif de la Bretonne, *Les nuits de Paris*, ed. Michel Delon (Paris: Gallimard, 1986), pp. 163–6. Rétif says that he 'mixes' in the crowd to watch the *parade*, but then immediately proceeds to enumerate the different social types of which the crowd is composed.

26 Vaillancourt, 'Le spectacle du lieu public', p. 234. Vaillancourt associates this kind of looking with the *cours* as opposed to the fair, yet I am convinced that the measured, sceptical looking that he ascribes to the *cour* may also have been possible at the fair, particularly during the eighteenth century. *Cf.* also Jonathan Conlin, 'Vauxhall on the boulevard: pleasure gardens in London and Paris, 1764–1784', *Urban History* 35:1 (May 2008), 24–47. Albeit focused on a slightly later moment, Conlin gathers accounts of public pleasure gardens, including the Wauxhall at the Foire Saint Germain (1768–83). Conlin suggests that the Wauxhalls encouraged a form of self-surveillance and policing, transforming class into an orderly spectacle.

27 On 'la combinaison des notions de théâtralité et de ville' see Vaillancourt, 'Le spectacle du lieu public', p. 206.

28 John Shovlin, 'The cultural politics of luxury in eighteenth-century France', *French Historical Studies* 23:4 (2000), 577–606, here pp. 580–84.

29 For the classic account, see Peter Burke, *The Fabrication of Louis XIV* (New Haven, CT: Yale University Press, 1992).

30 Nemeitz, *Séjour de Paris*, 1:171: 'se postent dans une boutique d'où ils font la revuë des passans'.

31 See for example, the designs for new booths at the Foire Saint-Ovide, drawn by P.-L. Moreau in 1771: Descat, 'La boutique magnifiée', p. 76.

32 See, for example, Jean Lepautre's print after Jean Bérain, published in the *Extraordinaire de Mercure galant* in January 1678, as part of an 'extraordinary' fashion supplement. Bérain depicts a stylish couple at a *boutique de galanterie* selling wigs, lace, and gloves.

33 Shovlin, 'The cultural politics of luxury', p. 578.

34 On the importance of the fair merchants in the seventeenth century and their role in developing a taste for Realism, see Mickaël Szanto, 'Les frères Le Nain à l'heure du marché de l'art; l'invention de la noble "gueuserie"', in Nicolas Milovanovic and Luc Piralla-Heng Vong (eds), *Le Mystère Le Nain* (Lens: Musée du Louvre-Lens, 2017), pp. 33–41. See also Antoine Schnapper, *Curieux du Grand Siècle: Collections et collectionneurs dans la France du XVIIe siècle* (1994; Paris: Flammarion, 2005), pp. 86–8.

35 Watteau's first dealer was Pierre Sirois, a merchant mercer who would also become his friend. Sirois owned a boutique in Paris and sold paintings, prints, and gilded frames, as well as glass panels. See Guillaume Glorieux, 'Pierre Sirois (1665–1726): le premier marchand de Watteau', in Jeremy Warren and Adriana Turpin (eds), *Auctions, Agents and Dealers: The Mechanisms of the Art Market 1660–1830* (Oxford: The Wallace Collection, 2007), pp. 87–98.

36 Heulhard, *La Foire Saint-Laurent*, p. 35.

37 Richard Andrews, *The Commedia dell'Arte of Flaminio Scala: a translation and analysis of 30 scenarios* (Lanham, MD: Scarecrow Press, 2008), pp. xi–xii.

38 On the nature of the Italian masks, see Gustave Attinger, *L'esprit de la commedia dell'arte dans le théâtre français* (Paris: Librairie théâtrale, 1950), pp. 37–46.

39 Napoléon-Maurice Bernardin, *La Comédie Italienne en France et les théâtres de la foire et du boulevard (1570–1791)* (Paris: Éditions de la 'Revue bleue', 1902), pp. 9–15.

40 Claude Parfaict and François Parfaict, *Histoire de l'ancien théâtre italien depuis son origine en France, jusqu'à sa suppression en l'Année 1697* (Paris: Chez Lambert, 1753), pp. 1–7.

41 On the complex origins of the mask, see Robert Storey, *Pierrot: A Critical History of a Mask* (Princeton, NJ: Princeton University Press, 1978), pp. 3–34. Storey identifies some of the Italian types that have been suggested as prototypes for Pierrot (Bertoldo, Bertoldino, and Cacasenno), but ultimately suggests a more purely French origin, in the theatre of Molière (see below).

42 *Arlequin Phaeton* in Gherardi, *Le théâtre italien*, 3:393.

43 Domestic servants were essential characters in the comic repertoire. In a study based on 250 French plays performed between 1610 and 1700, 784 domestic servants appear. They often functioned as confidant(e)s in addition to providing comic relief. See Jean Emelina, *Les valets et les servantes dans le théâtre comique en France de 1610 à 1700* (Grenoble: Presses Universitaires de Grenoble, 1975), p. 17. See also Jacqueline Sabattier, *Figaro et son maître: les domestiques au XVIIIe siècle* (Paris: Perrin, 1984).

44 On the literary representation of these kinds of transformations, see Amy Wyngaard, 'Switching codes: class, clothing, and cultural change in the works of Marivaux and Watteau', *Eighteenth-Century Studies* 33:4 (2000), 523–41.

45 Cissie Fairchilds, *Domestic Enemies: Servants & Their Masters in Old Regime France* (Baltimore, MD: Johns Hopkins University Press, 1984), pp. 102–3.

46 Sarah C. Maza, *Servants and Masters in Eighteenth-Century France: The Uses of Loyalty* (Princeton, NJ: Princeton University Press, 1983), pp. 174–6.

47 *La fille de bon sens* in Gherardi, *Le théâtre italien*, 4:83.

48 On clothing and the 'constitution of the social' during the Renaissance, see Ann Rosalind Jones and Peter Stallybrass, *Renaissance Clothing and the Materials of Memory* (Cambridge: Cambridge University Press, 2000), pp. 6–10.

49 Daniel Roche, *La culture des apparences: une histoire du vêtement XVIIe–XVIIIe siècle* (Paris: Fayard, 1989).

50 Jones and Stallybrass, *Renaissance Clothing*, pp. 175–206.

51 See *Mezzetin, Grand Sophy de Perse*, in Gherardi, *Le théâtre italien*, 2:345. When Colombine rebuts his advances, Pierrot exclaims: 'Voila ce que c'est que de n'avoir qu'un habit de toile'.

52 Leslie Clarkson, 'The linen industry in early modern Europe', in David Jenkins (ed.), *The Cambridge History of Western Textiles*, 2 vols (Cambridge: Cambridge University Press, 2003), 1.472–92, here pp. 486–8.

53 *Colombine Avocat Pour et Contre* in Gherardi, *Le théâtre italien*, 1:312.

54 Storey, *Pierrot*, pp. 18–20. Storey strongly believes that Molière's Pierrot provided crucial inspiration for the Italian type.

55 *Dom Juan ou le Festin de Pierre …*, in Molière, *Théâtre complet*, ed. Robert Jouanny (Paris: Garnier Frères, 1960), 1:707–76.

56 On Molière's interest in, and tendency to satirise the ribbons and feathers of male dress, see Jean-Pierre Lethuillier, 'Plumes et rubans à la Cour et sur le théâtre de Molière', in Carine Barbafieri and Alain Montandon (eds), *Sociopoétique du textile à l'âge classique: du vêtement et de sa représentation à la poétique du texte* (Paris: Hermann, 2015), pp. 279–302.

57 Molière, *Théâtre complet*, p. 728: 'tant de rubans, tant de rubans'.

58 Parfaict, *Histoire de l'ancien théâtre italien*, p. 268. The play was called *La Suite du Festin de Pierre*. Don Juan was a popular subject for theatre in the seventeenth century, and multiple versions of the story were staged during the period. Parfaict suggests that it was the Italians themselves who first represented the Don, in their early years in France, so in the mid-seventeenth century. There is also an account of the performance of *La Suite du Festin de Pierre* from the point of view of Dominique, the famous Arlequin of the Italian theatre: see Delia Gambelli (ed.), *Arlecchino a Parigi*, 3 vols (Rome: Bulzoni, 1993–7), 1.321.

59 Molière, *Théâtre complet*, p. 727: 'queuque gros, gros Monsieur, car il a du or à son habit tout depis le haut jusqu'en bas; et ceux qui le servont sont des Monsieux eux-mesmes'.

60 Gherardi, *Le théâtre italien*, 6:176: 'oranges de la chine, oranges. Des Rubans, des Fontanges'. *Fontanges* were artfully knotted bunches of ribbon used to decorate the hair.

61 Gherardi, *Le théâtre italien*, 6:179: 'se perdre à la Foire'.

62 Gherardi, *Le théâtre italien*, 6:179: 'un lieu public'.

63 Elizabeth Anne Honig, *Painting and the Market in Early Modern Antwerp* (New Haven, CT: Yale University Press, 1998), pp. 60–81.

64 On the market stage that is enacted at various points in Callot's episodic print see my account, Marika Takanishi Knowles, *Realism and Role-Play: the Human Figure in French Art from Callot to the Brothers Le Nain* (Newark, DE: University of Delaware Press, 2020), pp. 5–8.

65 Posner has also discussed the relationship to the curtain call: Donald Posner, 'Another look at Watteau's *Gilles*', *Apollo* 117 (February 1983), 97–9.

66 On this sequence of drawings, see Martin Eidelberg, *Watteau's Drawings: Their Use and Significance* (New York: Garland Publishing, 1977), pp. 30–34.

67 Marie-Claude Groshens, 'La pratique théâtrale foraine: contribution à l'étude de la fête marchande', *Ethnologie française* 17 (1987), 53–8.

68 Groshens, 'La pratique théâtrale foraine', 54: 'prestations et contre-prestations', 'de type "agonistique"'.

69 On vulnerability and the 'shame contract' between actor and audience in modern theatre, see Robin Bernstein, 'Toward the integration of theater history and affect studies: shame and the Rude Mech's *The Method Gun*', *Theater Journal* 64:2 (2012), 113–30, here p. 221.

70 Richard Sennett, *The Fall of Public Man* (1974; New York: W.W. Norton & Company, 1992), pp. 38–41.

71 Panofsky, '*Gilles* or Pierrot?', p. 339.

72 Honig, *Painting and the Market*, pp. 66, 72–81.

73 On changing retail strategies and shop design in the eighteenth century, see Claire Walsh, 'Shop design and the display of goods in eighteenth-century London', *Journal of Design History* 8:3 (1995), 157–76. Walsh argues persuasively that many of the 'modern retailing methods' associated with the nineteenth century were in fact invented in the eighteenth century. French shop design did not move as quickly

as that of England, but the overall movement was in the same direction – see Chapter 2.

74 On this dynamic, as well as a broader consideration of retail practices in eighteenth-century Paris, see Jones, *Sexing La Mode*, pp. 155–60. On this theme in the Italian context, see Evelyn C. Welch, *Shopping in the Renaissance: Consumer Cultures in Italy, 1400–1600* (New Haven, CT: Yale University Press, 2005), pp. 32–55. On the relationship between the presentation and the consumption of classed bodies in the marketplace, see also Sheila McTighe, 'Foods and the body in Italian genre paintings, about 1580: Campi, Passarotti, Carracci', *Art Bulletin* 86:2 (2004), 301–23. On the politics of looking at retailers and vendors, particularly the ambulatory vendors about which I will have much more to say, see Sheila McTighe, 'Perfect deformity, ideal beauty, and the *imaginaire* of work: the reception of Annibale Carracci's "Arti di Bologna" in 1646', *Oxford Art Journal* 16:1 (1993), 75–91; Katie Scott, 'Edme Bouchardon's "Cris de Paris": crying food in early modern Paris', *Word and Image* 29:1 (2013), 59–91.

75 Wolfgang Fritz Haug, *Critique of Commodity Aesthetics*, trans. Robert Bock (1971; Cambridge: Polity Press, 1986), p. 57.

76 Louis Hautecoeur, 'De l'échoppe aux grands magasins', *La Revue de Paris* 7 (1933), 811–841, here pp. 811–12. On shop design in Renaissance Italy, see Welch, *Shopping in the Renaissance*, pp. 123–63. On shop design, see also Nikolaus Pevsner, *A History of Building Types* (London: Thames and Hudson, 1976), pp. 257–72.

77 On the counter in eighteenth-century English shops, see Walsh, 'Shop design and the display of goods', 172. As Pevsner points out, the counter as an element of shop architecture has been in place since Imperial Rome, if not earlier: Pevsner, *A History of Building Types*, p. 257.

78 For a valuable discussion of this iconography, in relationship to the *Enseigne de Gersaint*, see Martin Eidelberg, 'Reconsidering Watteau's *Enseigne de Gersaint*', accessed 28 April 2023, http://watteauandhiscircle.org/Gersaint.htm.

79 For a detailed description of Gersaint's boutique and its relationship to Watteau's painting, see Guillaume Glorieux, *À l'enseigne de Gersaint: Edme-François Gersaint, Marchand d'Art sur le Pont Notre-Dame (1694–1750)* (Paris: Champ Vallon, 2002), pp. 66–84. Commentators have emphasised the relative novelty of depicting elite sociability as occurring in the shop of a merchant mercer, who sold paintings as well as furniture and toiletries: see Andrew McClellan, 'Watteau's dealer: Gersaint and the marketing of art in eighteenth-century Paris', *Art Bulletin* 78:3 (1996), 439–53, here pp. 439–44. See also Plax, *Watteau and Cultural Politics*, p. 156; Vidal, *Watteau's Painted Conversations*, pp. 165–202.

80 Knowles, *Realism and Role-Play*, pp. 57–62.

81 Knowles, *Realism and Role-Play*, pp. 57–62.

82 The presence of the counter, as well as the stage curtain and proscenium, distinguish the fair from the Rabelaisian carnival, as interpreted by Bakhtin: Mikhail Bakhtin, *Rabelais and His World*, trans. Hélène Iswolsky (Bloomington: Indiana University Press, 2009), pp. 303–67.

83 In the French context, these prints have been dealt with admirably by a number of scholars, including Sarah Cohen, Vincent Milliot, Pascale Cugy, David Pullins, and Paula Radisich. I cite here those sources that attempt to deal with the relationships between the multiple sub-genres of these prints, in an effort to create an overarching category. Vincent Milliot, *Les Cris de Paris ou le peuple travesti: Les représentations des petits métiers parisiens XVIe–XVIIIe siècles* (Paris: Publications de la Sorbonne, 2014);

Vincent Milliot, 'La ville au miroir des métiers. Représentations du monde du travail et imaginaires de la ville (XVIe et XVIIIe siècle)', in Claude Petitfrère (ed.), *Images et imaginaires dans la ville à l'époque moderne* (Tours: Presses universitaires François-Rabelais, 1998), pp. 181–204; Paula Radisich, 'The *cris de Paris* in the LACMA Recueil des Modes', in Kathryn Norberg and Sandra Rosenbaum (eds), *Fashion in the Age of Louis XIV: Interpreting the Art of Elegance* (Lubbock: Texas Tech University Press, 2014), pp. 55–71; David Pullins, 'Techniques of the Body: Viewing the arts and *métiers* of France from the workshop of Nicolas I and Nicolas II de Larmessin', *Oxford Art Journal* 37:2 (2014), 135–55; Pascale Cugy, *La Dynastie Bonnart: Peintres, Graveurs, et Marchands de Modes à Paris sous l'Ancien Régime* (Rennes: Presses Universitaires de Rennes, 2017), esp. pp. 197–267; Cohen, *Art, Dance, and the Body*, pp. 134–65.

84 Collectors amassed the prints under rubrics like '*Costumes, modes et habillemens*', '*Modes et habillements de divers états et de différentes Nations*', '*Pièces historiques, figures et habillements*', but also '*charges et caricatures*': Milliot, 'La ville au miroir des métiers', p. 185.

85 On the influence of the *Landsknecht* print, see Knowles, *Realism and Role-Play*, pp. 50–6. See also J.R. Hale, *Artists and Warfare in the Renaissance* (New Haven, CT: Yale University Press, 1990), pp. 52–61.

86 On the cries, see the decisive account by Milliot, *Les Cris de Paris*.

87 For a facsimile of Vecellio's volume as well as an up-to-date introduction, see Margaret F. Rosenthal and Ann Rosalind Jones, *The Clothing of the Renaissance World: Europe, Asia, Africa, the Americas: Cesare Vecellio's Habiti Antichi et Moderni* (London: Thames & Hudson, 2008). See also Jane Bridgeman, 'The origins of dress history and Cesare Vecellio's "pourtraits of attire"', *Costume* 44 (2010), 37–45.

88 Bronwen Wilson, 'Reproducing the contours of Venetian identity in sixteenth-century costume books', *Studies in Iconography* 25 (2004), 221–74, here pp. 261–4.

89 See Gillot's *Scène de la Comédie Italienne* (INV26754, recto), one of a number of drawings in the Louvre, many of which were etched and published by Gabriel Huquier *c.* 1730. This drawing, which does not appear to have been etched, shows a courtroom scene, with Scaramouche as judge and Arlequin as defendant. Pierrot appears behind Arlequin, a rifle resting on his shoulder.

90 On early fashion prints in France, see Raymond Gaudriault, *Répertoire de la gravure de mode française des origines à 1815* (Nantes: Promodis, 1988).

91 Cugy, *La dynastie Bonnart*, pp. 215–39, here p. 215. On the Bonnarts' *cris de Paris* and the overlap with other genres of fashion prints, see also Radisich, 'The *cris de Paris* in the LACMA Recueil des Modes', pp. 55–7.

92 Cugy, *La dynastie Bonnart*, p. 215: 'un vaste ensemble où communiquent des avatars élégants de toutes les couches de la société'.

93 Wilson, 'Reproducing the contours of Venetian identity', 257–65. For a discussion of the threshold or screen as the site of the inscription of social identity, see Kaja Silverman, *The Threshold of the Visible World* (New York: Routledge, 1996), pp. 18–20.

94 Cohen, *Art, Dance, and the Body*, p. 136.

95 Cohen, *Art, Dance, and the Body*, p. 148. See also Sarah R. Cohen, 'Body as "character" in early eighteenth-century French art and performance', *Art Bulletin* 78:3 (1996), 454–66, here pp. 458–60.

96 Cugy, *La dynastie Bonnart*, pp. 284–5. This was referred to as 'une estampe habillée'.

97 Molière, *Théâtre complet*, p. 729: 'sans reproche, des rubans a tous les marciers qui passont'.

98 Cugy, *La dynastie Bonnart*, pp. 241–2.

99 Roger-Armand Weigert, 'Sur les Larmessin et les costumes grotesques', *Nouvelles de l'estampe* 2 (1969), 67–75.

100 Weigert does not group the *Habit de la lingère* with the other *Costumes grotesques*, because he considers it a 'trade', which shows a figure in contemporary dress, rather than a garment entirely constructed from the figure's merchandise.

101 Pullins, 'Techniques of the body', 146.

102 On the *portrait déguisé* or *histoiré* see Marlen Schneider, *Belle comme Vénus: le portrait historié entre Grand siècle et Lumières*, trans. Aude Virey-Wallon (2015; Paris: Deutsches Forum für Kunstgeschichte, 2020).

103 Claude Parfaict and François Parfaict, *Mémoires pour servir à l'histoire des spectacles de la foire, par un acteur forain*, 2 vols (Paris: Briasson, 1743), I.33.

104 Hélène Adhémar, 'Watteau, les romans et l'imagerie de son temps', *Gazette des Beaux-Arts* 90 (1977), 165–72, here p. 172.

105 Julie Ann Plax has argued that this possibility should be taken seriously, which reflects her interest in Watteau's experiments with genre and his adaptation for elevated ends of unusual media like signboard paintings: Plax, *Watteau and Cultural Politics*, pp. 170–71.

106 A valuable account of signs was written by a historian of 'vieux Paris', Fournier. See Édouard Fournier, *Histoire des enseignes de Paris* (Paris: Libraire de la Société des Gens de Lettres, 1884).

107 Louis-Sébastien Mercier, *Tableau de Paris*, 2 vols, ed. Jean-Claude Bonnet (Paris: Mercure de France, 1994), I.1091–3.

108 Richard Wrigley, 'Between the street and the salon: Parisian shop signs and the spaces of professionalism in the eighteenth and early nineteenth centuries', *Oxford Art Journal* 21:1 (1998), 45–67, here p. 57.

109 Hélène Adhémar, *Watteau: sa vie, son œuvre* (Paris: Éditions Pierre Tisné, 1950), p. 229.

110 Henry Monnier, *Phénomènes*, Plate 2 of the *Galerie Théâtrale*, 1828, lithograph. British Museum, London. 1861,1012.823.

111 Jennifer M. Kilian, *The Paintings of Karel Du Jardin, 1626–1678, Catalogue Raisonné* (Amsterdam: John Benjamins Publishing Company, 2005), cat. no. 38, pp. 151–3.

112 For this association between street theatre and the images of the Italians in the street, see Jeffrey S. Ravel, 'Trois images de l'expulsion des comédiens italiens en 1697', *Littératures classiques* 82 (2013), 51–60.

113 This expression is borrowed from Jonas Barish, *The Antitheatrical Prejudice* (Berkeley: University of California Press, 1981), p. 213.

 **2**

Pierrot-co-co

In the decade prior to his death in 1715, Louis XIV retired from much of court life at Versailles, freeing his courtiers to return to their homes or to build new ones in Paris.[1] Liberated from the imposing symmetries and massive proportions of Versailles, elites redecorated their homes in a new style characterised by light colours and motifs drawn from the natural world, like the pebble and shell encrustations (*rocaille*) on the edge of a tidal pool. The resulting spaces were intimate and yet open to the natural world. Large windows looked out upon vistas of sunlight and greenery. Tall mirrors reflected what was seen through the windows, multiplying light, the rays of which played upon gilded frames and candlesticks. These interiors could feel like a 'forest clearing' or a gazebo overgrown with flowering vines.[2] It was the space of the *fête galante* made into a room. In these interiors that were also gardens, Pierrot arose, as he had once before, like a garden herm, awaiting the orders of his employers.

Eventually, towards the end of the eighteenth century, this 'modern taste' (*goût moderne*) would come to be called the rococo, which is how I refer to it here.[3] The rococo was both a style and a practice. As a style, it liberally used the c-curve, both in symmetrical and asymmetrical arrangements; it favoured light, pastel colours; it drew upon motifs from nature – shells, flowers, fluffy clouds – and incorporated into its painterly repertoire the materials of the luxury trades – satin and silk fabrics and cushions, strings of pearls, ribbons, gold and silver *objets d'art*. As a practice, rococo artists mixed and matched this repertoire of motifs in a range of media, including plaster and wood, precious metals, oil paint, ceramics, and tapestry. For human figures, artists drew upon the characters of the costume print. The masks of the Comédie Italienne, including Pierrot, were ubiquitous characters in the cast of the rococo. Marianne Roland Michel has described rococo artistic practice as drawing upon 'an international decorative repertoire' composed of a 'common stock of images', many of which were based on Watteau's works.[4] For Roland Michel, the artist's works were available as a common stock in no small part because of the way that his compositions and designs enabled the exchangeability of the figures they contained.[5]

Watteau's works were also available to rococo practice because of their dissemination as prints. Rococo artists both created and drew upon repertoires of figures and motifs made available to them through print. As a result, a new category of artist emerged, the *ornemantiste*, who was responsible for the creation of designs and patterns for ornament and ornamented objects, which were circulated as prints.[6] The chief source of prints after Watteau, from which myriad less expensive prints were copied and pastiched, was the *Recueil Jullienne*, a four-volume collection, published in 1735.[7] Commissioned, edited, and published by Jean de Jullienne, a wealthy collector and director of the Manufacture des Gobelins, the *Recueil Jullienne* contained prints after all of Watteau's known paintings, his designs for ornament, and a large selection of his drawings.[8] These expensive tomes, of which only a limited number were published, were intended for collectors, connoisseurs, and wealthy artists, who wished to admire Watteau's work at leisure.[9] Nevertheless, on a practical level, the *Recueil Jullienne* transformed Watteau's scattered *oeuvre* into a (comparably) compact repertoire.[10]

As a practice, the rococo is both figuratively and literally a *fête marchande* – figuratively because of the way it theatricalises its motifs and literally because it was a practice addressed to the marketplace. Coincident with the European 'consumer revolution' of the eighteenth century, the rococo was one of the first artistic styles to develop in tandem with the growth of a market for relatively inexpensive, prefabricated, luxury objects like ceramic figurines, snuff boxes, fans, ready-to-wear items of dress, and tableware. The rococo nourished luxury trades in Paris and encouraged a distinctive brand of Parisian decadence, one that 'trickled down' into the lower echelons of a nascent bourgeois society.[11] For those who could not afford an entire, purpose-built, rococo interior, tableware and porcelain figurines provided a taste of the style.[12] It is important to acknowledge that there were also deeply serious and erudite rococo objects, particularly the complex décors constructed for elite homes. Yet this is not the arena in which Pierrot thrives. He is a symptom and a hero of the 'down-market' rococo.

In this chapter, I want to think carefully about how Watteau's representations of Pierrot enabled the character's circulation and recurrence in rococo practice. Pierrot's theatrical address, to which I devoted Chapter 1, also characterises the address of many rococo artworks. As I will show, the theatrical address is built into both rococo marketplace practices and contemporary discursive constructions of the marketplace. In critical discourse of the period, negative connotations begin to accrue around a particular term, *étalage*, the displaying of things to attract attention. The marketplace is critiqued not only for its frivolity, but for the way that frivolity is exemplified by the *étalage* of merchandise. Pierrot's iterations in rococo form are key to understanding this convergence of theatricality, marketing, and a larger set of marketplace practices used to create goods for sale. Whereas Watteau's *Pierrot* (the large painting) reflects ambivalently upon the theatricality of the marketplace, the Pierrots in this chapter realise the promise of Watteau's figure as a marketplace actor. In the first half of the chapter, I explore the circulation and medial translation of four different figures of Pierrot, each created by Watteau and reproduced as a print in the *Recueil Jullienne*. This enables me to consider how Watteau's way of presenting Pierrot encouraged excerption and re-use, and how Watteau's strategies are emblematic of rococo practice more generally. In the second, more speculative part of the chapter, I consider the convergence of certain ways of conceptualising the mental space with the presentational mode of emergent retail strategies.

Arabesque

Perhaps the earliest Pierrot in rococo printed ornament appears in Louis Crépy's etching after a panel for a painted screen by Watteau (Figure 2.1). The print depicts a platform, suspended in mid-air by swags of drapery wrapped around a pair of herms (stone busts used in garden decoration) and two slender trees. This distinctive design, combining fanciful architecture, a central motif, and a playful, elaborate frame, was called an arabesque.[13] Watteau studied with Gillot and Audran, two early masters of the arabesque, whose designs are known both as prints and as the drawings from which the prints were made (see Figure 2.2). Circulated as a print, the arabesque could be copied and fitted to different surfaces, painted onto porcelain or the wall, woven into tapestry. Fans, upholstery, and fire-screens were all decorated with arabesques, but the most important surface for arabesques was the *boiserie*, the fitted wood-panelling that lined the walls of rooms. These tall, narrow panels were decorated with painted and sculpted elements; a carved and gilded wood frame hugged the edges of the panel.[14] Themes from inside the arabesques's central vignette – flora and fauna, musical instruments, hunting paraphernalia – might also appear in the frame, or in the 'trophies', bunches of objects bound in ribbon, which were hung throughout the design.[15] Within the vignette, gravity roots figures to the ground, but at the edges, motifs become weightless.[16] The entire woodland clearing is held aloft by a few delicate ribbons. The scallop shell, the bat's wing, the horn of plenty, the garland of flowers were examples of standard rococo design units, chosen for their decorative qualities and their ability to be scaled up or down in size, depending on the amount of space that needed to be filled.

'Arabesque for a screen, with Pierrot' was included in the fourth volume of the *Recueil Jullienne* in 1735, although the etching had been in circulation since 1727, when it was published, along with five other prints, each of which represented a single panel of the screen, by Edmé-François Gersaint. Three of the six designs in Gersaint's series feature a single figure from the Comédie Italienne (Pierrot, Colombine, and Arlequin), while the remaining three show more elaborate scenes that resemble small *fêtes galantes*.[17] Like Watteau's easel paintings, the arabesques that featured the Italian masks brought the fair, and its associations with the street and the popular, into the elite home.

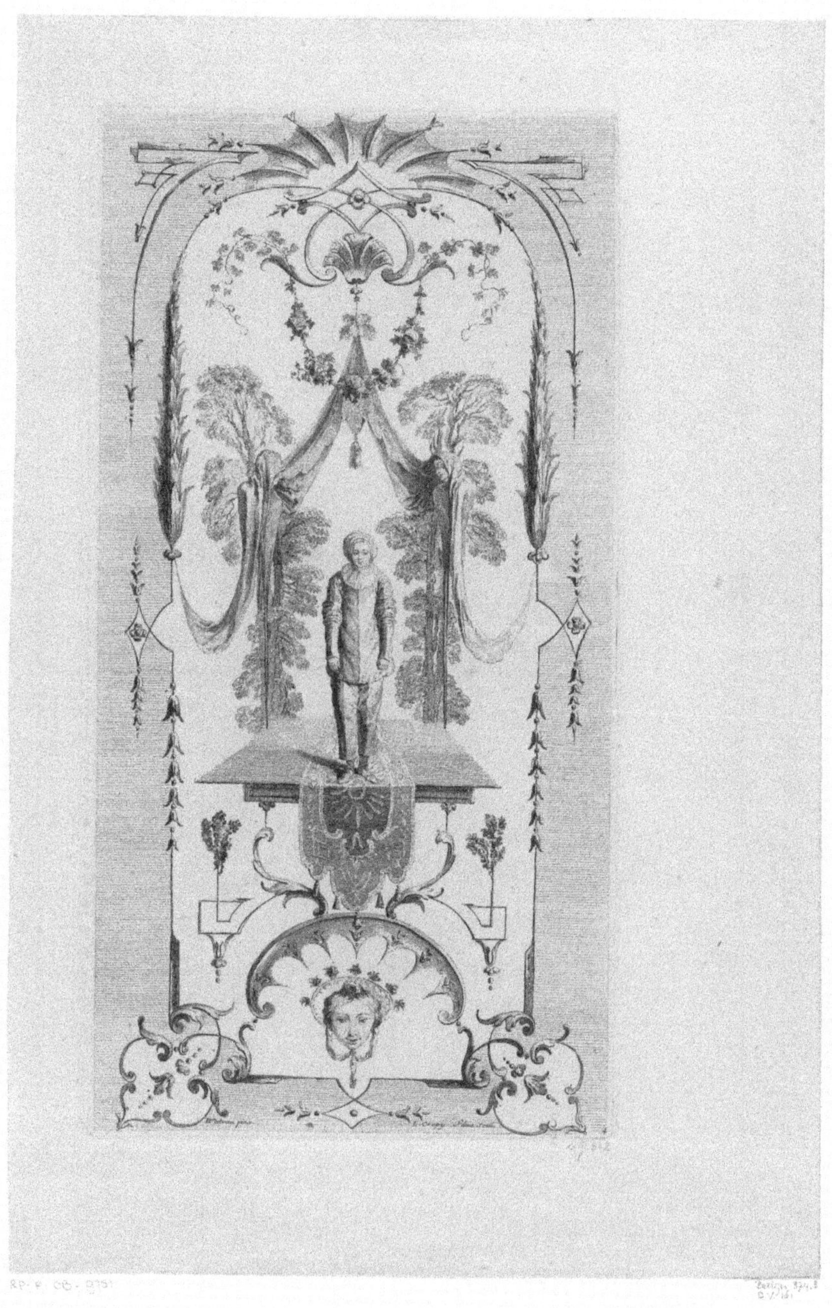

2.1   Louis Crépy after Antoine Watteau, *Arabesque for a screen, with Pierrot*,
ca. 1727. Etching, 39.2 × 19.8 cm. Source: Rijksmuseum, Amsterdam. RP-P-OB-9751
©Rijksmuseum.

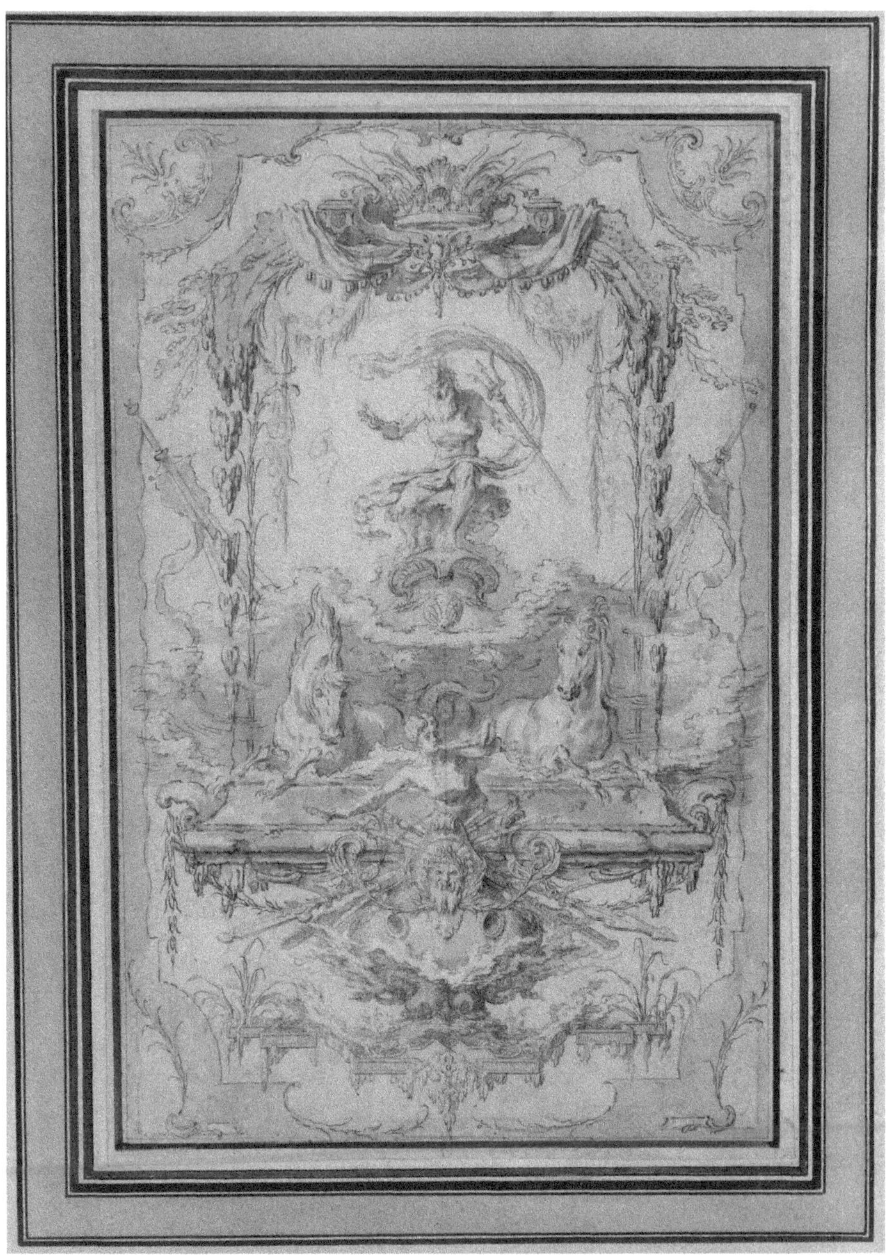

2.2   Claude Gillot, *Arabesque for a door frame, Neptune*, early eighteenth century.
Pencil, pen, and sanguine on a first-state etching, 28.4 × 18.4 cm. Source: Bibliothèque
Nationale de France, Paris. RESERVE B-6 (A,21)-BOITE ECU ©BNF.

In addition to the prints collected in Jullienne's volume, hundreds of arabesques 'after Watteau' were produced by print-makers during the eighteenth century. Often, this appellation merely referred to an arabesque in the 'spirit' of Watteau, as opposed to one that he had designed in full.[18] Print publishers were crafty manipulators of artists' drawings and designs, which they plundered for motifs to copy or to transform into ornament. Gabriel Huquier and Gersaint both engaged in the creation of arabesques 'invented by Watteau', but which were largely drawn by other artists working off a '*pensée*' left by Watteau.[19]

A painter or a decorator could have used Crépy's print as a model, as Watteau may have used one of Gillot's or Audran's arabesques as his own model, copying wholesale or picking and choosing different bits, stretching or compressing the forms depending on the size of the surface to be covered.[20] In addition, the printed design, an 'adaptable model', as Roland Michel has put it, could itself be re-used as a decoration by pasting it to the door of a cabinet, a trunk, or a fire-screen.[21] If the surface to be decorated was very small, a person could simply cut out Pierrot's figure, by itself. In an advertisement for the series published in the *Mercure de France* in November 1727, the author indicated this potential use: 'such subjects painted on white grounds are marvellously suited to cut-outs, with which ladies nowadays make such pretty objects'.[22] This kind of *découpage* was a popular pastime during the eighteenth century, thanks in part to a profusion of inexpensive prints.[23] An undated example of this kind of cutting and pasting is included in the *Recueil Valenciennes*, a print album conserved at the Musée des Beaux Arts, Valenciennes, which offers valuable insight into the way that collectors manipulated and assembled eighteenth-century prints (see Plate 8).[24] On this sheet, an unknown user has created an arabesque by combining a vignette of a hunt-inspired *fête galante* with garlands of ivy, flowers, scrollwork, and acanthus leaves. The scissors deployed were very nimble indeed, hugging the minute, irregular contours of the foliage and snipping whisper-thin vines.

The arabesque *découpée* performs an underlying formal principle of the rococo style, which is the exchangeability of recognisable motifs, like the acanthus swirl or the garland, in a mode of mix-and-match.[25] The arabesques attributed to Watteau had certain novel formal features when compared to the arabesques of Gillot. Watteau's arabesques were considerably airier, creating an open space around the central motif, and tending to hang objects individually, rather than bind things into a geometric pattern. In Gillot's *Neptune arabesque*, by contrast, the page is densely packed and the individual motifs more sculptural. Building atop a preliminary etched design, Gillot uses pen and wash to elaborate upon the underlying structure. Beneath the figure of Neptune, the torsos of two horses emerge from a grotto, but their hind legs disappear into the grotto's shadowy recesses. These horses are not extractable, nor do they seem to be suspended on the page. Mossy foliage, which drips off the trellis and the stone pediment, binds the architectural elements of the arabesque together. Watteau did create more verdant, exuberant designs for arabesques, but the Pierrot arabesque is comparably dry. Two neat sprigs of ivy sprout from the strapwork surrounding the palmette at the top of the design. But instead of drooping downwards and twining themselves around another element of the arabesque, the sprigs hover weightlessly against the white ground. Unlike Gillot's Neptune, whose figure is masterfully torqued, Pierrot offers a neat, symmetrical silhouette, poised at the very edge of the platform on which he stands. While the problem of attribution means that we do not know whether these designs can be attributed to Watteau, the features of the arabesques attributed to Watteau – frontality, crisp symmetry, a certain compositional aeration – are also the features of Pierrot's figure as the artist had designed it. Watteau's way of disposing figures may have inspired a new kind of arabesque, one that used a more frankly theatrical mode to offer its figures to the marketplace.

Figurine

In the large painting of Pierrot, his hat creates a perfect circle around his face, a straw halo. In another painting by Watteau, however, which is known as a print, *Arlequin, Pierrot and Scapin*, Pierrot appears with his hat angled to one side (Figure 2.3). This Pierrot's face is longer and more oval in form than the Pierrot of the large painting, yet he wears the same silky tunic with a row of tiny buttons and overlong sleeves, bunched up at the elbows, which he holds in place by pressing his arms to his sides. This Pierrot with angled hat also had an afterlife in the rococo. In the second half of the 1740s the Strasbourg-Haguenau faience manufactory, under the direction of Paul Hannong, produced a series of faience (glazed earthenware) figurines of the Italian masks, including a Pierrot that stands just over a foot tall, whose hat has been blown to one side (see Plate 9).[26] With his face elongated, his arms at his side, the faience Pierrot is clearly modelled on Watteau's figure, but now wrought in three dimensions, and lent a glossy surface, as well as several *mouches* (beauty spots made of black velvet) on his face. Diminutive ceramic figures were enormously popular rococo objects.[27] Available at a range of qualities and prices, the figurines were produced across Europe both in faience and porcelain.[28] Ceramic manufacturers sold the figurines alongside their other wares at fairs, in urban boutiques (*comptoirs*), and through catalogues (*catalogues marchands*).[29] At these outlets, vendors took orders, but they also sold from the stock displayed in the shop or on the stall. Customers were increasingly exposed to objects that were available to be purchased and packed up on the spot, moments after the sale had been concluded (not unlike the portrait of Louis XIV being boxed in *Gersaint's shop sign*). Ceramic figurines were originally inspired by sugar sculptures that served as table ornaments nestled amid arrangements of moss, flowers, mirrored trays, and candlesticks. Collections of figurines could also be displayed on dainty shelves above the fireplace, alongside other delicate *bibelots*, like vases, goblets, and clocks.[30] The Italian masks were a favourite repertoire from which to draw models for figurines. Frans Bustelli, working

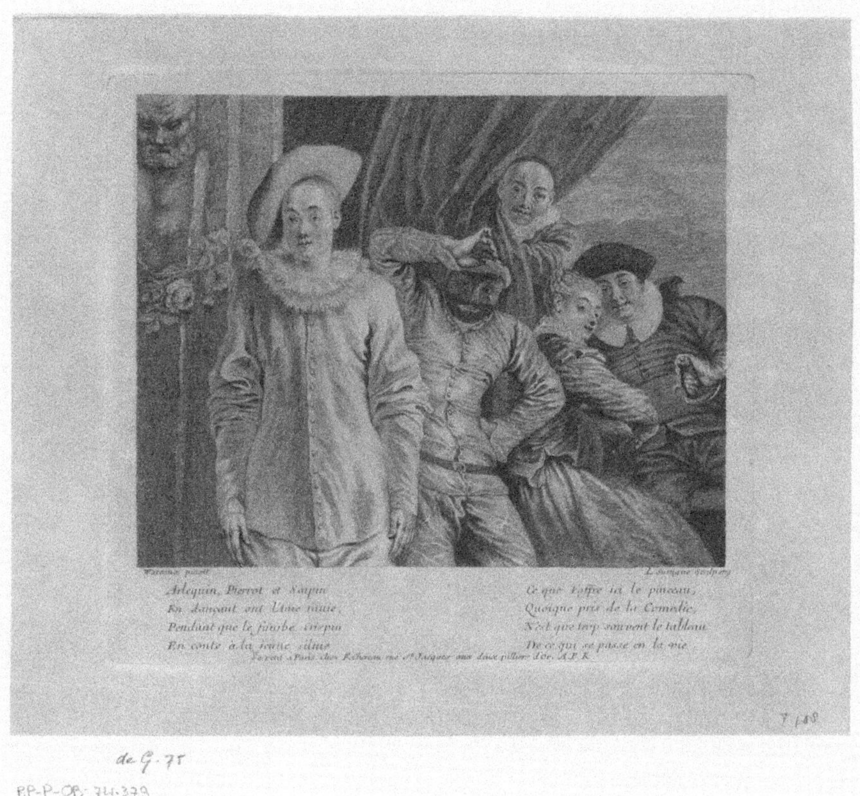

2.3   Louis Surugue after Antoine Watteau, *Arlequin, Pierrot and Scapin*, 1719.
Etching, 23 × 25.3 cm. Source: Rijksmuseum, Amsterdam. RP-P-OB-74.379
©Rijksmuseum.

at the Nymphenburg manufactory in the mid-eighteenth century, created an
entire Italian troupe in porcelain.[31] At Meissen, in response to the installation
of a troupe of Italian actors at the court of August III, Johann Joachim Kaendler
modelled groups of figurines featuring amorous Harlequins.[32] Other popular
figurines included monkeys playing musical instruments (it was possible to
acquire an entire 'money orchestra') and *chinoiserie* figurines, called 'buddhas',
'pagodas', or '*magots*'.[33]

Porcelain modellers combed print repertoires to discover attractive figures. Ceramic manufacturers maintained collections of prints, which were
used as models for figurines and painted décors. An inventory made at the
Sèvres manufactory in 1752 shows a collection of 88 paintings, 1,105 works
on paper, including drawings and prints, and 3 boxes of insects.[34] Meissen,
which was particularly known for its figurines and its 'Watteau decors', also
had a sizeable collection of prints intended for use as models.[35] While figurines
were modelled in wax, from which hard moulds were cast, ceramic painters

used prints to make *poncifs*, stencils or patterns, which could be pierced with small holes and used to establish the outlines of a design on the porcelain glaze.[36] The models preferred by the designers of figurines were taken from prints after Watteau, Gillot, François Boucher, and Jean-Baptiste Oudry, as well as the repertoires of *modes* discussed in Chapter 1. Although the surviving inventories are not detailed, manufactories' print collections of 'different figures and personages' probably referred to serial print repertoires, like costume prints, fashion prints, and 'criers'.[37] These types of figure were well suited to reflect the character of the rococo as a style of affluence, embellishment, and performative consumption. These figurines restaged the *fête marchande* in private homes.

The Strasbourg manufactory may have used Surugue's etching after Watteau's painting as a model for the figurine. This exquisite print, dating from 1719, was one of the ten etchings made after Watteau's paintings while the artist was still alive.[38] Included in the third volume of the *Recueil Jullienne*, it is typical of the outstanding quality of the prints Jullienne assembled and commissioned. Yet Hannong and his modellers could have easily used another, less expensive print. As with most published prints, the prints in Jullienne's volumes were quickly copied by less skilled artists and published by print sellers catering to a wide audience.[39] These copyists treated the prints after Watteau's paintings as open repertoires, from which they could select specific figures and motifs to re-use, reposition, and elaborate. For example, Christoph Weigel, a publisher active in Nuremberg, produced a series of etchings that reproduces all the figures from *Arlequin, Pierrot and Scapin*, but shown at full-length and each given their own plate. Alone, the figures strikes the same pose as seen in the larger composition, but the bottom half of the pose has been imagined by the etcher. Pierrot is named 'Brigella', an Italian clown whose costume very loosely resembles Pierrot's (see Figure 2.4), which suggests that Weigel's market was not overly familiar with the French types.[40] Hannong could have used either Surugue's or Weigel's print as his source for the faience figure.

While prints after the works of history painters like Poussin and Charles Le Brun were readily available, porcelain designers did not model figurines after these examples. Part of the reason for this preference lies in the rococo's taste for irregular and picturesque shapes, for dresses with ribbons or patches instead of the uniform pleats of a toga. Another important criterion was that the figures be intelligible and interesting when alone. Even if purchased as a set, the owner could put the figurines wherever they wanted, removing them from their companions, discovering new companions amid other *bibelots*. This mix-and-match quality meant that history painting's expressive poses, struck in order to act out events in a story, were undesirable. Pierrot, on the other hand, particularly as designed by Watteau, did very well on his own, with his self-contained pose and his neutral air. This can be put another way: certain figures performed their potential mobility better than others. Part of marketing, I have suggested, is the performance of availability – availability to be picked up,

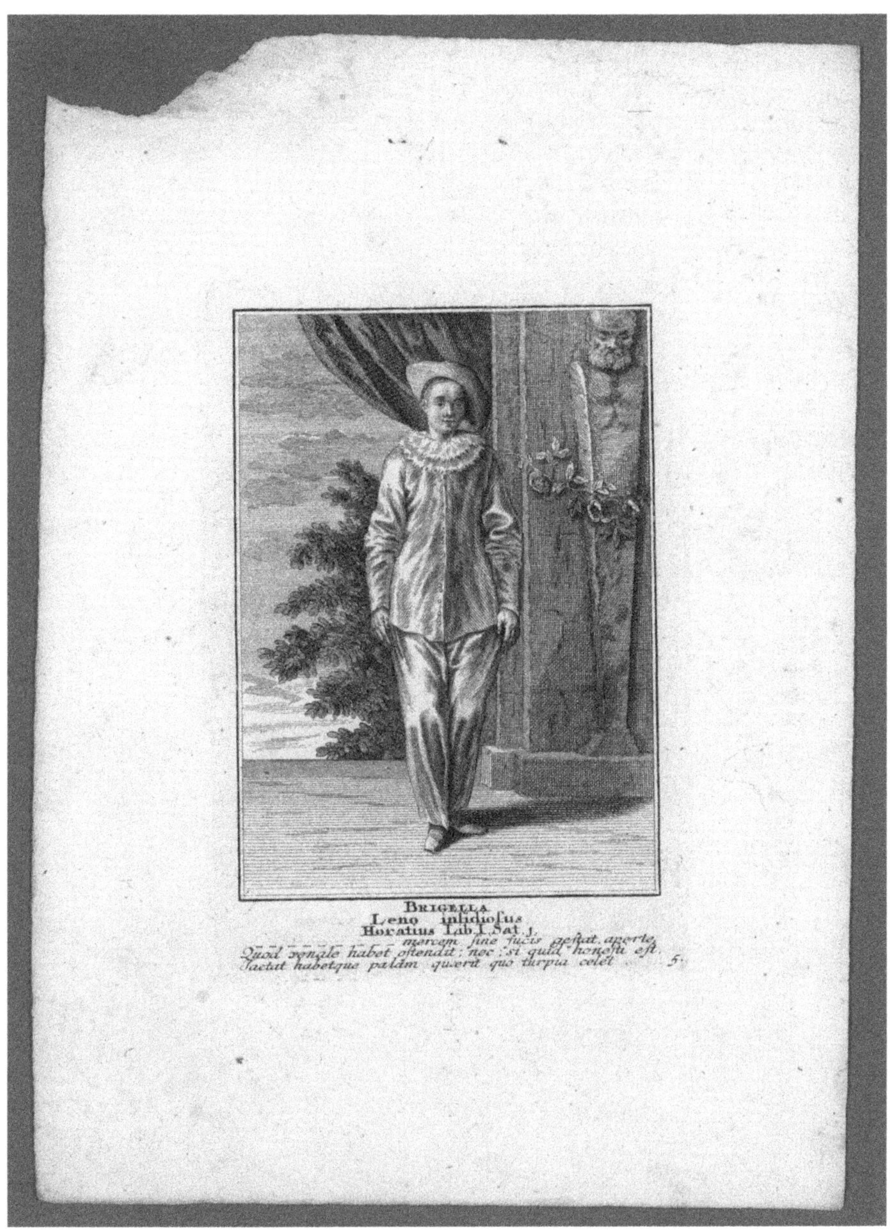

2.4   After Antoine Watteau, *Brigella*, mid-eighteenth century. Etching, 17.2 × 115 cm. Source: Rijksmuseum, Amsterdam. RP-P-1903-A-24069 ©Rijksmuseum.

taken away, and put elsewhere. Part of Pierrot's pathos had been his inability to pair up. His naïveté, his likelihood of being duped, means that Pierrot never gets the girl. Yet this also makes him mobile (no two-body problem for Pierrot), a mobility that is encoded in a pose that represents his self-sufficiency, his lack of engagement with others. The *Brigella* print, which markets Pierrot's figure to a wide range of users, fulfils the solitary destiny that is already encoded in Pierrot's figure in Watteau's original composition. Even so, to be solitary in the *fête galante* was to make merry in the *fête marchande*.

Faience

In Watteau's painted *oeuvre*, Pierrot appears playing the guitar in *Love in the Italian Theatre*, one of the rare nocturnal *fêtes galantes* by the painter. In this composition, Watteau used the guitar-playing Pierrot to fulfil his characteristic anchoring function, a stable presence towards the middle of a row of more mobile figures, whose colourful costumes shimmer in the light of a torch held by Mezzetin.[41] A fine print by Charles Nicolas Cochin after *Love in the Italian Theatre* was included in the *Recueil Jullienne* (Figure 2.5).[42] A mid-eighteenth-century faience plate from Marseilles shows this guitar-playing Pierrot, painted

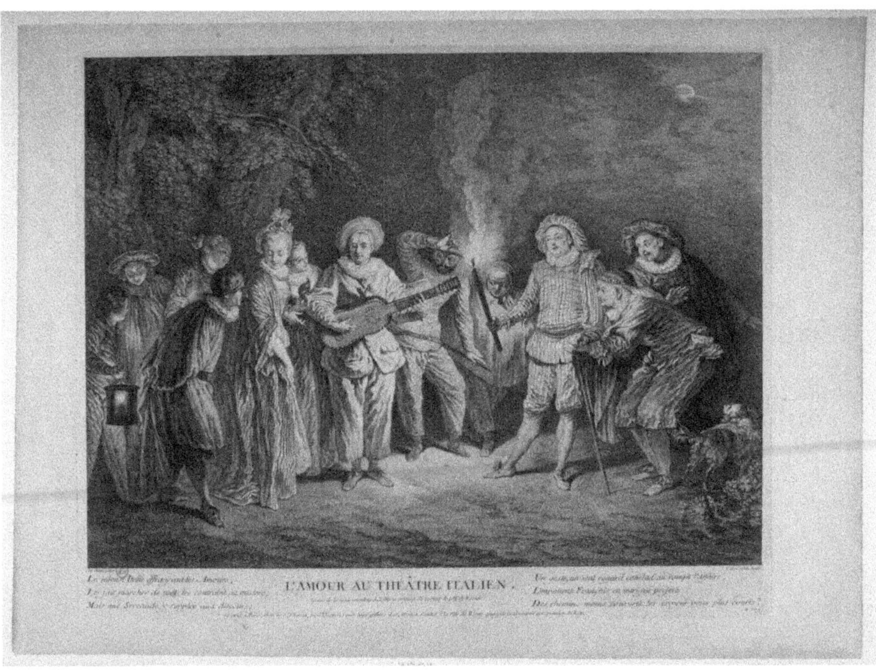

2.5   Charles Nicolas Cochin after Antoine Watteau, *Love in the Italian Theatre*, 1734. Etching, 37.2 × 48.5 cm. Source: Bibliothèque Nationale de France, Paris. RESERVE EE-15 (A,2)-FOL <P. 1> ©BNF.

in yellow cameo (*camaïeu jaune*), accompanying the dancing of a young couple (see Plate 10). This is a rather humble object, an assessment based on comparison with other examples of Marseilles faience, like those exquisitely painted specimens made by the prestige manufactory of the Veuve Perrin.[43] The décor could have been painted freehand or with a *poncif*. The plate belongs to a particular subset of faience known as a 'speaking' or 'singing faience', in which the lyrics of a song are painted onto the object. The caption around the plate's rim, presumably voiced by the cavalier to the sound of Pierrot's guitar, praises the virtues of wine.

Prints after paintings could also be used as the inspirations or sources for new paintings. In the years after Watteau's death, the inventories of painters and merchant mercers show plentiful 'Watteau subjects', which referred to inexpensive copies, based on prints, produced in large quantities and sold as decoration rather than cabinet paintings.[44] It is still possible to stumble across such compositions in the shops of French second-hand dealers. Moving up the ladder of cost and skill, the guitar-playing Pierrot also appears in at least two compositions by Jacques de Lajoue, the important mid-century rococo *ornemantiste* and painter. Lajoue worked in a later iteration of the *rocaille* style, which is sometimes referred to as the '*goût pittoresque*'.[45] While early rococo arabesques are symmetrical, Lajoue experimented with dramatic asymmetries, like those seen in *Fountain in a Park*, a painted overdoor, which would have been set into the *boiserie* above a door.[46] His composition features an elaborate, molluscy fountain capped by a tangle of sea nymphs brandishing Neptune's triton (see Figure 2.6). The oblique angle of the fountain leads the viewer's eye to an archway of trees on the right-hand side of the composition, beneath which Pierrot stands, playing his guitar. In another decorative painting featuring a more symmetrical composition, a kind of gazebo-stage topped by scalloped latticework, Lajoue again uses the figure of Pierrot playing the guitar (Figure 2.7). This time, however, Pierrot has been made into a statue, placed atop a pedestal at the back of the stage, but exactly in the centre of the composition.

Both the painter of the faience plate and Lajoue would have been familiar with the guitar-playing Pierrot from prints after Watteau's work. However, the faience painter probably drew his figure from further down the chain of printed knock-offs, a print more in the manner of the *Brigella*.[47] In addition, artists could have consulted yet another figure of a guitar-playing Pierrot, this one drawn from the second volume of the *Recueil Jullienne* (Figure 2.8). This Pierrot, etched by Jean Audran, appears alone within a thin black frame. Some small adjustments have been made to the angle of the hat, but the figure is otherwise nearly identical to the Pierrot in *Love in the Italian Theatre* (Figure 2.5), with the same bunching of the sleeves on the right arm over the top of the body of the guitar, and the same delicate, elongated fingers of the left hand pressed to the struts. None of the other figures from the painting are present in Audran's etching, however. In an adjoining frame, the same size as the one enclosing Pierrot, a young woman is seated on the ground, her face turned away from the viewer.

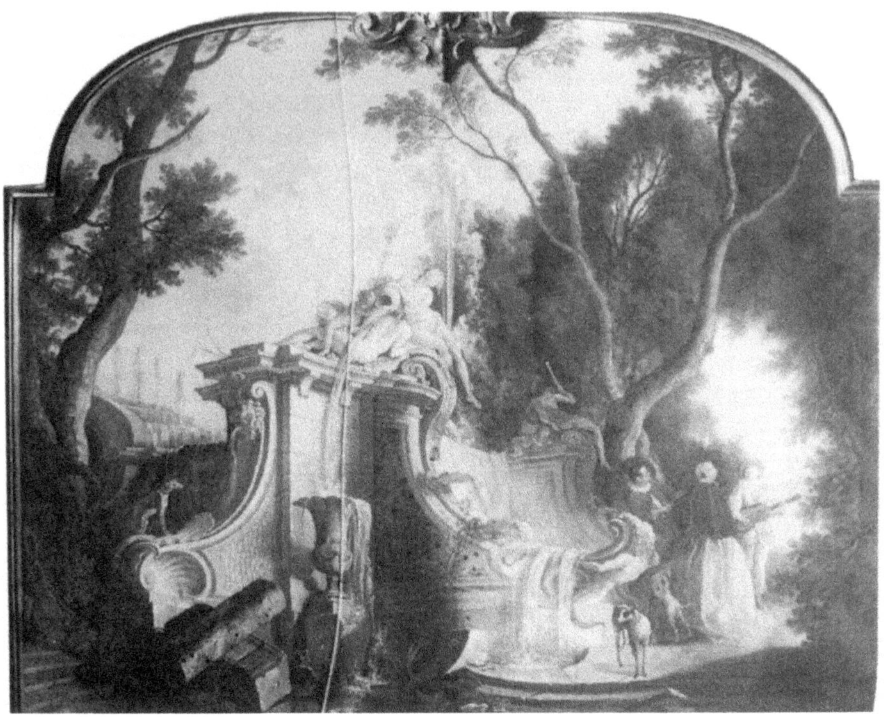

2.6   Jacques de Lajoue, *Fountain in a park*, eighteenth century. Oil on canvas,
110 × 140 cm. Source: Present location unknown ©the author.

She could be listening to Pierrot, as if the music floats across the page and
through the barrier of the frame.

These kinds of alterations, absences, and additions are typical of the first
two volumes of the *Recueil Jullienne*, which were published in 1726 and 1728,
and which are known as the *Figures of different characters* (*Figures de différents
caractères*). As a distinct part of the *Recueil Jullienne*, these volumes are particularly important for the functioning of this collection as a marketplace
repertoire. Upon Watteau's death, Jullienne had amassed a large number of
the drawings that the artist had left behind.[48] After scouring the sheets for
figures that he thought worthwhile to reproduce, Jullienne assigned individual figures to a fleet of etchers, including the young François Boucher.[49] In
the resulting volumes, Jullienne devised the arrangement of full-, half-, and
quarter-page plates. Like the guitar-playing Pierrot, many of the figures that
appear in the painted *fêtes galantes* can be found again in these pages, yet they
are presented against bare grounds, without any other surrounding figures
or landscape. According to Jullienne, the purpose of these volumes was to
commemorate Watteau's work as a draughtsman, but to fulfil this purpose, he
had transformed Watteau's extant *corpus* of drawings in ways that re-oriented
the drawings towards the marketplace.[50] By presenting each of the figures alone

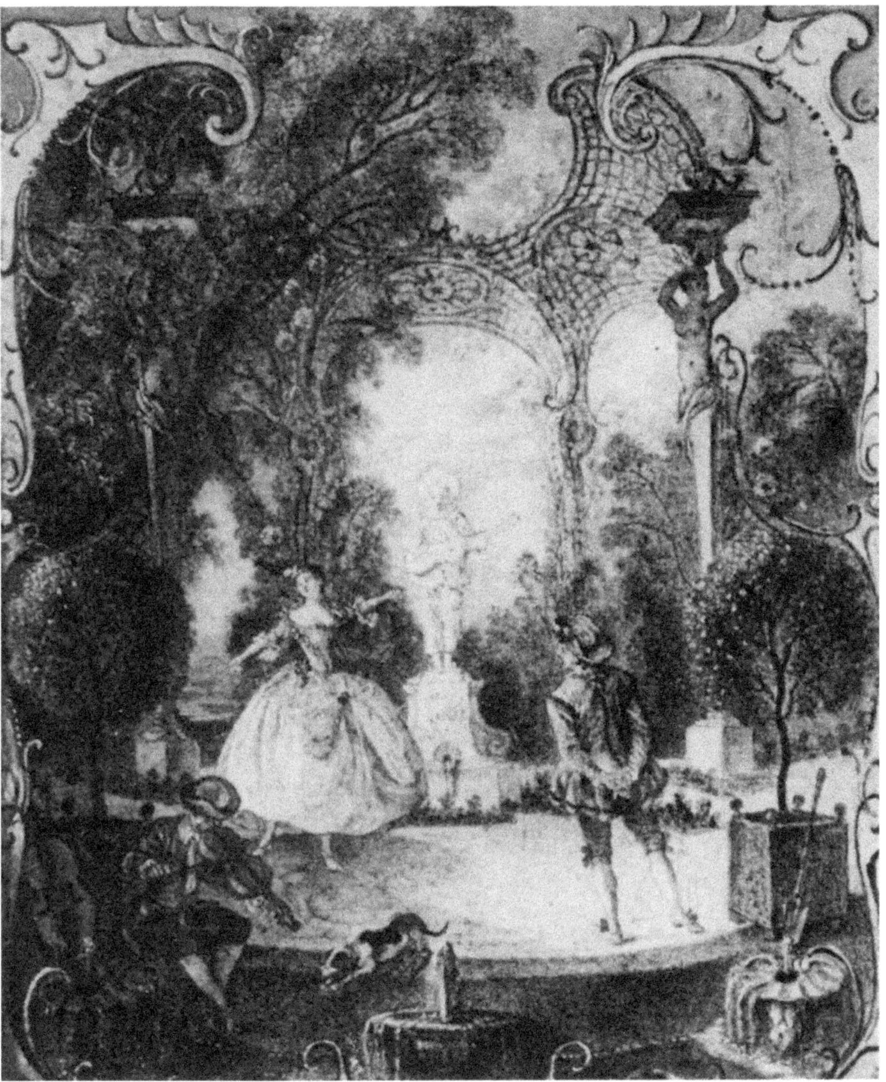

2.7   Jacques de Lajoue, *The Dance*, eighteenth century. 40 × 32 cm. Source: Present location unknown ©the author.

and by translating drawings made in red and black pencil and white chalk into etchings, Jullienne set these figures forth in a way that made them available both to rococo *ornemantistes* and to appreciative connoisseurs, whose practices will be discussed later in this chapter.

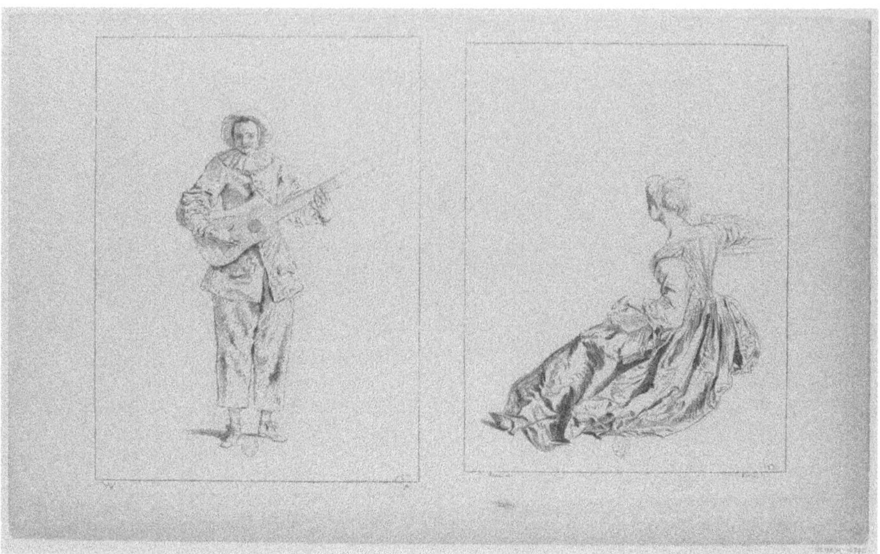

2.8   Jean Audran (L) and Benoît II Audran (R) after Antoine Watteau, Plates no. 187 (L) and no. 188 (R) from *Figures of different characters*, 1728. Etching, 51.5 × 36 cm. Source: Bibliothèque Nationale de France, Paris. RESERVE FOL-DB-15 (D,5) ©BNF.

Mask

Pierrot appears five times in *Figures of different characters*, more than any other Italian mask. In four prints, Pierrot appears at full length. The striking exception is a plate etched by Anne Claude de Caylus (the Comte de Caylus), in which Pierrot is shown as a solitary head, framed by his hat and ruff, but without any body (Figure 2.9). There is a beautiful drawing, which very likely provided a model for the shape of the head and the facial features (see Plate 11).[51] It is also possible that Caylus excerpted the head from a painting, *Happy Pierrot*, in which Pierrot wears the same silly grin.[52] In the painting, Pierrot appeared at full length. In the *Figures of different characters*, the suppression of Pierrot's body transforms him into a decorative motif known as a *mascaron*, which was in effect a disembodied head.[53] *Mascarons* were popular architectural ornaments. Carved in stone, they topped doorways and window frames on the façades of buildings. *Mascarons* also appeared frequently in the arabesque, as one of the motifs used to add weight to the top, bottom, and sides of the frame, where designers clustered ornament. For example, a *mascaron* of a female face, from which seven rosettes radiate, is placed at the base of Crépy's etching after Watteau's arabesque.

The presentation of Pierrot as a *mascaron* in the *Figures of different characters* creates a striking resemblance with the format of ornament prints.[54] These prints, which were usually published in series bound as booklets (*livrets*) but also sold as loose sheets, presented motifs – shells, birds, flowers, and acanthus

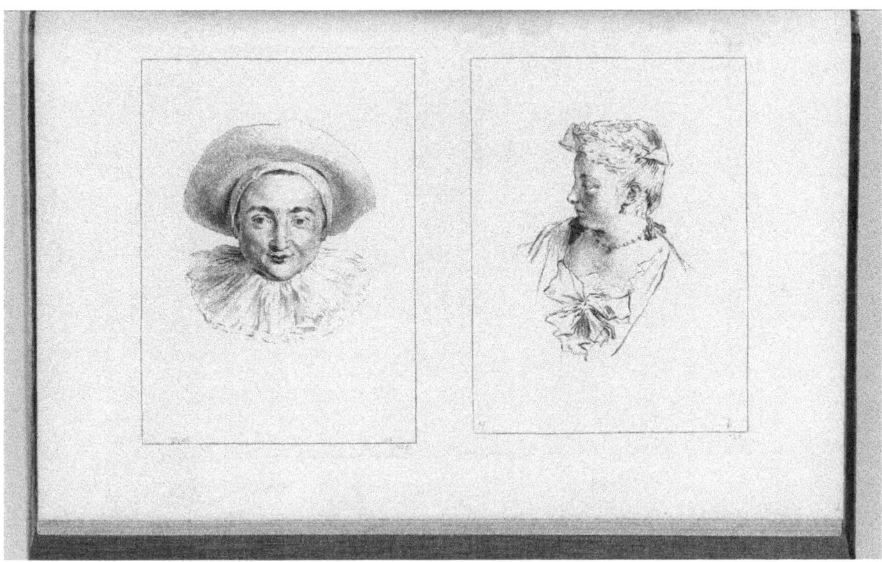

2.9   Anne Claude de Caylus (L) and François Boucher (R) after Antoine Watteau, Plates no. 323 (L) and 324 (R) from *Figures of different characters*, 1728. Etching, 51.5 × 36 cm. Source: Metropolitan Museum of Art, New York. 28.100.2 ©metmuseum.org.

leaves, for instance – as well as objects – candlesticks, tureens, inkwells, and saltcellars, say – transformed by the designer into a riot of texture, curves, and asymmetries.[55] Sometimes the designs, called 'pieces of fantasy' ('*morceaux de fantaisie*') or 'pieces of caprice' ('*morceaux de caprice*') did not even purport to represent a specific object, but offered marvellous and improbable architectures or bits of scrollwork, motifs intended for the most general kind of inspiration rather than as a template for a particular object.[56] Lajoue was known for such designs. He would have based the complex fountain in his painted overdoor on one of his own designs for ornament, most of which were published by Gabriel Huquier.[57]

A common form of ornament print presented the object against an empty ground, like Juste-Aurèle Meissonnier's designs for candlesticks and inkwells, also published by Huquier, or Alexis Peyrotte's 'Acanthus leaf', in which a very large swirl of scrolling leaf reigns in solitary splendour (Figure 2.10). The presentation of the motif against an empty ground facilitated its excerpting and re-use. This excerption could be performed literally, by scissors, or through copying and translation into another medium. Scaled up or down in size, the acanthus leaf could become plasterwork, the base of a candlestick, an encrustation on a silver serving vessel, or an ornament in a painted or printed arabesque. In its isolation on the page, the motif signalled the scope to combine it with other things – it had no pre-existing relationships. This isolation vividly performed the ornament print's address to the marketplace. Caylus's Pierrot

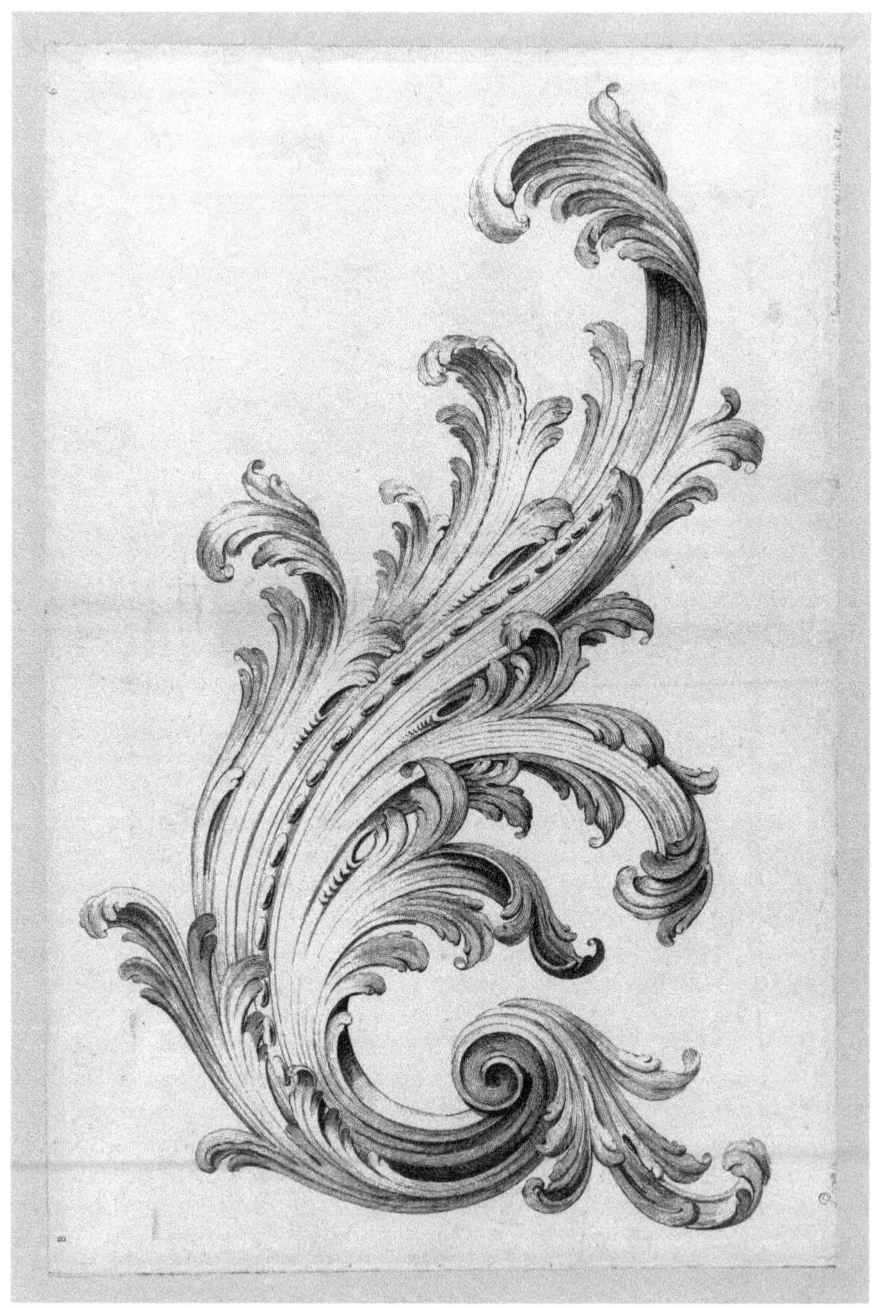

2.10   Gabriel Huquier after Alexis Peyrotte, *Acanthus leaf design*, from *Divers ornements, the era of Louis XV*, 1740. Etching on white laid paper, 30.7 × 48 cm. Source: Cooper Hewitt, Smithsonian Design Museum, New York. 1921–6-213–12 ©Smithsonian Institution.

mascaron presents itself in the same way. A smile on his lips, Pierrot faces the viewer, a facingness that also enables the symmetrical patterns that will allow the *mascaron* to be placed in arabesques. If, in Watteau's paintings, this facingness had performed Pierrot's awkwardness in relationship to the people around him, his social suspension in the print enables his theatrical address to the marketplace.

Rococo retail

In the *Recueil Jullienne*, the realisation of Watteau's *oeuvre* as a marketplace repertoire points to one of the arguments of the 'rococo reaction' or 'anti-rococo' critique, a discourse that evolved over the course of the eighteenth century. As Katie Scott has shown, the rococo 'exposed' itself to accusations of caprice, of frivolity, of vulgar materialism in part because of the way that print removed the style from its context, erasing the relational, discursive content that made rococo decorative interiors meaningful.[58] Scott defends the intellectual programmes, subversive and erudite, which were present in some of the more elaborate rococo interiors, particularly those commissioned in the 1710s and up to the 1730s. *In situ*, rococo decorative programmes could be both complex and irreverent.[59] Yet many rococo objects, particularly at the lower end of the market, circulated without predetermined contexts. Moved from shop to home, from one home to another, and back to the shop, these objects and figures were constantly unmoored. It is in this register of rococo production that Pierrot thrives. With the rococo, Pierrot found his footing amid the forms and the media of the marketplace – small, inexpensive, mobile, and promotional. He emerged as an emissary of the fusion between art, retail, and the 'consumer revolution' of the eighteenth century.[60] He returned through the world of goods.

Over the course of the century, Paris became a world-famous marketplace for luxury goods. These goods consisted of the moveable components of the rococo style: the accessories of home and person, from the paintings on the wall, to the toiletry sets on the dressing table (like the lacquer *nécessaire* on the counter in *Gersaint's Shop Sign*), to tableware, to clothing. As I have tried to show, using the example of Pierrot's figure, the mobility and the exchangeability of form were built into the rococo as a style and a practice. I want to present one final example of the mobility of forms in the rococo through the practices of rococo *marchands merciers* (merchant mercers). These market-facing retailers played a significant role in the dissemination, as well as the creation, of rococo aesthetics. They were also exemplary rococo practitioners, in the ways they manipulated a stock of existing things in order to produce novelty.

The merchant mercer sold a wide variety of goods for the adornment of the home and the performance of the elite lifestyle. Their inventories included furniture, mirrors, painting, *bibelots*, lacquer toiletry sets, writing sets, and jewellery.[61] Merchant mercers were not allowed to make anything from scratch; their corporation's statutes permitted them only to 'sell, buy, display, adorn, and prettify'.[62] Hence, to stoke the public's ravenous appetite for luxury, the merchant mercer resorted to 'design through assembly'.[63] Drawing from their stock of used and prefabricated goods and working with a network of importers and artisans, merchant mercers refurbished, arranged, and combined things to create objects that would pique the interest of even the most jaded consumer. This process was described as 'prettification' (*enjolivement*). Porcelain from Japan and China was set into European bronze mounts; lacquer was lifted from one surface and put onto another, where it could be framed by varnished panels or metalwork made in Europe.[64] The merchant mercers stocked large inventories of porcelain flowers, which could be affixed to a variety of supports, from clocks to salt cellars to snuff boxes. For example, a mantle clock now in the collection of the Metropolitan Museum of Art combines Meissen hard-paste figurines, a French timepiece crafted by Paul Gudin, soft-paste flowers made at Vincennes, and a bespoke gilded mount designed by a merchant mercer.[65] *Potpourri* holders were assembled out of Chinese porcelain teacups, bottles, and saucers, which were cut down, pierced, and then mounted in bronze to form a single unit. Ceramic inventory that was broken in transit was ideal for such repurposing. To diversify and expand their inventories, retailers traded in second-hand objects, which could be transformed with small improvements like new settings and varnishes, or which could be harvested for parts.[66]

A similar evolution was under way in the field of fashion retailing. Over the course of the eighteenth century, the trimming of dresses became an industry of its own, led by the emergence of the female fashion merchant (*marchande de modes*).[67] Originally a niche within the community of merchant mercers, to whom many of the *marchandes de modes* were related by kinship ties, the female fashion merchant (fashion merchants were overwhelmingly women) trimmed, rearranged, garnished, beribboned, and befeathered dresses, hats, gloves, hairpieces, shawls, collars, and any other kind of sartorial supplement.[68] Not to be confused with a tailor or a seamstress, who sewed up made-to-measure garments, she affixed things to dresses that had been made by others.[69] Like the merchant mercer, she coordinated between a number of industries – the sellers of fabrics, dress-makers, and hat-makers – to gather the elements of her design.[70] In her boutique, she sold ready-made shawls and mantillas and stocked an inventory of ribbons, lace, buttons, and braid. Echoing the merchant mercer's 'design through assembly', the fashion merchant authored by trimming, cutting, and folding. The practices of the female fashion merchant recall Pierrot's love of ribbons, as well as his description (ventriloquising Molière) of Don Juan as a figure whose matter was all lace, ribbons, buttons, gold braid.

These kinds of practice led to the famous epithet for the merchant mercers, 'sellers of everything, makers of nothing' ('*marchand de tout et faiseur de rien*'), published in the *Encyclopédie*.[71] While this label touched upon the reason why the merchant mercers could claim membership in the 'nobility of commerce' (*noblesse commerçante*), because they did not make anything with their hands, the phrase acquired increasingly negative associations over the course of the eighteenth century.[72] Moralists and critics were concerned not only about the perverse influence of luxury, but also about the locale of French genius and invention. As the first section of this chapter showed, assemblage was also a technique used by painters and designers of ornament. Lajoue's overdoor, for example, set the guitar-playing Pierrot from Watteau's *oeuvre* against a *rocaille* fountain inspired by one of his own designs (Figure 2.6). Sky and foliage fill in the gaps. This method of composition according to formal criteria – the arranging and disposing of figures and backdrops that complemented one another in purely visual ways – worried critics of art.[73] No moral purpose or didactic message lay behind the arrangement of forms. While a history painter disposed his figures to illustrate a dramatic action, the outcome of which was morally instructive, Lajoue composed according to taste and fancy. It is as if the artist, upon receiving a commission, had consulted the available 'stock', selected a figure and a fountain, and put them together.[74] For a painter, this stock lay in albums of sketches and collections of prints like the *Recueil Jullienne* or Huquier's publications of Lajoue's designs. For a merchant mercer, commissioned to design a mantle clock, the stock was in the warehouse or the back room. The female fashion merchant was an even riper target for accusations of vacuity. To create, she affixed ribbons and lace to existing garments, vesting sartorial identity not in a second skin but in a third, additional skin – the surface of trim. Certainly, it is difficult to make an argument in favour of the intellectualism of this rococo practice of design by assembly. Nevertheless, this was not a mindless practice; only, the mindfulness required was of a different nature than that necessary for the construction of historical tableaux. Taste and instinct, but also memory, were operative here. The building up of a 'stock' took place both physically, in the back rooms of boutiques, and virtually, in the minds of rococo practitioners. Trained in design by assembly, practitioners needed to be able to recall at speed a catalogue of forms. Printed volumes were essential in encouraging this mental repertoire, but skilled practitioners would have been able to do more: to call up a suitable figure in the blink of an eye.

Retail and connoisseurship

Jullienne himself would have been hesitant to acknowledge that the marketplace was the destination of his volumes. Publicly, he advertised a much loftier purpose: to solidify Watteau's reputation in the face of his early death and to create a medium through which the painter's work could be disseminated throughout Europe.[75] Jullienne knew that if Watteau were to enter the canon of European art, his works would have to reach the connoisseurs. These collectors and amateurs met in private homes to compare examples of work by great artists; reproductive prints after works by artists like Raphael were compared with drawings by Raphael or his students, prints after Raphael were compared with prints after other masters, and so on.[76] Participants rifled through portfolios and drawers and spread prints and drawings on tables. Some collectors bound their prints into volumes or bought pre-bound collections from dealers organised by artist or by school. Individual collectors had also begun to commission and publish prints after the works in their collections, creating printed galleries, of a sort.[77] Pierre Crozat, Watteau's most influential protector, had published such a collection in 1729 (Volume I) and 1742 (Volume II).[78]

As Andrew McClellan has pointed out, these kinds of gathering also encouraged consumption, building a market for drawings and prints.[79] Throughout a long and successful career, Gersaint, the canny merchant mercer who had once been Watteau's dealer, walked a fine line between the world of the shop and that of the connoisseur.[80] Gersaint organised sale previews to which distinguished collectors and amateurs were invited. The frontispiece to one of his catalogues depicted such a private viewing in the cosiest of terms, showing an elegant, well-lit room, with men seated at a table, looking at pictures on the wall, and leafing through portfolios, a few of which are casually strewn across the foreground of the composition. One of the goals of this frontispiece was to blur the line between the shop and a private 'cabinet', between shoppers and 'amateurs'.[81] Yet no matter the kinds of things that went on in the shop or the tone of its customers, Gersaint was running a retail operation.[82] The 'study material' that he offered at his sale previews was in fact his own stock. The 'amateurs' who attended his viewings were collectors and even speculators, who amassed mental repertoires as a form of market knowledge.

The ambivalent status of the *Recueil Jullienne* attests to the increasing difficulty of drawing clear lines between retail and practices that claimed to be disinterested. On one hand, Jullienne had created an object of knowledge for amateurs eager to learn more about Watteau's work. On the other hand, he had built an inventory of Watteau's works, which were now an available stock, a market repertoire. This condition was particularly amplified in the case of the *Figures of different characters*, in which the format of the individual prints was basically indistinguishable from the format of an ornament print. In allotting single figures to single plates, Jullienne had made Watteau's drawings, which were often packed with unrelated studies, amenable to re-use and medial translation.[83] He had also made them more likely to be remembered, by substituting crisply outlined, complete figures for Watteau's overlapping figures rendered in evocatively smudged chalk and pencil. For example, Caylus's Pierrot *mascaron* cites both the painting, *Happy Pierrot*, and a remarkable drawing, in which Watteau includes in the upper left-hand corner a perfectly round head, facing outwards, flush with the picture plane, the bare forehead framed by a wisp of white skullcap (Plate 11). The pronounced frontality of this figure, as well as the resemblance to the facial features of the Pierrot in the large painting, has led it to be identified as a Pierrot. As startling as this staring moon-like face is, it becomes infinitely more amenable to re-use when it is lent a hat and a ruff, placed in a frame of its own, and made available in the medium of print. In addition, the original drawing, which is typical of Watteau's productions as a draughtsman, combines Pierrot with figures sketched over the course of several years, in several different styles. Pierrot's chin brushes the top of the bow in the hair of a female toddler, while the curve of his cheek is echoed by the upward sweep of a line used to delineate a young man's cape. Studying this drawing could take a lifetime. (At the Louvre, researchers are only allowed to see this drawing once in their entire life.) Indeed, the passage of time is marked on the drawing's surface by the rising age of the figures, from the toddler at lower left, to the girl of seven or eight in the upper right, to the twenty-something Virgin at the top centre, and back to Pierrot at the top left. This experience – the invitation to linger, to follow each stroke of the red crayon, each flash of white chalk – does not carry over to Caylus's print. The drawing, so memorable, cannot be memorised.

When connoisseurs studied albums of prints in the back room of Gersaint's boutique, they followed the advice given by writers like Roger de Piles. De Piles, an influential French connoisseur active in the late seventeenth and early eighteenth centuries, had encouraged comparative looking as well as the use of prints and drawings to build up mental repertoires of images.[84] For de Piles, the essential task of a connoisseur was to see as many examples of an artist's work as possible, and thus to fill 'their memories with curious things of all times and all nations, while teaching them the diverse manners of painting'.[85] These stored-up images would be recalled upon viewing subsequent works and used as points of reference and grounds for judgement – this was to 'judge by comparison' (*juger par comparison*).[86] De Piles's description of storing images and recalling them when needed was probably influenced by theories of artificial memory. Roman treatises for orators, which were still widely read in the eighteenth century, described the art of memory as the selection of distinctive images or figures, each of which stood for a particular topic or thing. These images would then be arranged in a particular order in an imaginary place (*locus*), usually a house with multiple rooms.[87] When it came time to remember, the orator would recreate his movement through the house, and each image he came upon would remind him of his next topic.[88] These discussions of memory described the human mind, or a region of it, as a house hung with pictures. The mind was stocked with images as a warehouse might be filled with works of art.

The theatrical presentation of printed figures may have helped connoisseurs build mental repertoires of artworks. Many of the prints studied by connoisseurs at Gersaint's viewings would have reproduced tableaux by masters like Raphael and Poussin. They would not have resembled ornament prints except in their presentation in bound volumes. By the fact of being bound, however, the prints formed a repertoire and the repertoire resembled an inventory and an inventory resembled a stock, a series of resemblances that would have been encouraged by the setting of the gathering in Gersaint's back room. In other words, there was a growing closeness between cultural repertoires and retail inventories. Pierrot stands, as usual, at the threshold of the two practices. He is both for memory and for sale.

Rococo as étalage

Rococo retailers were aware of the importance of presenting their wares in a manner that would encourage customers both to remember and to buy. Although a far cry from the nineteenth-century department store, in which goods were liberally distributed and laid out in a profusion intended to resemble a cornucopia, eighteenth-century Parisian shops did offer displays (*étalages*), both inside and outside the shop.[89] Glass display cases were used; goods were hung on poles or hooks or pinned to fabric-covered boards. Although Gersaint's actual shop only very loosely resembled the spacious environment Watteau depicts in his painting, Gersaint owned ten glass display cabinets and hung objects from the shop ceiling.[90] Like other merchant mercers, he hung paintings and mirrors on the walls of his shop. In the fashion merchant's shop, velvet panels, above or between the drawers, showed samples pinned or dangling from strings and cords. On the Quai de la Mégisserie, where a clandestine market for old clothes operated on Sundays, trousers were hung on poles outside stalls, empty garments performing their need for a wearer.[91] The suspended trousers doubled as shop sign in the format of an improvised *potence*, the type of sign that was hung from a bracket extending over the street.

One of the most characteristic features of the *étalage* was the hanging, the suspending of goods. As Mercier put it in relationship to the advertising techniques of the stalls on the Quai de la Mégisserie, 'these suspended breeches invite the passerby'.[92] 'Suspension' is another term of note in relationship to the disposition of retail, because the state of suspension is also a state of uncertainty, of awaiting. As I have suggested, Pierrot has a kind of 'hang-dog' look to him; his costume 'hangs on him' as garments hang on a rack. Indeed, a hanging garment tends to assume Pierrot's position – arms at the side, legs together. The hanging object expresses a disposition of availability. The arabesque 'hangs' many of its elements. In the arabesque attributed to Watteau, a chain of bouquets hangs from strapwork extending from a scallop shell, while Pierrot's platform hangs from swags of drapery. This way of arranging the different motifs enabled separability; artists could evaluate and select which motifs they wished to copy. Moreover, the incongruity of objects in a single display reinforced the impression of each object's independence; there was no necessary connection between Pierrot standing on his platform and the garland of flowers suspended above him. An artist, or a customer, could take both, either, or neither.

Another element of the marketplace address was a certain kind of vacancy. The trousers can be hung because they are empty; empty, they advertise the ability to be filled. The lacquer *nécessaire* on the counter of Gersaint's shop would have been empty. A customer dreamed of filling it. The vacancy of the object addressed at the marketplace was beautifully articulated by a popular genre of ornament print: the cartouche. Essentially, cartouches were empty frames. As models for designers, they could be used, wholesale, for the frontispieces of books or woodwork motifs of the *boiserie* or the frames of chairs and mirrors.

Published in suites of a dozen or more, a collection of cartouches inundates the viewer with a reiteration of blanks. A cartouche like Meissonnier's, published by Huquier, addresses the viewer with its vacancy, as if issuing an invitation to be inscribed (Figure 2.11). Described as a frame for a dressing-table mirror (*miroir de toilette*), the design itself could be used for a number of purposes, including the frame of a chair or a firescreen. Morphologically, there is a notable resemblance to Pierrot, with his smallish head and sloping shoulders atop an oblong surface of white. This morphological resemblance is worth considering, not for any intentionality on the part of either artist, but for what it suggests about the nature of the figure's address to the marketplace. Both Pierrot and the cartouche are addressed to the marketplace; both are empty. In the context of the curtain call, upon which Watteau's painting is based, Pierrot is empty of remuneration, having not yet received the audience's verdict. The cartouche is empty of an inscription. Both await judgement and as a result, both are suspended. All that remains is for Pierrot to be hung, literally, a hanging that has already been imagined by those historians willing to consider the possibility that the large painting might have been a shop sign. While I do not believe that the painting was in fact a shop sign, I do find that Pierrot, as he appears in it, addresses the viewer in the manner of the shop sign.

The terms taken by the eighteenth-century critique of luxury, into which the anti-rococo critique was folded, attest to an awareness of the extent to which the marketplace address had come to characterise artistic practice. Critics targeted forms of display that addressed the marketplace, which were described as forms of *étalage*. Members of the Royal Academy of Painting and Sculpture were specifically forbidden to 'keep an open boutique in which to display (*étaler*) their works, to expose them in the window or in other places outside of their dwelling, or to affix any sign or inscription that indicates that works are for sale'.[93] When a critic wished to accuse a person or an image of ostentation, accusations of *étalage* were levelled. The Baronne d'Oberkirch described the fashion merchant Rose Bertin as having boastingly displayed (*étalé*) her affiliation with the queen on her trade bills.[94] When Étienne La Font de Saint-Yenne described the subjects of rococo portraits preening themselves ridiculously in their allegorical costumes, he used the verb *étaler*.[95] Throughout the *Encyclopédie*, *étalage* is used to describe excessive and frivolous forms of display. Diderot notes the 'vain and pompous display' of ancient Egyptian religion, while Faiguet de Villeneuve declares that the meaningless *étalage* of candles and decorations at funerals has replaced true piety.[96] Most definitively, Voltaire uses *étalage* to explain the negative associations of *faste*.[97] Derived from *fasti*, or festival days, festive or solemn occasions when Romans made a point of dressing up in their finest clothes, *faste* describes ceremonial demonstrations of status through clothing and accessories. From *fasti* to *fêtes* to *faste* was not a long journey: the fair as a *fête marchande* was regulated by the *jours de fête* of the Christian calendar. For Voltaire, sartorial demonstrations of status could very easily lead to 'revolting opulence' ('*opulence révoltante*') in a person's public appearance, which is the bad kind of *faste*. Finally, *faste* is the 'display (*étalage*)

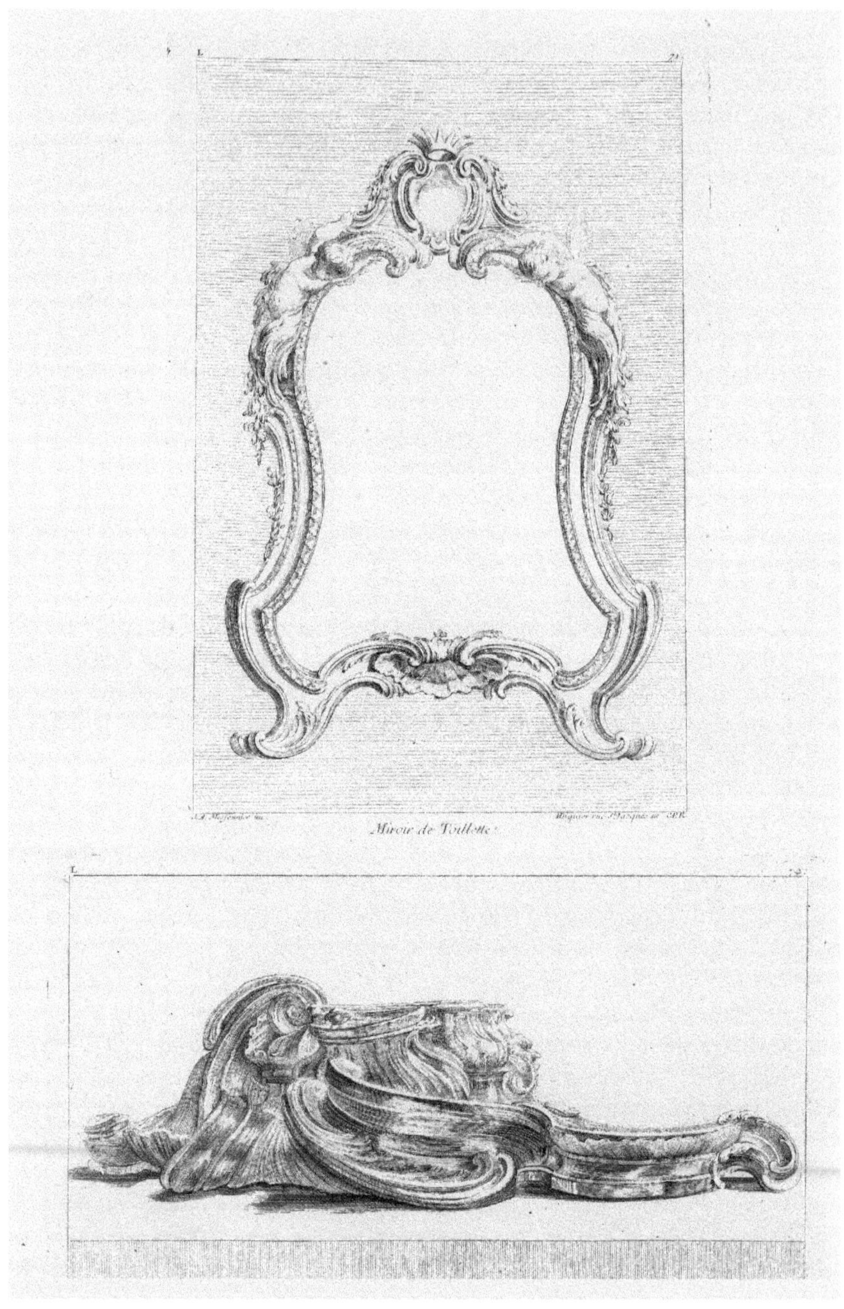

2.11   Gabriel Huquier after Juste-Aurèle Meissonnier, *Frame for a dressing-table mirror and view of the inkwell of Monsieur le Comte de Maurepas*, 1740. Engraving on white laid paper, 15.4 × 25.5 cm. Source: Cooper Hewitt, Smithsonian Design Museum, New York. 1921–6-212–30-b ©Smithsonian Institution.

of the costs of luxury'.[98] In Voltaire's definition, *faste* is a form of marketplace theatricality and *étalage* is its medium.

This discourse captures an abiding suspicion of forms of display that are turned towards the market, as well as recognition that this form of display deserves its own term. As I have shown, market-oriented display (*étalage*) runs through rococo artistic practice, infusing the very appearance of motifs as well as their mode of presentation. In this respect, the rococo, in most instances, is a deeply theatrical style, oriented outwards, towards the marketplace. Pierrot's proliferation in rococo repertoires is due, in no small part, to the way his figure encodes the theatricality of the marketplace address in its formal qualities of symmetry, frontality, and blankness. A kind of theatricality was also embedded in forms of connoisseurship, in which viewers internalised the images that they studied, arranging them in their mind as figures on a stage or in a house. Of course, the connoisseur was not supposed to favour one kind of figure over another but, as Jullienne's collection tellingly reveals, editors had strategies for making certain figures more memorable. These strategies were also those used by rococo retailers like Gersaint, whose career epitomises the crossover between merchants and connoisseurs.

For those who are familiar with Pierrot's character in late seventeenth- and early eighteenth-century theatre, his solitude can easily become a source of pathos. Yet this was not yet what was at stake in Pierrot's rococo instantiations, where what mattered more was the pleasant vacancy of his address to the mar-ketplace. In the nineteenth century, however, this would begin to change. In one nineteenth-century pantomime, Pierrot is hanged – executed. An etching shows him dangling from the gallows (*potence* – also the word for the bracket from which a shop sign was hung), a big white warning flag, but also a macabre sign, potentially, for a linens shop (Figure 2.12). More cheerfully, according to one of the accounts of the appearance of Watteau's *Pierrot* in the early nineteenth century (see Chapter 3), Denon saw the painting repeatedly before buying it, because it was being used as the sign for a shop that he passed every day on his way to his office in the Louvre. The author of this account, Louis Clément de Ris, says that the 'incessant call of this sign finished by getting on [Denon's] nerves'.[99] This is a familiar experience for many urban dwellers: an object in a shop window becomes the subject of fantasies of possession. Yet this is also an account that equates Pierrot's address to the viewer with the mournful address of an object that has failed to sell. According to de Ris, the owner of the shop had inscribed Pierrot's figure with the lines of a popular tune: 'how happy Pierrot would be/if he knew the art of pleasing you!' By writing upon the figure, the merchant has treated Pierrot as a cartouche. These responses to Pierrot's figure treat the marketplace not as a physical locale for commercial exchange, but as a mental stage registering the flows of consumer desire. Pierrot is not sad because nobody wants to partner up with him; he is sad because no one wants to buy him.

The eighteenth century is widely characterised as witnessing the advent of modern consumerism. The growth of cities and the middle classes as well as the

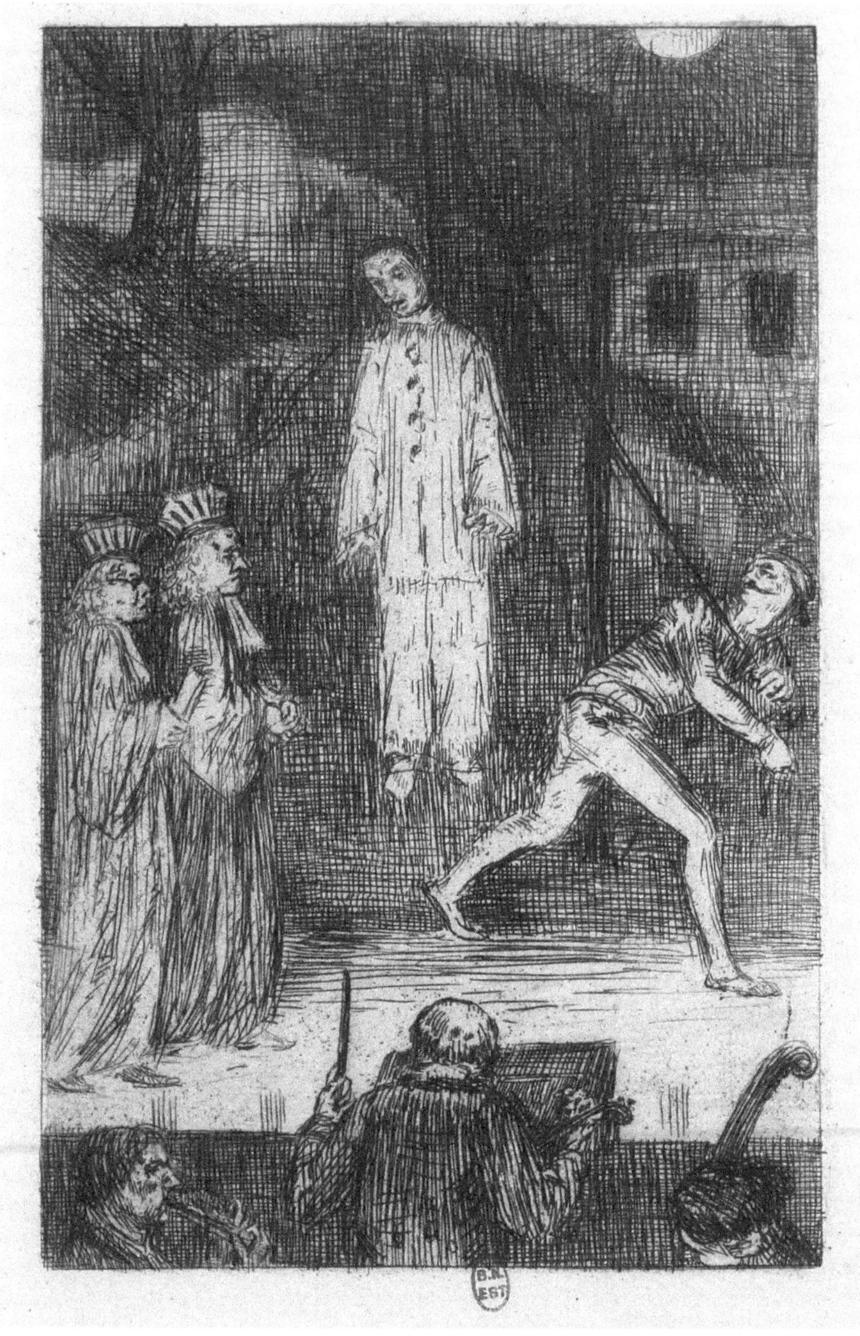

2.12   Alphonse Legros, *Pierrot hung*, 1860–65. Etching, 15.9 × 9.8 cm. Source: Bibliothèque Nationale de France, Paris. DC-310 (4)-FOL <ESTNUM-23969> ©BNF.

greater availability of inexpensive raw materials, thanks in part to colonial commerce, led to fuller purses and a wider range of goods from which to choose. More people could buy more than the bare necessities of life.[100] Certainly, the rococo objects discussed in this chapter catered to a wide variety of consumers with a range of budgets. In response to this emerging democratisation of consumption, moralists like Mercier both bemoaned and celebrated the world of retail.[101] Yet as Natacha Coquery puts it, 'Mercier's ethical perspective was blind to the desire people had for fancy goods, and for elegance – no longer an aristocratic preserve but the dream of less privileged classes'.[102] This desire and the dreams it encourages are particularly important to an understanding of Pierrot, whose first act on the French stage was to marvel at the ribbons of a rich man. During the nineteenth century, Pierrot will move continuously between physical marketplaces and what is increasingly recognised as their virtual correlate: the dream-world of consumers.

Notes

1 A crucial account of the rococo remains Fiske Kimball, *The Creation of the Rococo Decorative Style* (1943; New York: Dover Publications, 1980). For a more recent, extremely rich account of the style, which also provides detailed social context and interpretative readings, see Katie Scott, *The Rococo Interior: Decoration and Social Spaces in Early Eighteenth-century Paris* (New Haven, CT: Yale University Press, 1995).

2 Patrick Brady, 'Rococo and neo-classicism', *Studi Francesi* 22 (1964), 34–49, here p. 42.

3 For a useful history of the nomenclature, see Rémy G. Saisselin, 'The rococo as a dream of happiness', *Journal of Aesthetics and Art Criticism* 19:2 (1960), 145–52, here p. 145.

4 Marianne Roland Michel, *Watteau: An Artist of the Eighteenth Century*, trans. Richard Wrigley (London: Trefoil Books, 1984), p. 294.

5 Roland Michel, *Watteau*, p. 291.

6 On the *ornemantiste*, see Marianne Roland Michel, *Lajoue et l'art Rocaille* (Neuilly-sur-Seine: Arthena, 1984), pp. 142–4. An excellent example of an *ornemantiste* is Juste-Aurèle Meissonnier, who trained as an architect, but devoted most of his time to designing ornament. See Peter Fuhring, 'Juste-Aurèle Meissonnier and His patrons', in Sarah D. Coffin (ed.), *Rococo: The Continuing Curve, 1730–2008* (New York: Smithsonian Cooper-Hewitt National Design Museum, 2008), pp. 22–39.

7 For specifications on the *Recueil*, see Émile Dacier and Albert Vuaflart, *Jean de Jullienne et les graveurs de Watteau au XVIIIe siècle*, 4 vols (Paris: Les Auteurs, 1921–9), Vol. II for the history of production and technical specifications. The Louvre has recently published a useful introduction to the prints after Watteau: see Marie-Catherine Sahut and Florence Raymond, *Antoine Watteau et L'Art de l'Estampe* (Paris: Musée du Louvre, 2010).

8 For a recent, nuanced study of Jullienne and the milieu of collectors in which he moved see Isabelle Tillerot, *Jean de Jullienne et les collectionneurs de son temps: un regard singulier sur le tableau* (Paris: Editions de la Maison des sciences de l'homme, 2010).

9 Only 100 copies of the final two volumes were printed. Dacier and Vuaflart, *Jean de Jullienne*, I.233.

10 See Roland Michel's crucial discussion of this transformation, including detailed comments on the different extant versions of the *Recueil*. Roland Michel, *Watteau*, pp. 243–77.

11 On trends in consumption and luxury goods, see Daniel Roche, *France in the Enlightenment*, trans. Arthur Goldhammer (Cambridge, MA: Harvard University Press, 1998), pp. 548–77. On the 'trickle-down' effect see Cissie Fairchilds, 'The production and marketing of populuxe goods in eighteenth-century Paris', in John Brewer and Roy Porter (eds), *Consumption and the World of Goods* (London: Routledge, 1993), pp. 228–48.

12 Natacha Coquery, 'The language of success: marketing and distributing semi-luxury goods in eighteenth-century Paris', *Journal of Design History* 17:1 (2004), 71–89, here pp. 86–7.

13 On the genealogy of the arabesque, see André Chastel, *La grottesque* (Paris: Le Promeneur, 1988), pp. 65–75.

14 On the history and the technique of the *boiserie* see Anne Forray-Carlier, *Les Boiseries du Musée Carnavalet* (Dordan: Vial, 2010).

15 On the movement of motifs between vignette and ornamental frame in the rococo style, see Hermann Bauer, *Rocaille: Zur Herkunft und Zum Wesen einer Ornament-Motivs* (Berlin: Walter de Gruyter, 1962), pp. 6–9.

16 On weightlessness as a characteristic of the arabesque, see Katie Scott, 'Playing games with otherness: Watteau's Chinese cabinet at the Chateau de la Muette', *Journal of the Warburg and Courtauld Institutes* 66 (2003), 189–248, here p. 206.

17 Dacier and Vuaflart, *Jean de Jullienne*, III.79–80, cat. nos 158–163.

18 On Watteau's arabesques see Léon Deshairs, 'Les arabesques de Watteau', in *Mélanges offerts à M. Henry Lemonnier* (Paris: Champion, 1913), pp. 287–300.

19 On Gersaint's activities as a print editor of Watteau, see Guillaume Glorieux, *À l'enseigne de Gersaint: Edme-François Gersaint, Marchand d'Art sur le Pont Notre-Dame (1694–1750)* (Paris: Champ Vallon, 2002), pp. 179–206. Huquier almost certainly had other artists create the borders, drawing only the central motif, if anything, from Watteau's repertoire. On Huquier's interventions see Yves Bruand, 'Un grand collectionneur, marchand et graveur du XVIIIe siècle, Gabriel Huquier, 1695-1772', *Gazette des Beaux Arts* (July–September 1950), 99–114. See also Martin Eidelberg, 'Gabriel Huquier – friend or foe of Watteau?' *The Print Collector's Newsletter* 15 (1984), 157–64; Martin Eidelberg, 'Huquier in the guise of Watteau', *On Paper* 1 (1996), 28–32; for Huquier's similar treatment of drawings by Oppenord, see Jean-François Bédard, 'Prints by Gabriel Huquier after Oppenord's decorated "Ripa"', *Print Quarterly* 29:1 (2012), 37–43.

20 On these kinds of adjustments, see Glorieux, *À l'enseigne de Gersaint*, pp. 213, 219–21.

21 Roland Michel, *Watteau*, p. 292.

22 *Mercure de France*, November 1727, 2491–2, here p. 2492: 'De pareils sujets peints sur des fonds blancs, conviennent à merveille aux découpures, dont les Dames font aujourd'hui de si jolis meubles.'

23 Peter Fuhring, 'The print privilege in eighteenth century France – I', *Print Quarterly* 2:3 (1985), 175–93, here pp. 191–2. On the use of prints after Watteau as *découpures*, see Dacier and Vuaflart, *Jean de Jullienne*, II.154.

24 On this album, see Pierre Rosenberg, 'Watteau: le recueil de Valenciennes', *La Revue du Louvre* 415 (1986), 286–9.

25 On this kind of mobility and its effect on the motif, see Hermann Bauer, *Rokokomalerei: Sechs Studien* (Mittenwald: Mäander Kunstverlag, 1980), p. 50. Scott describes this as a 'scrap-book' mode of composition. See Scott, *The Rococo Interior*, p. 133.

26 For a history of the Hannong family and its various eighteenth-century faience concerns, see Jacques Bastian and Marie-Alice Bastian, *Faïences de Strasbourg: Manufacture Hannong* (Riggisberg: Abegg-Stiftung, 2013). See also Antoinette Faÿ-Hallé et al., *Faïences françaises, XVIe–XVIIIe siècles* (Paris: Éditions de la Réunion des Musées Nationaux, 1980), pp. 274–8; Jacques Bastian, *Strasbourg: faïences et porcelaines, 1721–1784*, 2 vols (Strasbourg: Éditions M.A.J.B., 2002).

27 On the French production of porcelain figures, see Svend Eriksen and Geoffrey de Bellaigue, *Sèvres Porcelain: Vincennes and Sèvres 1740–1800* (London: Faber and Faber, 1987), pp. 63–9, 107–11, 88–90.

28 On English figurines, see Arthur Lane, *English Porcelain Figures of the Eighteenth Century* (London: Faber and Faber, 1961).

29 Bastian, *Strasbourg: faïences et porcelaines*, p. 21.

30 Annik Pardailhé-Galabrun, *La naissance de l'intime: 3000 foyers Parisiens XVIIe–XVIIIe siècles* (Paris: Presses Universitaires de France, 1988), pp. 393–7.

31 On Bustelli see Lothar Altmann, *Die Figuren des F.A. Bustelli* (Munich: Scaneg, 1993).

32 *Frühes Meissener Porzellan: Kostbarkeiten aus deutschen Privatsammlungen*, exh. cat. (Munich: Hirmer Verlag, 1997), pp. 71–80.

33 On *chinoiserie* figures, which were particularly popular at the Chantilly soft-paste manufacture, see Geneviève Le Duc, *Porcelaine tendre de Chantilly au XVIIIe siècle* (Paris: Hazan, 1996), pp. 89–99. See also Daniëlle Kisluk-Grosheide, 'The reign of *magots* and pagods', *Metropolitan Museum Journal* 37 (2002), 177–97. *Magot* was a derisive term: it was used to describe apes and large monkeys as well men deemed particularly ugly. As a descriptor for figurines purporting to represent Asians, *magot* was intended to connote the bizarre, the grotesque, and the bestial.

34 Joanna Gwilt, *Vincennes and Early Sèvres Porcelain from the Belvedere Collection* (London: V&A Publishing, 2014), p. 27.

35 *Frühes Meissener Porzellan*, pp. 269–70. On Meissen's Watteau décors see Maureen Cassidy-Geiger (ed.), *Fragile Diplomacy: Meissen Porcelain for European Courts ca. 1710–63* (New York: Bard Graduate Center and Yale University Press, 2007), pp. 161–2.

36 Bastian, *Strasbourg: Faïences et porcelaines*, I.99–103, I.121–8, I.129–49 on the prints used as models for the *poncifs*.

37 See Gwilt, *Vincennes and Early Sèvres*, p. 27. The 1752 inventory lists sixty-one prints and drawings of 'figures et personnages différens'. Bustelli produced a series of criers at Nymphenburg. The Mennecy Villeroy soft-paste manufactory made criers as well as hybrid winged-*putto*-criers. See Nicole Duchon, *Tendre porcelaine de Mennecy Villeroy* (Mennecy: Maury Imprimeur, 2016), pp. 69, 215, 243. The Meissen manufacture released its own series of criers, modelled by Kaendler after drawings by Christophe Huet, between 1756 and 1763: see *Frühes Meissener Porzellan*, pp. 258–60.

38 Dacier and Vuaflart, *Jean de Jullienne*, III.47, cat. no. 97.

39 Dacier and Vuaflart, *Jean de Jullienne*, II.145–52.

40 *Cf.* Glorieux's comments on the emptying out of significance of Watteau's motifs as they travelled into the decorative arts. Glorieux, *À l'enseigne de Gersaint*, pp. 214, 220.

41 Sarah Cohen has discussed the anchoring function performed by Pierrot in Watteau's compositions and the way he lends himself to the design of arabesques; Cohen sees the arabesque as the inspiration for the structures of the paintings featuring Pierrot. Sarah R. Cohen, *Art, Dance, and the Body in French Culture of the Ancien Régime* (Cambridge: Cambridge University Press, 2000), p. 266.

42 Dacier and Vuaflart, *Jean de Jullienne*, III.114, cat. no. 271.

43 Danielle Maternati-Baldouy et al., *La faïence de Marseille au XVIIIe siècle: La manufacture de la Veuve Perrin* (Marseille: Musées de Marseille/Editions Agep, 1990).

44 Glorieux, *À l'enseigne de Gersaint*, pp. 233–38.

45 Kimball, *The Creation of the Rococo*, p. 152.

46 This is a technique called *scena per angolo*, borrowed from Italian stage designs. See Michel, *Lajoue et l'art Rocaille*, p. 125. See also Bauer, *Rocaille*, pp. 72–73.

47 Copyists favoured the compositions featuring the Italian characters. See Dacier and Vuaflart, *Jean de Jullienne*, II.145–52.

48 Pierre Rosenberg and Louis-Antoine Prat, *Antoine Watteau 1684–1721: Catalogue raisonné des dessins*, 3 vols (Milan: Leonardo Arte, 1996), pp. xii–xiii.

49 On the commissioning and the design of the *Figures*, see also Isabelle Tillerot, 'Graver les dessins de Watteau au XVIIe siècle', in Emmanuelle Delapierre and Sophie Raux (eds), *Quand la gravure fait illusion: Autour de Watteau et Boucher, Le Dessin Gravé au XVIIIe siècle* (Valenciennes: Musée des Beaux-Arts, 2006), pp. 27–31. See also Rosenberg, 'Le recueil de Valenciennes', pp. 286–9.

50 For a detailed account of these changes, see Roland Michel, *Watteau*, pp. 243–59. See also Marianne Roland Michel, 'Watteau et les *Figures de différents caractères*', in François Moureau and Margaret Morgan Grasselli (eds), *Antoine Watteau (1684–1721): le peintre, son temps et sa légende* (Paris: Clairefontaine, 1987), pp. 117–27.

51 Antoine Watteau, *Masque de Pierrot, fillettes vues en buste, homme drape et visage de femme*, sanguine and white pencil on gray paper. Musée du Louvre, Paris. INV 33366, Recto.

52 Antoine Watteau, *Pierrot content, c.* 1712, oil on canvas. Museo Nacional Thyssen-Bornemisza, Madrid. 1977.75.

53 André Chastel, 'Les temps modernes: masque, mascarade, mascaron', in *Le Masque*, exh. cat. (Paris: Musée Guimet, Éditions des Musées Nationaux, 1959), pp. 87–93.

54 On the ornament print and the relationship between designers and publishers like Gabriel Huquier, see Marianne Roland Michel, 'L'ornement rocaille: quelques questions', *Revue de l'art* (1982), 66–75. See also Gail S. Davidson, 'Ornament of bizarre imagination: rococo prints and drawings from Cooper-Hewitt's Léon Decloux Collection', in Coffin (ed.), *Rococo: The Continuing Curve*, pp. 40–71.

55 For a useful list of types of ornament prints, see the list of eighteenth-century French applications for privileges to publish ornament prints in Peter Fuhring, 'The print privilege in eighteenth century France – II', *Print Quarterly* 3:1 (1986), 19–33, here pp. 22–9. This list is by no means comprehensive, as most print-makers simply commissioned and published without applying for privilege.

56 Juste-Aurèle Meissonnier published such a collection in 1734: see Kimball, *The Creation of the Rococo*, p. 161.

57 See, for example, the *Second Livre de tableaux d'ornemens et rocailles, c.* 1734. Cooper Hewitt Museum, New York. Acc. 1921–6–327–8.

58 See Scott's excellent description of the diffusion of the style through prints, Scott, *The Rococo Interior*, pp. 241–52.

59 See also Bédard's comments on the meaningful nature of Oppenord's marginalia for Cesare Ripa's *Iconologies*, the irony and wit of which was lost when Huquier transformed the drawings into ornament prints: Bédard, 'Prints by Gabriel Huquier', pp. 40–42.

60 This was a phrase first used to apply to English society in the eighteenth century in classic accounts like Neil McKendrick, John Brewer and J.H. Plumb, *The Birth of a Consumer Society: The Commercialization of Eighteenth-Century England* (London: Hutchinson, 1983). It has also been argued that France underwent its own consumer revolution. See Roche, *France in the Enlightenment*, pp. 548–77. On the kinds of goods that populated Parisian interiors and reflected the growing volume of consumption, see Pardailhé-Galabrun, *La naissance de l'intime*. See also the work of Sargentson and Coquery, as cited in this chapter.

61 The essential source on the merchant mercer is Carolyn Sargentson, *Merchants and Luxury Markets: the marchands merciers of eighteenth-century Paris* (London: Victoria and Albert Museum, 1996); see also Carolyn Sargentson, 'The manufacture and marketing of luxury goods: the *Marchands Merciers* of late 17th- and 18th-century Paris', in Robert Fox and Anthony Turner (eds), *Luxury Trades and Consumerism in Ancien Régime Paris* (Aldershot: Ashgate, 1998), pp. 99–137; Pierre Verlet, 'Le commerce des objets d'art et les marchands merciers: à Paris au XVIIIe siècle', *Annales, Histoire, Science Sociales* 13:1 (1958), 10–29.

62 Verlet, 'Le commerce', p. 11: 'vendre, achepter, estaller, parer, et enjolliver' [*sic*].

63 Sargentson, *Merchants and Luxury Markets*, pp. 52–6.

64 Sargentson, *Merchants and Luxury Markets*, pp. 64–73.

65 Metropolitan Museum of Art, New York. Acc. 1974.356.411.

66 Natacha Coquery, 'The social circulation of luxury and second-hand goods in eighteenth-century Parisian shops', in Ariane Fennetaux, Amelie Junqua and Sophie Vasset (eds), *The Afterlife of Used Things: Recycling in the Eighteenth Century* (New York: Routledge, 2014), pp. 13–24, here pp. 14–16.

67 Daniel Roche, *La culture des apparences: une histoire du vêtement XVIIe–XVIIIe siècle* (Paris: Fayard, 1989), pp. 291–3. See also Pamela A. Parmal, 'Fashion and the growing importance of the *marchande des modes* in mid-eighteenth-century France', *Costume* 31:1 (1997), 68–77.

68 Clare Haru Crowston, *Fabricating Women: The Seamstresses of Old Regime France, 1675–1791* (Durham, NC: Duke University Press, 2001), p. 67.

69 Clare Haru Crowston, *Credit, Fashion, Sex: Economies of Regard in Old Regime France* (Durham, NC: Duke University Press, 2013), pp. 207–10.

70 Crowston, *Fashioning Women*, p. 68.

71 'Mercerie', 10:369, in Denis Diderot and Jean le Rond d'Alembert (eds), *Encyclopédie, ou dictionnaire raisonné des sciences, des arts et des métiers, etc.*, eds Robert Morrissey and Glen Roe (University of Chicago: ARTFL Encyclopédie Project), http://encyclopedie.uchicago.edu/, accessed 28 April 2023.

72 In her valuable article, Mimi Hellman explores the meaning of 'garnishing' with flowers as a form of performative, artistic activity on the part of the *marchand mercier*: Mimi Hellman, 'The nature of artifice: French porcelain flowers and the rhetoric of the garnish', in Alden Cavanaugh and Michael Yonan (eds), *The Cultural Aesthetics of Eighteenth-Century Porcelain* (Farnham: Ashgate, 2010), pp. 39–64.

73 On the anti-rococo, see Scott, *The Rococo Interior*, pp. 252–62; Roland Michel, *Lajoue et l'art rocaille*, pp. 126–36; Christian Michel, '*Le goût contre le caprice:* Les enjeux des débats sur l'ornement au milieu du XVIIe siècle', in *Histoires d'ornement: Actes du colloque de l'Académie de France à Rome, 27–28 Juin 1996* (Paris: Klincksieck, 2000), pp. 203–14, here pp. 204–6. In addition to Voltaire's *Temple du goût* (1731), an influential critique of the Rococo was Étienne La Font de Saint-Yenne's *Reflexions sur quelques causes de l'état présent de la peinture en France, avec un examen des principaux ouvrages exposés au Louvre le mois d'Août 1746* (The Hague: Jean Neaulme, 1747). See McClellan's discussion of this text and its impact: Andrew McClellan, *Inventing the Louvre: Art, Politics, and the Origins of the Modern Museum in Eighteenth-Century Paris* (Cambridge: Cambridge University Press, 1994), pp. 19–20.

74 There was concern that the artist and the *marchand* were becoming dangerously intertwined categories, and that commercial genius was becoming the backbone for the dissemination of artistic form. See Roger Laufer, *Style rococo, style des lumières* (Paris: José Corti, 1963), p. 22.

75 On Jullienne's motivations, see Colin Bailey, 'Toute seule elle peut remplir et satisfaire l'attention: the early appreciation and marketing of Watteau's drawings, with an introduction to the collection of modern French drawings during the reign of Louis XV', in Alan Wintermute (ed.), *Watteau and his World: French Drawing from 1700–1750* (London: Merrell Holberton, 1999), pp. 68–92. See also Christian Michel, *Le 'célèbre' Watteau* (Geneva: Droz, 2008), pp. 34–7.

76 On connoisseurs' use of prints as tools for study see Kristel Smentek, 'Entrepreneurial art history: Pierre-Jean Mariette and the *Recueil d'estampes* in eighteenth-century Europe', in Cordélia Hattori, Estelle Leutrat and Véronique Meyer (eds), *À l'origine du livre d'art: Les recueils d'estampes comme entreprise éditoriale en Europe (XVIe–XVIIIe siècles)* (Milan: Silvana Editoriale, 2010), pp. 131–9. On the comparison of drawings, see Christian Michel, 'Le goût pour le dessin en France au XVIIe et XVIIIe siècle: de l'utilisation à l'étude désintéressé', *Revue de l'art* 143 (2004), 27–34. For a contemporary source praising the utility of careful comparative studies of prints, see Pierre-Jean Mariette, 'Lettre sur Leonard de Vinci, peintre florentin, à Monsieur le C[omte] de C[aylus]', in *Recueil de Testes de caractere et de charges dessinées par Leonard de Vinci Florentin et gravées par M. le C. de Caylus* (Paris: J. Mariette, 1730), pp. 1–22, here p. 19.

77 Patrick Michel, *Peinture et Plaisir: Les Goûts Picturaux des Collectionneurs Parisiens au XVIIIe Siècle* (Rennes: Presses Universitaires de Rennes, 2010), pp. 141–5.

78 On this project, see Benedict Leca, 'An art book and its viewers: the "Recueil Crozat" and the uses of reproductive engraving', *Eighteenth-Century Studies* 38:4 (2005), 623–49.

79 Andrew McClellan, 'Watteau's dealer: Gersaint and the marketing of art in eighteenth-century Paris', *Art Bulletin* 78:3 (1996), 439–53, here pp. 450–51.

80 This is one of the underpinning arguments of the magisterial study by Glorieux, *À l'enseigne de Gersaint*, cited throughout this chapter.

81 On efforts to blur these distinctions see Coquery, 'The language of success', pp. 76–8.

82 On *marchands merciers* as picture dealers, see Patrick Michel, *Le commerce du tableau à Paris dans la seconde moitié du XVIIIe siècle* (Villeneuve d'Ascq: Presses Universitaires du Septentrion, 2007), pp. 29–32.

83 On Watteau's tendencies as a draughtsman and the relationship to composition, see the valuable essay by Alan Wintermute, 'Le pèlerinage à Watteau: an introduction

to the drawings of Watteau and his circle', in Wintermute (ed.), *Watteau and His World*, pp. 8–49, here pp. 28–32.

84 Roger De Piles, *L'Idée du peintre parfait* (1699; Paris: Gallimard, 1993), p. 91.

85 De Piles, *L'Idée du peintre parfait*, p. 91: '[les estampes] rempliront leur mémoire des choses curieuses de tous les tems et de tous les Pais: et en leur apprendront les diverses manières dans la Peinture'.

86 De Piles, *L'Idée du peintre parfait*, p. 92.

87 Frances Yates, *The Art of Memory* (London: Penguin, 1966), pp. 18–41. Yates' volume remains one of the most important accounts of artificial memory to date.

88 The popular Roman text *Ad Herennium* (BCE 86–82) encouraged the selection of images that were as grotesque and as striking as possible, because these images would be remembered more easily, by imprinting themselves more forcefully upon the mind. Yates, *The Art of Memory*, pp. 25–32.

89 Sargentson, 'The manufacture and marketing of luxury goods', pp. 127–30.

90 Glorieux, *À l'enseigne de Gersaint*, p. 80 (on the difference of the sign), p. 163 (on the furnishings of the boutique).

91 Louis-Sébastien Mercier, *Tableau de Paris*, 2 vols, ed. Jean-Claude Bonnet (Paris: Mercure de France, 1994), I.1204–7, here p. 1205.

92 Mercier, *Tableau de Paris*, I.1207: 'ces culottes suspendues invitent les passants'.

93 'Relation de ce qui s'est passé en l'établissement de l'Académie royale de peinture et de sculpture', cited in Michel, *Le commerce du tableau à Paris*, p. 32: 'tenir boutique ouverte pour y étaler ses ouvrages, de les exposer aux fenêtre ou autres endroits extérieurs du lieu de sa demeure, ou d'y apposer aucune enseigne ni inscription pour en indiquer la vente'.

94 Sargentson, 'The manufacture and marketing of luxury goods', pp. 133–4.

95 La Font de Saint Yenne, *Reflexions*, p. 24.

96 Diderot, 'Egyptiens', in Diderot and d'Alembert (eds), *Encyclopédie*, p. 5:434; Faiguet de Villeneuve, 'Epargne', in Diderot and d'Alembert (eds), *Encyclopédie*, p. 5:748.

97 Voltaire, 'Faste', in Diderot and d'Alembert (eds), *Encyclopédie*, pp. 6:418–19.

98 Voltaire, 'Faste', p. 6:419: 'l'étalage des dépenses que le luxe coûte'.

99 Louis Clément de Ris, *Les Amateurs d'autrefois* (Paris: E. Plon et Cie, 1877), p. 446: 'l'appel incessant de cette enseigne finit par lui agaçer les nerfs'.

100 On the higher 'participation rate' in eighteenth-century consumerism, see Grant McCracken, *Culture and Consumption: New Approaches to the Symbolic Character of Consumer Goods and Activities* (Bloomington: Indiana University Press, 1988), pp. 16–22.

101 Describing the bejewelled novelties produced by the famous boutique, the Petit Dunkerque, Mercier complains about the wasted expenditure and vaunts the ingenious craftsmanship: Mercier, *Tableau de Paris*, II.67–70.

102 Coquery, 'The language of success', 83.

☙ 3 ❧

Manet bric-à-brac

The rococo presented Pierrot in a state of pristine freshness: his costume sparkling white, his ribbons jaunty. He seemed always new, even though he was now quite old, based on a figure invented in the first two decades of the eighteenth century. Around 1860–61, a rather dirty and worn Pierrot appeared in a painting by Édouard Manet, *The Old Musician* (see Plate 12). There is no question that the boy, second from the left in Manet's painting, is based on Watteau's prototype of a figure wearing loose trousers and shirt, hands hanging by his side, round face framed by a round straw hat, brim flipped up. Having seen Watteau's *Pierrot* when it was exhibited in Paris in 1860, Manet placed the character in a painting that is filled with figures cribbed from other paintings. This new Pierrot is very much the worse for wear, despite being younger (he looks about eight or nine years old). His clothing appears grimy and unwashed, streaked with dirt and grease; the too-large trousers must be balled up at the waist, but they still sag over his shoes. Claiming that Manet's figures were 'dirty' was one way of targeting his unusual manner of painting, in which shadows often remained unblended, but nevertheless it seems likely that this Pierrot's clothing is not supposed to appear recently laundered.[1] The figure's expression is also noticeably down in the mouth. Sometimes Watteau's Pierrot yields a hint of a smile, but Manet's Pierrot is far more tense, on guard, a little surly. Indeed, the boy offers a vision of what Pierrot might look like if he did absorb the wear and tear of time. His costume, worn by a hundred Pierrots before him, is showing its age. Such visible marks of wear were unacceptable to the rococo aesthetic, but by the early 1860s much had changed. Thanks to the upheaval of the French Revolution, the marketplace for second-hand goods had blossomed. Paris became a vast junk shop, overflowing with used household goods, aristocratic libraries and wardrobes, and works of art. As a result, old things acquired a new patina and a new poetics, which it is the object of this chapter to trace.

In *The Old Musician*, Manet uses both composition and iconography to pay tribute to this cult of old things. Most noticeably, he presents an array of recognisable social types, nearly all of whom were regulars in the

98

physiognomies, social repertoires of word and image that were used to characterise the new marketplace. The young Pierrot is also the *gamin de Paris*, the streetwise urchin, orphan of revolutions. Found in the centre of the painting is a gypsy musician, a representation of bohemian itinerance and marginality.[2] At the right-hand edge is the mythic type of the Wandering Jew, the condemned persecutor of Christ, a type closely associated with itinerant old-clothes sellers. Finally, second from the right, Manet places a top-hatted *flâneur-cum*-ragpicker, a fetishised type in the literature of modernity.[3] This popular iconography has been explored by Theodore Reff, Marilyn Brown, and Anne Coffin Hanson, among others.[4] As Reff and Michael Fried have shown, these social types are also citations of the art of the past, through which Manet announces his debt to Watteau, Velazquez, and the brothers Le Nain.[5] Here, I add to these accounts by situating these social types, as well as these citations of the art of the past, within the culture of the marketplace for second-hand things. I describe both the marketplace itself, and the way this marketplace was theatrically personified through a repertoire of social types. Walter Benjamin referred to this repertoire as 'panoramic literature'.[6] I understand the 'panoramic' to encompass the qualities, discussed in Chapter 2, of the display of merchandise (*étalage*). Through the *physiognomies*, Paris was laid out for sale as a repertoire of social types.

The ragpicker, the old-clothes seller, and the *gamin* all dealt in the second-hand markets that catered to the growing population of Paris. In the mythology of the marketplace for old and forgotten things, Watteau's *Pierrot* (the large painting) had played a role of its own. At least one account, published in 1877, suggested that the painting was sold by a bric-à-brac merchant. I refer in this chapter both to a 'poetics of old things' – strategies for characterising derelict and dilapidated objects – and to the 'aesthetics of bric-à-brac'. As a catch-all term for catch-all inventories, bric-à-brac was a deliberately cultivated aesthetic of mish-mash and pell-mell, in which objects from numerous historical eras and geographic regions were placed side by side. In this period, the contexts in which works of art were marketed and evaluated were increasingly characterised by bric-à-brac: auction houses, the shops of painting and curiosity merchants (*marchands de tableaux et de curiosités*), the quays of the Seine. As a result, the behaviour of consumers changed. In *Bricabracomania: The Bourgeois and the Bibelot*, Rémy Saisselin argues that nineteenth-century bourgeois collectors valued tactility, quantity, and thingness. Overwhelmed by the experience of a city crammed with objects, images, and people, overstimulated collectors amassed objects in a kind of frenzy.[7] For Saisselin, nineteenth-century collectors were shoppers, not connoisseurs. The shopper is mobile, instinctive, and easily swayed (a neurotic modern subject); the connoisseur is rational and measured. Dominique Vivant Denon, the first known owner of Watteau's *Pierrot*, had different ways of relating to works of art. But when he bought *Pierrot*, he was shopping.

In this chapter, I situate Denon's discovery of Watteau's *Pierrot* within the post-Revolutionary marketplace for second-hand goods. I then turn to the

Théâtre des Funambules, where a very different, new kind of Pierrot was fast becoming a Romantic legend. This Pierrot, as played by the mime Gaspard Deburau, would feature in 1855 in a new medium, photography. Yet newness was not on the lips of the critics who frequented the Funambules and spread Deburau's fame in books and literary journals. Instead, these critics were deeply interested in bric-à-brac as a mode for understanding 'the people'. In the second part of this chapter, I explore representations of the ragpicker, the old-clothes seller, and the *gamin*. In panoramic literature, these figures are represented as skilled interlocutors of the Parisian marketplace. They are the poetic interpreters of a bric-à-brac urbanity; it is in this guise that they reappear in Manet's painting.

Denon the curious

On the streets of post-Revolutionary Paris, it was impossible to escape old things, most of which were for sale. For every new Revolutionary government, more old things were thrown out onto the streets and the market, as the next wave of enemies of the state were exiled or executed. As turmoil continued, with the downfall of Napoléon and the revolutions of 1830 and 1848, more things lost their owners and ended up on the market. It was in this milieu that Watteau's large painting of Pierrot made its first appearance in the historical record. The painting's history in the eighteenth century is a complete blank.[8] The painting is not included in the *Recueil Jullienne* or mentioned in any period accounts of Watteau's life, of which there were several, written by men who knew Watteau personally.[9] It does not appear in any contemporary inventories. If the painting served as a sign for Belloni's café, as has been suggested, surely Watteau's friends would have noted this very public event, as they noted the fact that he created a painting to serve as the sign for the shop of his dealer Gersaint. In addition, if Belloni had owned the painting, upon his death in 1721 (the same year Watteau died) one of Watteau's collectors, like Gersaint or Jullienne, would have snapped it up, just as they bought up and resold the contents of the painter's studio.[10] What is likely is that the painting ended up in a private home outside Paris, where it went unnoticed by the connoisseurs who remained interested in Watteau throughout the eighteenth century. Many elites staged amateur theatricals and *parades* in their country homes and built intimate, jewel-box theatres to match. Possibly, the painting served as a decoration, an elevated version of the paintings with which nomadic performers decorated their makeshift trestle stages. If the painting was outside Paris, buried in the countryside, this may explain how it could have gone unremarked for such a long time.

It makes its first historical appearance in a drawing by Denon, which can be dated to between 1815 and 1825 (see Plate 13). The sheet depicts Denon's drawing room in his home on the Quai Voltaire, where he lived after the fall of Napoléon. The walls of his salon are thickly hung with paintings, drawings, prints, and watercolours. Men, women, and children wearing the latest fashions cluster throughout the room, leaning casually on chair-backs, conversing, and working away at sketchbooks and drawing pads. Denon includes a self-portrait, on the right-hand side of the drawing; he appears as a little man with untidy hair, beaming at his guests. At the back of the room, two large doors have been flung open, revealing a small anteroom, where larger paintings, placed high on the wall, can be glimpsed. Here, hanging above two vases and a stuffed parrot, is Watteau's large *Pierrot*, unmistakable even when represented by a few light pencil strokes.

There is no record of where or when Denon acquired the painting. The first published account of Denon's discovery of it dates to 1845, twenty years after Denon's death. According to its author, Pierre Hédouin, the painting

> belonged, forty years ago, to M. Meuniez, *marchand de tableaux*, who had kept it for many years without being able to place it. To attract the eyes and flatter customers, he had written in white crayon, on the ground of this painting, two verses of a once popular song: 'How happy Pierrot would be/if he knew the art of pleasing you!'.[11]

The 'Meuniez' to whom Hédouin refers could be 'Meunier', 'Marchand de tableaux et de curiosités', listed in a period almanac.[12] From 1800–08, Meunier had a boutique at 11 Quai Voltaire. The Quai Voltaire was where Denon lived out the last decade of his life, as well as the locale of several other picture dealers (*marchands de tableaux*). In 1877, the amateur and curator Louis Clément de Ris, whose account was also discussed in Chapter 2, told the story slightly differently, claiming that Denon found the painting in the Carrousel du Louvre. Neither Hédouin nor Clément de Ris cites the source of their account. It is possible that this was Denon's version of events, told to friends, who passed it on, until it became old lore in circles of collectors and dealers. It was a good story, after all, and Denon loved to tell stories. If we cannot learn where the painting was actually acquired from these stories, we can nevertheless learn much about the figure of the post-Revolutionary collector and the mechanics of the *trouvaille*, the stunning discovery of an overlooked masterpiece.

Denon lived in an era when such discoveries were possible. Born into a noble family in 1747, the first epoch of De Non's life was courtly and cosmopolitan.[13] Living in Italy when the Revolution began, he returned to France in 1793 to avoid being labelled an *émigré*. Now Denon, he arrived in Paris during the early months of 1794, not long after the beheading of Marie-Antoinette. In February of that year, he moved into an apartment in one of the capital's most bustling corners, the Hôtel Bullion, a former *hôtel particulier* that had been transformed into an auction house during the late eighteenth century.[14] The Hôtel Bullion's daily sales reflected a market fuelled by the collections seized from 'enemies of the Republic', a category that included nobility, *émigrés*, and clergy, along with any other individuals deemed unpatriotic. The volume of merchandise passing through the Revolutionary marketplace was immense; the furnishings and décor of Versailles alone, which were sold *in situ* in approximately twenty thousand lots, took a year to auction off.[15] Confiscated collections went first to one of several Revolutionary depots, where bureaucrats versed in the arts assessed and catalogued the spoils.[16] Some choice items were put in newly founded museums, charged with educating Revolutionary subjects,[17] and thousands of seized objects, not deemed worthy of the museum, were sold.[18] Proceeds went to the government, with hefty cuts taken by the dealers and auctioneers who organised the sales.[19] The result was that France, and Paris in particular, was flooded with art, *bibelots*, tableware, houseware, and tapestries – all the appurtenances of eighteenth-century luxury.[20]

At the Hôtel Bullion, Denon was in heaven. He attended the frequent sales and set up a secondary market in the two rooms of his apartment. He covered his walls in pictures and objects, resold them to his visitors, and used the profits to buy more things.[21] He wrote to his muse in Venice, Bettine (Isabella Teotochi), bragging that he had become *un marchand*, whose rooms were an 'open boutique', 'well-decorated with curiosities'.[22] He delighted in the perpetual renewal of the inventory, the variety of the goods, and the efficiency with which they were shown, sold, and packed off; it was, in his words, both a 'spectacle' and a 'revue'.[23] Denon found his feet at the Hôtel Bullion, yet this was only the beginning of his Revolutionary career. He renewed a friendship with Jacques-Louis David. When David ended up in prison after the fall of the Montagnards, Denon remained unscathed. Within a few years, he had become indispensable to Napoléon Bonaparte, whom he accompanied to Egypt in 1798.[24] The military mission was a failure, but Denon transformed the trip into a cultural triumph by publishing, upon his return in 1802, a hugely popular illustrated account, *Voyage in Upper and Lower Egypt during the Campaigns of General Bonaparte*.

In 1802, Napoléon appointed Denon General Director of the Arts, a coveted post whose purview included the Musée Napoléon (now the Musée du Louvre), the Musée des Monuments Français, the Musée Spéciale de l'École Française at Versailles, the galleries of the Palais du Gouvernement, medal- and print-making, and studios for stone engraving and mosaics.[25] In addition, Denon served as the personal 'decorator' for the homes of Napoléon and Josephine, which included the chateaux at Fontainebleau, St Cloud, Compiègne, the Tuileries, and Josephine's private residence at Malmaison.[26] For these projects, the Revolutionary warehouses were at his disposal. Paintings and porcelain seized from the nobility reappeared in the Imperial residences. As the Napoleonic armies campaigned victoriously across Europe, sweeping through Belgium, the German and Italian principalities, and Spain, Denon travelled in the wake of the conquerors, selecting works to be brought back to France for exhibition in the Musée Napoléon. He had become the world's curator; his museum was the only museum; all roads ended in Paris, at the door of the Louvre, at the foot of his collection.

At the height of Denon's power, the museums of Europe became his personal warehouse, a saleroom in which he was the only bidder. Yet Denon continued to haunt the second-hand shops of Paris. These shops had flourished during the Revolutionary period, stocked by the same flow of goods as the plusher auction houses.[27] They clustered around and on the quays, from the boutiques on the Quai Voltaire to the open-air stalls (*échoppes*) radiating along the Seine from the Pont Neuf. Sometimes a mere blanket, laid with piles of porcelain, paintings, and books, would serve as a shop's premises. Visitors to Paris, surveying the results of the Revolution, compared the city to an overstocked junk shop.[28] This trade had its own vocabulary and its own myths. Many aristocratic commentators, who had seen their property ransacked by the revolutionaries, strongly deplored the character of the new market.[29] For detractors, the bric-à-brac markets along the Seine and in the alleys of Paris loomed large as a representation of the disrepair and disrepute into which taste, connoisseurship, and the art market had fallen. Picture merchants were grouped with *brocanteurs*. Once a purely descriptive term, for those who bought and resold second-hand goods, *brocanteur* had become a category laced with disrepute.[30]

More optimistically, there also circulated myths of the great treasures to be found within this chaos. The tale of Denon's discovery of Watteau's painting fell into this genre. The painting is neglected, overlooked. Hédouin names a seller of paintings and curiosities, not an elite dealer (the most upscale dealers did not keep shops); Clément de Ris names an 'obscure bric-à-brac seller'. In both accounts, Pierrot is on *parade*, desperate to attract clients. In Clément de Ris's account Pierrot is literally outside the shop, as the *parade* was outside the theatre. As Clément de Ris describes it, Pierrot 'calls' to Denon. In the poetics of old things, old artworks often speak. Louis-Sébastien Mercier, the indispensable chronicler of Paris, described the *dépôt* at the Petits-Augustins, before it became the Musée des Monuments Français, under the charge of Alexandre Le Noir. This depot was crowded with large, bulky pieces of sculpture, many of which had been torn off civic monuments or the walls of cathedrals by Revolutionary mobs. Mercier lauds the temporal disorder that resulted from the statues being thrown together, prior to any classificatory efforts. Into this 'unique spectacle, the most curious, the most important, the most novel that had struck at once my eye and my imagination, saints and mythological gods, heroes, virgins, the ancients, cardinals, Etruscan vases, stoups, medals, columns, busts, the colossal statues of Charlemagne and Saint Louis', have been 'thrown at random'.[31] The result, he says, is poetic and sublime disorder, magnificent and precious confusion.[32] 'All these statues spoke to me, because chance had disposed them in an eloquent manner.'[33] Yet, having been arranged in Le Noir's museum, in rooms organised by century, the statues 'have become mute again'.[34] Mercier advocates surrender to the disorder brought on by Revolutionary upheaval. Rather than bemoan the chaos, he argues that it is precisely because of the confusion that the sculptures speak to him.[35]

The speaking artwork, addressing the viewer, is theatrical. When arranged pell-mell, the sculptures are unable to address one another, as in a tableau. They are forced to address the viewer. Mercier's desire to be addressed by the artworks may reflect an era in which many objects were silent, having lost their back stories, provenance, and context. A talkative work helped to redress these gaps. Denon also engaged imaginatively with works of art, particularly those works that he reserved for his large and eccentric personal collection. He owned paintings, drawings, prints, sculptures in marble and bronze, architectural fragments, medals, lacquer-ware, and engraved gems.[36] In addition, he also collected 'curiosities' in the form of objects, artefacts, and specimens of natural history from Asia and Africa, including woven baskets, pieces of fabric, and kitchen utensils.[37] After his death, the auctioning-off of his estate lasted sixteen days.[38] Amongst Denon's collection, there were a few masterpieces, but the majority of the collection was not particularly valuable or historically noteworthy.[39] For his private collection, Denon often picked works with which he could imagine an emotional connection. When he was living at the Hôtel Bullion, he wrote to Bettine: 'I have found a tableau that represents a beautiful angel as large as life and that resembles you as if I had commissioned it, … it is the first thing I see when waking and I believe I am still dreaming'.[40] He admitted that the work was not well painted, yet it was the only work he refused to sell. If he had company, he placed the painting on an easel and moved it into the salon, to make 'Bettine' a further member of the party.

Denon also used the objects in his collection to create imagined relationships with persons of the past. In one of the trunks he had brought back from Egypt, he had stowed a little mummy's foot, which he described as 'the foot of a young woman, of a princess, a charming being, whose form, never altered by a shoe, was perfect; it seemed to me that I had obtained a favour, and gained a furtive lover in the lineage of the pharaohs'.[41] Denon's relationship to the objects in his collection was playful, and personal, in the literal sense of the work as a medium for an imagined encounter between its owner and another person. The story that circulated, in which Denon was 'addressed' by Pierrot, calling to him from Watteau's canvas, depicts Pierrot as a theatrical emissary, whose call to Denon establishes a relationship, where before there had been silence.

These kinds of personal relationship to works of art had long been a subject of satire. Collectors fell into different categories, each with its own set of associations. There were *amateurs*, *connoisseurs*, *collectionneurs*, and *curieux*.[42] In the eighteenth century, *amateurs* enjoyed a high level of esteem as persons of disinterested taste; the *connoisseur* was associated with judgement, knowledge, and discernment, which could be the result of professional activities.[43] *Curieux* was an ambivalent term and continued to be so.[44] It was associated with irrational, passionate habits, an impulse to accumulate, and the pursuit of rarity.[45] In the late seventeenth century, La Bruyère had delivered a scathing portrait of the *curieux* as one for whom the objects of the collection rose up to form a phantasmagoric alternative society. La Bruyère's collector of birds, for example, 'meets his birds again in his sleep: he himself is a bird, he is crested, he warbles, he perches; he dreams the whole night that he moults or that he warms his eggs'.[46]

The tendencies of the *curieux* were perfectly suited to the post-Revolutionary art world. The ability to welcome what might be characterised as 'irrational' sensations, when encountering works of art, was now a helpful skill.[47] In a satire of art market actors, the author Champfleury would make fun of the tendency to overimagine: one type of collector, the *dreamer*, assigns the names of great masters to 'canvases that a *brocanteur* on the quay of the Hôtel-Dieu would not dare to display'.[48] Denon did, indeed, misattribute many works in his own collection, including several that hung adjacent to Watteau's *Pierrot*. Given the post-Revolutionary context, however, even mistaken attributions could be understood as palliative. Part of the challenge for the post-Revolutionary generation, confronted with thousands of masterpieces crowding the magazines of the Louvre on the one hand, and the odd assortment of bric-à-brac and curiosities arranged pell-mell in the courtyard of the same museum on the other, was how to lend form to the fragments, how to attribute and construct meaning for decontextualised objects, and how to do so without falling into outright storytelling. Denon was adept at such efforts (although occasionally he did simply make things up).[49] As has recently been suggested, the upheaval of the Revolution gave birth to a new kind of history by expediency, for which source material was no longer texts or archival materials, since many libraries had been destroyed or were hopelessly disorganised, but rather objects found in second-hand marketplaces like the quays of the Seine. These 'informal resources' had been enriched by Revolutionary turmoil, giving birth to the 'historian collector', for whom the material artefact, like an autograph, a faience plate, or a print, provided a new kind of evidence of the past.[50]

Yet Denon appears to have resisted the impulse to project a strong historical narrative onto Watteau's large painting. He chose not to etch the painting for the *Monuments des Arts du Dessin*, a massive work that he spent the last ten years of his life composing, which would describe the history of art as a succession of schools, illustrated with engravings after works drawn from Denon's own cabinet. Denon died before the work could be finished, but it was completed by Amaury Duval, and published in 1829, still without a reproduction of the large painting of Pierrot.[51] In omitting it from the official narrative of his collection, Denon allowed Pierrot to remain in the poetic disorder of the bric-à-brac shop, this eloquent pell-mell that had also characterised Mercier's description of the *dépôt* of the Petits-Augustins. Here, in the disorder of the ages, Pierrot would still be able to speak.

Displacement and neglect, as well as the lack of a historical narrative, characterise the presentation of the figures in *The Old Musician*. As scholars have shown, almost every figure in the painting is a reference to other, older paintings or sculptures. The gypsy musician, with his violin on his lap, refers to a seated piper by the brothers Le Nain as well as a Roman copy of a Greek statue of the stoic philosopher Chrysippos.[52] The pair of companionable little boys, their bodies oriented towards the viewer, is a reference to the same painting by the Le Nains, also known as a print, *The Village Piper*.[53] Citations of Velazquez and what Fried has termed 'Spanishness' also run through the painting:[54] the arrangement of seated and standing figures in a nondescript setting, with a dirt ground, and the leafy bough in the left-hand corner, create a composition that resembles Velazquez's *Triumph of Bacchus*.[55] Finally, the seated ragpicker is both an exact quotation of a previous painting by Manet himself and a nod to Watteau's *The Indifferent One* through the dance-like arrangement of the feet. Fried has argued that these citations reflect a deliberate effort on Manet's part to establish a unique genealogy for artistic Frenchness as a theatrical take on Realist (Spanish) subject matter.[56] I would add yet another layer, which is the post-Revolutionary art market in which such a programme of reference became possible or thinkable. The juxtaposition of eras, styles, and artists reflects the incongruities produced by post-Revolutionary *dépôts* and second-hand retailers. These incongruities were a source of poetic confusion for a writer like Mercier, but they could also register an undercurrent of dejection, as is the case in both the accounts of Denon's discovery of Watteau's over-looked painting. At least some of this dejection characterises the tone of *The Old Musician*, a painting that is hardly as merry as the *Triumph of Bacchus*, in which the figures are tightly laced together as they reach for the same cup of wine, held by a grinning man. Manet's figures have not quite overcome the distance that separates their sources. They are lined with the same embarrassment that affects the objects on the clearance rack, the bargain bin outside the shop, where things that have not been able to please are obliged to sing for their supper.

Bric-à-brac taste

The Carrousel du Louvre, where Clément de Ris located Denon's discovery of Watteau's painting, was a key locale in the aesthetics of bric-à-brac. Over the course of the nineteenth century, the Carrousel emerged as both the literal and the figurative epicentre of the 'bric-à-brac taste' (*goût bric-à-brac*).[57] The 'bric-à-brac taste' in collecting and decoration consisted of the intentional juxtaposition of periods and styles. During the 1830s, this taste became the favoured style of bohemian Paris, a milieu that was energetically asserting itself following the disappointing results of the Revolution of 1830. A generation of young Romantics, who Paul Bénichou has described as the 'School of Disenchantment', were deeply disillusioned by the events of 1830, when one constitutional monarchy was replaced by another branch of the same family.[58] By turning their backs both on politics and on bourgeois careers in law or bureaucracy, these young men performatively rejected the status quo. The bric-à-brac taste was the chosen decorative style of this coterie, which included Gérard de Nerval and Théophile Gautier. During the 1830s Nerval and Gautier lived with the painter Camille Rogier and the critic Arsène Houssaye in a dilapidated flat, the sole attraction of which was an intact eighteenth-century *boiserie*.[59] The flat was located in the Impasse Doyenné, a dead-end street in the ancient neighbourhood of the Carrousel du Louvre. These streets no longer exist; they stood inside the courtyard of the Louvre in the space now occupied by I.M. Pei's pyramids. A print by H. Toussaint shows the mish-mash of buildings, one of which has had to be buttressed, obscuring the western façade of the Louvre's Cour Carré, with its distinctive central pavilion. An advertisement for vinegar is painted on the side of one building, while a series of low shopfronts appear on the right (Figure 3.1).

Taking advantage of the fresh glut of inventory in the aftermath of 1830, the group furnished their flat with a few mismatched pieces, including a 'Louis XIII chair', 'a renaissance bed', a 'medici console', and a hammock.[60] As would later be recalled in numerous accounts, the friends threw a housewarming party and invited the artists they knew to paint directly onto the walls, in the spaces in the *boiserie*. The resulting decorations were heteroclite, including bacchanals by Adolphe Leleux and Célestin Nanteuil, two narrow Italian landscapes by Corot, a Diana in her bath by Théodore Chassériau, a 'Watteau or Lancret' pastiche by Gautier (who also dabbled in painting), 'hoffmanesque fantasies' by Rogier, and a palm tree by the Orientalist painter Prosper Marilhat.[61]

The delight in the eighteenth-century panelling, as well as the inclusion of a 'Watteau' dashed off by Gautier, reflects the renewed fashionability of the rococo, a 'revival' that followed the neo-classical severity of the Revolution and the Empire.[62] Gautier, Houssaye, and Nerval all wrote admiringly of the rococo and of Watteau, whose work they regarded as full of 'fantasy' and elegance. Gautier and Nerval were invested in the way that the rococo had survived in the form of objects hidden away in dusty attics or displayed on the quays of the Seine.[63] In a poem describing an encounter with eighteenth-century pastel portraits displayed on a quay, Gautier plays on the way that the age of the objects is reflected in the appearance of the pastels' subjects.[64] As the portraits have been exposed to the elements, the women's complexions have been aged by 'the wind of winter', their beauty spots replaced by mud splatters ('you have now only *mouches* of mud'), 'and on the quays you lie all dirtied'.[65] Their bouquets of flowers are 'a little pale, as suits flowers that are a hundred years old'.[66]

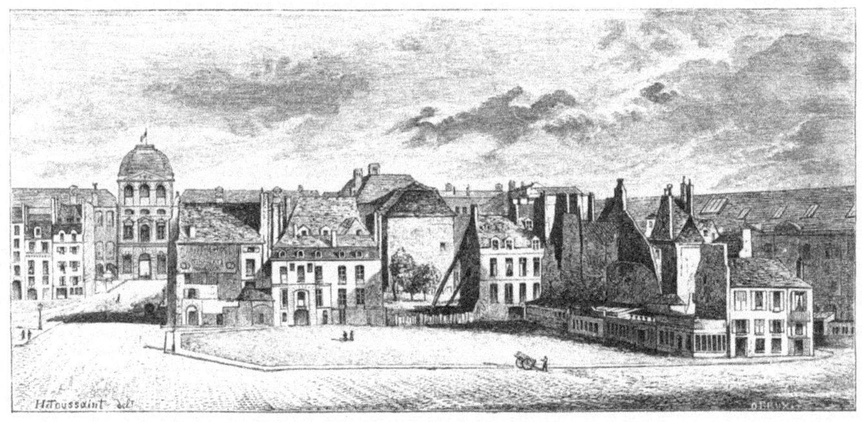

3.1   H. Toussaint, *Place du Carrousel in 1850*, mid-nineteenth century. Etching. Source: Private collection ©Look and Learn/Bridgeman Images.

Gautier makes the material traces of the object's age into part of his experience of the image. His eloquence is inspired by the dilapidated state of the object, which he takes great care to mention and to elaborate, as well as the melancholy fact of pastness: 'it is past, the sweet reign of beauties'.[67] In this version of the rococo revival material evidence of age was a desirable, even a necessary criterion. By addressing the work, Gautier attempts to theatricalise it. Once again, we have evidence not so much of a work that is inherently theatrical (although the portrait is a theatrical genre), but of a viewer who wants very badly to believe that it is. This desire to animate the work, and in so doing, to theatricalise the marketplace, is one of the tendencies of the poetics of old things.

In addition to the apartment where the Cenacle du Doyenné took up its residence, the Carrousel du Louvre featured a variety of second-hand shops and stalls. Drawings and prints were sold in the Carrousel, as were old-clothes, bric-à-brac, and live birds. In Baudelaire's 'The Swan', published in the revised edition of *Les fleurs du mal* (1861), the poet remembers the old Carrousel, the 'encampment' of stalls, a pile of architectural fragments (capitals and shafts of columns), weeds, and 'shining in the window-panes, the confusion of bric-à-brac'.[68] In this poem, he allows the Carrousel to stand for all of 'vieux Paris', the historic Paris that existed before Haussmann's renovations. As this suggests, the Carrousel had acquired a mythic status, helped along by Gautier, Nerval, and Houssaye, who all published retrospective accounts of their bohemian escapades in Rogier's flat. The contrast between the richness of the Louvre and the shabbiness of the neighbourhood within was not lost on the inhabitants of the flat in the Impasse. This spatial incongruity was another form of bric-à-brac. The pervasiveness, and persuasiveness, of these accounts may explain why Clément de Ris, in 1877, placed the bric-à-brac seller from whom Denon bought Watteau's *Pierrot* in the Carrousel du Louvre.

Gautier's obituary of Marilhat was published in 1848 and again in *L'art moderne* in 1856. *Les fleurs du mal*, which Baudelaire dedicated to Gautier, was published in 1857 and a revised edition, including 'Le Cygne', in 1861. Nerval's *Petits châteaux de Bohême* appeared in 1853. In this sense, it was not necessarily during the 1830s itself that the bric-à-brac taste emerged as a distinctive poetics, but rather during the 1850s, as an alternative to yet another disappointing Revolution. It was not until 1860, in fact, when Manet most likely began work on *The Old Musician*, that critical attention was paid to *Pierrot, dit Gilles*, Denon's find from the Carrousel. Exhibited in 1860 at the Galerie Martinet, as part of an exhibition of the 'Old French School', the large canvas was remarked upon by numerous critics, including Gautier.[69] During the 1830s, when Gautier and Nerval were hosting parties in the Carrousel, the large Pierrot had again languished in relative obscurity. The painting did not find a buyer at Denon's posthumous sale, although it was advertised in the sale catalogue as 'the most important painting, of the most original character that ever left the brush of this excellent colourist'.[70] Denon's nephew, Brunet-Denon, inherited the painting. From Brunet-Denon's collection of mediaeval curiosities, the painting finally found its way to the cabinet of Louis La Caze, who had built a significant collection of seventeenth- and eighteenth-century French art, including works by the Le Nains and Watteau.[71] According to his guests, La Caze claimed that Pierrot often popped out of his frame for a chat and a tour of the salon. Perhaps Pierrot's belated debut coincided with the nostalgic mood of the aged bohemians, who were finally ready, in 1860, to answer his cry.

Broken faience at the Théâtre des Funambules

The inhabitants of the Doyenné could have capped off their night of revelry with a trip to the Théâtre des Funambules, where they would have seen a Pierrot that hardly resembled the figure in Watteau's painting. This is the Pierrot who would appear, in 1855, in Nadar's sleek photographs, exhibited at the Palace of Industry in the context of triumphant modernity. Yet influential accounts of the 'original' of this Pierrot, Baptiste Deburau (father of Charles, who is pictured in the photographs), had woven Pierrot into a dense texture of old things. The Théâtre des Funambules was located on the Boulevard du Temple in the modern-day 3rd and 10th *arrondissements* of Paris, near what is now the Place de la République. Theatres had begun to appear on the Boulevard in the late 1760s and 1770s.[72] In addition to its theatres, the Boulevard had a boisterous street life made up of the *parades* performed in front of or on the façades of the theatres, sideshow attractions that squeezed their tents into the gaps between theatres, and lively, if seedy, cafés and outdoor terraces. The growing number of theatres pushed down the prices of performances, making these accessible to a new audience. Members of the working classes, who could now see more than just the *parade*, stood cheek-by-jowl in the theatres' highest balconies, which were referred to as 'the Gods', 'the paradise', or 'the chicken coop'.

The Funambules began as a theatre of tightrope walkers and gymnasts, which then added pantomimes to its repertoire. The pantomimes featured the old masks of the Comédie Italienne and the fair theatres: Columbine, Arlequin, and Pierrot. In the early 1820s a young actor named Baptiste Deburau began to moonlight in the role of Pierrot. By 1826, he had officially taken over the role, which he played daily to a packed house, with his most devoted audience to be found in the paradise.[73] His popularity made Pierrot into the pantomime's central figure, who nevertheless tended to remain peripheral to love plots. Deburau's costume was different from the one worn by Watteau's Pierrot. Most importantly, Deburau jettisoned the floppy straw hat in favour of a skull-cap, which drew attention to his long, expressive face (Figure 3.2). When Deburau first began playing the role, no speaking at all was allowed on stage. The actors used gesture, movement, and facial expression to mime the emotions of the stock characters and stock scenarios: falling in love, jealousy, eating and drinking too much, stealing, avarice, kicking and punching. In one particularly popular pantomime genre, the harlequin-fairy-pantomime (*pantomime-arlequinade-féerique*), these rather hackneyed plot elements were supplemented by complex, garish, and fanciful scenic décor. The Funambules

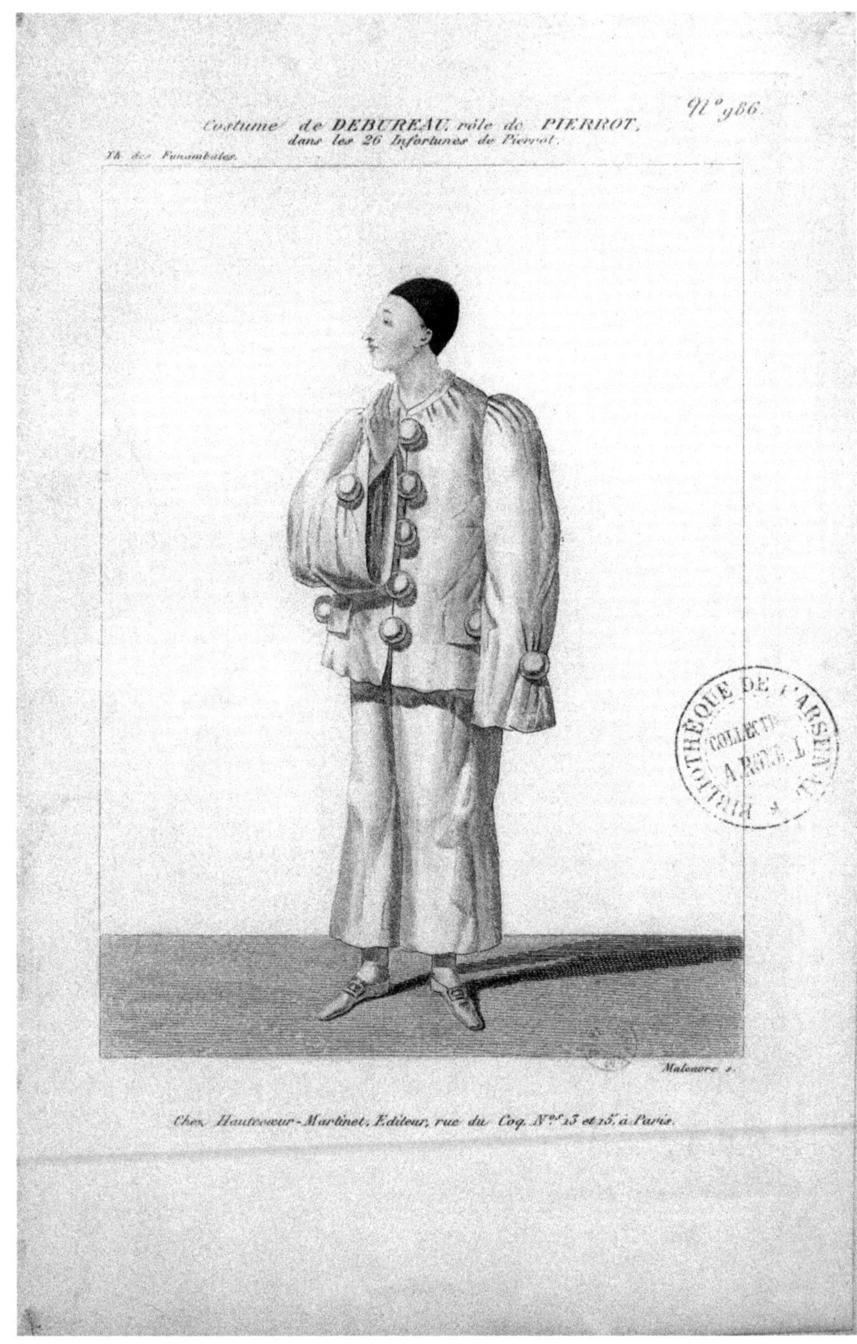

3.2   Atelier Maleuvre, *Baptiste Deburau in The twenty-six misfortunes of Pierrot*, 1833. Hand-colored etching, 23 × 14.5 cm. Source: Bibliothèque Nationale de France, Paris. DIA-ICO COS-8840 ©BNF.

also boasted certain 'special effects', the ability to simulate fire, real fireworks, and the lightning-quick disappearance of characters who would then reappear in entirely new costumes.[74] These magical transformations, or 'changes in view' (*changements à vu*), were supervised by a fairy (*fée*), from whom the *féerique* appellation of this genre was derived.[75]

Rumour of Deburau's tremendous popularity with a working-class audience aroused the interest of the literary elite.[76] In 1828 Charles Nodier, an author, bibliophile, and librarian of the Arsenale, published a laudatory article on Deburau in *Le Pandore*, one of the many 'little journals' that had sprung up in nineteenth-century Paris. By 1830 Jules Janin, a prolific and influential theatre critic, had begun to champion Deburau. In 1832 Janin published a biography entitled *Deburau, History of the Theatre at 4 Sous, as a sequel to the history of the Théâtre-Français.*[77] The title alluded both to the inexpensive price of the tickets and to the decadence of the French theatre, which the pantomime promised to replace. In the 1830s Nerval and Gautier became denizens of the Funambules, to which they were followed by Champfleury in the early 1840s. Deburau died in 1846; George Sand penned a lengthy commemorative essay.[78] In 1854, Champfleury published *Souvenirs des Funambules*, which consists mostly of previously published reviews, short stories, lists, and summaries of pantomime scenarios.[79]

Focusing on Janin and Champfleury, I attend here to the way that these critics' interest in Deburau intersected with their curiosity about bric-à-brac and the marketplace for old things. For both these critics, the representation of second-hand things provided a screen for the popular and 'the people' (*le peuple*). As a blanket category, *le peuple* massed together both rural agricultural labourers and the urban working classes. Janin was interested in the latter, the teeming proletariat, while Champfleury's preference was for the former, the simple inhabitants of the countryside. Descriptions of *le peuple* varied widely in tone, from condemnations of their moral depravity to rhapsodic tributes to their purity of spirit.[80] Janin belonged in the rhapsodic category. Particularly attuned to Parisian manifestations of the popular, Janin viewed the people as essentially picturesque, living in shabby attics, of mercurial temperament, swinging from joy to rage, from piety to blasphemy, yet fundamentally present, immediate, and instinctive.[81] This was also Janin's Pierrot:

> after his grimace, after this vengeance with which he contents himself while awaiting better, see how he gambols with greater flair, how he becomes drunk again, quarrelsome, moody, mean, good; it is always the instinct of the people, the spirit of the people, the life of the people.[82]

In his first published discussion of Deburau, Janin offered a list of places where the people were likely to be found: cheap hotels, church-sponsored pawnbrokers (*monts de piété*), attics, cabarets, the Place de Grève (the site of a weekly market for used linens), outdoor boutiques from stalls (*échoppes*) to the quays (*quais marchands*).[83] These locales reflected the author's interest in Parisian secondary markets for resale and re-use. He cherished the *petits métiers*, those open-air professions, distinctive to the urban fabric, which included itinerant vendors (criers) and all those responsible for clearing the streets of dirt, sewage, and rubbish, from *regratteurs* who sought bits of iron between the paving stones (fallen off carriages and horseshoes), to the sellers of old clothes and ragpickers. In his essay on the *petits métiers* in *Le livre des cent-et-uns*, Janin described a vast second-hand marketplace, from the clever salesgirl who bought, on Monday, the lace worn by a countess on Sunday, to the clerk who purchased a marked-down ticket from a duke who had watched only the first half of a performance.[84] Parisians, the critic believed, possessed the ingenuity and flair necessary to make the best of scarce resources, which were continually changing hands, travelling down the ladder of Parisian society, until they landed in the gutters, where they were picked up by ragpickers, night-soil men, and *regratteurs*.

It particularly delighted Janin that Deburau was prop master at the Funambules, in charge of a well-stocked closet. Janin devoted an entire chapter of his biography to an inventory of this closet, an absolutely remarkable text, in the form of a list which reads like a phantasmagoria of a junk shop.[85] Alongside a leather valise, a crucifix, seven coffee cups with matching saucers, a large mallet, two crystal carafes, and an iron key are a host of objects made out of inexpensive materials like wood, copper, and papier-mâché, including goblets, trophies, chandeliers, and platters, all covered in gilded paper. There are two papier-mâché pâtés, a roast chicken made of the same, and a 'thunderclap made of 30 leaves of sheet-metal'.[86] As a device, the transcription of the list allows for the presentation of a heteroclite collection of things, which do not need to be fitted into any overarching organisation except that of the prop closet. This is bric-à-brac as a literary aesthetic, expressive of abundance and randomness. This was also the impression created by pantomimes at the Funambules, in which many things happened, but little logic strung those things together.

It is a string, or a rope, that is strung across the top of the Funambules' stage in a print by Alphonse Legros, which illustrates the 1859 edition of Champfleury's *Souvenirs des Funambules* (Figure 3.3). Legros shows Pierrot, Arlequin, Cassandre, and Columbine, who have come to the edge of the stage to take their bow. The etcher has streaked Pierrot's surface with rough hatchings, a reflection of a crowded stage picture, viewed in dim, smoke-wreathed lighting. Above the actors is the rope, hung with what appears to be a collection of the theatre's props: a letter sealed with wax, a doll, a wine bottle, and perhaps a few papier-mâché sausages and baguettes. This odd detail, which does not appear in any other descriptions of the theatre, is reminiscent of old-fashioned storage mechanisms, in which food, as well as paper, was stored on strings affixed to the wall or the rafters, out of the reach of mice (mice nibbled paper as well as sausages). Yet it also offers a reflection of the pantomime's structure, which was not so much a coherent architecture as a string or a wire that held together disparate things: things, not events, because at the Funambules things provided the pretence for events. A papier-mâché roast chicken was in itself an event, as was a wine bottle, or a letter. It was things that held the potential for consumption, or transfor-mation, that were the *modus operandi* of the pantomime's stories: Pierrot eats a

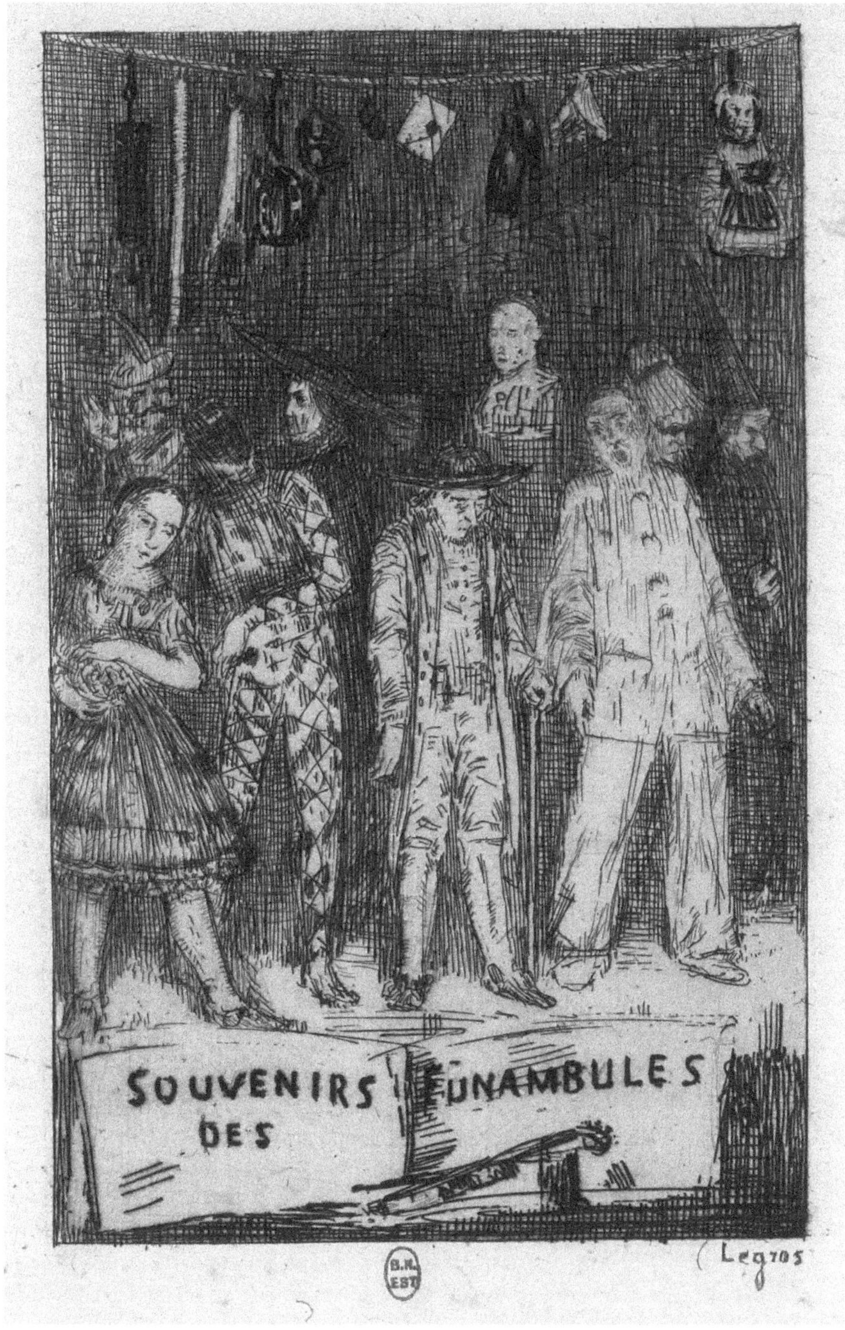

3.3   Alphonse Legros, Frontispiece for *Souvenirs des Funambules* (unpublished edition), 1860–65. Etching, 15.9 × 9.8 cm. Source: Bibliothèque Nationale de France, Paris. DC-310 (4)-FOL <ESTNUM-23969> ©BNF.

chicken; or Pierrot is about to eat the chicken, but the chicken transforms into a fairy. Janin's Pierrot moves through a world inhabited by shabby, used things, the second-hand furnishings of working-class households. The critic preferred this décor to the bourgeois salon, the setting of many a melodrama or a vaudeville, with its 'modern intrigue' played out between bankers, financiers, politicians, and their wives and daughters.[87] In an echo of Mercier's description of the fruitful pell-mell at the Dépôt des Saint-Augustins, 'the confusion of ideas and things' at the Funambules encourages Janin's imagination, engendering a 'waking dream'.[88]

Champfleury, the author and collector who took up Pierrot's cause during the 1840s and 1850s, shared Janin's interests in old things.[89] Champfleury's tribute to the pantomime theatre, *Souvenirs des Funambules*, is another intentionally pell-mell kind of volume. Many of the texts in this book had been previously published, but Champfleury gathered them for the occasion and put them together with little regard for continuity or logical sequence, creating a motley literary composition, which he described as 'tales sewn together with white thread'.[90] He admitted that there was no 'method' to their arrangement: 'all these little papers, these tales, these pantomimes, which I have lined up the one after the other, I believed in them when I wrote them, and that is my only justification'.[91] As Champfleury pointed out, a similar kind of randomness characterised the writing of pantomime scenarios. Invited to 'write' a pantomime, he is given a box filled with little bits of paper, cardboard, and string. Each piece of board represents a *truc*, a trick or a transformation, like a rifle that changes into a ladder, or an *armoire* into a chair.[92] Instead of writing words, he is asked to string together the *trucs*. The result is the *féerie*, amid the frenzy of which it is impossible 'to recognise the *idea* that could have presided over this heap of events'.[93]

Champfleury was an ardent collector of artefacts of popular culture, which he tended to identify with old, broken, and discarded things.[94] He haunted the quays and the *marchands de tableaux et de curiosité*. He was particularly fond of French faience, which he regarded as both rustic and delicate.[95] Like Denon, Champfleury was able to tease stories out of the objects he collected. In *Souvenirs des Funambules*, the critic lovingly describes one of the treasures of his collection: a *plat-à-barbe*, a shallow dish used for shaving, with an indentation on its wide rim, into which a man would place his chin. On his travels, the plate broke into six pieces, which Champfleury insisted upon saving, refusing to throw them in the *'coin d'une borne'*, which refers to the Parisian practice of heaping trash beside the stone bollards (*bornes*) that were affixed to the sides of buildings, in lieu of pavements.[96] Finally, an itinerant dish seller pieced the plate back together using strands of wire. In a demonstration of the richness of 'the naïve arts', Champfleury teases from this 'melancholy *plat-à-barbe*', an entire 'little country drama', in which the members of a rural village, including the curate, the schoolteacher, and the mayor, are shaved by the local barber.[97]

The broken pieces of faience provide another image for the piecing together of parts, which Champfleury claims characterises both the writing of pantomimes and the writing of his book.[98] With these comparisons, he places his project for remembering Pierrot under the sign of the second-hand. It is the jauthor's task to identify the old thing, as Champfleury found the faience *plat-à-barbe* deep in the countryside; and, if necessary, to put it back together. The author was attached to this trope of the broken dish, which he had already used once, in 1853's *Aventures de Mademoiselle Mariette*, a novel about Parisian bohemia and its flighty, transitory inhabitants. In this telling, a painter finds half of a faience salad bowl (*saladier*) in a pile of rubbish on the street.[99] A moment later, he sees a ragpicker plucking from the bottom of the heap the other half of the bowl. For two sous (half the price of a ticket to the Funambules), the painter buys that half from the ragpicker. The salad bowl is repaired by an unspecified artisan who 'fastens things' ('l'homme qui met des attaches') and ends up on the wall of the painter's studio, 'shining like a sun'.[100] This version of the broken faience vessel introduces the ragpicker, one of the most important figures in the nineteenth-century poetics of old things.

Published in 1854 as *Contes d'Automne* and in a new edition, with the title *Souvenirs des Funambules* in 1859, Champfleury's account of the Theatre was yet another retrospective text, which exemplified the culture of bric-à-brac in the years leading up to Manet's painting. Janin's and Champfleury's literary treatments of the Funambules amplify the aesthetics of randomness and belabour the dilapidated character of the objects in the milieu of the Theatre. The world of *le peuple*, as imagined by these authors, is crammed with objects and unnavigable by the ordinary outsider. It is Pierrot, however, who offers a way in, a 'white thread'. Offstage, Deburau, as prop master, reigned over a cabinet of old things, an ersatz *marchand de bric-à-brac*. Onstage, Pierrot put the pieces together; he is the 'idea' that 'presides', to riff on Champfleury. If all else fails, an expressive wink from Pierrot to his audience in the paradise will smooth over the seams of a plot gone haywire because a papier-mâché turkey has become Cassandre, Pierrot's tyrannical boss. It is not the relationships between characters on stage that tie things together, but the fact of Pierrot's being there for his audience. Bric-à-brac is reimagined in these accounts as a popular practice, enabling suggestive parallels between the bourgeois collector – like Champfleury, his attics crammed with broken bits of faience – and the ragpicker. For Janin and Champfleury, Pierrot was not so much a representative figure of *le peuple* as a kind of emissary or relay, a privileged interlocutor of a dense world of old things. This was also the role of figures like the ragpicker, who had risen to exemplary status through forms of 'panoramic' representation.

Rags and *physiognomies*

Through another citation, this time of his own work, Manet included a ragpicker in *The Old Musician*. In 1859, Manet had submitted a painting, *The Absinthe Drinker*, to the Salon. It was refused. The sole inhabitant of this rejected painting was exactly the same figure who is seated second from the right in *The Old Musician*, wearing a top hat pulled over his eyes and a tattered cape. The model for this figure was a man called 'Collardet', who may have worked as a ragpicker.[101] With his narrow-legged grey trousers, however, and his elegant black leather shoes, the 'absinthe drinker' is certainly an up-market type of ragpicker. Nor does he carry a basket or a hook, the ragpicker's signature tools. Yet contemporary representations of the ragpicker, like the lithograph by Charles-Joseph Traviès de Villers, often paired a top hat with tattered clothes, a sign of the way the type combined poetic nobility and material wretchedness (Figure 3.4). Traviès's print was one of a series of *physiognomies* published in *La Caricature* in 1840. Sometimes also called *physiologies*, these serial publications had become a preferred vehicle for representing the urban working classes.[102] These series, which combined word and image in varying proportions, were the clear heirs of the *costumes* and *modes* discussed in Chapter 1. The most famous of these *physiognomies* was *Les Français peints par eux-mêmes*, published by Léon Curmer in eight volumes between 1840 and 1843 (five volumes covered Paris and three the provinces and colonies). In addition to such luxury publications, hundreds of *physiognomies* in inexpensive, pamphlet form also proliferated.[103] Like the *costumes*, the *physiognomies* presented a repertoire of social types. These selected, stylised types became a screen for the entire population of Paris, enabling a 'panoramic' view of society.[104] In addition to being more detailed than the *costumes*, the *physiognomies* were distinctly 'intermedial', in that they tended to pair different media, usually text and image. In *The Old Musician*, Manet includes references to three types taken from the *physiognomies*: the ragpicker, the old-clothes seller, and the *gamin*. The first two types – the ragpicker and the old-clothes seller – were key figures in the poetics of old things.

Until the late nineteenth century, European paper-makers were entirely dependent upon pulp made from old cloth.[105] Ragpickers (*chiffonniers*) roamed the urban streets and the countryside, sorting through rubbish heaps and collecting scraps of linen and hemp cloth to be used to make paper. Findings were deposited in wicker baskets (*hottes*) worn strapped to the back. Ragpickers also scavenged other cast-offs, including discarded pieces of bone, wood, metal, and the pelts of dogs and cats.[106] Although historical records suggest that they lived in family groups, and that at least a third of ragpickers were women, it was the lonely and intoxicated male ragpicker who figured in the repertoires of artists, poets, novelists, and journalists.[107] In a move that is emblematic of the poetics of old things, poets and novelists frequently compared themselves to ragpickers, suggesting analogies between searching for rags and searching for literary material. Most famously, in 'The Wine of the Ragpicker', a poem included in the first printing of *Les Fleurs du Mal* (1857), Baudelaire compared a drunken ragpicker to a poet, a misunderstood outcast obsessed by vivid dreams.[108] Some of the imagery of the poem had already appeared in articles of his praising intoxicating substances: in 'On wine and hashish' Baudelaire depicts the ragpicker as a both collector and poet – 'all that the great city has rejected, all that it has lost, all that it has disdained, all that it has broken, [the ragpicker] catalogues it, he collects it'.[109] Janin would proudly compare himself to a ragpicker, reporting on his willingness to source his literary material 'in the street', on foot, plucking 'scraps of prose and verse' from the rubbish piles.[110]

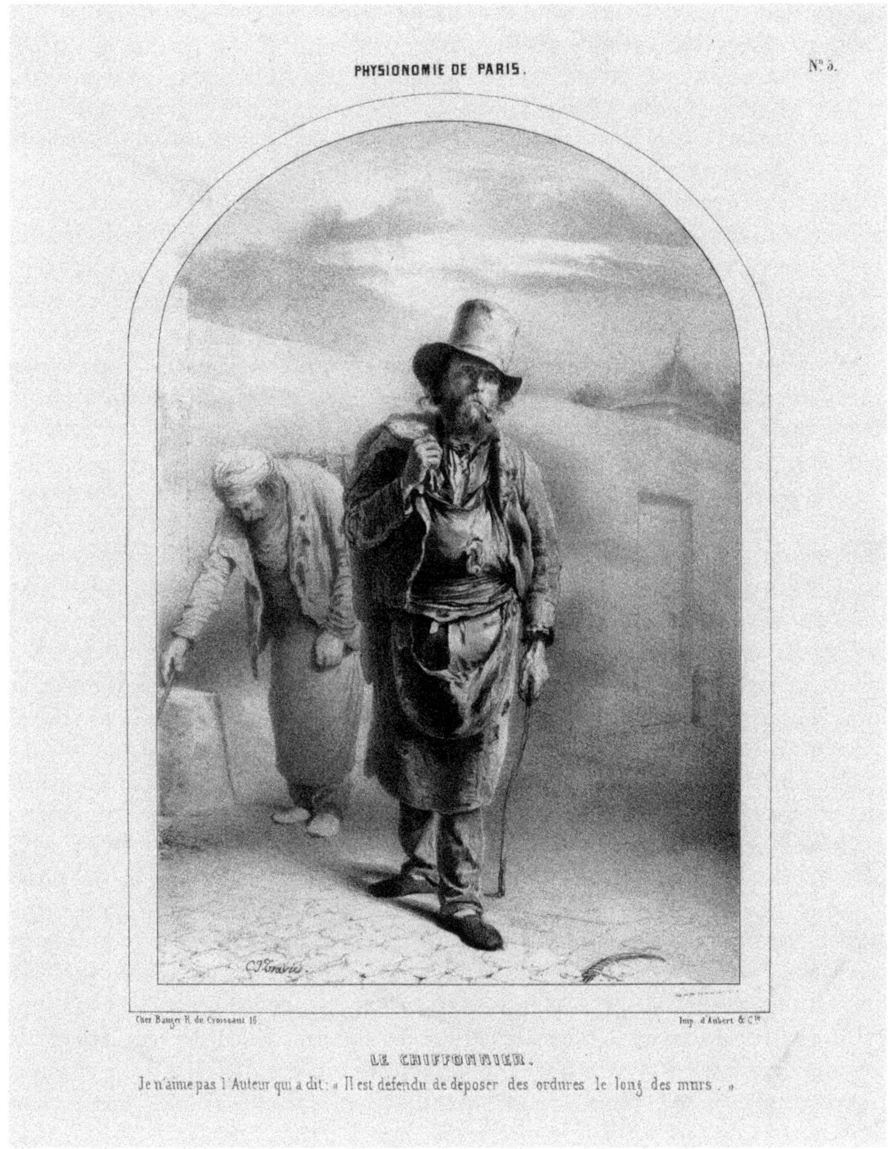

3.4   Charles-Joseph Traviès de Villers, *Le Chiffonnier*, no. 5 from *Physionomies de Paris*, 1840. Lithograph, 36 × 27.5 cm. Source: Musée Carnavalet, Paris. G.24727 ©Les musées de la ville de Paris.

Comparisons between writers and ragpickers were also used as insults.[111] Critics accused Realist authors like Champfleury, and later Émile Zola, of finding their urban and working-class subjects amongst trash that even ragpickers would disdain to pick. In March 1859, Nadar, who had long been at odds with

Champfleury, cruelly caricatured the critic as picking through Balzac's trash, moments after that author's death, like a ragpicker.[112] Nadar accompanied this textual sketch with a cover-page lithograph of Champfleury as a ragpicker, a wicker basket on his back and his hook reaching into a pile of broken ceramics.[113] Yet Nadar's mockery did not deter Champfleury from publishing, six months later, *La mascarade de la vie parisienne*, a serial novel set in a community of Parisian ragpickers.[114] One of the novel's characters, Topino, is a ragpicker who collects posters (*affiches*), which he glues together so as to create decorative partitions in his home.[115] The partitions, which function as papier-mâché room dividers, are both colourful and didactic. Topino uses the posters to teach neighbourhood children, including the offspring of ragpickers, how to read. Champfleury christens Topino 'an artist in the medium of rags'.[116] The artist as ragpicker is also the artist as ragpicker collector: 'as soon as a striking new poster made itself known in Paris, [Topino] rubbed his hands together like a lover of paintings who discovers a Raphael at a bric-à-brac shop'.[117]

In addition to his symbolic associations, the ragpicker is crucial to understanding *The Old Musician* because of his status as the 'master figure' of the *physiognomies* as a particular style of literary representation. In Gavarni's frontispiece to *Diable à Paris* (1845–6), a multi-authored collection of caricatural *physiognomies*, Gavarni's frontispiece shows an agent for the devil, Flammèche, surveying a map of Paris, a ragpicker's *hotte* strapped to his back.[118] It is Flammèche's job to assess Parisian society and determine why so many Parisians are ending up in hell. The frontispiece cleverly likens the ragpicker to the editor, whose chosen *physiognomies* make up the ensuing volume. Studying a map spread on the ground before him, Flammèche fulfils his task in a mode that Benjamin would describe as 'panoramic'.[119] Panoramas, a form of spectacular entertainment, consisted of a large painted canvas, usually representing an elevated or aerial view of a city, landscape, or military battle.[120] Installed in a rotunda, the panorama was viewed from a central platform, on which viewers were free to move about. To call the *physiognomies* 'panoramic' was to emphasise the resemblance between the way the panorama laid out a landscape for a viewer's perusal and the way the *physiognomies* laid out social types. As a novel form of leisure, the panorama encouraged a particular kind of looking, one that was associated with the boulevards, the passages, and department stores.[121] This style of visual experience reflected 'the desire of the public to see its social space like a scene or a gallery', in which what was seen was also for sale: 'the city as an assembly of different specialties in a shop window' (*vitrine*).[122]

Like the bric-à-brac taste, panoramic literature did not build links between types, but rather presented (and marketed) differentiation as an attribute of the market and its 'ranges'.[123] The result was what Nicholas Green describes as a 'picture built up from individuated objects and images'.[124] The nature of this picture can be grasped in a lithograph advertising a shop front for the publishing enterprise of Aubert, who worked with both Philipon and Traviès, the maker of this print (Figure 3.5). A crowd gathers to study the caricatures and *physiognomies* pinned to the façade of a shop, the name of which, 'Aubert

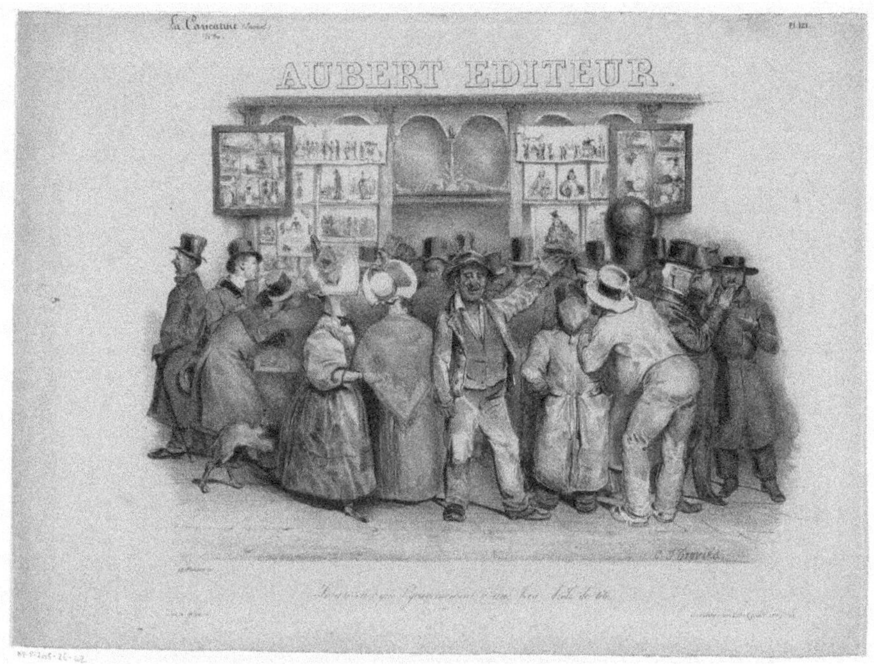

3.5   Charles-Joseph Traviès de Villers after Charles Philipon, *The publisher Aubert*, 1831. Lithograph, 25.9 × 33.7 cm. Source: Rijksmuseum, Amsterdam. RP-P-2015–26–102 ©Rijksmuseum.

Editeur', is written in large capitals. As the caption suggests, many of these figures would have been caricatures of the government, but other prints suggest the more generic types of *physiognomie*, which would have been displayed in the same way. To echo the address of the display, a man is poised at the edge of the crowd, facing the viewer and lifting his hand to indicate the goods for sale. Here, the address of the figures in the prints doubles the address of the objects themselves, which have been placed on the threshold of the market-place. Traviès plays brilliantly upon the contrast between the crowd of densely packed figures, a mass of shawls and top hats, and the neat silhouettes of the lithographed figures. What the crowd wants to see is not, in fact, a mirror of its own confusion, but rather an abundance of distinct figures, clearly labelled and set apart. The exemplary nature of the lithographed figures is vividly represented by the fact that they, unlike the crowd, have arrived at a place where they are not obliged to rub shoulders with strangers.

Deburau often took the opportunity to transform Pierrot into recognisable popular types, an array of which are illustrated in the commemorative litho-graph, *Galerie de Deburau* (Figure 3.6).[125] Here, Deburau's roles are arranged as mannequins in a shop window, each labelled with the specific pantomime. By casting Pierrot as a soldier, a shoe-maker, a grocer's boy, a hunter, a priest,

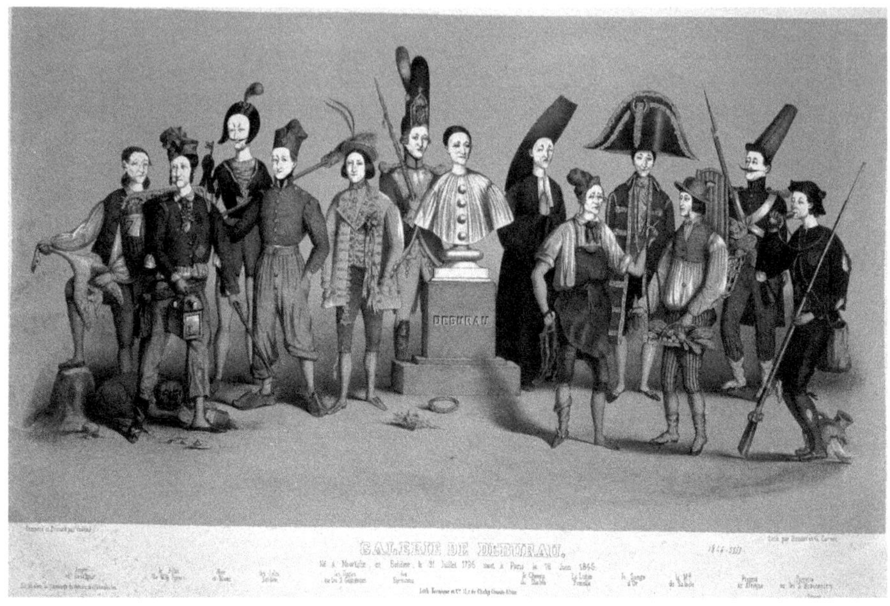

3.6   G. Cornet after Louis-Michel Vautier, *Gallery of Deburau*, 1846. Lithograph.
Source: Private collection. ©Leonard de Selva/Bridgeman Images.

the pantomime offered its own version of panoramic literature as a 'gallery' introducing its viewers to a range of social types differentiated by costume. In the gallery, Deburau appears, second from the left, in the costume of a ragpicker, with his *hotte* on his back, his lantern, and his crook in his hands. Pierrot the ragpicker was the hero of the pantomime *The 1000-franc note*, in which, after a morning spent drinking and eating *brioche*, the character does indeed find a 1,000-franc note, which he uses to transform himself into a brilliant dandy.[126] Quickly tricked out of his riches by Robert Macaire (Macaire was another popular type, a criminal speculator and confidence man), Pierrot is forced to enlist as a soldier. As the lithograph suggests, the Funambules could both spoof the *physiognomies* – every 'different' type is, in fact, just another version of Pierrot – while still participating in its classificatory mode. The differences between social types are presented as an attraction, a spectacle, as well as a series of choices freely made – which role will Pierrot play tonight? This panoramic bric-à-brac of social types and costumes is overseen by the bust of Pierrot in his 'default' costume of white tunic and black skullcap. As the only one of the figures presented as a sculptural bust, rather than a full-length figure, this decision is perhaps intended to reflect the commemorative nature of the plate, made upon Deburau's death in 1846. The 'original' Deburau has receded to the realm of the funerary bust, but the social costumes he wore live on as phantasmagorical skins, now shed.

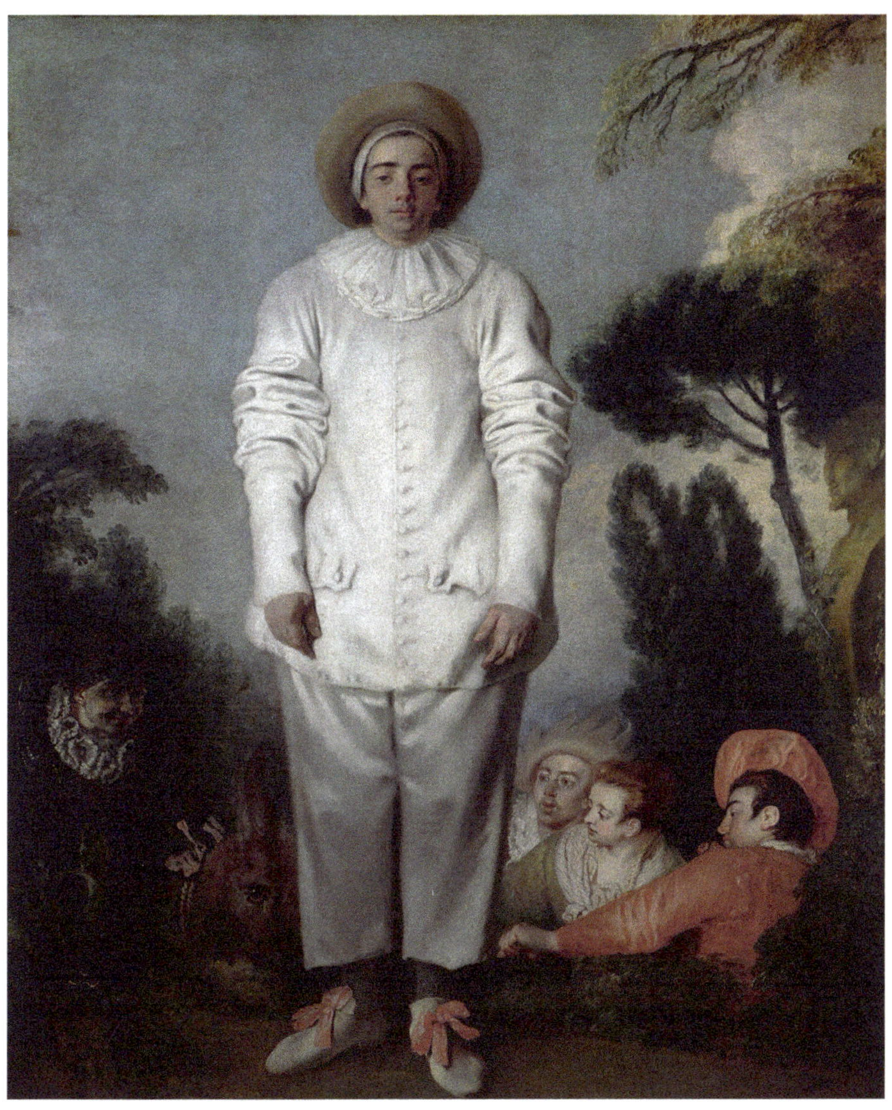

1   Antoine Watteau, *Pierrot*, c. 1718–19. Oil on canvas, 185 × 217 cm. Source: Musée du Louvre, Paris.

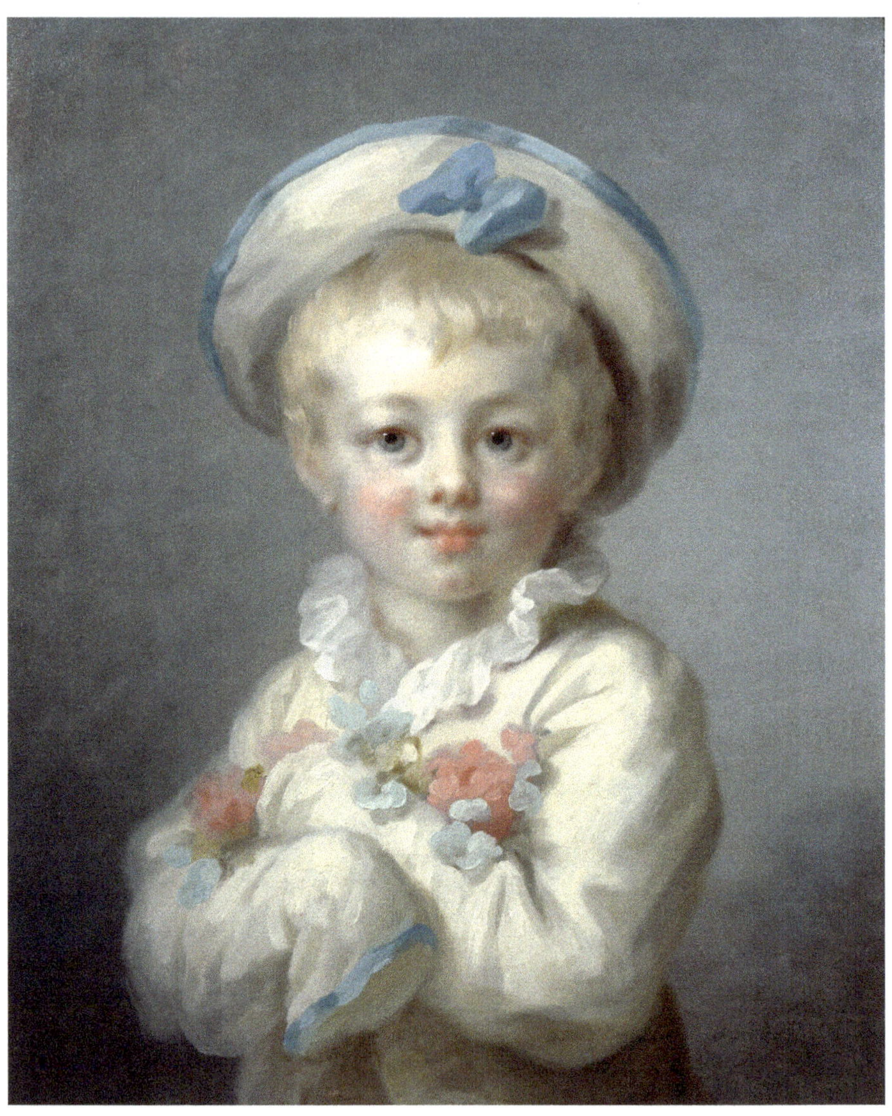

2   Jean-Honoré Fragonard, *A Boy as Pierrot*, *c.* 1785. Oil on canvas, 59.8 × 49.7 cm. Source: Wallace Collection, London.

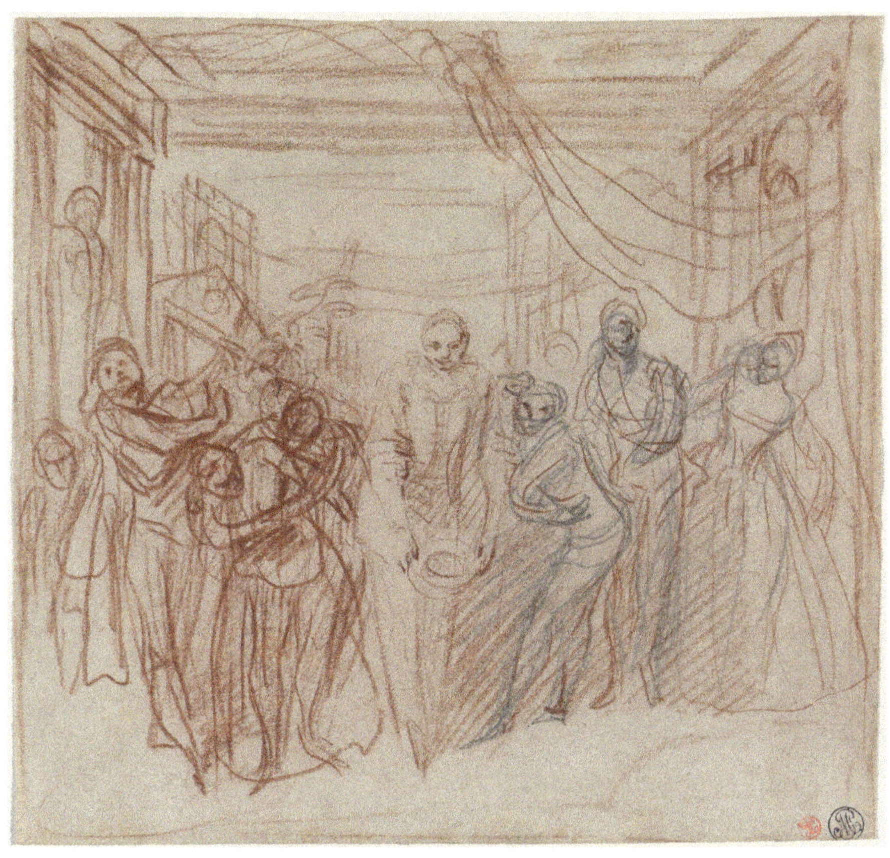

3   Antoine Watteau, *Italian Comedians Taking Their Bows*, c. 1718. Red chalk and graphite on cream laid paper, 17.8 × 18.5 cm. Source: National Gallery of Art, Washington, DC.

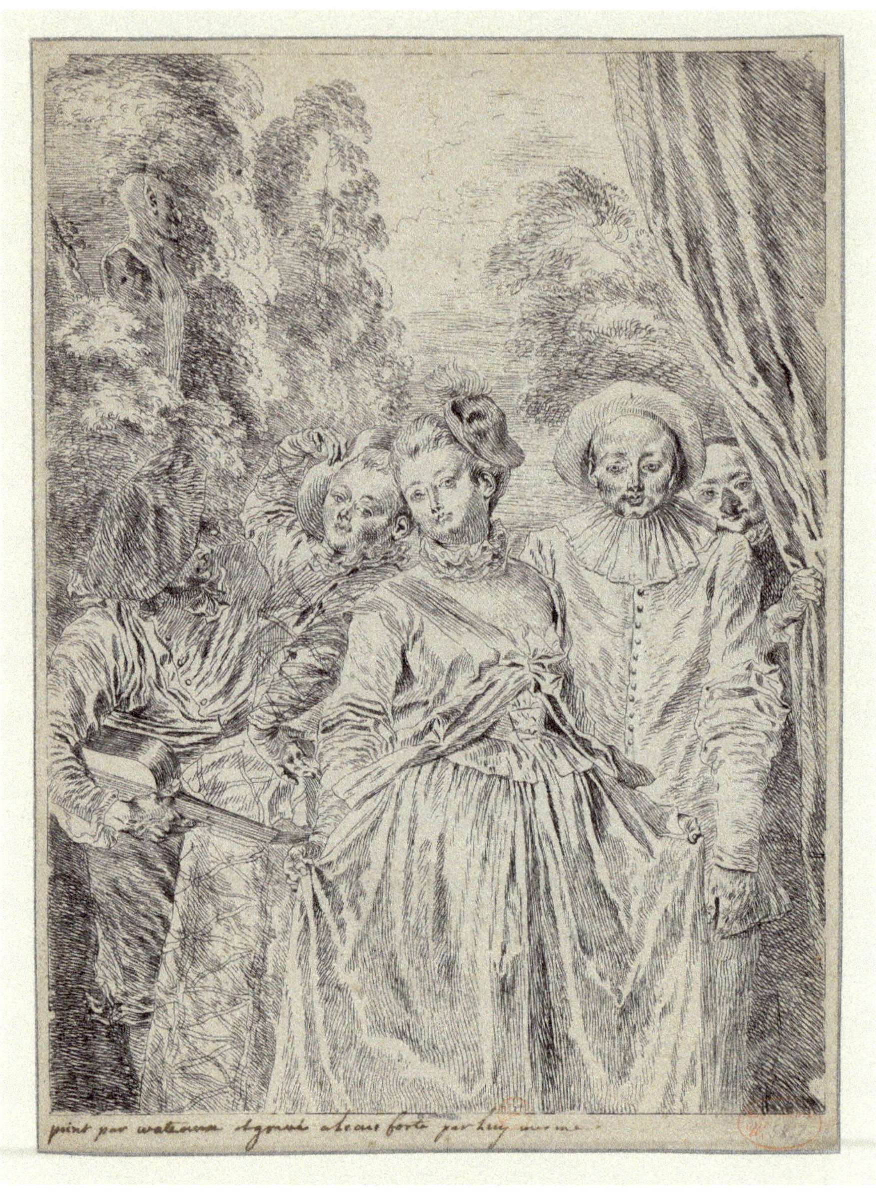

4   Antoine Watteau, *The Costumes are Italian*, c. 1715–16. Etching, 29.5 × 20.1 cm. Source: Bibliothèque Nationale de France, Paris.

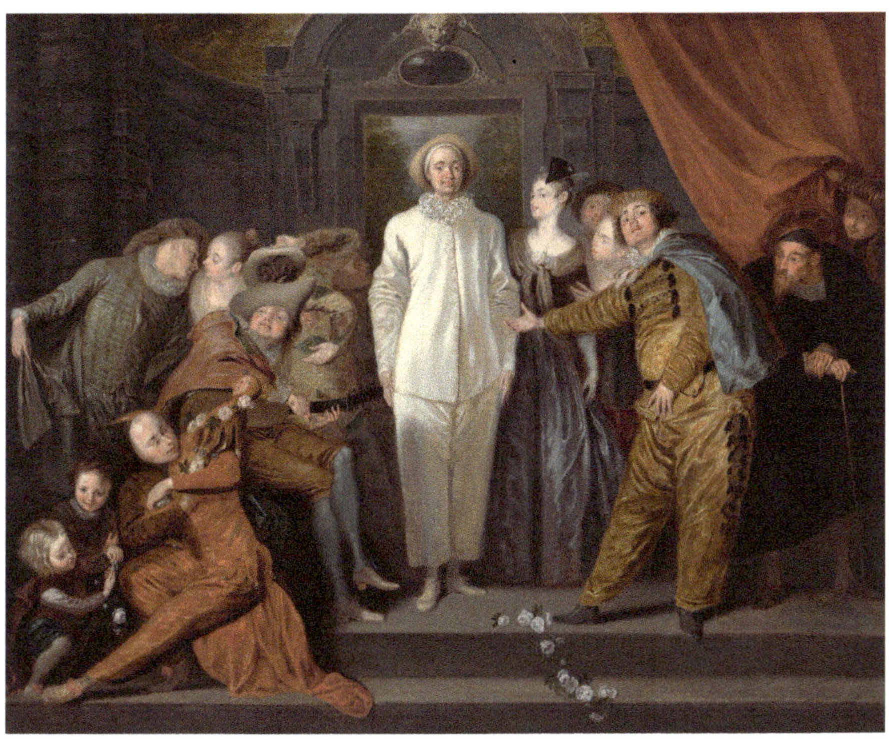

5   Antoine Watteau, *The Italian Comedians*, 1720. Oil on canvas, 63.8 × 76.2 cm.
Source: National Gallery of Art, Washington, DC.

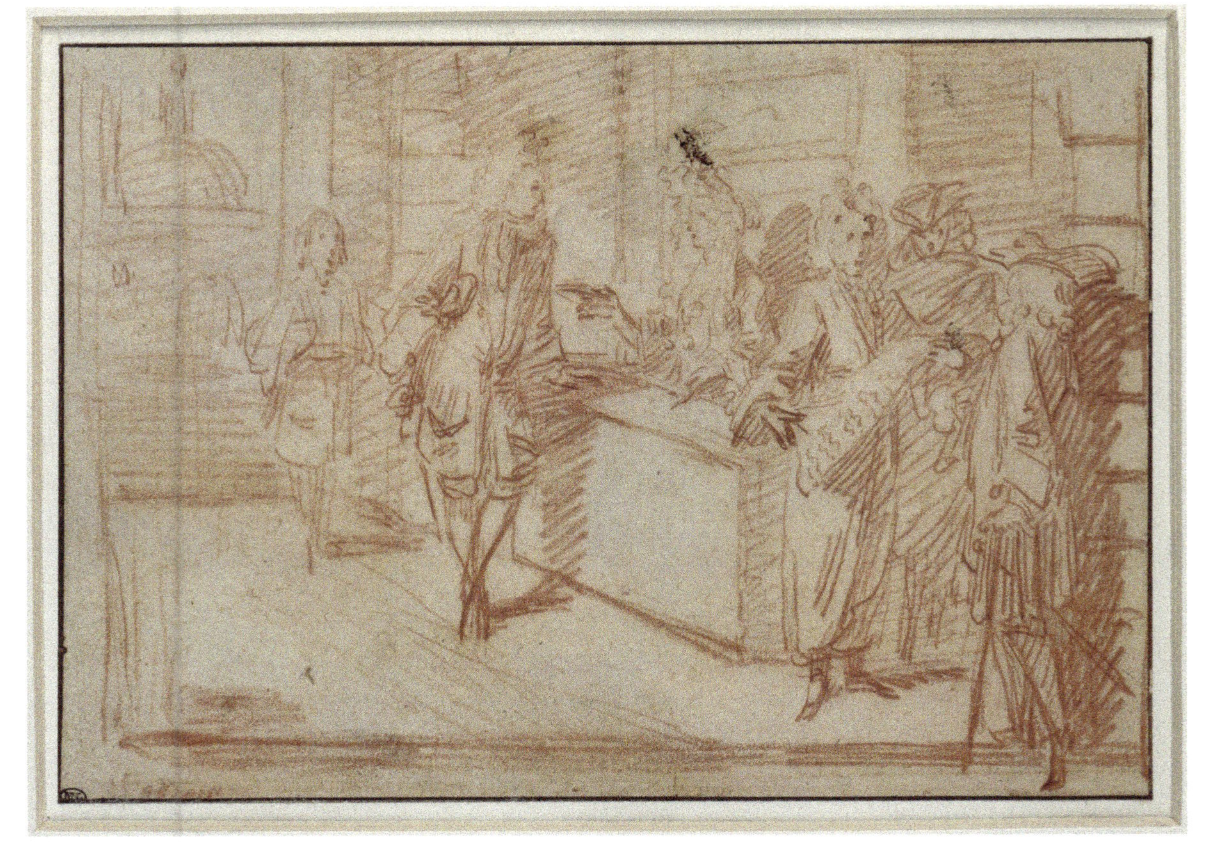

6 Antoine Watteau, *A draper's shop*, c. 1705–11. Red chalk on paper, 12.2 × 33.4 cm. Source: Musée du Louvre, Paris.

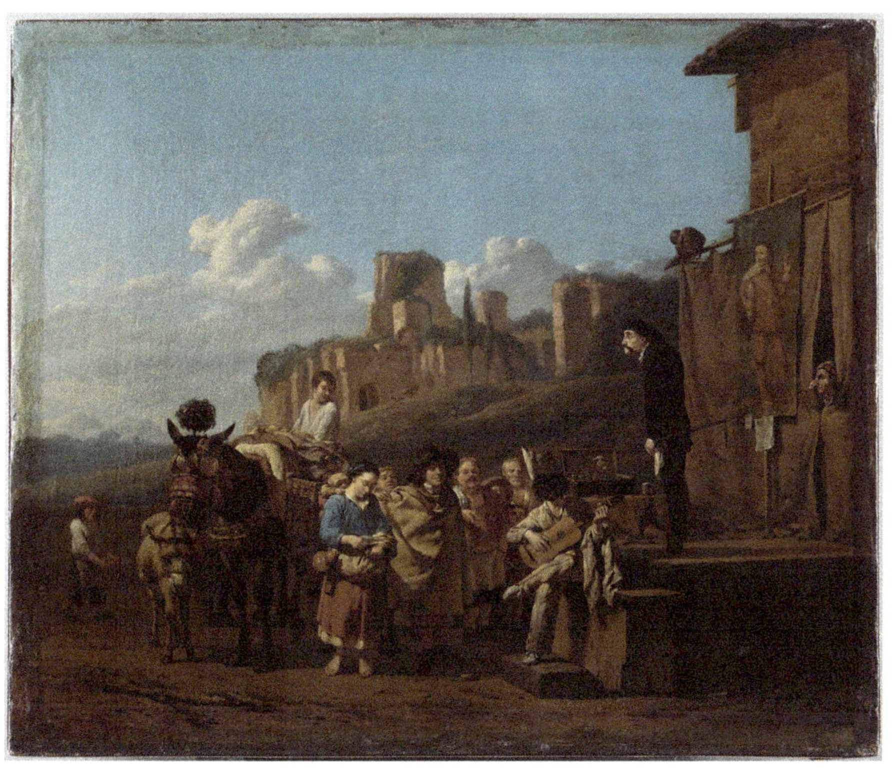

7   Karel Dujardin, *The Italian Charlatans*, 1657. Oil on canvas, 64 × 52 cm.
Source: Musée du Louvre, Paris.

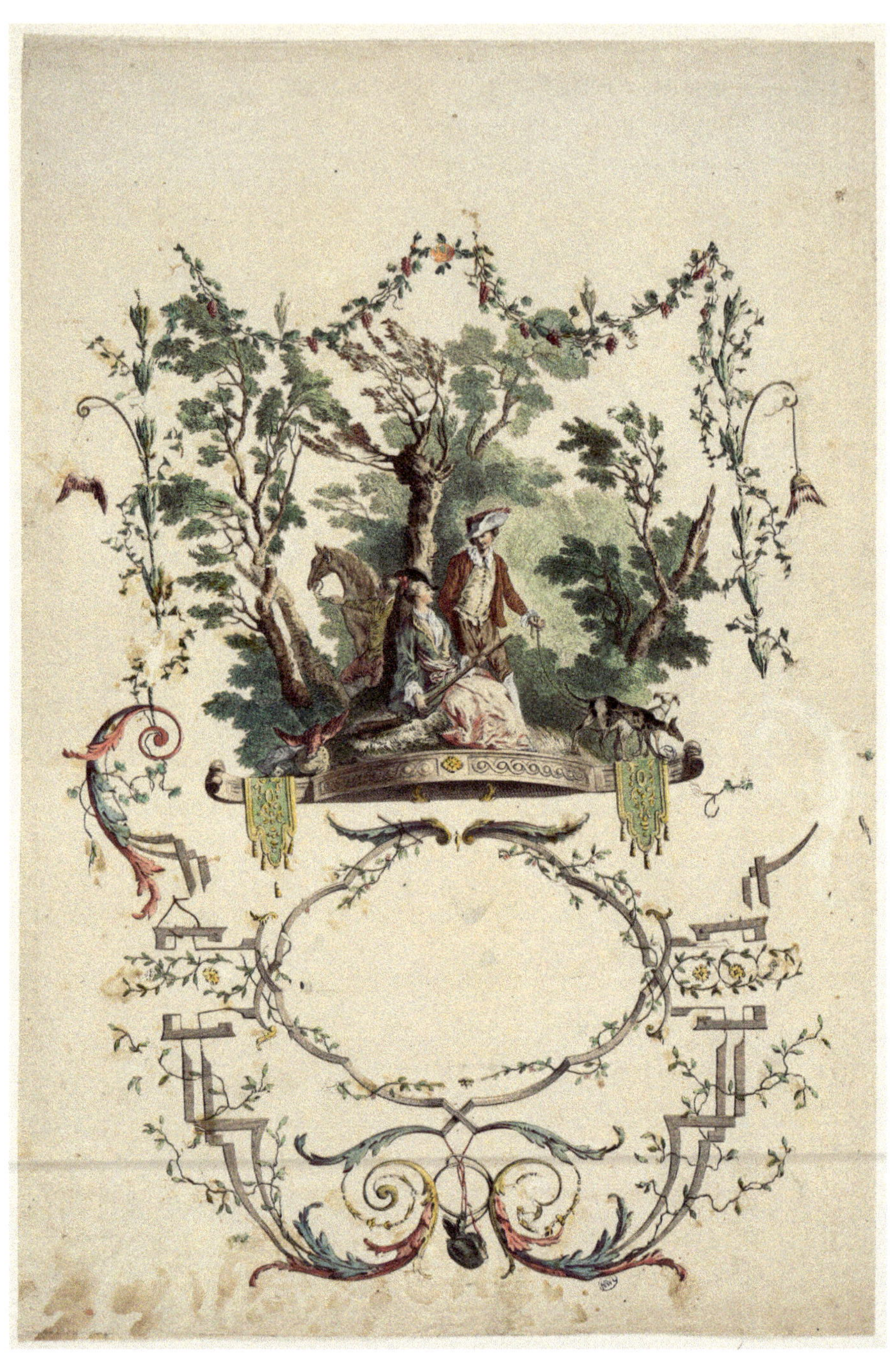

8 *Arabesque: the hunting party*, eighteenth century. Watercolor and etching. Source: Musée des Beaux-Arts, Valenciennes.

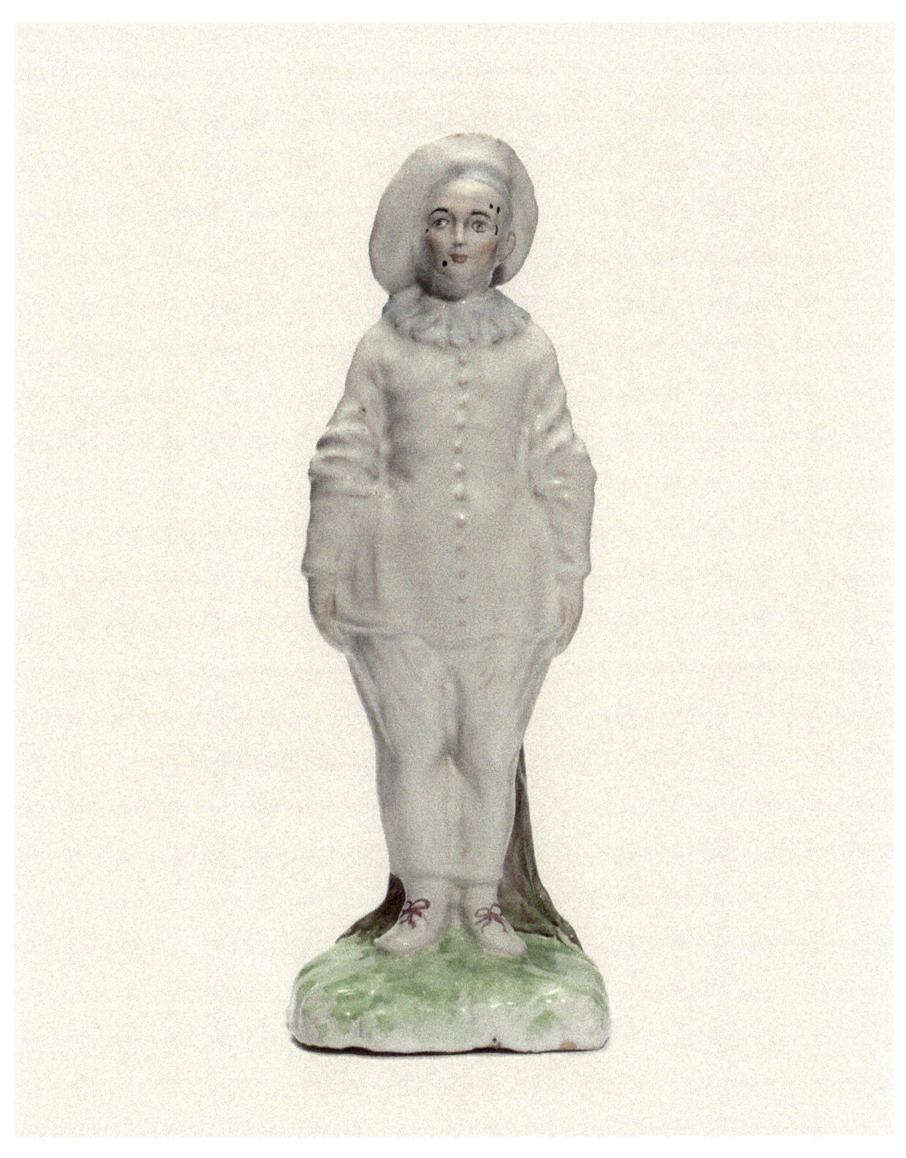

9   Manufacture Hannong, Strasbourg, *Pierrot*, *c.* 1745. Faience, h: 33 cm.
Source: Private collection.

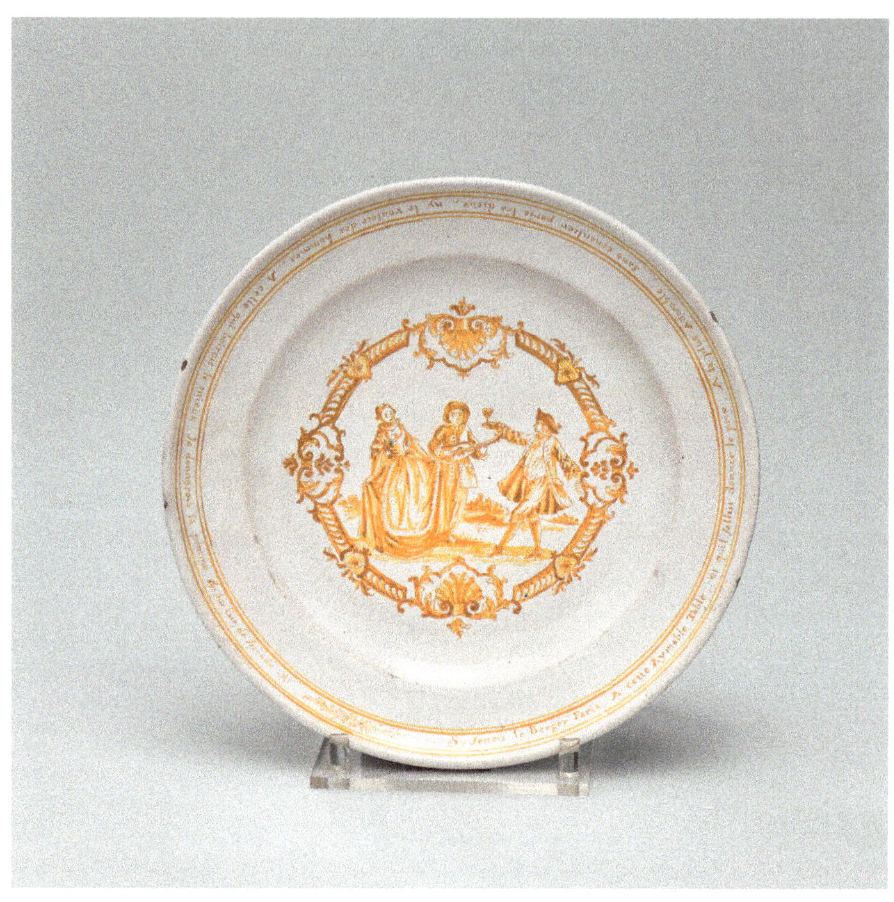

10   Manufacture de Marseilles, *Plate in camaïeu jaune*, eighteenth century. Décor du grand feu, faïence, 25 × 23 cm. Source: Manufacture et musée nationaux, Sèvres.

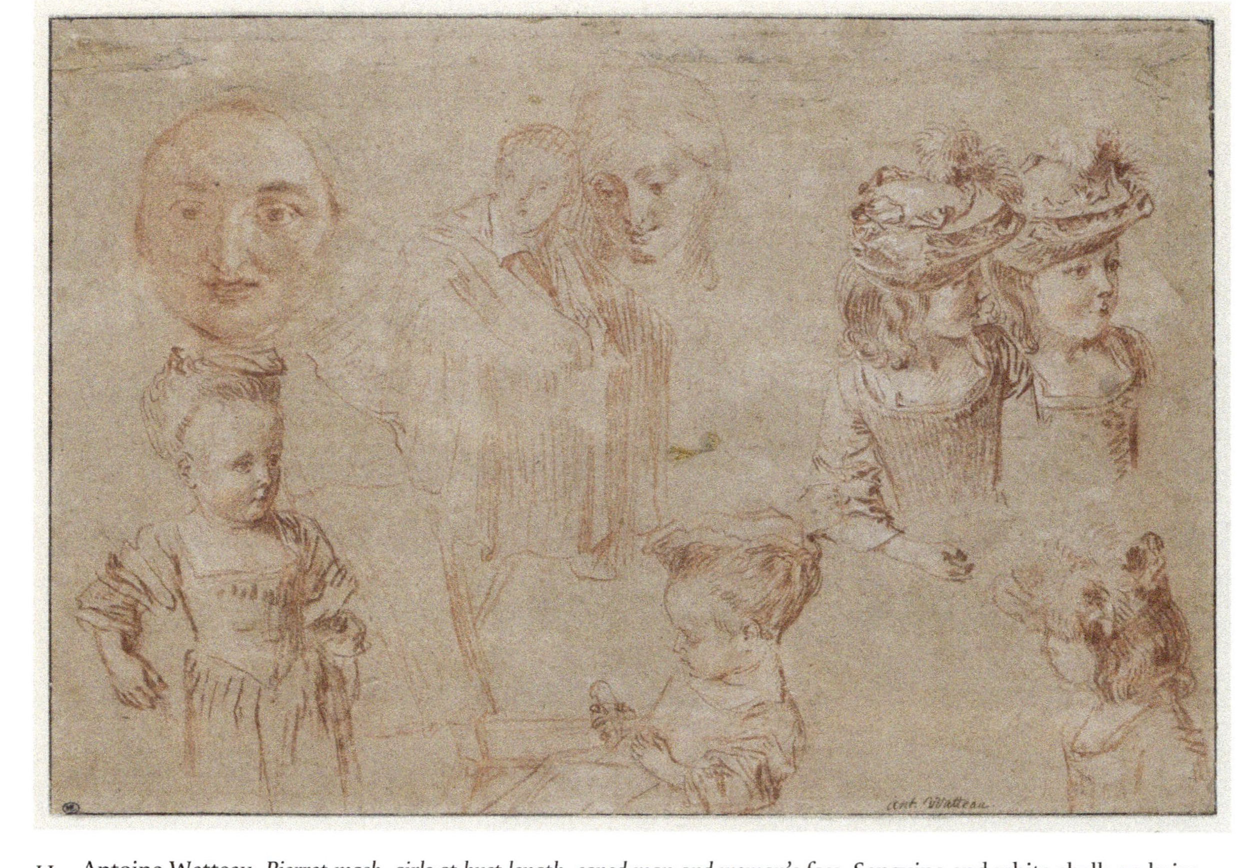

11   Antoine Watteau, *Pierrot mask, girls at bust-length, caped man and woman's face*. Sanguine and white chalk on beige paper, 27.1 × 40 cm. Source: Musée du Louvre, D.A.G., Paris.

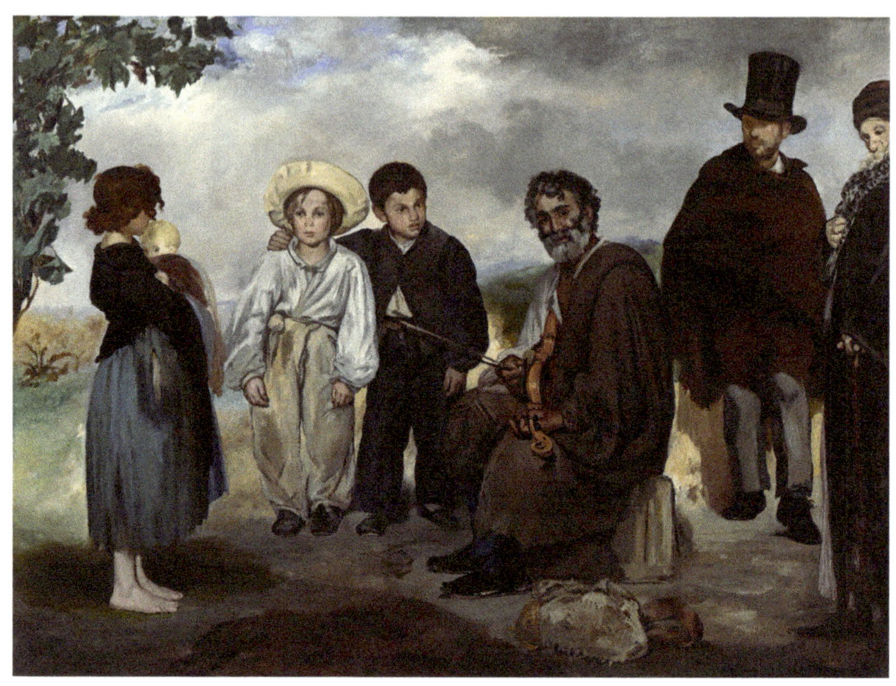

12　Édouard Manet, *The Old Musician*, 1862. Oil on canvas, 187.4 × 248.2 cm. Source: National Gallery of Art, Washington, DC.

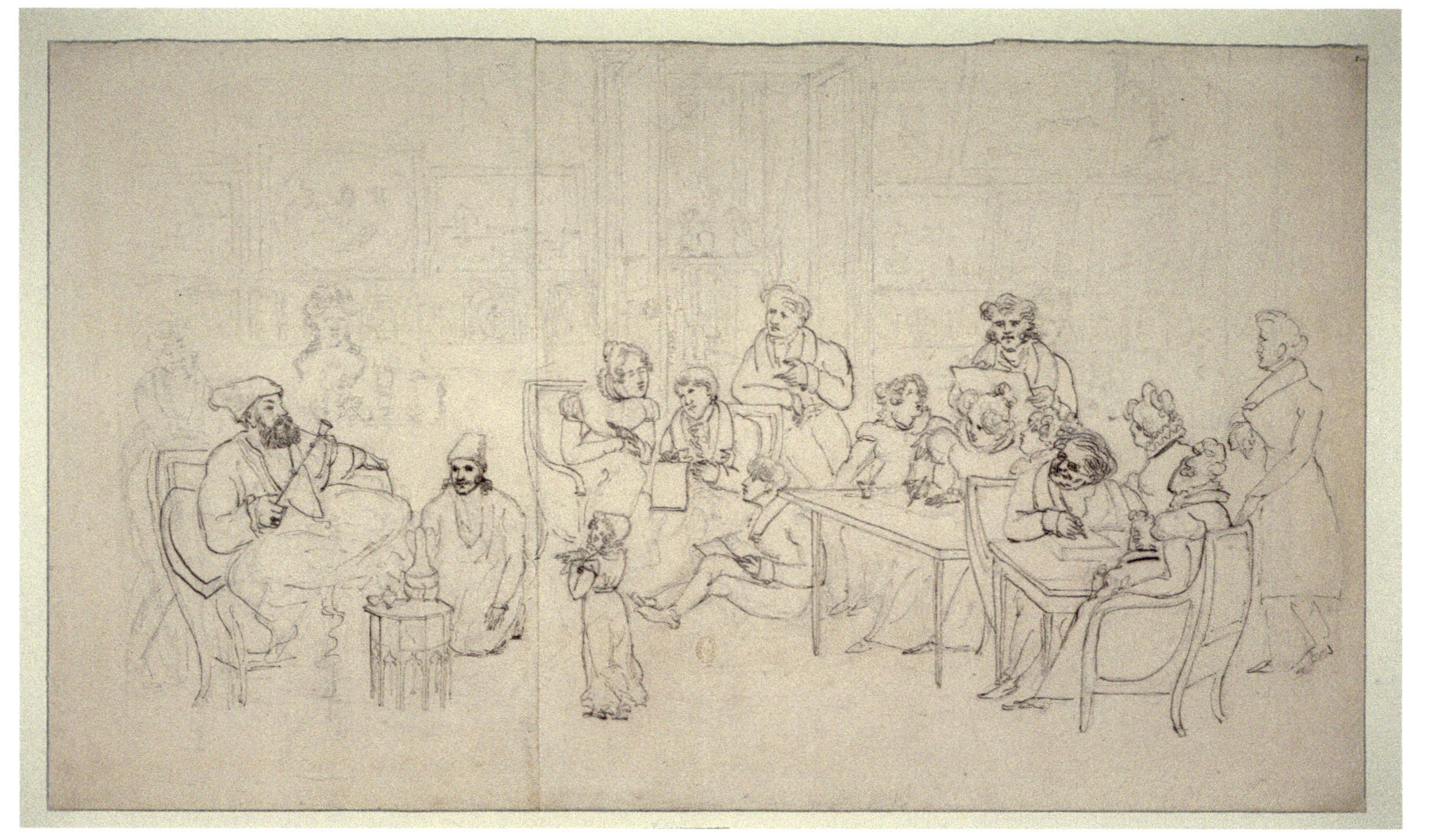

13   Dominique Vivant Denon, *Denon at home*, 1815–25. Pen and pencil on paper, 46 × 62 cm. Source: Bibliothèque Nationale de France, Paris.

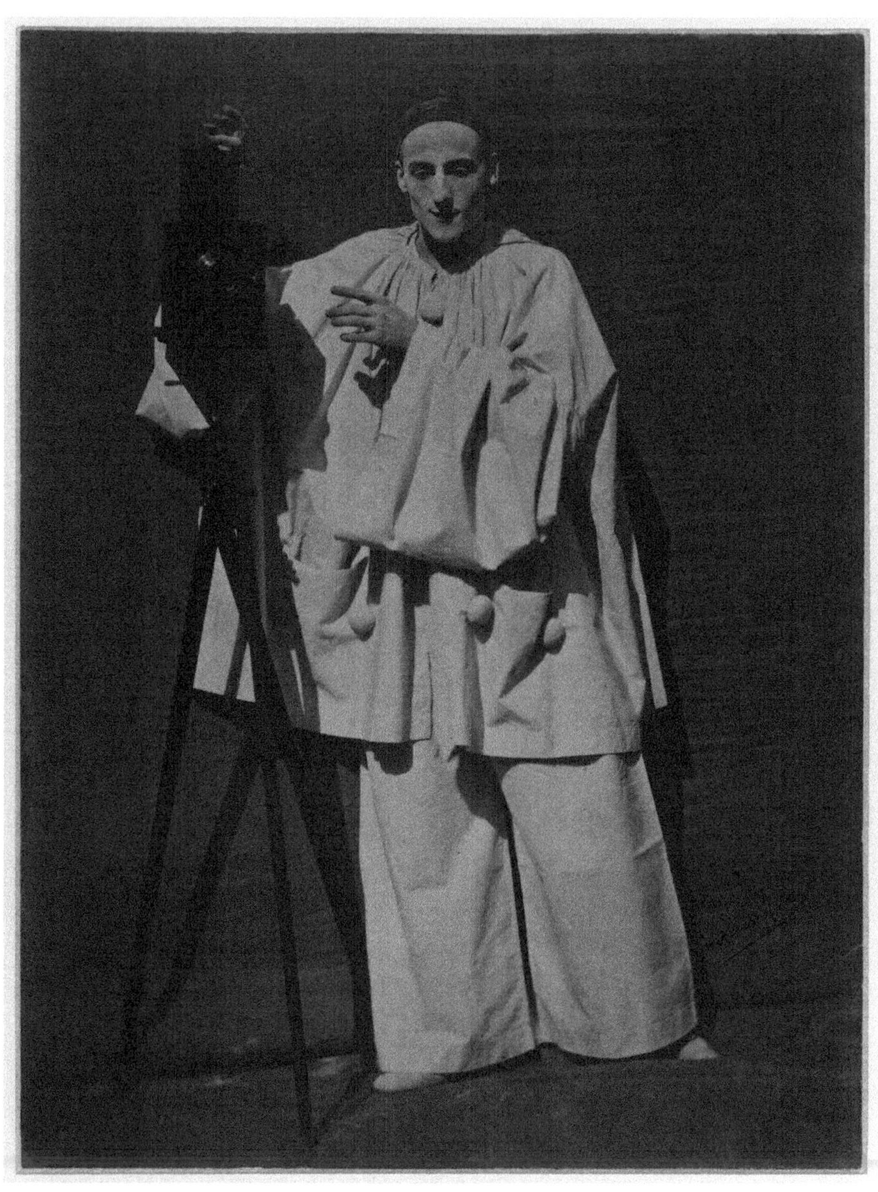

14   Nadar and Adrien Tournachon, *Pierrot the photographer*, 1854–55. Salted paper print, 27.3 × 20.1 cm. Source: Musée Carnavalet, Paris.

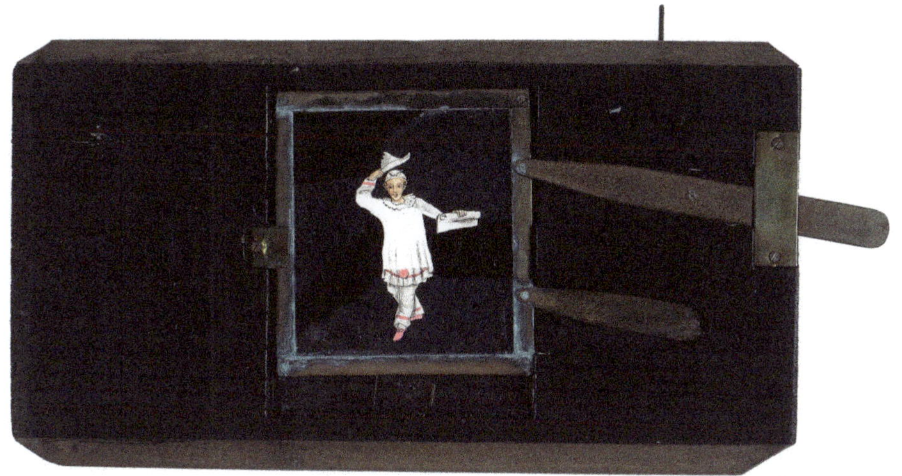

15   Magic lantern slide with two levers, *Pierrot says bonsoir*, late nineteenth century. Painted glass, 28.1 × 15.3 cm. Source: Cinémathèque française, Paris.

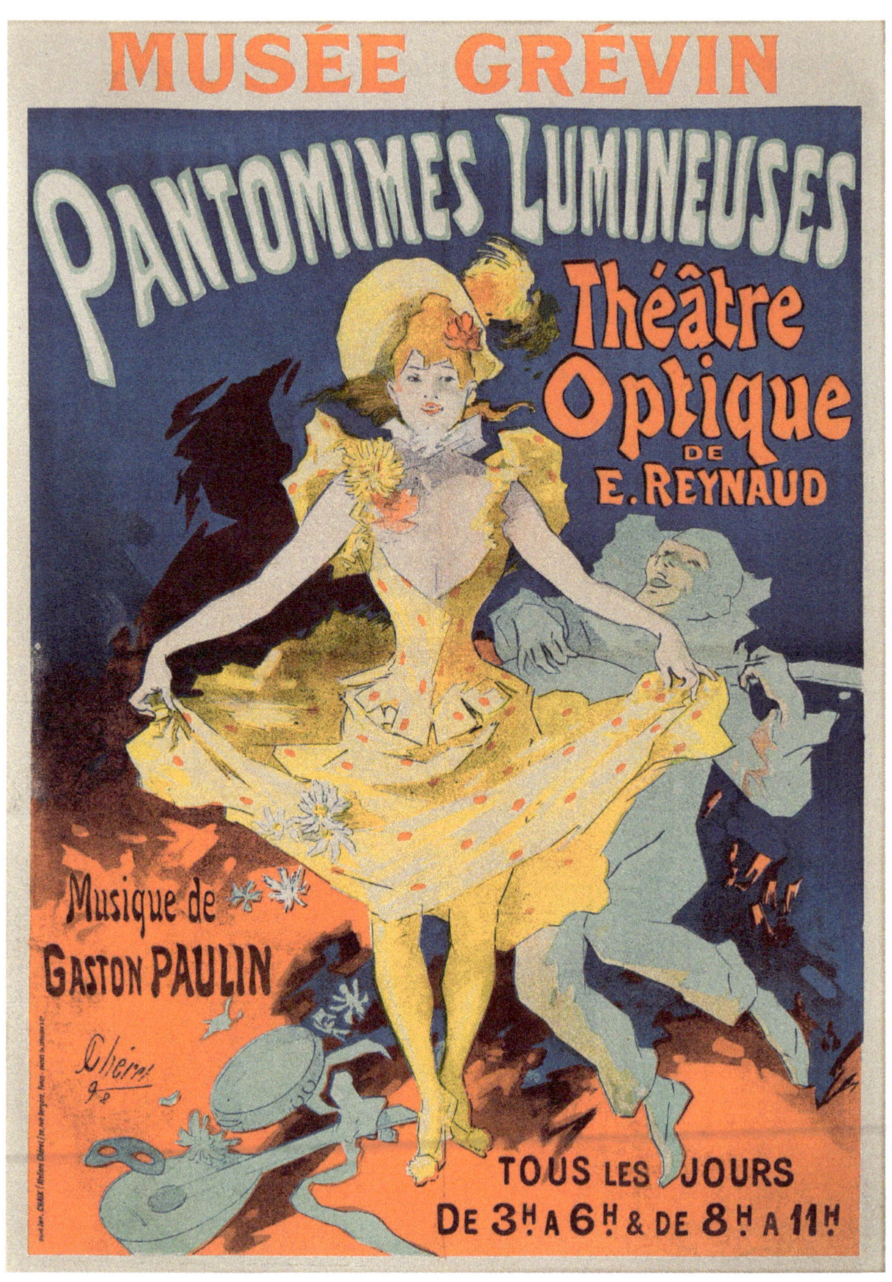

16   Jules Chéret, *Pantomimes lumineuses, théâtre optique de E. Reynaud*, 1892. Coloured lithograph, 88 × 124.6 cm. Source: Rijksmuseum, Amsterdam.

Pierrot *gamin*

Visitors to the Funambules claimed that Deburau's most devoted audience were the *gamins* of the quarter. A recurrent type in the *physiognomies*, the *gamin de Paris* was a young boy without a stable family life. He was truant, brazen, and cunning, an agile navigator of Parisian streets.[127] George Sand described the extensive, mute communication between the children in the paradise and Deburau on the stage of the theatre.[128] In Sand's account, the *gamin*, possessed of a special intelligence, which he shares with Deburau, observes the mime with great seriousness: 'they do not laugh much; they examine, they study'.[129] Sand's account represents the *gamin* as another privileged interpreter of modern visuality, in this case the special kind of expressiveness of Deburau's pantomime. Outside the theatre, these skills helped the *gamin* navigate the Parisian marketplace. In Ernest Bourget's *Physiologie du gamin de Paris, galopin industriel* (1842), he writes of the *gamin* who uses his street smarts to become a 'merchant of bric-à-brac', although his inventory is more sundry (toiletries and cigarettes) than second-hand.[130] Like the ragpicker, the *gamin* knows how to sift through the information presented by the street, to seize what is useful and ignore what is not. The *gamin* is often both duplicitous and theatrical in his self-presentation. A wood engraving accompanying Bourget's text shows a round-faced *gamin*, his hands in his pockets, clothed in ragged jacket and trousers, begging for 'five sous' for his household (Figure 3.7).[131] On a blanket in front of him sits a dish to collect coins, reminiscent of Pierrot's empty hat in Watteau's early studies for the curtain call. Bourget notes the *gamin*'s 'commercial tactic' of always 'shivering with cold even when it is twenty degrees'.[132] Manet's Pierrot does not have a blanket or a bowl, but like the *gamin* he addresses the marketplace by putting himself forward in an attitude that is both expectant and a bit miserable. Through the *gamin*, *The Old Musician* acknowledges yet another Parisian marketplace type, one with well-known links to the Funambules.

We are coming closer to seeing the many ways that *The Old Musician* registers and inflects the poetics of old things and the bric-à-brac taste. The composition of the painting itself is a patchwork, in which these figures made up of worn fabric surfaces are strung together like sausages and saucepans on a string above the stage of the Funambules. Manet has picked each of these rags and he presents them as Topino would: sorted and arranged according to type, not according to a story. Like the connoisseur of bric-à-brac, Manet has assembled a group of imperfect pieces from different eras. He has put them together in a panoramic gallery of the margins. With the same nonchalance that his ragpicker performs as he lifts his feet in a dance, Manet puts these figures together with performative negligence, as if he does not have the time to give their clothes a brushing or their faces a wash. The state of the figures' clothing is telling indeed, hinting at the presence in the painting of yet another figure from the *physiognomies* and the pantomime – the old-clothes seller.

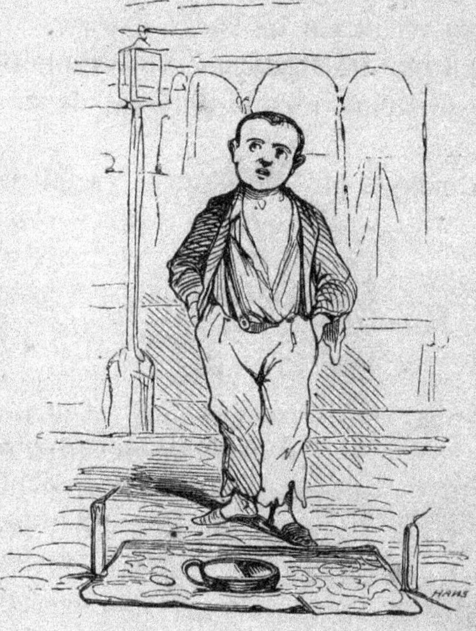

3.7   Louis Marckl, *Physiologie du gamin de Paris*, p. 11 (Paris: J. Laisné), 1842.
Lithograph. Source: Bibliothèque Nationale de France, Paris. 8-LI6–73 ©BNF.

Masquerade and old clothes

Manet's system of references is not stable or singular; figures in the painting refer to pieces of multiple traditions, as the old musician represents both the Greek philosopher and Velazquez's drinker. In this vein, the top-hatted ragpicker, Manet's citation of his own work as well as Watteau's, also suggests the old-clothes seller, another type featured in the *physiognomies*.[133] Like the ragpicker, the old-clothes seller was often shown wearing a top hat, which he had presumably bought off one of his clients (Figure 3.8). Old-clothes sellers purchased and resold used clothing, as well as the occasional non-textile fabric item. Honoré Daumier's old-clothes seller has also nabbed a guitar with which a young student might dress as a courtier from a *fête galante*. The lithograph's caption suggests that his business booms during carnival, but their merchandise was also bought as everyday attire.[134] They negotiated with clients in their homes and either sold on the garments to *fripiers*, who kept shops where old and new clothes were sold, or sold the clothes themselves on their peregrinations through the streets of Paris.[135] Walking through the streets, old-clothes sellers carried their merchandise slung over one arm, as Daumier's lithograph suggests, or hanging from a long pole, a kind of flag. Like most of the *petits métiers*, old-clothes sellers were depicted as acute readers of the urban landscape. As they trolled the streets, voicing their distinctive cry – 'seller of old clothes and braid!' ('*marchand d'habits galons!*') – they watched for movement at the windows of the buildings that lined the street. They detected the slightest flick of a curtain or movement of a shutter, the 'imperceptible sign' that an inhabitant of the building might be considering selling some of their clothes.[136] Occasionally, the old-clothes seller made a *trouvaille*, perhaps an eighteenth-century frock coat, the former garment of a *grand seigneur*, passed down from 'master to lackey, from the lackey to his children, from these to their distant relatives, surviving four generations'.[137] Joseph Mainzler, who wrote the *physiologie* of the old-clothes seller for *Les Français peints par eux-mêmes*, described the old-clothes seller, at such a moment, as experiencing 'the joy of a bibliophile resuscitating some old forgotten manuscript, or of a gourmet who pulls from the depths of a cave a bottle cloaked in ancient dust'.[138] With this description, the old-clothes seller is placed firmly within the poetics of old things, as possessed of the same kind of intelligence and sensibility as the bibliophile, the collector, and the ragpicker. Here is yet another type who knows how to appreciate what is old and how to distinguish between what is merely old and what is in fact a treasure.

The absinthe drinker in *The Old Musician* could be a ragpicker or an old-clothes seller. Certainly, the characters of the painting would have obtained their clothing second-hand, in the vast market for old clothes adjoining the Rotonde du Temple, or off the arm of the old-clothes seller.[139] Of particular note are the skirt and jacket worn by the girl on the left-hand edge of the composition, a barefoot figure represented in *profil perdu*, holding a blonde infant to her chest. A source for this figure has been identified in a contemporary print of a gypsy encampment.[140] Another possible precedent from the *physiologies* is the

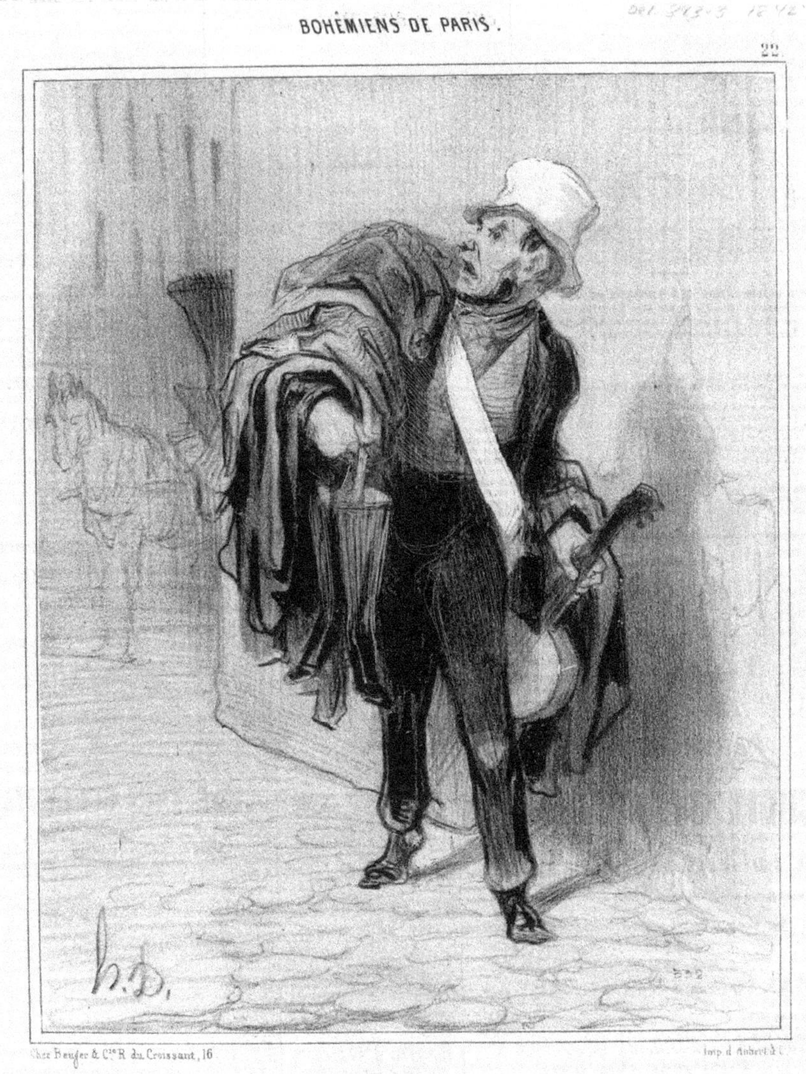

3.8   Honoré Daumier, *The old-clothes seller*, 1842. Lithograph on newsprint. Source: National Gallery of Art, Washington, DC. 1979.49.39 ©Courtesy the National Gallery of Art, Washington.

grisette, the young woman who has worked in shops or as a chorus girl (*figurant*) before being set up in a (modestly) furnished room by a lover.[141] Certainly, the figure in Manet's painting has lost her room. She has got drunk and quarrelled with her lover, or slept with her tailor, or had a child – the very one she holds in the painting. Yet a certain pert *chic* can still be identified in this girl, traceable to the *grisette* as a former milliner's assistant perhaps, and thus a skilled trimmer of used garments, lace, and ribbons, which she has bought at the Marché du Temple.[142] Her dress consists of the cast-offs of a better world, which she has caught as they fell. The jacket is a deep black, of a lustre that suggests velvet. It is neatly cut, nipped in at the waist with a little fantail. Equally interesting is the skirt, which is extremely ragged at the hem, but which appears to be made of one of the more expensive fabrics to be represented in the picture, an iridescent taffeta, a silk weave combining threads of blue and green. In painting the skirt in long strokes of black, green, and blue, Manet mimics the palette and the technique of eighteenth-century pastels. Yet he uses the darker strokes to evoke the mud that has been splashed onto these pastels over years. The suggestion of this mud has become part of the patina of the medium, part of the poetics of age. This skirt, perhaps, was once an old-clothes seller's *trouvaille*.

There is still another figure in the painting who alludes to the trade of the old-clothes seller. Noticeably cropped at the right edge of the canvas, the tall, narrow figure, with his fluffy white beard, turban-like head wrap, and speckled scarf, is recognisable as the Wandering Jew. The Wandering Jew was a popular Romantic archetype, but the 'legend' of this perpetual wanderer, condemned because he had refused the cross-bearing Christ a drink of water, had been widespread in European literature and lore since at least the early seventeenth century.[143] Having been cursed by Christ, the Wandering Jew had spent hundreds of years studying the world, contemplating his bad deed, and warning others not to follow his example. Manet's Wandering Jew corresponds almost point by point to Champfleury's description of the type in his *Histoire de l'imagerie populaire* (1869), the first chapter of which is entirely devoted to the Wandering Jew.[144] The author cites the Baron de Reiffenberg's account of the Wandering Jew as 'a man with a grey beard half-clad in a ragged tunic, covered down to his eyes in a dirty turban'.[145] Even more interestingly, this Wandering Jew, who turns up in Frankfurt, presents himself at the shop of a second-hand clothes dealer, a *fripier*, where he tries to use an ancient Roman coin to buy a fur-lined, satin robe.[146] The appearance of the Wandering Jew at the *fripier* is significant because this type would increasingly become associated with the figure of the old-clothes seller. Across the Channel in England, the old-clothes seller was already a Semitic type, referred to as the 'Jew Old-Clothes Man' in Henry Mayhew's *London Labour and the London Poor* (1861).[147]

The appearance of the Wandering Jew at the edge of the composition is one of the ways the painting thematises nomadic, itinerant lives. It is likely that Manet found his models in Little Poland, a shantytown on the outskirts of the Batignolles, the neighbourhood in which the painter had recently rented a studio. These gatherings of shacks and tents were built on the border of the encroaching city and the receding countryside. They gave shelter to the people who had been pushed out of the centre of the city by Haussmann's projects. Ragpickers made their homes there out of the materials they scavenged. Jean Lagrène, a Romani who lent his features to the figure of the musician, lived in Little Poland; Collardet may have lived there as well.[148] Manet's painting encodes the doubleness of panoramic vision. On the one hand, the panoramic view captured the vibrant spectacle of the new city's shop windows, with their colourful goods laid out to be seen. On the other, the panoramic mode was also necessary to capture those members of society who found themselves displaced and unfixed by the building of the boulevards. They too, were mobile, but in a different way.

The apparition of the Wandering Jew is also a sign that one way to read this painting is as a story of costume, of the surfaces that happen both in cloth and in paint, and of the feelings that line the wearing of these garments. Through old clothes, the painting returns to the theme of costume as a threshold of the market stage. I have focused on the classificatory and presentational aspect of the *physiognomies*, yet these were also representations that relied upon garments as identificatory surfaces, through which class and social type could be reliably interpreted. As Catherine Nesci has shown, the panorama of urban life was also figured through the language of cloth in the form of *chiffons*, a term that meant both rags (ragpickers were *chiffonnières*) and fabric.[149] Authors like Balzac, Janin, and Nerval were well-versed in this language, which compared the spectacle of Paris to a parade of cloth surfaces. These surfaces included rags, but also feminine finery like ribbons, shawls, and lace: the 'decorative surplus of the feminine masquerade'.[150] From some points of view, the figures in *The Old Musician* are dejected, at a loose end, yet there is also a way that they are deliberate, insistent in their presentation of themselves, and none more so than the tough little figure of Pierrot, with one fist clenched. He is not at ease in his costume, which is too big for him, but he is determined to stand there and present himself. This array of figures, plucked from the pages of the *physiognomies*, has an air of the costume ball, a patchy and reluctant approximation of glitzier festivities, but nevertheless a little ball held in the open air, a dusty *fête galante*. The old-clothes seller, or the old-clothes sellers, because there are two – the absinthe drinker and the Wandering Jew – attend the party both as purveyors of costume and as costumes themselves.

In *Marchand d'habits*, a pantomime performed in 1842 and probably written by Gautier, Pierrot murders an old-clothes seller in order to procure the costume of a nobleman.[151] While his crime buys him a meteoric social rise, ending with his engagement to a beautiful countess, the ghost of the old-clothes seller haunts him. In the end, Pierrot and the old-clothes seller tumble together into hell, skewered on the same sword, which had been one of the old-clothes seller's wares. This pantomime will only increase in importance as the years pass, becoming closely associated with Pierrot in the *fin-de-siècle* and one of the two pantomimes re-enacted at length in the film *Children of Paradise* (1945), which is discussed in Chapter 5. Some of Pierrot's desperate, menacing desire for new clothes (even if these 'new' clothes are second-hand) is legible in Manet's figure. Like the ragpicker in Traviès lithograph, Pierrot stares into the distance, dreaming of possession. He holds himself stiffly, committed to his surface, even in its poverty. Pierrot, once he sees the clothes on the old-clothes seller's arm, can never forget. Nor could Molière's Pierrot forget Don Juan's ribbons.

Old, Old Musician

Much has been made, and rightly so, of the novel spectacle of luxury goods for sale in the new Paris, a panorama of commodities in which 'the most unlikely objects were drawn into the same perceptual place', including 'glazed fruits at Tortoni's, fashionable dresses on the boulevards and the phantasmagoria of toys, paperweights and pictures in Susse or Giroux'.[152] I will turn to this vision of retail in Chapter 4. Yet, as the current chapter has emphasised, many of the things for sale in Paris were old. A vast marketplace for second-hand things unfolded alongside, or just beneath, the market for new things. For all the fruits at Tortoni's, there were the *arlequins*, the pot-luck of leavings from upper-class tables, sold by servants to taverns; for the all the precious little pictures in the window of Giroux, restored to a high varnish and set in glittering frames, there were the mud-streaked pastels on the quays or the 'Watteaux' sitting in the dirt outside the bric-à-brac shop. Finally, for all the beautiful people walking the passages, there were the working classes and the *classes dangereuses*, the families living in one room, with one cracked basin in which to wash, with one set of worn clothes. I want to emphasise that the marketplace for second-hand things was just as poeticised and mythologised as the marketplace for new things. Yet its poetics offered far more fertile ground to those critics who believed that they were too discerning to want new things, things without history, things that did not speak.

The Old Musician is steeped in this second-hand world, a tribute to the aesthetics of bric-à-brac and the poetics of old things. The painting presents its popular types as second-hand things. They are displayed as they might be in a shop window, laid out (*étalé*). It is a mixed lot. Manet's Pierrot is literally on the ground ('*étalé par terre*'), which was how Clément de Ris described Watteau's painting in the Carrousel du Louvre. The figures in *The Old Musician* are pre-used, both figuratively – borrowed from other works – and materially – they are tattered and shabby. This was how such types were expected to be seen; this was how they made sense to viewers who were used to the *physiognomies* and to the culture of bric-à-brac, these two presentational, panoramic modes that asked viewers to 'single out, sift, and move across'.[153] Yet Manet also lends gravity and weight to these figures, by presenting only six of them, each of whom is given a remarkable solidity, a dense texture of buttery paint, carefully modelled faces, built up out of viscous strokes. This treatment is very different from that allowed to the dense crowd of figures in the same artist's *Music in the Tuileries*, a much smaller painting, which he painted either at the same time, or immediately following *The Old Musician*. The contrast between these two paintings is significant. Arguably, they are pendants to one another, despite their difference in size. *Music in the Tuileries* is stuffed with figures: Gautier, Champfleury, and Baudelaire are all included, among others. Faceted as if seen through Baudelaire's kaleidoscope are top hats, cravats, patches of flesh, foliage, veils, and ribbon. It is possible to pick out the individual portraits if one knows where to look, but the overlapping figures are squeezed together, rendered with a modicum of strokes, all that can be fit onto faces that are not much bigger than small coins. While *Music in the Tuileries* represents the 'new Paris' and *The Old Musician* the 'old', it is the new and the old together that make up Manet's vision of the modern city. To represent the old, he cultivates slowness rather than speed, monumentality rather than fleetingness. This fits the territory, but what is new is Manet's willingness to show the age of the old things, to register in the texture of their garments their long journeys into the present. In 1860, he would have seen Watteau's *Pierrot* in the triumphant *parade* of French artistic achievement at the Galerie Martinet. However, the citation in *The Old Musician* embeds the painting's present success within the context of the marketplace and its vicissitudes, as well as its occasional serendipities. In *The Old Musician*, meaning accrues to Pierrot not just as a citation of a figure by Watteau, but as a citation of an object – the unwieldy painting that had once been unable to find a buyer. Manet's Pierrot, like Watteau's outside the bric-à-brac shop, has been waiting a long time.

Notes

1 T.J. Clark, *The Painting of Modern Life: Paris in the Art of Manet and his Followers*, rev. edn (Princeton, NJ: Princeton University Press, 1999), pp. 93–8.

2 Marilyn Brown, 'Manet's "Old Musician": portrait of a gypsy and naturalist allegory', *Studies in the History of Art* 8 (1978), 77–87.

3 On the ragpicker in this painting, see Ewa Lajer-Burcharth, 'Modernity and the condition of disguise: Manet's "Absinthe Drinker"', *Art Journal* 45:1 (1985), 18–26.

4 Anne Coffin Hanson, 'Manet's subject matter and a source of popular imagery', *Art Institute of Chicago Museum Studies* 3 (1968), 63–80; Anne Coffin Hanson, 'Popular imagery and the work of Édouard Manet', in Ulrich Finke (ed.), *French 19th Century Painting and Literature, with Special Reference to the Relevance of Literary Subject-Matter to French Painting* (Manchester: Manchester University Press, 1972), pp. 133–63; Theodore Reff, 'On "Manet's sources"', *Artforum* 8:1 (1969), 40–48.

5 Michael Fried, *Manet's Modernism, or, The Face of Painting in the 1860s* (Chicago: University of Chicago Press, 1996), pp. 23–135. This essay was originally published in *Artforum* (1969), after which Reff published his response, 'On "Manet's sources"', in the same journal.

6 Walter Benjamin, 'Panorama', in *Das Passagen-Werk*, ed. Rolf Tiedemann (Frankfurt am Main: Suhrkamp Verlag, 1982), 2:655–65. On this category and Benjamin's discussion of it in *The Arcades Project*, see Margaret Cohen, 'Panoramic literature and the invention of everyday genres', in Leo Charney and Vanessa R. Schwartz (eds), *Cinema and the Invention of Modern Life* (Berkeley: University of California Press, 1995), pp. 227–52, here pp. 228–30.

7 Rémy Saisselin, *Bricabracomania: The Bourgeois and the Bibelot* (London: Thames & Hudson, 1985). The French version of this text was available to me, so I have consulted that: Rémy G. Saisselin, *Le bourgeois et le bibelot*, trans. Jacqueline Degueret (Paris: Albin Michel, 1990).

8 For some archival leads into the eighteenth-century locale of the painting, see Jeannine Baticle, 'Pierrot, Gilles, et les autres', in François Moureau and Margaret Morgan Grasselli (eds), *Antoine Watteau (1684–1721): le peintre, son temps et sa légende* (Paris: Clairefontaine, 1987), pp. 37–41. Ultimately, Baticle's suggestions cannot be confirmed and significant objections have been raised regarding her proposal.

9 These arguments are summarised in Christian Michel, *Le 'célèbre' Watteau* (Geneva: Droz, 2008), p. 269.

10 It is Michel who suggests that Jullienne and Gersaint bought the remainder of Watteau's studio, which they asked Jean-Baptiste Pater to complete: Michel, *Le 'célèbre' Watteau*, pp. 43–4.

11 Pierre Hédouin, 'Watteau III', *L'Artiste*, ser. 4, 5:5 (1845), 78–80, here p. 79.

12 J. de la Tynna, *Almanach du Commerce de Paris, des Départements de l'Empire Français, et des Principales Villes du Monde* (Paris, L'an VII – 1808). Period orthography often confused 'r's and 'z's.

13 For a comprehensive biography of Denon, see Jean Chatelain, *Dominique Vivant Denon et le Louvre de Napoléon* (Paris: Librairie Académique Perrin, 1973).

14 The powerful dealer and advisor to the crown, Alexandre-Joseph Paillet, founded the auction house at the Hôtel Bullion in 1778. See Patrick Michel, *Le commerce du tableau à Paris dans la seconde moitié du XVIIIe siècle* (Villeneuve d'Ascq: Presses Universitaires du Septentrion, 2007), pp. 249–50.

15 Michel Beurdeley, *La France à l'encan, 1789–1799: exode des objets d'art sous la Révolution* (Paris: Librairie Jules Tallandier, 1981), p. 95.

16 David A. Wisner, 'Jean Naigeon at the Dépôt de Nesle', *Journal of the History of Collections* 8:2 (1996), 155–65.

17 On the conflicts of interest at the heart of the formation of the new national collections, see Charlotte Guichard, 'Le marché au coeur de l'invention muséale? Jean-Baptiste-Pierre Lebrun au Louvre (1792–1802)', *Revue de synthèse* 132:6:1 (2011), 93–117.

18 On the circulation of artworks during the Revolutionary era, see Roberta Panzanelli and Monica Preti-Hamard (eds), *La circulation des oeuvres d'art 1789–1848* (Rennes and Los Angeles: Universitaires de Rennes and Getty Research Institute, 2007).

19 Gabriele Sprigath, 'Sur le vandalisme révolutionnaire (1792–1794)', *Annales historiques de la Révolution française* 52:242 (1980), 528–31.

20 For an outstanding description of the Revolutionary and post-Revolutionary art market, see Tom Stammers, *The Purchase of the Past: Collecting Culture in post-Revolutionary Paris, c1790–1890* (Cambridge: Cambridge University Press, 2020), pp. 27–68.

21 On Denon's activity as a buyer and seller of paintings see Benjamin Peronnet, 'Denon, collectionneur typique ou atypique?', in Daniela Gallo (ed.), *Les vies de Dominique-Vivant Denon: actes du colloque organisé au Musée du Louvre* (Paris: la Documentation française, 2001), pp. 741–59.

22 Fausta Garavini (ed.), *Lettres à Bettine* (Arles: Actes Sud, 1999), letter of 24 February 1794, pp. 290–92: 'boutique ouverte' and 'bien-garnies de curiosités'.

23 Garavini (ed.), *Lettres à Bettine*, letter of 13 February 1794, p. 285: 'revue perpétuelle'; letter of 3 March 1794, p. 293: 'un spectacle fort intéressant'.

24 Chatelain, *Dominique Vivant Denon*, pp. 88–93.

25 For an authoritative catalogue of Denon's Imperial career, see Marie-Anne Dupuy (ed.), *Dominique-Vivant Denon: l'œil de Napoléon* (Paris: Réunion des Musées nationaux, 1999). On Denon's official functions and occasional conflicts of interest with David, see Pierre Lelièvre, *Vivant Denon: Homme des Lumières, "Ministre des arts" de Napoléon* (Paris: Picard, 1993), pp. 101–14.

26 On Denon's role as a decorator, see Chatelain, *Dominique Vivant Denon*, p. 192, pp. 207–8. See also related letters in Marie-Anne Dupuy (ed.), *Vivant Denon, directeur des musées sous le Consulat et l'Empire: correspondance 1802–1815* (Paris: Réunion des musées nationaux, 1999), letters no. 427, 493–4, 496, 509, 515, 726, 964. On Denon's work as a dealer for Josephine, see Alain Pougetoux, 'Le directeur et l'impératrice', in Gallo (ed.), *Les vies de Dominique-Vivant Denon*, pp. 105–17.

27 On the emergence of the second-hand market for luxury goods, see Natacha Coquery, 'Luxury goods beyond boundaries: the Parisian market during the Terror', in Johanna Ilmakunnas and Jon Stobart (eds), *A Taste for Luxury in Early Modern Europe: Display, Acquisition and Boundaries* (London: Bloomsbury Academic, 2017), pp. 283–302.

28 Stammers, *The Purchase of the Past*, pp. 56–7.

29 Pierre Gault de Saint-Germain, for example, viewed most dealers and collectors as motivated solely by greed: Stammers, *The Purchase of the Past*, pp. 62–5. Many dealers and auctioneers did act unscrupulously, fiddling with inventories and valuations in order to secure the best prices for themselves, funnelling treasures across the Channel to avid English buyers: Sprigath, 'Sur le vandalisme révolutionnaire', p. 530.

30 Stammers, *The Purchase of the Past*, pp. 56–60. See also the interesting description in Edmond Bonnaffé, *Le commerce de la curiosité* (Paris: Honoré Champion, 1895), p. 65.

31 Louis-Sébastien Mercier, 'Sur le dépôt des Petits-Augustins, dit le Musée des Monuments français', *Journal de Paris*, 2 October 1797, 42–3, here p. 42: 'un spectacle unique, le plus curieux, le plus imposant, le plus neuf qui ait frappé a la fois mon oeil et mon imagination; les Saints & les Dieux mytologiques [sic], Les héros, les vierges, les antiques, les cardinaux, les vases étrusques, les bénitiers, les medaillons, les colonnes, les bustes, les statues colossales de Charlemagne et de Saint Louis', 'jeté au hasard'.

32 I am paraphrasing here: Mercier, 'Sur le dépôt des Petits-Augustins', 43: 'cette collection magnifiquement confuse, poétiquement désordonnée'.

33 Mercier, 'Sur le dépôt des Petits-Augustins', 43: 'toutes ces statues me parloeint [sic], parce que le hazard les avoit disposés d'une manière éloquente'.

34 Mercier, 'Sur le dépôt des Petits-Augustins', 43: 'sont redevenues muettes'.

35 In negotiating the spectacle provided by the depot, Mercier uses the techniques that he cultivated as a narrator of Paris, the results of which he had published in the two-volume *Tableau de Paris*. See Jean-Claude Bonnet, 'Mercier et l'art du recyclage', *Revue d'histoire littéraire de la France* 118:3 (2018), 517–22.

36 'Vente du cabinet de M. Denon', *Le Globe*, 6 May 1826.

37 C. Harmand, *Manuel de l'amateur des arts dans Paris pour 1824* (Paris, 1824), pp. 161–3.

38 A.N. Pérignon, *Description des objets d'arts qui composent le cabinet de feu m. le baron V. Denon* (Paris: Hippolyte Tilliard, 1826).

39 Denon was a much more responsible, systematic collector for Napoléon's Louvre, where he amassed and displayed choice masterpieces from the different European

schools: Andrew McClellan, *Inventing the Louvre: Art, Politics, and the Origins of the Modern Museum in Eighteenth-Century Paris* (Cambridge: Cambridge University Press, 1994), pp. 140–48.

40 Garavini (ed.), *Lettres à Bettine*, letter of 24 February 1794, p. 290.

41 Chatelain, *Dominique Vivant Denon*, p. 91.

42 On these categories in the eighteenth century, see Krzysztof Pomian, 'Marchands, connaisseurs, curieux à Paris au XVIIIe siècle', *Revue de l'art* 43 (1979), 23–36.

43 Patrick Michel, *Peinture et Plaisir: Les goûts picturaux des collectionneurs parisiens au XVIIIe siècle* (Rennes: Presses Universitaires de Rennes, 2010), pp. 17–19; Charlotte Guichard, *Les Amateurs d'art à Paris au XVIIIe siècle* (Seyssel: Champ Vallon, 2008), pp. 15–17.

44 See, for example, Adolphe Thibaudeau, 'Lettre à l'auteur, sur la curiosité', in Charles Blanc, *Le trésor de la curiosité* (Paris: Jules Renouard, 1857), 1:i–cxxxii, here 1:iii–vii.

45 Guichard, *Les amateurs d'art à Paris*, p. 17.

46 Jean de La Bruyère, *Les caractères ou les mœurs de ce Siècle*, ed. Robert Pignarre (1691; Paris: Garnier-Flammarion, 1965), p. 338: '[i]l retrouve ses oiseaux dans son sommeil: lui-même il est oiseau, il est huppé, il gazouille, il perche; il rêve la nuit qu'il mue ou qu'il couve'.

47 Adams has discussed the new emphasis, in the post-Revolutionary art market, on 'a personal connection with the artist's work': Steven Adams, '"Noising things abroad": art, commodity, and commerce in post-Revolutionary Paris', *Nineteenth-Century Art Worldwide* 12:2 (2013), www.19thc-artworldwide.org/autumn13/adams-on-art-commodity-and-commerce-in-post-revolutionary-paris, accessed 28 April 2023.

48 Champfleury, *L'hôtel des commissaires-priseurs* (Paris: E. Dentu, 1867), p. 64: 'des toiles que n'oserait étaler un brocanteur du quai de l'Hôtel-Dieu'.

49 On Denon as a mythologist, see Marie-Hélène Girard, 'Denon et la notion de monument', in Francis Claudon and Bernard Bailly (eds), *Vivant Denon: colloque de Chalon-sur-Saône, 14 et 15 Mai 1999* (Chalon-sur-Saône: Université pour tous de Bourgogne, 1998), pp. 35–50. On a famous forgery by Denon, see Elaine Williamson, 'A *vraie-fausse* statue of William the Conqueror: representation and mis-representation of Anglo-French history', *Franco-British Studies* 19 (1995), 21–5.

50 Tom Stammers, 'The bric-à-brac of the *ancien régime*: collecting and cultural history in post-Revolutionary France', *French History* 22:3 (2008), 295–315.

51 On Amaury Duval's participation in the project and possible changes to the text resulting from his intervention, see Barbara Steindl, 'La documentation graphique sur la collection de Vivant Denon et *Les Monuments des Arts du Dessin*', in Gallo (ed.), *Les vies de Dominique-Vivant Denon*, 771–807.

52 Alain de Leiris, 'Manet, Guéroult and Chrysippos', *The Art Bulletin* 46:3 (1964), 401–4.

53 Reff, 'On 'Manet's sources'", p. 43. See also my own discussion of citations in this painting: Marika Takanishi Knowles, 'Affect, citation, and rapt looking in Manet's *The Old Musician*', *Word & Image* 34:2 (2018), 111–25.

54 Fried, *Manet's Modernism*, pp. 28–48.

55 Juliet Wilson-Bareau, 'Manet and Spain', in Gary Tinterow and Genevieve Lacambre (eds), *Manet/Velazquez: The French Taste for Spanish Painting* (New York: The Metropolitan Museum of Art, 2003), pp. 203–51.

56 Fried, *Manet's Modernism*, pp. 71–84.

57 On this extraordinary neighborhood, see Carl de Vinck, *Place du Carrousel* (Paris: Société d'Iconographie Parisienne, 1931).

58 Paul Bénichou, *L'école du désenchantement: Sainte Beuve, Nodier, Nerval, Gautier* (Paris: Gallimard, 1992).

59 Marika Takanishi Knowles, 'The microcosm as interior in Théophile Gautier's "Marilhat"', in Anca I. Lasc (ed.), *Visualizing the Nineteenth-Century Home: Modern Art and the Decorative Impulse* (New York: Routledge, 2016), pp. 3–18. See also René Jasinski, *Les années romantiques de Théophile Gautier* (Paris: Librairie Vuibert, 1929).

60 Gérard de Nerval, *Petits châteaux de Bohême* (Paris: Eugène Didier, 1853), pp. 7–8, p. 12. On the post-1830 market for second-hand things, see Tom Stammers, 'Scavenging rococo: *trouvailles*, *bibelots* and counter-revolution', in Katie Scott and Melissa Hyde (eds), *Rococo Echo: Art, Theory and Historiography from Cochin to Coppola* (Oxford: Oxford Studies in the Enlightenment, 2015), pp. 71–85, at pp. 76–7.

61 Théophile Gautier, *L'Art Moderne*, ed. Corinne Bayle and Olivier Schefer (1856; Lyon: Fage éditions, 2011), p. 98.

62 Carol Duncan, *The Pursuit of Pleasure: The Rococo Revival in French Romantic Art* (New York: Garland Publishing, 1976), pp. 18–19, 28–9. See also Jacques-Henry Bornecque, *Lumières sur les fêtes galantes de Paul Verlaine: avec le texte critique des Fêtes galantes* (Paris: Nizet, 1959), pp. 24–34.

63 On Nerval's interest in the rococo, see Marika Takanishi Knowles, 'Time-chaste damsels: Ingres, Nerval, and *Sylvie*', *RES: Anthropology and Aesthetics* 73/74 (2020), 140–54, here pp. 151–3.

64 Théophile Gautier, *Poésies Complètes* (Paris: Charpentier, 1858), p. 181.

65 Gautier, *Poésies Complètes*, p. 181: 'le vent d'hiver', 'vous n'avez plus que des mouches de boue', 'sur les quais vous gisez tous salis'.

66 Gautier, *Poésies Complètes*, p. 181: 'un peu pâles, comme il convient à des fleurs de cent ans'.

67 Gautier, *Poésies Complètes*, p. 181: 'il est passé le doux règne des belles'.

68 Charles Baudelaire, *Oeuvres complètes*, ed. Claude Pichois (Paris: Gallimard, 1975), 2:85–6.

69 On the critical response in 1860, see Knowles, 'Affect, citation, and rapt looking', 115–17.

70 Pérignon, *Description des objets d'art*, pp. 86–7, cat. no. 187.

71 On Brunet Denon's collection see A.J., 'Collections de curiosités et d'objets d'art: Cabinets de MM. Denon, Sauvageot et de Guignes', *L'Artiste*, ser. 1, 9:12 (1835), 141–3. In 1838, Brunet Denon sold the painting to the Marquis de Cypierre, an amateur of distinguished lineage who bought, restored, and sold eighteenth-century canvases. Sometime before his death in 1844, Cypierre sold the painting, at a loss, to Louis La Caze or his intermediary. Cypierre's log book indicates that he bought the painting in 1838 from Brunet-Denon for 4,000 francs and sold it to an unknown buyer – probably la Caze or his agent – for 2,500 francs: H. Demoriane, 'Le *Gilles* de Watteau', *Connaissance des Arts* 270 (1974), 34–5.

72 Victor Fournel, *Les spectacles populaires et les artistes des rues* (Paris: E. Dentu, 1863), p. 372.

73 Edward Nye, 'The pantomime repertoire of the Théâtre des Funambules', *Nineteenth Century Theatre and Film* 43:1 (2016), 3–20, here p. 5. Older, but useful biographical sources on Deburau include Louis Péricaud, *Le Théâtre des Funambules*,

ses mimes, ses acteurs et ses pantomimes, depuis sa fondation, jusqu'à sa demolition (Paris: Léon Sapin, 1897); Tristan Rémy, *Jean-Gaspard Deburau* (Paris: L'Arche, 1954).

74 On nineteenth-century theatres, décors, tricks, and other special effects, see M.J. Moynet, *L'envers du théâtre: machines et décorations* (Paris: Hachette, 1873); Georges Moynet, *La machinerie théâtrale: trucs et décors* (Paris: Librairie Illustrée, 1893).

75 The *féerie* was a major genre in nineteenth-century popular theatre; see Roxane Martin, *La féerie romantique sur les scènes parisiennes, 1791–1864* (Paris: Honoré Champion, 2007). On the décor of the *féerie* see Marie-Françoise Christout, 'La féerie Romantique au théâtre: de la *Sylphide* (1832) à *La Biche au bois* (1845), chorégraphies, décors, trucs et machines', *Romantisme* 12:38 (1982), 77–86.

76 For an analysis of Deburau's popularity both with 'le peuple' and the critics, see Edward Nye, 'Jean-Gaspard Deburau: romantic Pierrot', *New Theatre Quarterly* 30: 2 (2014), 107–19.

77 For the first edition see Jules Janin, *Deburau, l'histoire du théâtre à quatre sous* (Paris: C. Gosselin, 1832). This text was stitched together from Janin's *feuilletons* about Deburau, although some new material was added. For the most part, I cite directly from those publications rather than the collection.

78 George Sand, 'Deburau' (February 1846), in *Questions d'art et de littérature* (Paris: C. Lévy, 1878), pp. 215–22.

79 Champfleury, *Contes d'Automne* (Paris: Victor Lecou, 1854). When he published it in 1854, it was called *Contes d'Automne*, but the text is identical to that published under the new title in 1859: Champfleury, *Souvenirs des Funambules* (Paris: Michel Lévy frères, 1859). Citations are from the 1859 edition.

80 Gérard Fritz, *L'idée de peuple en France du XVIIe au XIXe siècle* (Strasbourg: Presses Universitaires de Strasbourg, 1988), pp. 80–92 for the negative characterisation of *le peuple* in the early nineteenth century, pp. 93–116 on the more positive views from the same period. Jules Michelet, George Sand, and the socialist Pierre-Joseph Proudhon were important advocates of a relatively new kind of humanitarianism, which ascribed both misery and innate nobility to *le peuple*.

81 Bertrand Tillier, 'Jules Janin, chiffonnier, antiquaire et naturaliste de Paris', *Revue d'Histoire littéraire de la France* 118:3 (2018), 599–610, at p. 608.

82 Jules Janin, 'Théâtre Français: première représentation du *Nègre*, drame en quatre actes et en vers libres, par M. Ozanneaux', *Journal des débats*, 1 November 1830, 1–3, here p. 3.

83 Janin, 'Théâtre Français', p. 3.

84 Jules Janin, 'Les petits métiers', in *Paris, ou le livre des cent-et-uns* (Paris: Chez Ladvocat, 1832), 4:317–42, here 4:329–31.

85 Janin, *Deburau*, pp. 234–52.

86 Janin, *Deburau*, p. 246.

87 Janin, 'Théâtre Français', p. 3.

88 Janin, 'Théâtre Français', p. 3.

89 On Champfleury see the old, but still essential Émile Bouvier, *La bataille réaliste* (Geneva: Slatkine Reprints, 1973). On Champfleury and the Funambules, see Robert Storey, *Pierrots on the Stage of Desire: Nineteenth-century French Literary Artists and the Comic Pantomime* (Princeton, NJ: Princeton University Press, 1985), pp. 36–73.

90 Champfleury, *Souvenirs des Funambules*, p. ii. Republishing previously published material was not an unusual practice for authors who published frequently in the *feuilleton*.

91 Champfleury, *Souvenirs des Funambules*, p. 263.

92 Champfleury, *Souvenirs des Funambules*, pp. 5–6.

93 Champfleury, *Souvenirs des Funambules*, p. 86, italics original.

94 On Champfleury's collection, see the useful catalogue by Luce Abélès (ed.), *Champfleury: L'art pour le peuple* (Paris: Réunion des Musées Nationaux, 1990).

95 Bernard Vouilloux, 'Champfleury, ou l'écrivain-collectionneur en chiffonnier', *Revue d'histoire littéraire de la France* 118:3 (2018), 623–36, here p. 632.

96 Champfleury, *Souvenirs des Funambules*, p. 79.

97 Champfleury, *Souvenirs des Funambules*, pp. 80–81.

98 On Champfleury's fragmentary mode of composition, see Sara Pappas, 'The lessons of Champfleury', *Nineteenth-Century French Studies* 42:1–2 (2013–14), 51–73.

99 Champfleury, *Les aventures de mademoiselle Mariette*, 3rd edn (Paris: Michel Lévy, 1857), p. 76.

100 Champfleury, *Les aventures de mademoiselle Mariette*, p. 76.

101 Hanson, 'Manet's subject matter', p. 72. Hanson cites A. Tabarant, *Manet et ses oeuvres* (Paris: Gallimard, 1947), p. 28, which is not an entirely reliable source, but given the widespread iconography of the ragpicker as a top-hat-clad drinker, there is at least some intention to evoke the type, if not to replicate it entirely.

102 Richard Sieburth, 'Une idéologie du lisible: le phénomène des physiologies', *Romantisme* 47 (1985), 39–60. See also the useful discussion of the *physiologies* in Antoine Compagnon, *Les chiffonniers de Paris* (Paris: Gallimard, 2017), pp. 209–43.

103 Sieburth, 'Une idéologie du lisible', p. 42.

104 Dietmar Rieger, '"Ce qu'on voit dans les rues de Paris": marginalités sociales et regards bourgeois', *Romantisme* 59 (1988), 19–29, here pp. 20–22.

105 Louis André, *Machines à Papier en France 1789–1860* (Paris: Éditions de l'école des hautes études en sciences sociales, 1996), pp. 21–54.

106 Barrie M. Ratcliffe, 'Perceptions and realities of the urban margin: the rag pickers of Paris in the first half of the nineteenth century', *Canadian Journal of History* 27 (1992), 197–233, here p. 214.

107 The vogue for ragpickers as emblematic urban scavengers began during the Revolution, when popular prints represented ragpickers as members of 'the research committee', an early instrument of Revolutionary surveillance: Compagnon, *Les chiffonniers de Paris*, pp. 191–201.

108 For the text of the poem as it appeared in the 1861 edition of *Les fleurs du mal*, see Claude Pichois and Jacques Dupont (eds), *L'atelier de Baudelaire: Les Fleurs du Mal, édition diplomatique* (Paris: Honoré Champion, 2005), 2:2825–6.

109 Charles Baudelaire, 'Du vin et du hachish, comparés comme moyens de multiplication de l'individualité', *Le Messager de l'Assemblé*, 8 March 1851. A facsimile of this text is reproduced in Pichois and Dupont (eds), *L'atelier de Baudelaire*, 2:2810–12, here 2:2811. Walter Benjamin believed Baudelaire recognised the affinity between poet and ragpicker because both 'derive their heroic subject' from the city's waste: Walter Benjamin, *Charles Baudelaire: A Lyric Poet in the Era of High Capitalism*, trans. Harry Zohn (London: Verso, 1973), p. 79.

110 Jules Janin, 'Horace et le chiffonnier', *Les Guêpes*, February 1843, 56, cited in Compagnon, *Les chiffonniers de Paris*, p. 333.

111 Ségolène Le Men, 'Chiffonniers de papier', *Revue d'histoire littéraire de la France* 118:3 (2018), 559–70, here p. 564.

112 Compagnon, *Les chiffonniers de Paris*, p. 343.

113 See the cover of the *Journal Amusant*, 166, 5 March 1859.

114 The first instalment of the novel appeared in *L'opinion nationale* on 5 September 1859.

115 On Topino and his poster museum, see Emma Bielecki, '"Un artiste en matière de chiffons": the rag-picker as a figure for the artist in Champfleury's *La Mascarade de la vie Parisienne*', *Nineteenth-century French Studies* 37:3–4 (2009), 262–75; Ségolène Le Men, 'Le portrait du collectionneur en chiffonnier, vu par Champfleury (1859)', in Jacques Guillerme (ed.), *Les collections: fables et programmes* (Seyssel: Champ Vallon, 1993), pp. 275–82.

116 Champfleury, 'L'oncle Topino (Suite), *La mascarade de la vie parisienne*', *L'opinion nationale*, 17 September 1859, 1–3, here p. 1.

117 Champfleury, 'L'oncle Topino, *La mascarade de la vie parisienne*', *L'opinion nationale*, 16 September 1859, 1–3, here p. 2.

118 Compagnon, *Les chiffonniers de Paris*, pp. 281–8.

119 Sieburth, 'Une idéologie du lisible', p. 42.

120 Patrice Thompson, 'Essai d'analyse des conditions du spectacle dans le Panorama et le Diorama', *Romantisme* 38 (1982), 47–64, here pp. 52–3.

121 I am particularly indebted to the remarkable account of the spectacle of commodities in Nicholas Green, *The Spectacle of Nature: Landscape and Bourgeois Culture in Nineteenth Century France* (Manchester: Manchester University Press, 1990), pp. 28–41, here p. 31. On the transformation of viewing Paris into viewing images, and the permeability of seeing and 'imagerie' see Philippe Hamon, *Imageries: littérature et image au XIXe siècle*, rev. edn (Paris: José Corti, 2001), pp. 27–31.

122 Sieburth, 'Une idéologie du lisible', pp. 41, 50: 'désir du public de voir son espace comme une scène ou une galerie', 'la ville comme un assemblage de différentes spécialités en vitrine'. See also Saisselin, *Le bourgeois et le bibelot*, pp. 39–51.

123 On this kind of differentiation and its orientation towards the market, see the remarkable article, Jillian Taylor Lerner, 'The French profiled by themselves: social typologies, advertising posters, and the illustration of consumer lifestyles', *Grey Room* 27 (2007), 6–35, here pp. 22–6.

124 Green, *The Spectacle of Nature*, p. 31.

125 Edward Nye, 'The romantic myth of Jean-Gaspard Deburau', *Nineteenth-Century French Studies* 44:1–2 (2016), 46–64, here p. 50.

126 Émile Goby, *Pantomimes de Gaspard et Charles Deburau* (Paris: E. Dentu, 1889), pp. 227–42.

127 Marilyn Brown, *The Gamin de Paris in Nineteenth-Century Visual Culture: Delacroix, Hugo, and the French Social Imaginary* (New York: Routledge, 2017). This source is absolutely key.

128 On Deburau's style of pantomime, which combined the aesthetic transformation of gesture with a kind of visual *argot*, see Judith Wechsler, *A Human Comedy: Physiognomy and Caricature in Nineteenth Century Paris* (Chicago: University of Chicago Press, 1982), in particular Chapter 2, 'Deburau and the Théâtre des Funambules, the literary marionettes'.

129 Sand, 'Deburau', p. 217: 'ils ne rient pas beaucoup; ils examinent, ils étudient …'.

130 Brown, *The Gamin de Paris*, p. 57.

131 Brown has noted the resemblance between this figure and Manet's Pierrot: Brown, *The Gamin de Paris*, p. 82.

132 Ernest Bourget, *Physiologie du gamin de Paris, galopin industriel* (Paris: J. Laisne, 1842), p. 11: 'notez bien qu'il grelotte toujours de froid même par vingt degrés de chaleur. – Ceci est une recommandation maternelle et toute commerciale.'

133 As a type, the old-clothes seller was related to the ragpicker; the two were occasion-
    ally confused, or attributes exchanged between them: Compagnon, *Les chiffonniers
    de Paris*, pp. 295–301, at p. 296.

134 Joseph Mainzler, 'Le marchand d'habits', in *Les Français peints par eux-mêmes.
    Encyclopédie morale du dix-neuvième siècle* (Paris: L. Curmer, 1841), 5:250–56.

135 On *fripiers* see Daniel Roche, *La culture des apparences: une histoire du vêtement
    XVIIe–XVIIIe siècle* (Paris: Fayard, 1989), pp. 327–8.

136 Mainzler, 'Le marchand d'habits', 5:253.

137 Mainzler, 'Le marchand d'habits', 5:254: 'du maitre au laquais, du laquais à ses
    enfants, de ceux-ci à des collatéraux, survivant à quatre générations'.

138 Mainzler, 'Le marchand d'habits', 5:254: 'la joie du bibliophile ressuscitant quelque
    vieux manuscrit oublié, ou celle du gastronome qui tire des profondeurs d'un
    caveau une bouteille parée d'une poudre semi-séculaire'.

139 On the Rotonde du Temple, see Philippe Perrot, *Les dessus et les dessous de la
    bourgeoisie, une histoire du vêtement au XIXe siècle* (Paris: Fayard, 1981), pp. 78–92.

140 Hanson, 'Popular imagery', p. 146. The work is a painting by Henri-Guillaume
    Schlesinger, *The Kidnapped Child*, exhibited at the Salon in 1861 and published as a
    wood engraving in *Le magasin pittoresque* the same year.

141 On the *grisette* see Abigail Solomon-Godeau, 'The other side of Venus: the visual
    economy of feminine display', in Victoria de Grazia and Ellen Furlough (eds), *The
    Sex of Things: Gender and Consumption in Historical Perspective* (Berkeley: University
    of California Press, 1996), pp. 113–50, here p. 141.

142 On *grisettes* and other women haunting the second-hand clothes markets in Paris,
    see Perrot, *Les dessus et les dessous de la bourgeoisie*, p. 80.

143 George K. Anderson, *The Legend of the Wandering Jew* (Providence, RI: Brown
    University Press, 1965), pp. 53–9. On the Wandering Jew in Courbet and Realism,
    see Linda Nochlin, 'Gustave Courbet's meeting: a portrait of the artist as a
    Wandering Jew', *The Art Bulletin* 49:3 (September 1967), 209–22.

144 Champfleury, *Histoire de l'imagerie populaire* (Paris: E. Dentu, 1869), pp. 1–104.

145 Champfleury, *Histoire de l'imagerie populaire*, p. 18.

146 Champfleury had been amassing material on the Wandering Jew for two dec-
    ades prior to his book's publication. Manet could have encountered this passage
    through Champfleury, or through the original source by the Baron de Reiffenberg.
    See Frédéric Auguste Ferdinand Thomas de Reiffenberg, *Souvenirs d'un pélerinage en
    l'honneur de Schiller* (Bussels and Leipzig: C. Muquardt, 1839).

147 Compagnon, *Les chiffonniers de Paris*, pp. 181–2.

148 Marilyn Brown, 'Manet's "Old Musician"', p. 79.

149 Catherine Nesci, *Le flâneur et les flâneuses: les femmes et la ville à l'époque romantique*
    (Grenoble: Université Stendhal, 2007), pp. 171–231, 391–4.

150 Nesci, *Le flâneur et les flâneuses*, p. 202: 'le surcroît décoratif de la mascarade
    féminine'.

151 Théophile Gautier, 'Shakespeare aux Funambules', in *L'art moderne* (Paris: Michel
    Lévy, 1856), pp. 167–79.

152 Green, *The Spectacle of Nature*, p. 31.

153 Green, *The Spectacle of Nature*, p. 31.

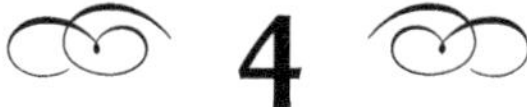

Nadar charlatan

'You will have to be free of any entanglements', 'Colonel' Tom Parker tells the singer in the Baz Luhrmann biopic *Elvis* (2022), 'the fans need to believe that you are always available'. Young Elvis gives his assent and, with a jerk, the seat of the Ferris wheel in which he is suspended flies upwards. The camera pans out, showing the seat as it swings through the sky above the twinkling lights of a carnival. This schlocky moment has a lot to say about Pierrot's history in the second half of the nineteenth century. The single, unpartnered celebrity lends themself to the fantasies of their audience. This freedom from entanglements enables the celebrity 'to fly' – Elvis tells his manager he is 'ready to fly' – a metaphor that confuses the celebrity's imagined life in the mind of their fans with the arc of their actual career. Except that these are, increasingly, the same. The most famous performer is the one who burns most vividly in the minds and memories of their audience.

Within a few years of its invention in 1839, photography had become instrumental in helping celebrities fly, by circulating the image of the celebrity far and wide. A key event in the partnership between photography and celebrity was the Universal Exposition (*Exposition universelle*) of 1855, where the Tournachon brothers (Félix and Adrien) exhibited a series of photographs of Charles, the son of Baptiste Deburau, in the costume of Pierrot. The photographs crystallised nascent strategies for publicising literary and artistic celebrity, many of which had been pioneered by Félix, the older of the two brothers, who would go on to be known by the moniker 'Nadar'. Towards the end of *Elvis*, 'Colonel' Tom Parker is revealed as a charlatan, a term that deserves parsing in this context because Nadar, as I will argue, was also a charlatan. Parker is a charlatan because he is an impostor who claims to be American and to have served in the military. Yet more importantly, for my purposes, he is a charlatan in the sense of a hawker who markets his wares through fictions and performances. As for the goods he sells, Parker trades in the image of his performer, which he multiplies through a vast merchandising campaign. To call Nadar, the most famous and esteemed photographer of nineteenth-century France, a charlatan is not to castigate his work but to emphasise his embeddedness within a world in which celebrity personalities were made and marketed. In this crucial series of photographs of Charles Deburau as Pierrot, Nadar freed Charles, and Pierrot, of entanglements.

It should be noted that the Tournachons' 'new' Pierrot preceded Manet's 'old' Pierrot by at least six years. I discussed Manet's painting first because it is about what came before the photographs, reference to which Manet rather pointedly omits from *The Old Musician*. Yet it could have been the photographs themselves, or the spectacle of the Universal Exposition, which spurred Manet's turn to another kind of marketplace. In this chapter, I situate the Tournachons' photographs within the context of the Universal Exposition, a massive marketplace for the promotion of France as a cosmopolitan, industrial, world capital. While Watteau's *Pierrot* would enter the Musée du Louvre in 1870, the Pierrot that emerged through photography, at the Universal Exposition, would continue the character's address to the marketplace through the *fin-de-siècle* and the emergence of cinema. To prosper in these media, Pierrot would become increasingly spectral, his groundlessness visualised as weightlessness. The Tournachons' photographs are at the start-point of this trajectory, for having discovered that Pierrot lends himself to dreams of flight.

Marketing photography at the Universal Exposition

The Universal Exposition was organised by the administration of the emperor Napoléon III, who hoped to rival Britain's Grand International Exhibition of 1851, at Crystal Palace. The primary displays were housed in the 'Palace of Industry', which boasted an Italianate limestone façade enveloping a central hall of iron and glass.[1] Exhibitions of agriculture and horticulture lay outside the hall, as well as an exhibition of machines, a sales hall, and a purpose-built hall for an enormous show of fine arts.[2] Nearly 5 million tickets were sold to the Palace of Industry, while close to a million visitors attended the exhibition of fine arts, where Ingres, Delacroix, Vernet, and Descamps were presented as the mastheads of the French School.[3] In the Palace of Industry, goods were arranged by country of manufacture and by category. Among the French industries featured were printing, porcelain, pottery, metalwork, shoe-making, woodwork, glass, and crystal. Exhibitions of textiles took up nearly half of France's ground-floor real estate: types of fabric included merinos, velvet, lace, crinolines, different types of cotton, linen, and hemp (*toile*).

The pre-eminence of fabric is a reminder of the kinship between the Universal Exposition and the eighteenth-century fairs, particularly the Foire Saint-Germain, which originated as a fabric market. Like the fair, the Palace of Industry was a purpose-built structure, set aside from the city and offering the display of goods as a form of spectacle and a leisure-time activity. Booths, stalls, and counters were arranged in a grid-like fashion, recalling the neat rows of boutiques at the fair (see Figures 1.3 and 4.1).

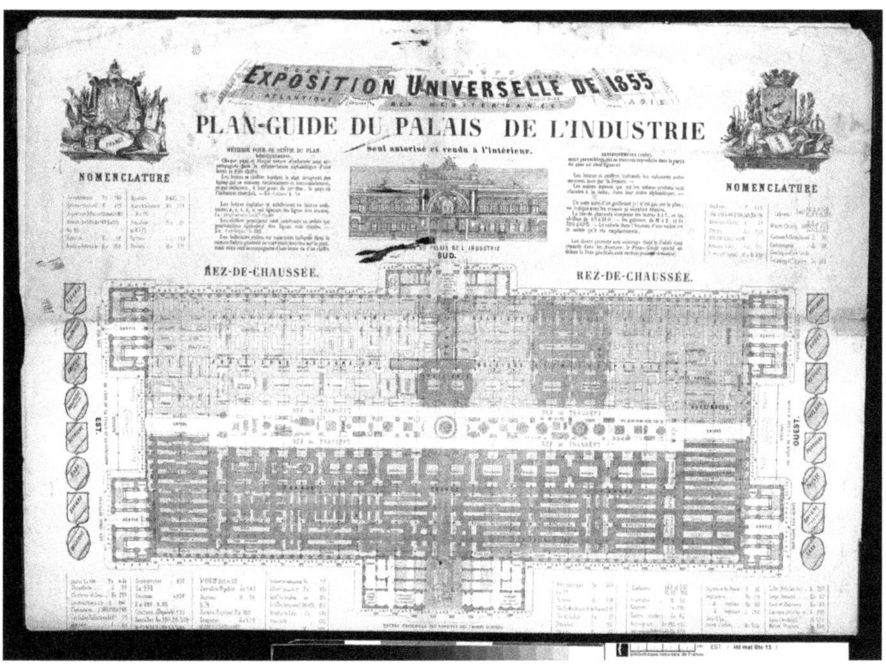

4.1   *Plan-guide to the Palace of Industry*, 1855. 49 × 40 cm. Source: Bibliothèque Nationale de France, Paris. HD MAT1-BT 13 ARCHITECTURE CIVILE ©BNF.

Members of a range of social classes attended the exhibition, although the cost of admission excluded the poorest Parisians. There were crucial differences, however, between the fair and the Exposition. There were no theatres within the Palace of Industry, no jugglers, acrobats, or other live performers. The goods displayed in the palace could not be bought on site because they were samples. Nevertheless, many objects were exhibited with price tags, a nod to the fixed prices of the Parisian department store, the first of which had opened in 1852.[4] Presumably, goods displayed in the Palace of Industry could be ordered or bought at the salesroom (*comptoir des ventes*) located across the Allée d'Antin. Finally, while the Foire Saint-Germain had hosted the boutiques of *marchands de tableaux*, there were no paintings displayed or for sale in the Palace of Industry. To an extent, this absence reflected the fact that, in the years that separated Watteau's frequenting of the Parisian fairs and the Universal Exposition, painting had succeeded in attaining the coveted status of a liberal art, as opposed to an artisanal practice catering to the marketplace. Over the course of the eighteenth century, the exhibition of painting had become an important foundation of Parisian public life, an opportunity for the performance of disinterested aesthetic discourse.[5] Of course, as Chapter 3 showed, works of art both new and old remained goods for sale, exhibited in the windows of picture dealers and bric-à-brac sellers. In 1855, the existence of a separate locale for the display of fine arts drew a distinction that may in fact have remained somewhat tenuous.

For the moment, however, the teenaged medium of photography was still rooted in the marketplace. It was in the Palace of Industry that photographs were exhibited, classified under 'Design and plastic arts applied to industry' (*Dessin et plastique appliqués à l'industrie*).[6] The French section featured the works of around forty French photographers and studios.[7] In the different national sections further photographs could be found, with the English having staged a particularly ample display. The French display consisted of two, facing structures of three-and-a-half bays each, as well as the outer walls, where more photographs were hung. To the north, the photography section was flanked by displays of hemp (*toile*), ropes, and instruments for carding and spinning fabric; to the south it was adjacent to displays of ivory and furniture. On walls draped in black velvet, framed paper prints and daguerreotypes were densely packed. Genres exhibited included portraits, landscapes, architectural photographs, and still lifes. Reproductive photography, or the photography of famous works of art, was another important category at the exhibition, which featured photographs of works by Rembrandt, Marc-Antonio Raimondi (after Albrecht Dürer), and Jean Le Pautre.[8] As an art 'applied to industry', the photographic exhibition also included photographs of things made by industry, from exquisite Sèvres vases to swatches of fabric and samples of furniture.[9] Photographs of flowers or still lifes including plants also offered industrial applications, if used as models by designers of ornament or textile patterns.

The most popular photographic displays were the portraits of political and theatrical celebrities.[10] These were money-makers for photographers. Photographs of celebrities could be sold to journals for reproduction as prints, which could also be sold as loose sheets in printer's shops, like the boutique shown in Traviès' lithograph (see Figure 3.5). As photography on paper increasingly superseded the daguerreotype, photographic portraits could be printed in multiples (without having to be translated into engraving or lithography) and sold directly from the photographer's studio. In printed frames emblazoned with the name of the photographer, these portraits advertised both the celebrity and the studio.

The photographs of Pierrot, exhibited in the booth of 'Nadar jeune', were one of the exhibition's most popular attractions. According to Ernest Lacan, who wrote a multi-instalment review of the photography exhibition for *Lumière*, 'amongst all these specimens, those that have most excited the interest of the public, and before which few visitors pass without stopping, are the *Pierrots*, as they are called by the crowd'.[11] The display included at least eight large-format photographs on paper, printed from glass negatives.[12] Pierrot, in these photographs, was played by Charles Deburau, the son of Baptiste Deburau, the Pierrot who had made the role iconic at the Théâtre des Funambules. Charles wears his father's version of the Pierrot costume, although with expanded proportions and more structural volumes: a trapeze tunic with overstuffed buttons, wide-legged trousers (see Plate 14). Like his father, Charles sports

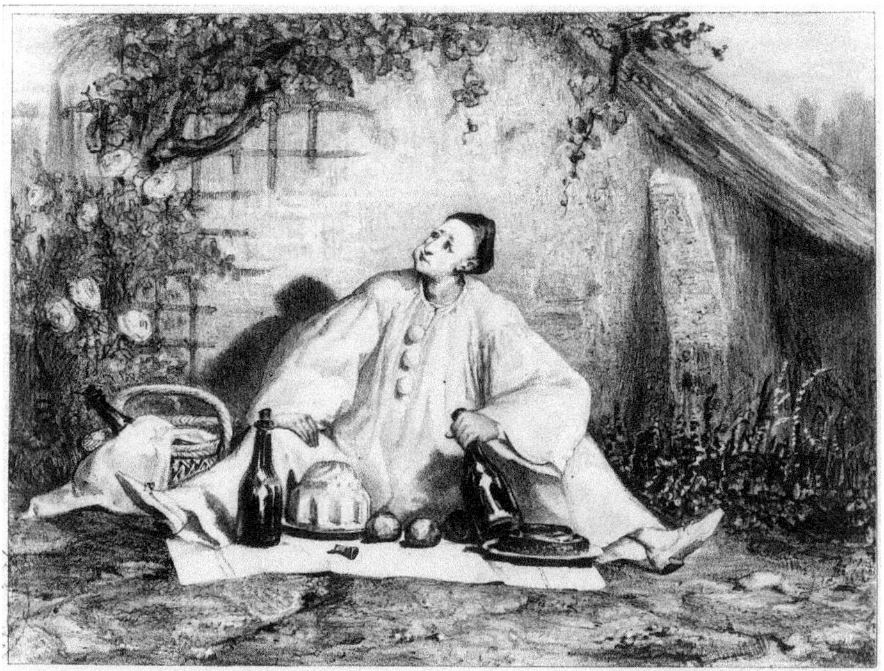

4.2   Delaunois after Auguste Bouquet, *Pierrot's feast in Le Boeuf enragé*, 1826.
Lithograph, 15 × 22 cm. Source: Bibliothèque Nationale de France, Paris. 4-RO-11521
©BNF.

a skullcap framing a long, narrow face powdered in a thick layer of white.
During Baptiste's heyday at the Funambules, portraits and other illustrations
of him had frequently appeared in books and in the popular press.[13] Baptiste
was shown 'at home' in an opulent study or leaning over a stone balustrade.
He was shown onstage, in his role, surrounded by the props from his closet
(Figure 4.2). The Tournachons' photographs, however, announce a bold new
aesthetic, eliminating Pierrot's historical setting as well as any stage décor,
except, in the series' most famous photograph, a camera (see Plate 14). It is as
if the dark fabric backdrop behind Charles is present, at worst because it has
to be – the glass plates were square – and at best as a source of pure contrast,
against which Pierrot can stand out. As a result, these photographs market
Pierrot alone, not Pierrot of the Funambules. Two different sets of artists –
Tournachons and Deburaus – contributed to the genesis of these unusual photographs, the motivation for which was in no small part market-driven.

Tournachons and Deburaus

As the end of 1854 drew near, Félix Tournachon, known in Paris as 'Nadar',
was still looking for his big break. A journalist, caricaturist, and theatrical

impresario, Nadar had long been a fixture of Parisian bohemia, the world of writers, courtesans, actors, artists, and the wealthy individuals whose money supported these lifestyles in various degrees of comfort. Like other bohemians, Nadar frequented the Funambules, where he met Champfleury, Nerval, and Gautier. In 1854, Nadar had been working for about five years as a successful caricaturist, a close collaborator of the media entrepreneur Charles Philipon, who ran the journals *La Caricature* and *Journal pour Rire*, and who had also published as many as half of the Parisian *physiognomies*.[14] One of Nadar's most celebrated contributions to *Journal pour Rire* was his series the *Lanterne magique des auteurs et journalistes*, caricatures of contemporary literati who appeared as if projected by a magic lantern slide (Figure 4.3). By at least 1853, Nadar was also dabbling in photography.[15] In early 1854, he installed his ne'er-do-well younger brother Adrien as a commercial photographer in a studio on the Boulevard des Capucines.[16] Always alert to opportunity, Nadar may have hoped to use Adrien as a test case for the financial and creative potential of the new medium. In addition, he may have wanted Adrien to assist him in his most recent undertaking, an intermedial Comédie Humaine, the 'Panthéon Nadar'.[17] This hugely ambitious scheme was planned as a series of four very large lithographic prints, to be accompanied by a textual component, the intended character of which remains unknown.[18] Each print would assemble portrait charges of the celebrities of a different branch of French arts: literature, theatre, the fine arts, and music. The *Panthéon* was envisioned as a caricatural Parnassus, of sorts, offering not only a catalogue of contemporary French creativity, but as well the potential of caricature to represent history. It was also intended to make money.

The *Panthéon* was a strange, clunky project in which Nadar insisted on his particular vision of celebrity. In the first sheet, the only one to be realised, the literary celebrities are cast in a parade that snakes its way down the sheet as if in a feast day procession (Figure 4.4). This is very different from the lithographic portrait in an illustrated journal, in which a Balzac or a Lamartine appears distinguished and at home, elegantly dressed, lost in thought. Instead, the bodies of the authors jostle against one another as they make their way through a stony terrain. Nadar's *Lanterne magique* had also used a 'processional' approach, placing the full-length figures of each black-suited author in a row, each hanging onto the coattails (literally) of the author before him, with Victor Hugo reluctantly leading the way. The parade of figures enabled a panoramic mode, in which figures are presented side by side, while also offering a very loose sense of temporal progression.[19] Both the *Panthéon* and the *Lanterne magique* represent Nadar's insistence, at this point in his career, that celebrity be marketed as a full-length human figure who would be presented to their public in a theatrical mode. Part of the consequence of presenting the authors at full length meant that they were seen as if on a stage. While this mode of presentation was of course indebted to the costume print, there was little that was distinctive in the authors' dress. All the stakes of showing the full-length figure fell then on the way that this format made the author available – as a

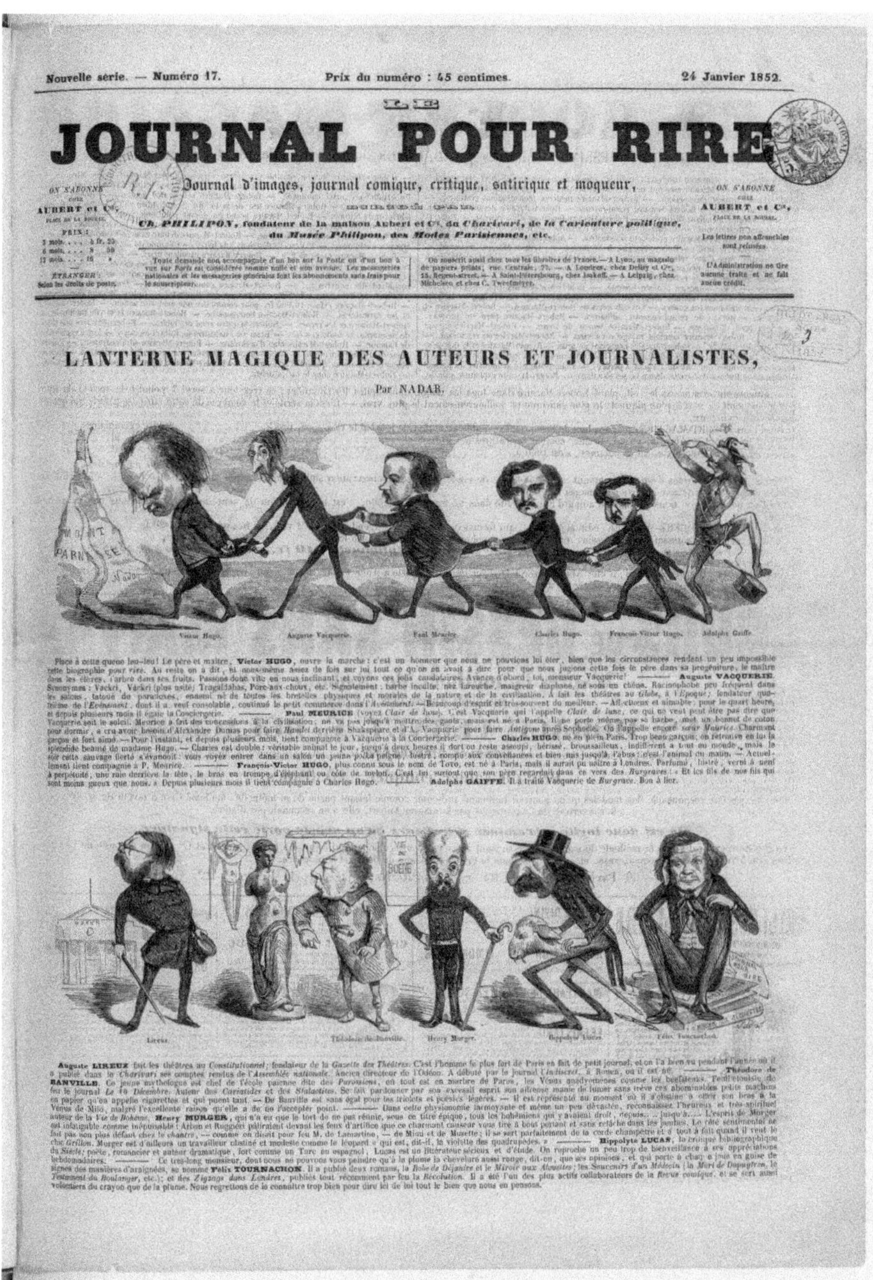

4.3   Nadar, *Magic Lantern of Artists and Journalists*, 1852. Wood engraving. Source: Bibliothèque Nationale de France. FOL-LC2–1681 ©BNF.

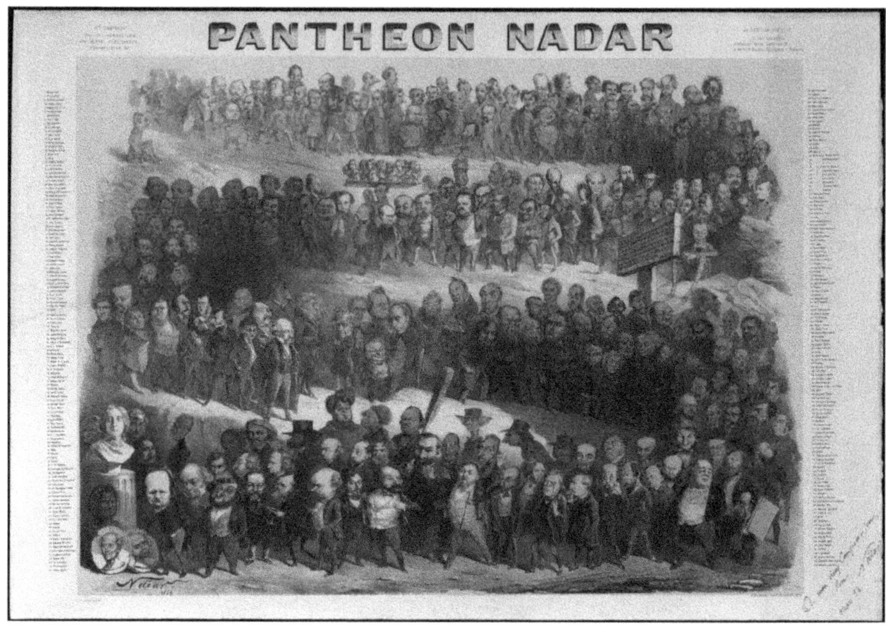

4.4   Nadar, *Panthéon Nadar*, 1854. Lithograph, 81.9 × 114.9 cm. Source: Metropolitan Museum of Art, New York. 1993.1079 ©metmuseum.org.

figure – to the viewer. The lithographic process for producing the *Panthéon* was laborious, requiring every one of the hundreds of celebrities to be drawn from life and then transformed into a *charge*, a large head atop a tiny body.[20] Despite being widely publicised 'in the windows of all the print merchants', as Gautier reported, sales were disappointing.[21] To add to Nadar's troubles, by September 1854 Adrien's photography studio was already mired in financial difficulty. Nadar, recently married, began to spend most of his time at the studio at 11 Boulevard des Capucines.

Meanwhile, at the Théâtre des Funambules, Charles Deburau, son and heir of Baptiste, was also struggling. The heyday of the Romantic pantomime was long past. Baptiste had died in 1846. Some accounts claimed this beloved Pierrot had been fatally injured when he fell through a trap on the stage at the Funambules.[22] Charles had been trained by his father, to whom he bore a remarkable resemblance. The Deburaus had long, oval faces and sharp features. When covered in a thick layer of white stage makeup, they produced astonishingly expressive grimaces that could be seen from a good distance. Tall and thin, they flitted about the stage like spidery ghosts. Nevertheless, Charles struggled to attain his father's supremacy at the Funambules. Baptiste had been both elegant and hysterically funny. He could project the 'grace of a marquis' at one moment, devour a roast chicken in two bites, and then writhe on the ground with horrible indigestion.[23] According to contemporary accounts, Charles had the refinement of his father, but lacked the earthier comic touch.[24] Without this, it was difficult for him to earn the loyalty of the crowd that packed the paradise. Nor was Charles the only Pierrot in Paris; he had a significant rival in another of his father's protégés, Paul Legrand.[25] The heavy-set Legrand was a different kind of Pierrot, jollier than the Deburaus, less physically supple, but gifted with excellent comic timing. The Romantic accounts of Pierrot had insisted upon the importance of Deburau's milieu: his seedy, dim theatre that smelled of gas, his raucous audience in the paradise. Yet in 1855, owing to the continuing rivalry with Legrand, Charles was considering a departure from the Funambules in order to self-produce at his own theatre.

The details of the collaboration between the Tournachons and Charles are unclear. Both parties needed a boost, a means to distinguish themselves from rivals – other Pierrots, other family members, other photographers. In 1848, Nadar had penned a 'republican pantomime', *Pierrot ministre*, for Charles.[26] This existing relationship suggests that Nadar may have initiated the series, rather than Adrien. Whatever the case, in the winter of 1854–5, Charles posed for Félix and Adrien in full makeup and costume, standing against a plain cloth background. For each of the photographs, Charles strikes a different pose: he runs (Figure 4.5), he begs for money from his master, he examines a basket of exotic fruits (Figure 4.6), he gasps in surprise, he grimaces and clutches his belly (Figure 4.7), having eaten and drunk too much. Shadow picks out Charles's angular features, his strong brows and prominent cheekbones. The fabric of his costume is stiff and architectural, the shape of the tunic like a pyramid, the creases harbouring valleys of darkness.

The generic affiliation of these photographs is difficult to pin down. This is at least one of the reasons why this series is regarded as crucial to emergent theories of photography as a 'fine art', because the series demonstrates photography's ability to reference and to subvert a variety of purposes.[27] Arranged by an artist who had long worked as a caricaturist, the photographs may have been intended to spoof the physiognomic series. Adrien had recently collaborated on such a series with the scientist Duchenne de Boullogne. As '*têtes d'expression*', Charles's photographs were goofy rather than grave, preferring to present comic states like indigestion rather than the emotions associated with serious intrigues. The series may also provide a meditation on wordless communication, as Rosalind Krauss has suggested.[28] Deburau *père* had been renowned for his ability to communicate without words, using his face primarily. The photographs of his son explore the expressive potential of the entire surface of Pierrot's costume, with its ripples and valleys of shadow, its pendulous buttons. The story that I wish to trace here, however, is about the way these photographs enact the theatricality of the marketplace.

Photography and commercial culture

In 1855, many photographers and critics were troubled by the Exposition's classification of photography as an industrial art.[29] The critical treatises devoted

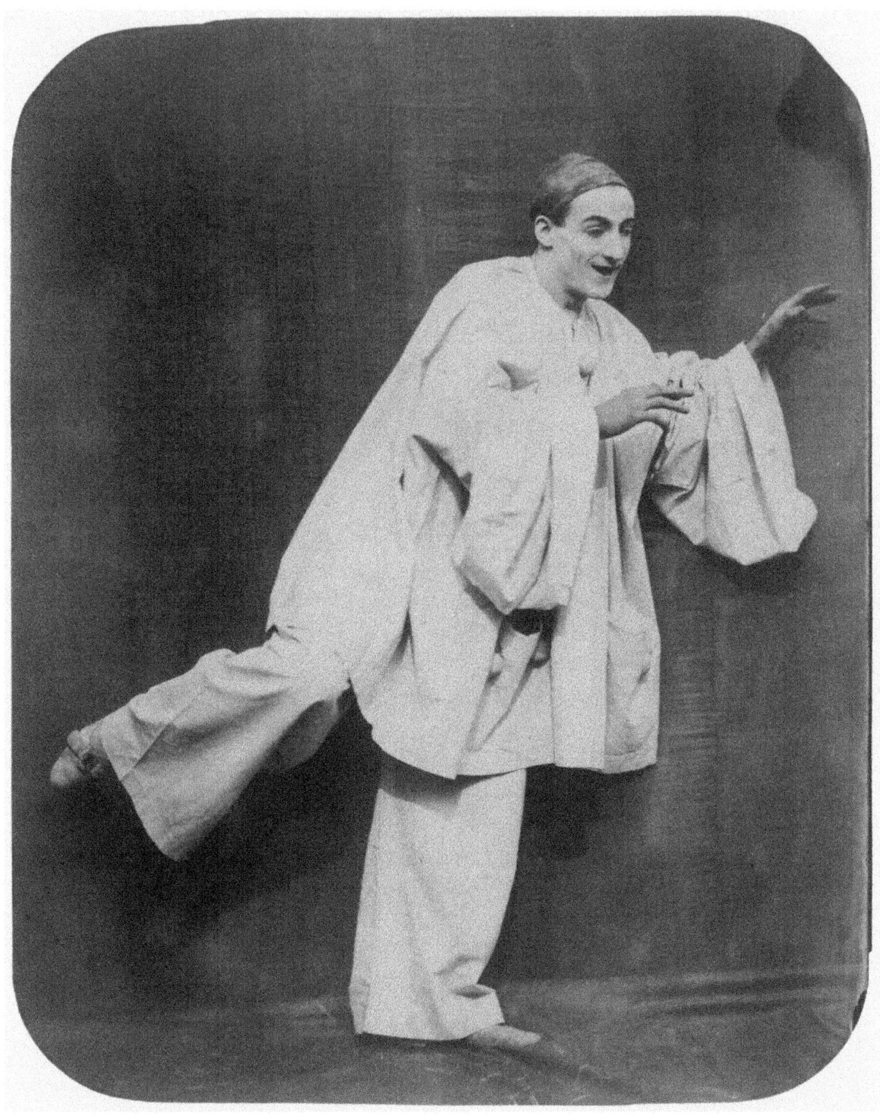

4.5　Nadar and Adrien Tournachon, *Pierrot running*, 1854–5. Albumen silver print from a glass negative, 26.5 × 20.8 cm. Source: Metropolitan Museum of Art. 2005.100.43 ©metmuseum.org.

to the exhibition by distinguished amateurs of photography made a point of distinguishing between photographers who deserved the title of artists and hacks who did not. Defenders of photography as art argued that taste and a painterly eye were necessary for producing attractive compositions. Adrien's compositions, for example, were frequently praised for the harmonious,

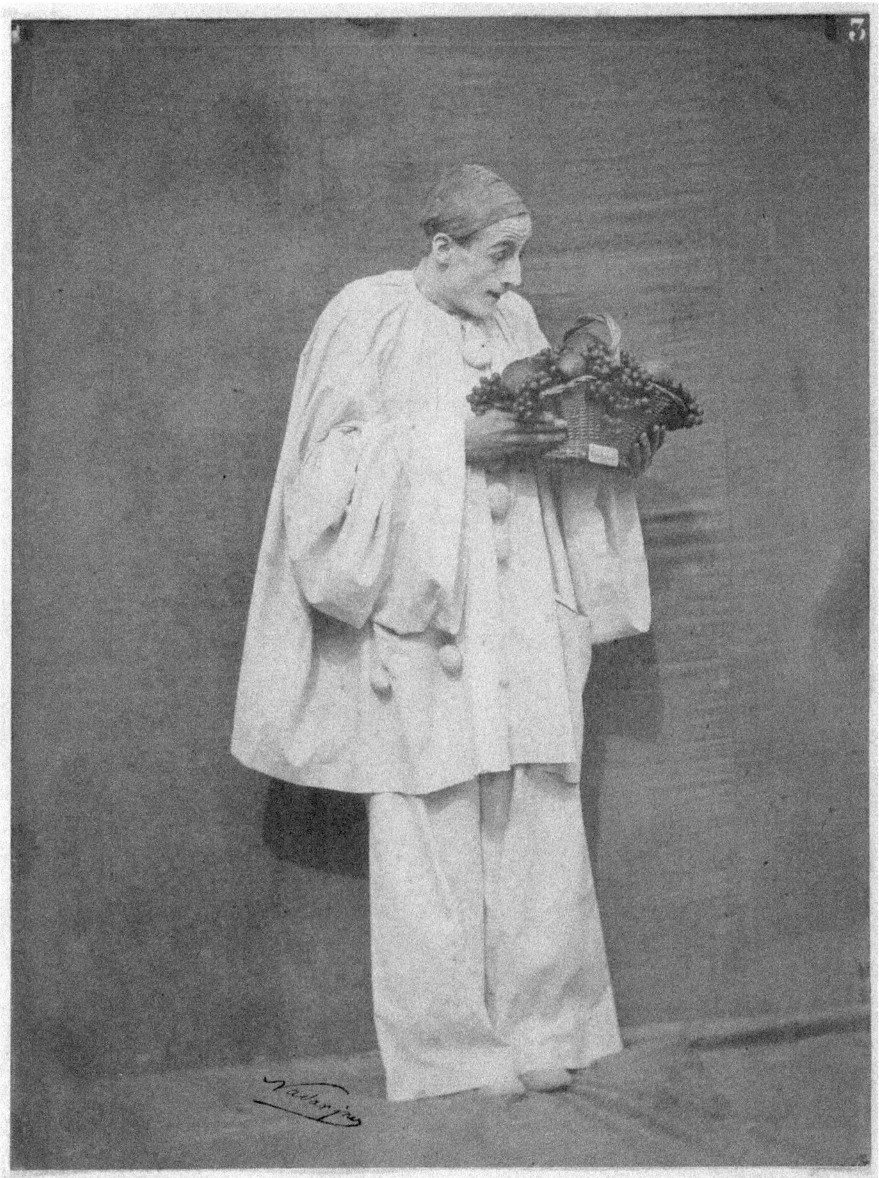

4.6   Nadar and Adrien Tournachon, *Pierrot with a basket of fruit*, 1854–5. Salted paper print, 28.7 × 21.2 cm. Source: Musée d'Orsay, Paris. PHO1991–1-3 ©RMN-Grand Palais (musée d'Orsay)/Hervé Lewandowski.

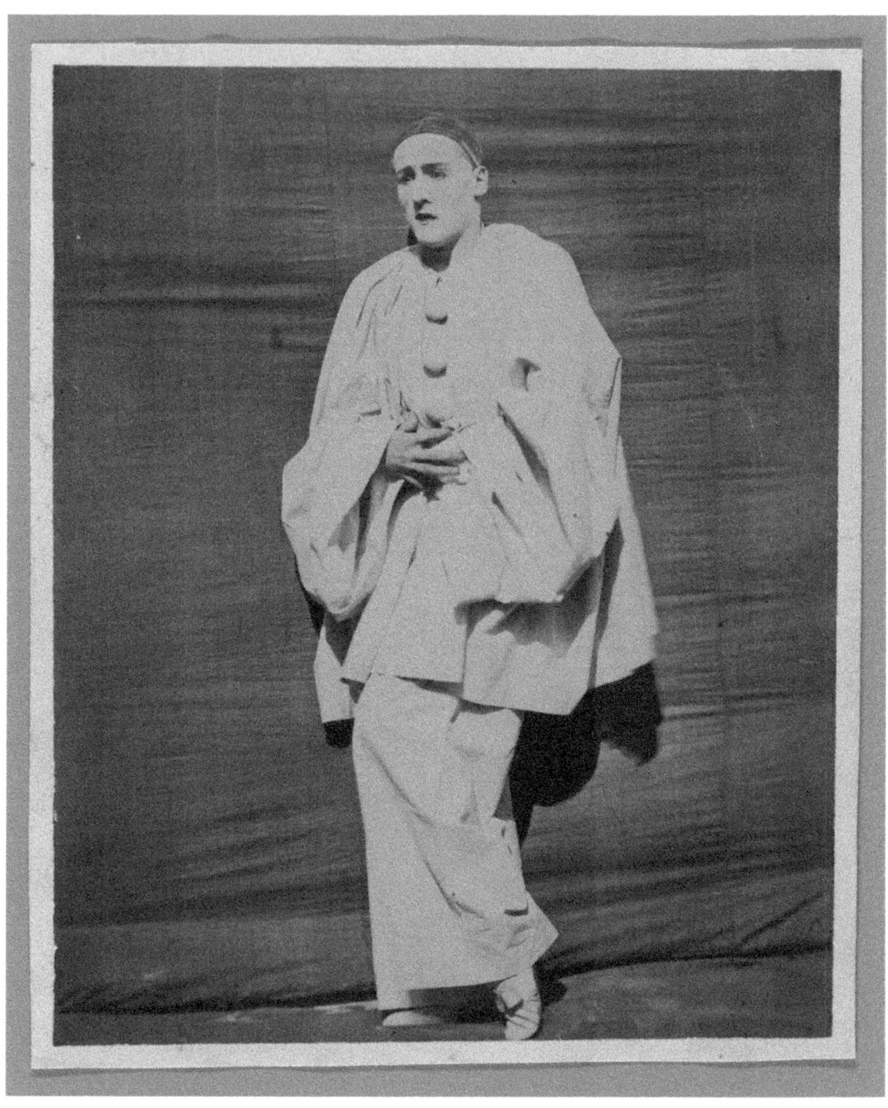

4.7   Nadar and Adrien Tournachon, *Pierrot in pain*, 1854–5. Albumen silver print from a glass negative, 25.6 × 20.4 cm. Source: Metropolitan Museum of Art, New York. 2005.100.255 ©metmuseum.org.

painterly arrangement of swathes of light and dark.[30] In the manner of portraiture, these critics argued, skilled photographers possessed the ability to either stage appropriate poses or inspire their models to strike such poses. As these treatises insisted, it was not merely a matter of knowing how to operate a camera and develop a print; the photographer also needed an artistic instinct, a certain flair. For these reasons, many members of the photographic community believed that photography should have been included in the exhibition of fine arts, on the Avenue Montaigne.

However, despite these protestations, the lion's share of the photographers in the French exhibition ran commercial studios. This was particularly true of the portrait photographers, like Mayer and Pierson, whose display boasted photographs of the tragic actresses Rachel and 'La Ristori' and portraits of the emperor and empress. While painters and sculptors sold their works, no 'fine artists' operated large-scale commercial enterprises like the portrait studios, which were located on the new boulevards, and which advertised their works in glass vitrines on the ground floor, or in the windows of shops along the boulevard.[31] The advertising techniques of commercial studios made the boulevards into an important space for the exhibition of photography. In their reviews of the photography display in 1855, the critics often refer to previously seeing the same photographs in vitrines or shop windows: Paul Périer, commenting on a photographic still life by Boitouzet, adds that he had already been 'struck' by this photograph upon its exhibition in a vitrine on the Boulevard Italien.[32] Ernest Lacan mentions that Gerothwol's and Tanner's photographic portrait enlargements had been on view at Susse Frères, a former stationer that had transformed into a retailer of paintings and a maker of luxury *objets d'art*, including bronze figurines.[33] Susse Frères had a boutique in the Place de la Bourse, with a 'public exhibition space' on the first floor.[34] This is presumably where Lacan saw the enlargements, which he says were attracting the attention of the passersby.[35] Périer also makes a negative allusion to vitrines as a space of empty commercial show. When complaining about retouched and painted photographic portraits, the critic sarcastically thanks the Exposition's organisers for separating photography from the 'vitrines of Lyon and the displays of *parfumeries*'.[36] The fabric sellers of Lyon would not have been able to compete with the painted creations of so-called photographers, Périer implies. The suggestion here is that photography has gone too far in its appeal to the street, becoming nothing other (and in fact much more) than a display of fabrics and cosmetics. Ferdinand de Lasteyrie, writing in *Le Siècle*, also complains about photographic 'commerce' on the boulevards, where photographers display their work in the same vitrines used to post menus for *prix-fixe* dinners.[37]

The vitrines, like the *parades*, were intended to 'entice' customers to enter the studio or the theatre. In his own commentary on the Exposition, the successful portraitist and inventor of the *carte de visite*, Adolphe Disdéri, claimed that photographers used their vitrines as a means to entice and flatter (*allécher*) the public, cajoling the passerby into entering the studio, which was usually located up several flights of stairs.[38] In the Tournachons' photographs, Pierrot performs the *parade*. Placed in the vitrine of Adrien's, or Nadar's, studio, the photographs would have attracted the attention of the passersby on the Boulevard des Capucines or the Boulevard des Italiens, to which Adrien's studio soon moved. In a testament to the spatial economies of the boulevard, in one photograph Pierrot eyes a luxuriant basket of fruit, his lips forming a little 'o' of anticipation

(Figure 4.6). A card bearing the name 'Couturier' is tucked into the basket, a product placement for the fruit-seller Couturier, whose shop was situated nearby.

In addition to performing the *parade* for the Tournachons' studio, the photographs in the vitrine would have advertised Charles Deburau. Theatrical celebrities were among the first to seize upon the possibilities of photography as a way of circulating their image. The presence of actors in the vitrines, advertising both themselves and the shop, brought this practice back to the activities of the charlatan and his clown, using jokes to hawk specious medical remedies. Charlatanry was also on the lips of the critics of the photographic Exposition in 1855. Lacan reported on the 'charlatanism' of an American photographer who sold subscriptions to his photographic recipes and disappeared with the proceeds.[39] In *Pierrot the Photographer*, in which he appears to demonstrate what it is to take a photograph, Pierrot does indeed perform the role of the hawkers' clown, demonstrating the efficacy of his boss's product. In addition, Pierrot previews the 'play' that will take place inside the shop, when a customer crosses the threshold and pays for their photograph.

Charlatanry was also evoked by the spatial origins of one of the pioneers of photography, Jacques-Louis Daguerre, who had perfected his technique on the Boulevard du Temple, in his *cabinet* above his Diorama. The showman Daguerre wanted his photographic process to be presented in as theatrical a manner as possible.[40] It may be for this reason that it was a theatre critic, none other than Pierrot's greatest champion Jules Janin, who published the first descriptions of Daguerre's process.[41] As a critic, Janin was also a promoter. Indeed, his ardent accounts of Pierrot had led to comparisons between Janin's newspaper columns and the theatrical *parade*.[42] In the journal *L'Artiste*, Janin spared none of his flair in detailing the photographic process, which Daguerre demonstrated for him during an exclusive *séance*. Janin's description builds to a theatrical climax, when the photographic image appears as if conjured up by the brush (or the wand) of 'queen Mab, queen of the fairies'.[43] By this point, Janin was indelibly associated with Pierrot and the Funambules, where fairies served as Pierrot's guides in the pantomime. Sixteen years later, Pierrot would replace the fairy as the public's guide to photography, when he performs the photographic process with mock solemnity in *Pierrot the Photographer*.

After, if not before the end of the Exposition, Nadar and Adrien quarrelled. Adrien claimed full responsibility for 'The Pierrots' and for the first-class medal, awarded by the jury. Against his brother, Nadar asserted creative responsibility for the photographs of Deburau and claimed his right to the exclusive use of the Nadar moniker. The Bibliothèque Nationale de France now attributes the photographs entirely to Adrien. However, Nadar was undoubtedly working alongside his brother, in the same studio, when the photographs were made, and it was Nadar who had known connections with Charles Deburau. In addition, the photographs bear the impress of Nadar's distinctive style and his treatment of the human figure in *Le lanterne magique* and the *Panthéon*. At the core of this style lay the insistence on the full-length presentation of the human figure.

The marketing of celebrity and the full-length figure

As Nadar's previous work for Philipon suggests, Nadar was well versed in the techniques of editorial publicity including the *réclame*, the puff piece inserted in a journal that promoted an actor, an author, or a product.[44] By combining portrait charge and a few lines of snappy text noting the achievements for which the subject was known, Nadar had pioneered a form of caricatural *réclame*.[45] He was also an experienced stager and promoter of theatrical events: in 1854, he had produced a theatrical production entitled *Les binettes contemporains*, a kind of caricatural review that animated his eponymous collection of visual and textual caricatures. For this performance, Nadar painted the theatre's *toile de fond* with large caricatures, including one of himself, in the very centre of the composition (Figure 4.8).[46] These figures, which floated on the curtain like projections from a magic lantern, reinforced the connection between caricatural figurations of the body at full length and Nadar's promotional tactics. Nadar understood that the celebrity must be presented as a figure 'free of any entanglements'. Placed at the back of the stage rather than the front, the *toile de fond* was not a curtain. Yet it does appear to have marked a threshold of sorts, given that immediately

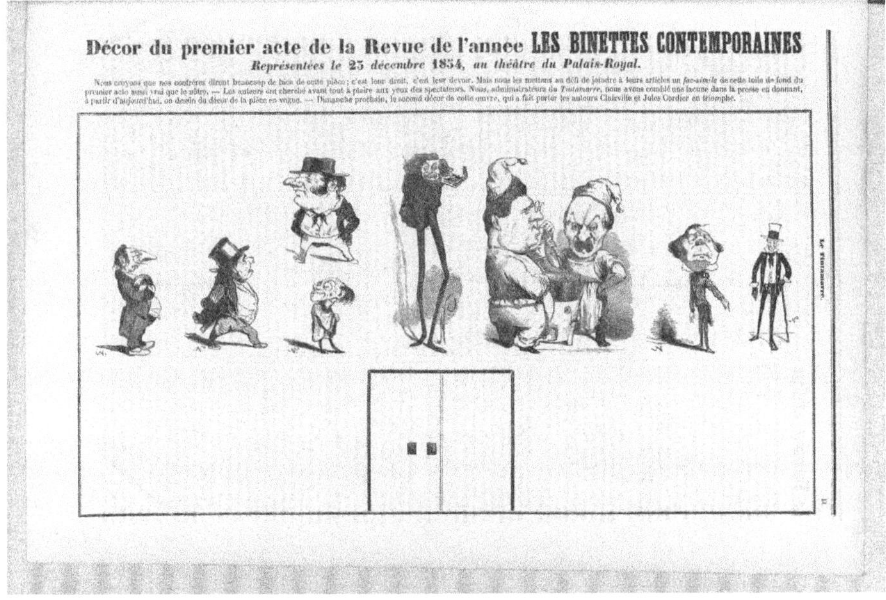

4.8   Nadar, *Design for the curtain of Les Binnettes contemporains*, in *Le Tintamarre*, 24 December 1854. Lithograph. Source: Bibliothèque Nationale de France, Paris. FOL-Z-23 ©BNF.

beneath Nadar's long-legged figure there is a double door, through which the actors may have made their entrances. Drawing attention to the threshold as a place of suspension, the figures preview the show as the setting forth of a series of figural performances – a revue of personalities rather than a scripted drama. Nadar had also featured Pierrot on an invitation to one of his *soirées*, a 'Feste Champestre' organised in 1840 (Figure 4.9). Paired with a caricature of Nadar himself, Pierrot holds one end of the *banderole* announcing the festivities. (The evening, a satire of Romantic excess and dandyism, did feature a Pierrot, who Nadar identified as Baptiste Deburau, but it was in fact a musician from the Funambules who greatly resembled Deburau.[47]) In the heading, Pierrot both personifies and bears the invitation as an address to the recipient. His relationship to the cartouche as a source of expectant vacancy is also articulated in this print, where he holds one side of a fringed shawl serving as a cartouche upon which the title of the event is inscribed. Pierrot, as usual, finds himself in the position of the front man, at the door of the theatre or the party, holding up the sign for what lies inside.

Interestingly, neither of the Tournachon brothers used the full-length format for their immediately contemporary portraits. When, after the Universal Exposition, Nadar began to turn his attention exclusively to photography, he jettisoned, initially, the promotional strategies he had used as an illustrator. Instead, he made a name for himself with an intimate three-quarters style of photographic portraiture. This style both stimulated and reproduced intimacy between the sitter and the viewer, which reflected the fact that Nadar chose to photograph his own friends: artists and writers to whom he enjoyed privileged access.[48] In the near future, whenever Nadar used the full-length format there was usually an element of either theatre or ethnography, genres that relied upon the presentation of costume. He photographed his wife Ernestine in 'oriental' dress at full length in 1860; in 1863 he photographed himself at full length as an 'eskimo'. In 1862, the members of the Japanese diplomatic mission also received full-length portraiture. By the mid-1860s, preoccupied with his hot air balloon (*le géant*), which he used to photograph Paris from the sky, he ceased to pay much attention to the format of the celebrity 'editions' his studio churned out. Adrien, whose early portraits used the three-quarters format, would use the full-length format for similar purposes, for example to photograph Italian musicians in regional costume in 1856, Arab shepherds and cavaliers in the same year, and circus performers in 1861.

Soon after the Universal Exposition, the full-length photograph would become the preferred format for the *carte de visite*. Invented by Adolphe Disdéri, *cartes-de-visite* were made using a multi-lensed camera, which enabled a glass plate negative to record up to eight exposures in a grid format. The exposures could be made separately, by sliding the plate through a frame fixed with shutters, or all at once. The resulting print would be cut up and each of the photographs mounted on cards. Disdéri had first offered *cartes-de-visite* in 1854, but the craze for these pocket-sized photographs would not take off until late in that decade. During the heyday of the *carte-de-visite*, individuals

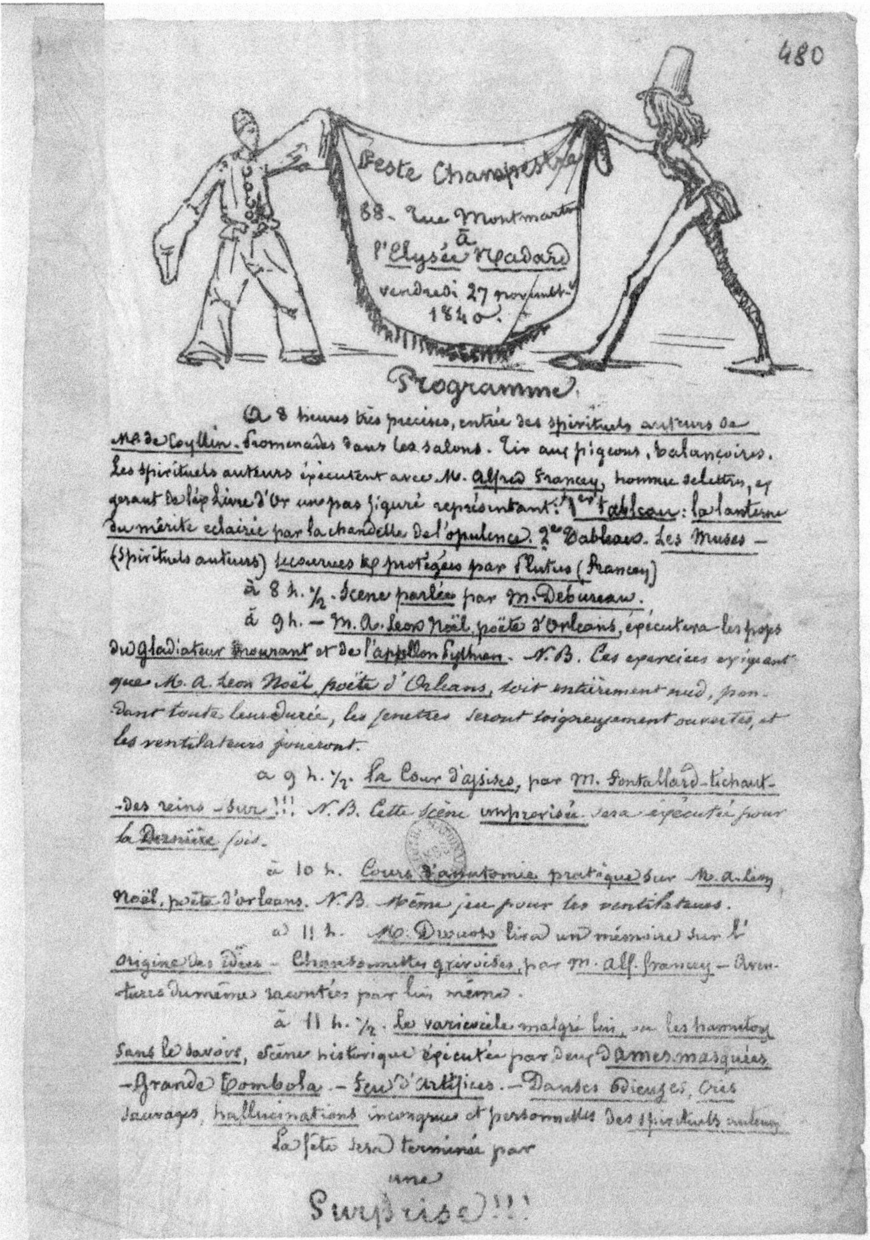

4.9   Nadar, *Invitation to a 'Feste Champestre'*, 1840. Lithograph. Source: Département des manuscrits, Bibliothèque Nationale de France, Paris. NAF 24988 Folio 48or ©BNF.

collected *cartes* of family members, celebrities, and social types, which they arranged in purpose-made albums.[49] *Cartes-de-visite* offering the figures of theatrical performers circulated widely. Disdéri produced his own albums or 'galleries', preconstructed volumes of *cartes-de-visite* in which the artistic, financial, and political celebrities of the Second Empire displayed their finest clothes and most studied poses.[50] Pictured at full length, the subjects of *cartes-de-visite* performed their address to a wide public, beyond the horizon of family and friends. Whether or not this audience existed for those thousands of private individuals who commissioned *cartes-de-visite*, the format of the *carte* signalled the subject's willingness to assume a role, to be pictured across the threshold (the costume) of social type and social class. The address of such costumes, as I have argued throughout this study, was the marketplace, where costumed appearance circulated as a form of social credit or currency. More intimate forms of photographic portraiture continued to thrive, but the *carte-de-visite* became an essential mode – a mode of photography as well as a mode of social existence. Dress, bearing, and gesture all contributed to elaborate a repertoire of types: the young, marriageable woman, the matron, the sleek man-about-town, the soldier, the man of letters.

The photographs of Pierrot by Adrien and Nadar were far larger than *cartes-de-visite*, but they articulated the underlying stakes of this soon-to-be mass medium by linking the *parade*, marketing, and the exhibition of a full-length figure. Arguably, they do so better than Disdéri's actual *cartes-de-visite* representing Charles' rival, Paul Legrand (Figure 4.10). These *cartes* show Legrand goofing off in a well-furnished bourgeois sitting room, provided courtesy of Disdéri's studio. While the Tournachons' photographs of Pierrot offer a commentary upon the presentational stakes of the *carte-de-visite*, Disdéri's uncut sheet exemplifies the genre in its most ubiquitous, unreflective form. The sheet offers variety, a range of poses and expressions from which a buyer could choose. A collector might purchase several of the *cartes*, to make a set. Pasted to card, *cartes-de-visite* had a material heft that blurred the distinction between image and object. The relative smallness of the standard *carte-de-visite* also helped in this regard. A *carte* had a satisfying feel in the hand; it could be popped into a pocket or a purse. Moreover, the presentation of the full-length but miniaturised human figure also blurred the distinction between object and person. By purchasing *cartes*, a collector amassed 'celebrities' or 'Legrands' or 'Pierrots' the way they might build a collection of figurines. Where cropping the figure would have reminded the viewer of the fact of the image, the presentation of the full-length figure offered the impression of immediate, unlimited access.

Nadar emphasised his difference from Disdéri in his own photograph of Legrand as Pierrot (Figure 4.11). This portrait exemplifies the characteristics of Nadar's most fêted portraits of Parisian bohemia. Legrand stands close to the camera, his hands raised to his ears, as if he is pinching them, or perhaps indicating that he is listening. The photograph is closely cropped, so that the white tunic occupies the breadth of the composition, showing off its thousands

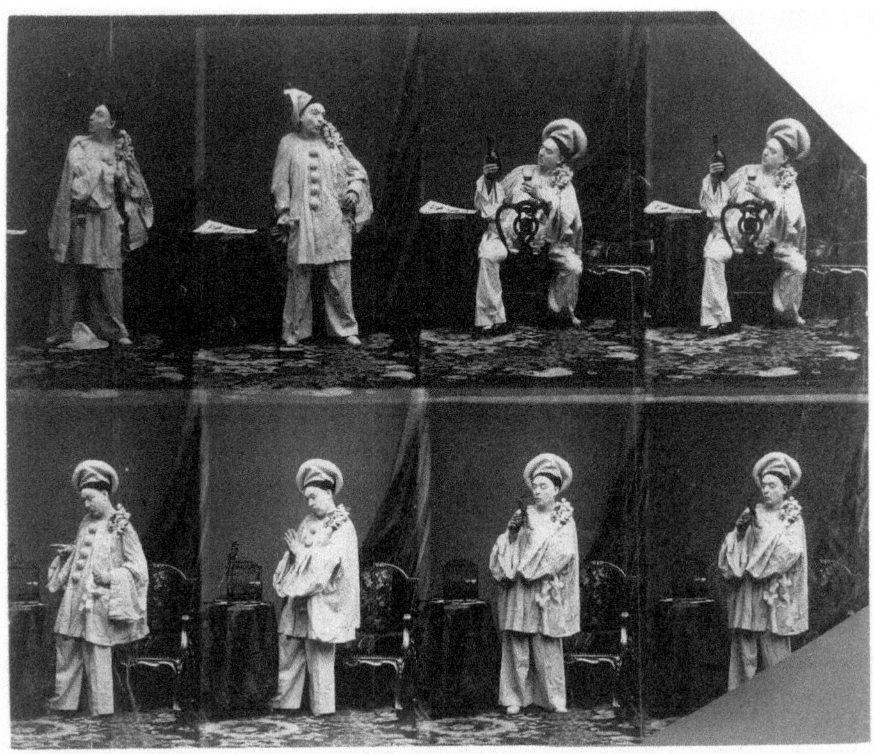

4.10   André-Adolphe-Eugène Disdéri, *Paul Legrand in eight poses*, c. 1860. Albumen paper print, 20 × 23 cm. Source: Musée d'Orsay, Paris. PHO1995–27–96 ©Musée d'Orsay, Dist. RMN-Grand Palais/Alexis Brandt.

of little folds. This is not a photograph that would lend itself to the needs of publicity. Information about the silhouette of Legrand's costume, about the way he carries himself on stage, is at a minimum in this photograph. Instead, Nadar offers a tracing of finely wrought detail. Each wrinkle of Pierrot's tunic reminds the viewer of Legrand's presence before the camera. His strange expression, as if he is pulling his face into a smile by grasping his ears, is far from the generic poses of Disdéri's *carte*. The photograph rewards prolonged looking, through which the eye dwells on Legrand's surface as it might a map, seeking out nooks and crannies, or jolts of recognition. Examination reveals fascinating *studia*, for example the discovery that Legrand's ruff is separable from his tunic, fastened with a small, flat button, the same small buttons that sit just under the larger, overstuffed buttons, which are revealed to be purely decorative. This is a photograph that makes itself known as a deliberate composition and as a record of light and shadow. Pierrot is the subject of the photograph, but he is not presented as an object. Even when the photograph was reproduced as a *carte-de-visite*, as part of Nadar's endless remarketing of his studio's stock of images,

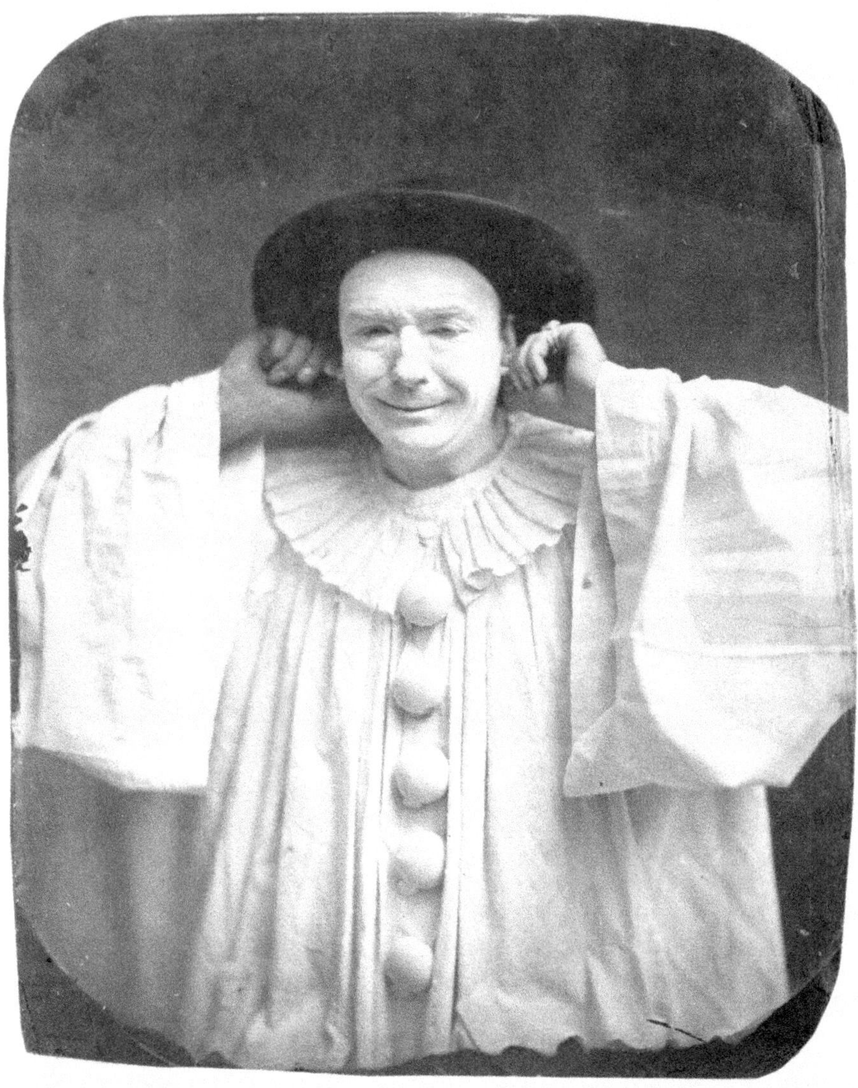

4.11   Nadar, *Paul Legrand*, 1855–59. Salted paper print, 26.4 × 20.8 cm. Source: Musée d'Orsay, Paris. PHO1991–2-64 ©Musée d'Orsay, dist. RMN-Grand Palais/Patrice Schmidt.

the viewer cannot imagine grasping this Pierrot the way the little Legrands in Disdéri's sheet can be imagined as a series of Pierrot figurines.[51]

It is unknown whether the photographs of Charles appeared in the vitrine of Adrien's new space, the photographic 'salons' at 17 Boulevard des Italiens. Yet in 1856 Alcide-Joseph Lorentz's lithographic poster advertising the new studio featured the figure of Pierrot and his camera as its central motif (Figure 4.12). In this re-use the original photograph is made to serve as an

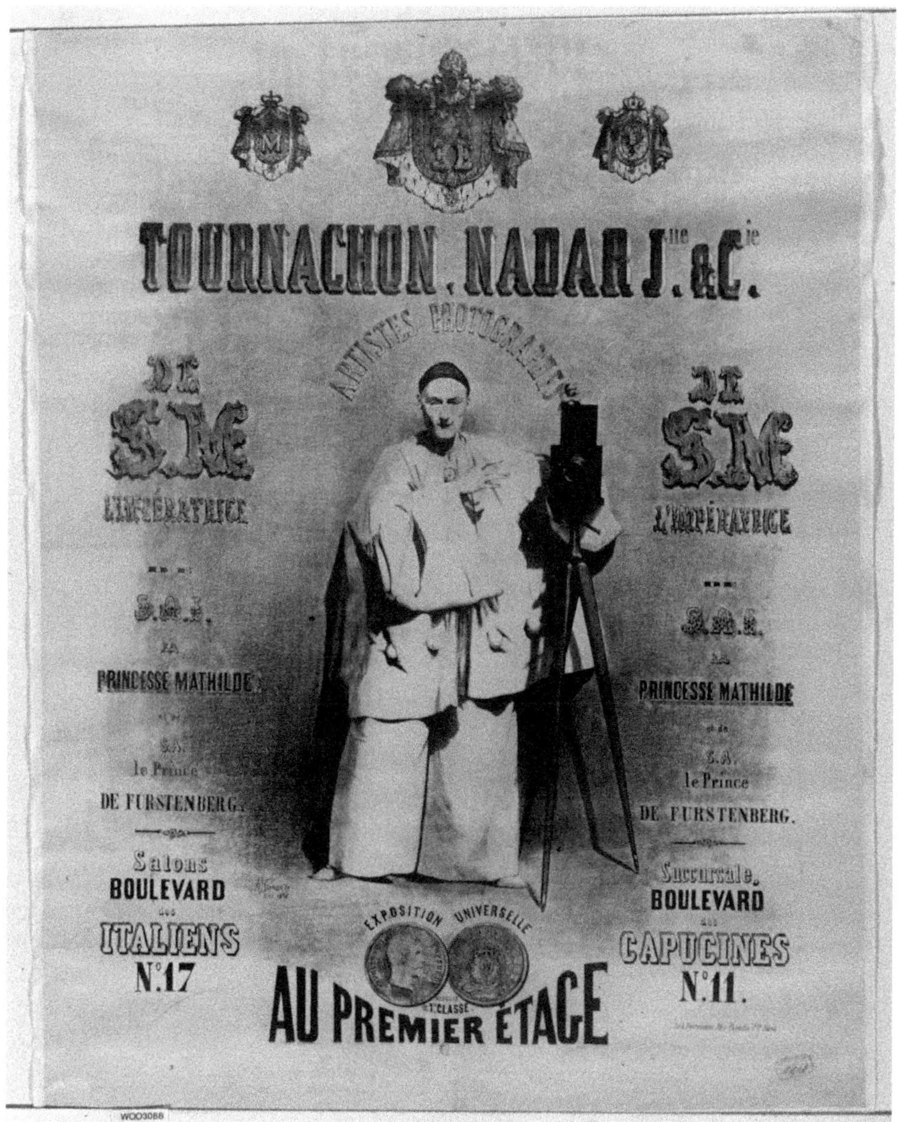

4.12   Alcide-Joseph Lorentz, *Publicity Poster for the Studio of Adrien Tournachon*, 1856. Lithograph, 102 × 76 cm. Source: Bibliothèque Nationale de France. ENTAD-1-FT6 ©BNF.

ornament print, from which a motif can be excerpted and placed in a different context. The choice of this photograph as a motif for the poster was an obvious one. The original photograph enacts the passage into photographic appearance. Pierrot lifts the shutter, exposing the plate inside the camera, just as a stage curtain is drawn aside to reveal an actor. Again, Pierrot is closely aligned with the threshold of appearance. In Watteau's repertoire, Pierrot was coincident with the curtain that withdrew to reveal the row of actors; in addition, the fabric expanse and frontality of the character made him a kind of human curtain, marking the threshold between the stage and the *salle*. In the costume print, as I have suggested, it is upon this threshold, this surface, that appearance takes place. The costume print condenses the threshold of the stage (and the market) in the surface of a figure, which is also the surface of the print, or the photograph. That surface is visible in the Tournachons' photograph as the black square of the shutter, which alludes to the glass plate inside the camera, as well as to the rectangular format of the resulting photograph, a dark square in which Pierrot appears. Yet the charge of this photograph is somewhat muted in Lorentz's poster design, which takes care to render Pierrot's figure in full, sculptural volume, exaggerating the splay of the camera's legs to emphasise the depth of the space represented in the vignette. Pierrot's costume is billowier than in the photograph, his trouser legs even wider. He recedes from the threshold. His brazenness is muted. It makes sense that it was likely Adrien alone, *sans* Félix, who supervised this poster's design, after having quarrelled with his brother. It was Nadar who was the gifted promoter and marketer, who knew what it took to make a figure fly.

Exposition, phantasmagoria

The Exposition was a vast marketplace, an accumulation of goods intended to perform prosperity as well as the civility of commerce.[52] Designed as a show-piece for the orderly society of the Second Empire, the exhibition was a place of controlled eclecticism: a place 'of bric-à-brac and organisation', a 'place of diversion' as well as 'display of knowledge', 'exemplary' but also 'provisional, removeable, transitory'.[53] Through the display of merchandise, the world took on the character of a 'well-organised department store'.[54] Consumption offered access to distant cultures, which could be represented both by objects and by foreign visitors, whose attendance at the Exposition was proudly reported in the Parisian press.[55] In this context, the displays of the photographic exhibition offered a stock of human figures, a repertoire of authors, politicians, artists, and actors, made available to the customer through photography. In other words, despite claims to the contrary by photographers anxious to be granted the status of 'artists', the Exposition tended to underline the relationship between photography and the marketplace. Taking his cue from the exhibition, Nadar himself would go on to amass significant capital in the form of a 'stock' or 'inventory' of celebrity portraits, which he reprinted and marketed as *cartes-de-visite* and sold to journals to be lithographed or engraved.[56] The negative of the large-format photograph of Legrand, for example, would be put to such use, offered by the Nadar studio as a print in two formats, each cropped differently.

As commodities photographs were distinctive because they offered the marketplace not one, but two forms of merchandise: the photograph itself and the celebrity subject. The celebrity subject was consumed differently than the photograph as a material object. The destination of the celebrity was not the wall of the living room, but the wall of the mind. The double offering of the celebrity photograph grants it an important status in light of later discussions of the Universal Exposition as a key moment in the history of the commodity in nineteenth-century France. Famously, Benjamin used the Universal Exposition as an example of a 'phantasmagoria'. After abandoning the 'dialectical image', Benjamin made phantasmagoria the master term for the *Arcades Project*, his unfinished account of nineteenth-century Paris.[57] In his characteristically opaque, but evocative prose, Benjamin described the phantasmagoria as a 'thingish representation' (*'représentation chosiste'*), through which civilisation represented itself, to itself, as a series of thing-apparitions, many of which were commodities for sale.[58] Benjamin's phantasmagoria was made of solid things that were also, simultaneously, weightless. The world manifested itself as a collection of marketable goods, yet because the value of commodities lay in the imaginary powers ascribed to them, these things were also ghostly and apparitional. In other words, Benjamin's interest lay in the spectral character of the commodity, the way it occupied the stage of memory and the imagination.

As Benjamin knew, the first phantasmagoria was Étienne-Gaspard Robertson's Parisian 'Fantasmagorie', which opened its doors in 1798.[59] To produce its promised 'apparitions of spectres, phantoms, and revenants', Robertson's phantasmagoria used magic lanterns to project both sculpted and painted bodies. Magic lanterns were boxes with a single, often circular opening. A light source placed inside the box projected the image painted on a transparent glass plaque fixed to the lantern's window. The magic lantern was by no means a new technology. By the mid-eighteenth century, itinerant magic lantern operators, trolling the streets of Paris with their lanterns strapped to their backs, were already regular figures in the *cris de Paris*. Traditionally, magic lantern shows offered a range of entertainments, including landscapes and cityscapes. One of the medium's most ubiquitous offerings was the human figure at full length, projected against a plain sheet or an empty wall, which served as the background. Long, narrow, glass slides painted with multiple figures were also common. By sliding the glass past the lantern's window, a procession of figures could be projected. Or, if a single figure was repeated multiple times in slightly different poses and the slide moved through a metal frame equipped with a shutter, a jerky kind of movement could be suggested (Figure 4.13). This device was called the choreutoscope. Arlequins and Pierrots, as well as the dwarf clowns (*gobbi*) invented by Callot in the early seventeenth century, were popular figures in magic lantern repertoires. Some slides had moving panels, which allowed the figure's pose to change. In at least two extant magic lantern slides, Pierrot appears holding a paper *banderole*, which is unfurled when levers are used to move the panels, which also raise and lower his hat. On one of the slides, the *banderole* reads 'bonsoir',[60] but on the slide shown here, it remains blank, which suggests that operators could write in what they wished (see Plate 15). Once again, Pierrot is found positioned at the threshold of the performance. In this case, he bids the audience good evening, but he could also

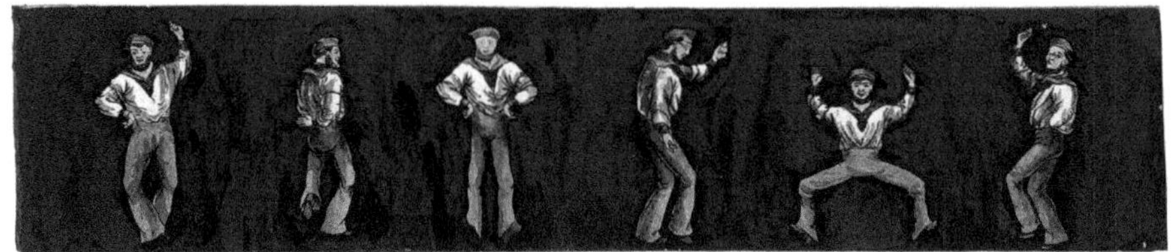

4.13   Magic lantern slide for a choreutoscope, *Sailor in blue and white*, late nineteenth century. Painted glass, 19.8 × 43 cm. Source: Cinémathèque française, Paris. PLM-00601–008 ©Cinémathèque française.

have wielded his *banderole* as a frontispiece, advertising the name of the ensuing show or the price of entry. Pierrot is quite a friendly figure in these slides, but magic lantern artists also painted hundreds of fantastic, monstrous creatures, like those used in Robertson's show.

Period illustrations suggest that Robertson's phantasmagoria projected its figures at full length, above the heads of spectators seated in a darkened hall. As a result, the figures appeared to be airborne. Seizing upon the macabre atmosphere of post-Terror Paris, Robertson offered to revive the victims of the guillotine. By combining the projections of mobile magic lanterns (the devices were mounted on wheels) with actors who crept among the spectators, Robertson both terrified and delighted his audience. The apparatus itself was concealed behind a curtain, which also served as a screen to receive the projections. By transforming real bodies into 'aesthetic apparitions, fantastic nightmares of an evening's entertainment', Robertson's phantasmagoria lightened the weight of history.[61] Heads that had fallen with a thud into the guillotine's basket escaped the pull of gravity and flew through the air. For Benjamin, the Universal Exposition's phantasmagoric nature lay in the apparitional and theatrical character of the commodity, enhanced by the way its display distanced goods from sites of making and use.[62] Looked at, but neither touched nor held, the things on display became ghosts seen through glass. Indeed, one of the Exposition's most vaunted attractions was a gargantuan piece of plate glass set in a gilded frame.[63]

The display of photographs, where Pierrot reigned, would have encouraged Benjamin's meditations, by offering the marketplace as a repertoire of mobile, theatrical human figures. In his précis for 'Paris: capital of the nineteenth century', Benjamin described *physiognomies*, like *Les Français peints par eux-mêmes*, as 'phantasmagorias of the marketplace, in which men appear only in their typical aspect'.[64] The author alighted here on the apparitional character of the *physiognomies*, their concentration of identity in a two-dimensional surface, as well as their tendency to present, in the panoramic mode, a range of different types, whose relationship to one another is not illustrated. The relationship between *physiognomies* and the magic lantern is further suggested by the fact that Philipon, editor of *physiognomies* who had commissioned Nadar's *Lanterne magique*, had created a magic lantern show of caricatures based on his own publication, *Le Musée ou magasin comique de Philipon* (1842).[65] The *physiognomies* as a representation of the marketplace is not surprising. What is new, however, is the addition of light-based projection as a medium for displaying and perceiving the repertoire.

Over the course of the nineteenth century, the phantasmagoria was increasingly evoked as a model for mental activity. The imagination cast figures on the wall of the mind; thought was represented as a 'spectral process', the images of which floated like ghosts.[66] As Benjamin's discussion suggests, the phantasmagoria is also representative of marketplace practices, which increasingly acknowledge the mind as a kind of image theatre. The trick is to offer the thing as a brilliant, seductive apparition: to cast it into the mind's eye, where it will stick. Photography, as a medium for fixing the image projected by light, offers to materialise this practice. As Janin crowed of the photograph's chemical fixation of the image, *'as soon taken, as soon hung'* (italics original).[67] In the Tournachons' photographs, Pierrot appears against a cloth backdrop, as if his figure were cast on the curtain stretched before a magic lantern. Deburau himself, however, is relatively firmly rooted on the floor of the studio, even if the use of the curtain represents an attempt to conceal the break between the backdrop as a floorless, two-dimensional (back)ground and the floor as a physical, three-dimensional ground. Moving forward into the late nineteenth century, however, Pierrot would become increasingly airborne, eliminating the need for a ground on which to stand.

Theatre of shadows

In the lead-up to the Lumières' premiere of the *cinématographe* in 1895, Pierrot enjoyed a resurgence as a favourite figure in key related technologies: light-based projection and animation.[68] While direct influence is impossible to trace, the Tournachons' series had at the very least drawn attention to ways that Pierrot's figure was particularly suited to these practices, while offering a template for visual experiments to come. As a scholarly field, the literature on early cinema is extremely rich; I do not pretend to add to it here in any substantive way. I merely want to make note of Pierrot's recurrence throughout the history of this medium, as a favoured figure to be projected, serialised, photographed, and animated.

In the late 1880s, the magic lantern became the focal point of a new entertainment, the 'Shadow Theatre', at the Chat Noir cabaret in Montmartre.[69] Under the directorship of the charismatic Rodolphe Salis, the Chat Noir offered a variety of entertainments, including music, theatre, and poetry, as well as the spectacle of Montmartrois bohemian life. The Shadow Theatre, which debuted in 1887 in the cabaret's new quarters on the Rue de Laval, featured a sculpted proscenium in the form of a neo-baroque explosion of angels and golden rays of light. A coloured décor served as a backdrop for the projections of a magic lantern. Instead of painted glass slides, however, the lantern projected black zinc silhouettes, which had been cut into a series of figures. Music and the narration of Salis accompanied the movement of the figures against the fixed décors.[70]

Pierrot featured in at least two of the shadow plays performed at the Chat Noir, *L'âge d'or* by Adolphe Willette and *Pierrot pornographe* by Louis Morin.[71] In *L'âge d'or*, Pierrot, dressed in a black tuxedo, does his best to woo an indifferent Colombine. He pleads, plays the violin, paints her portrait at full length, eventually loses all his money, becomes a gardener (Figure 4.14), and dies. In the final scene, a skeletal Pierrot rises from the grave to offer Colombine a coin. Only then, finally, does she pay attention. Some of the silhouettes, which Willette designed, were jointed and could make simple movements, much like the Pierrot of the magic lantern slide unfurling his *banderole*. Only a single silhouette was used for each 'scene', with a total of eight to ten silhouettes presented over the course of the performance.

Many of the artists who gathered at the Chat Noir were socially conservative, a reflection of the rightwards shift of *fin-de-siècle* bohemia. I will discuss these politics further in Chapter 5. Willette claimed to reject contemporary capitalist society in favour of a bohemian life on the 'Butte'. In his *oeuvre*, which will be discussed further in Chapter 5, he cast Pierrot as the emblem of the French *peuple* oppressed by tricky capitalists and spurned by Dame Fortune. The Shadow Theatre, for Willette, represented a naïve, popular entertainment that disdained the pretension of mainstream theatres.[72] Rather than offer a spectacle of materialism thinly veiled by a melodramatic plot, the Shadow Theatre presented silhouettes abstracted from the contemporary.[73] There was also a spectral character to these performances. As two-dimensional designs in black and white, the silhouettes were dematerialised through projection, transformed from a piece of metal to a shadow thrown by light.

In his thousands of representations of Pierrot, most of which took the form of journal illustrations, Willette frequently played with weightlessness or suspension or showed Pierrot as airborne. Pierrot appears perched atop the blade of a Montmartrois windmill;[74] or little winged infant-Pierrot heads fly through the air to pay tribute to a young woman in a decoration Willette painted from the Auberge du Clou on the Avenue Trudaine, just south of Pigalle.[75] In a more macabre vein, he often represented Pierrot hanged, whether floating from a noose on the cover of his book *Pauvre Pierrot* (1884), or having hanged himself outside a woman's window, presumably because she has rejected him in favour of a rich man.[76] For Willette, Pierrot's suspension – whether weightless or weighted – represented his unsuitability for earthly life, at least in its urban, capitalist form. To chronicle Pierrot's adventures, the artist devised a form of illustration that he called 'stories without words' (*histoires sans parole*). These featured eight to twelve vignettes presenting a simple tale, usually involving capers in Montmartre and Pierrot's mistreatment by women and agents of authority. For example, Willette published 'L'âge d'or' as a story without words in his journal, *Le Pierrot* (Figure 4.15). The zinc silhouettes are reproduced in Willette's fluid lithographic style and arranged in four rows, each of which features two scenes.

The Tournachons' series may have encouraged the visual storytelling practised in the *histoires sans parole*. If a few of the prints from the photographic

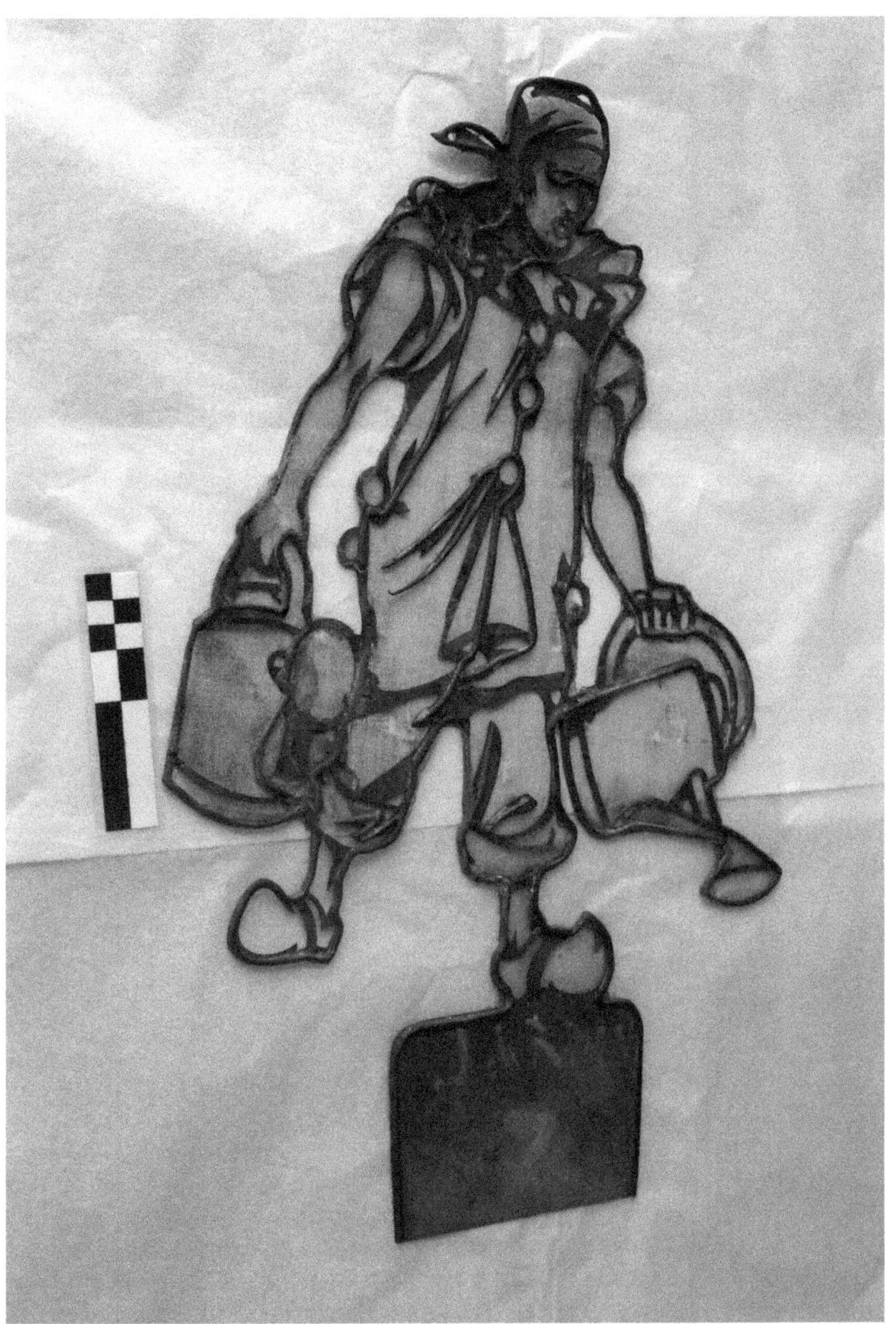

4.14   Adolphe Willette, *Pierrot waters his garden*, c. 1887. Zinc-cut silhouette, 50.2 × 30.5 cm. Source: Musée de Châtellerault. INV1998.6 ©Musée de Chatellerault, Estelle Sénelé.

series were to be joined together, a little wordless history could be created: from Pierrot examining fruit, to Pierrot eyeing a jar of medicine (fruit and medicine both stolen), to Pierrot getting sick from drinking the medicine, to Pierrot running away. During the 1830s and 1840s, the theatrical press had reproduced scenes from Deburau's latest comedies in a similar way, illustrating only the actors and omitting the scenery, while placing several vignettes on a single page.[77] However, paragraphs of text were used to break up the vignettes. Willette tends to omit text entirely. In addition, he rarely chooses to section the page with a grid or with lines, which might indicate the ground on which the figures supposedly stand. As a result, the vignettes float on the sheet like birds in the air. Without a guiding ground, the viewer's eye is also untethered, roving up and down, left to right, an erratic movement that expresses the zany, manic spirit of Willette's Pierrot. Meanwhile, the character's lean, wiry figure hardly seems subject to gravity. He is as thin and as flexible as a metal silhouette.

Willette is an unattractive character whose cultural politics will be addressed in Chapter 5. However, the stories without words reflect a formal development worth noting. Pierrot's figure bears the burden of the expressive pantomime, without the assistance of a depicted environment. Early techniques for visualising motion would also fix upon a single figure, the serial presentation of which would be key to animation.[78] Moreover, Willette presents Pierrot using a graphic language of weightlessness and suspension. This is intended to express the character's detachment from the material concerns of modern life – he has not a penny in his pocket to weigh him down, although he is heavy enough to hang himself when life becomes too much. The state of being unentangled and untethered is vital to Pierrot's persona throughout the second half of the nineteenth century. Yet the expressive valences of this state would be interpreted quite differently. Willette saw the essence of bohemianism; Charles Deburau saw the apotheosis of himself as Pierrot; Nadar (who would eventually take photographs from a hot air balloon) saw the upward trajectory of his career and his business empire.

Pantomimes and posters

One of the most significant precursors of the *cinématographe* was the praxinoscope, invented by Émile Reynaud and used during the 1890s to screen 'luminous pantomimes' featuring as their hero none other than Pierrot. Reynaud had begun his career in light-based technologies with magic lantern projections of scientific lectures, a fashionable late-nineteenth-century technique termed 'pedagogy by projection'.[79] Eventually, the spectacular, visual aspect of his lectures began to overwhelm their scientific content, and Reynaud moved on to theatrical entertainment and animation. The luminous pantomime consisted of two, superimposed projections. One magic lantern projected a stationary décor. A second projector cast the moving figures of Colombine, Arlequin, and Pierrot against this décor. This feat was accomplished by the substitution of a flexible, transparent gelatin band for the glass slide of the magic lantern.

Affixed to a hand-turned wheel, the strip passed before the light source at closely spaced intervals, was reflected by mirrors mounted on a revolving carousel, and projected onto a screen (Figure 4.16).[80]

On 28 October 1892 Reynaud's luminous pantomime *Pauvre Pierrot* debuted in the *cabinet fantastique* of the Musée Grévin.[81] A boyish Pierrot serenades Colombine in the walled courtyard of a house. Arlequin, however, steals Pierrot's wine, beats him, and runs off with Colombine. The pantomime required that hundreds of little Pierrots, Colombines, and Arlequins be painted against the transparent ground of the strip: in total, five hundred images compose the band (funnily enough, this is only twice the number of figures that appear in Nadar's *Panthéon littéraire*). The band can be seen spooling along a track, its movement controlled by Reynaud, in the illustration published in *La Nature* (Figure 4.16). Reynaud's Pierrots have none of the graphic complexity of Willette's writhing, acrobatic subjects. Instead, these Pierrots are simple, wooden figures; the appearance of Reynaud's painted band resembles the choreutoscope magic lantern slide in which a figure is represented serially, in increments of movement. While the visual qualities of Reynaud's Pierrots are not particularly eloquent, the existence of the strips themselves attests to a willingness to imagine the human figure in a spatial vacuum, as if movement took place in the air instead of on the ground. The luminous pantomime is indicative of the way that early experiments in 'moving pictures' leaned heavily upon moving figures – figural movement rather than the movement of the apparatus. This reflected the theatrical model, where the boundaries of the stage were fixed. Early forms of cinema were based on this premise of a fixed frame, within which figures would move. The frame held the figure's movement, providing a visual field against which the movement would take place, as opposed to a ground from which the movement sprang. The sailor on the choreutoscope magic lantern slide reproduced in Figure 4.13 moves as if immersed in water, or as if airborne.

Increasingly, artists conceptualised liberating forms of movement as taking place in an airy, groundless realm, where normal principles of gravity did not apply. This aesthetic would also characterise late-nineteenth-century poster design, including the promotional posters that Jules Chéret produced to advertise Reynaud's luminous pantomimes. These lithographic posters epitomised Chéret's signature combination of striking typography, bright, contrasting colours, and figures that floated and danced amidst the promotional text.[82] In the most iconic of these posters, a ginger-haired Colombine appears in a yellow dress with red polka dots (see Plate 16). Her toes pointed, she is suspended against a ground of red flames and a midnight-blue sky. Chéret places Pierrot immediately behind her, his back arched, floating on the waves of the music he plays. In 1900, the artist would re-use and re-arrange these figures on the curtain that he painted for the Musée Grévin's Petit théâtre. Here, the airborne Pierrot and Colombine were suspended on the theatrical threshold, offering both a *parade* prior to the entertainment proper, as well as a performance of the liminality that unites encounters in the theatre and the marketplace.

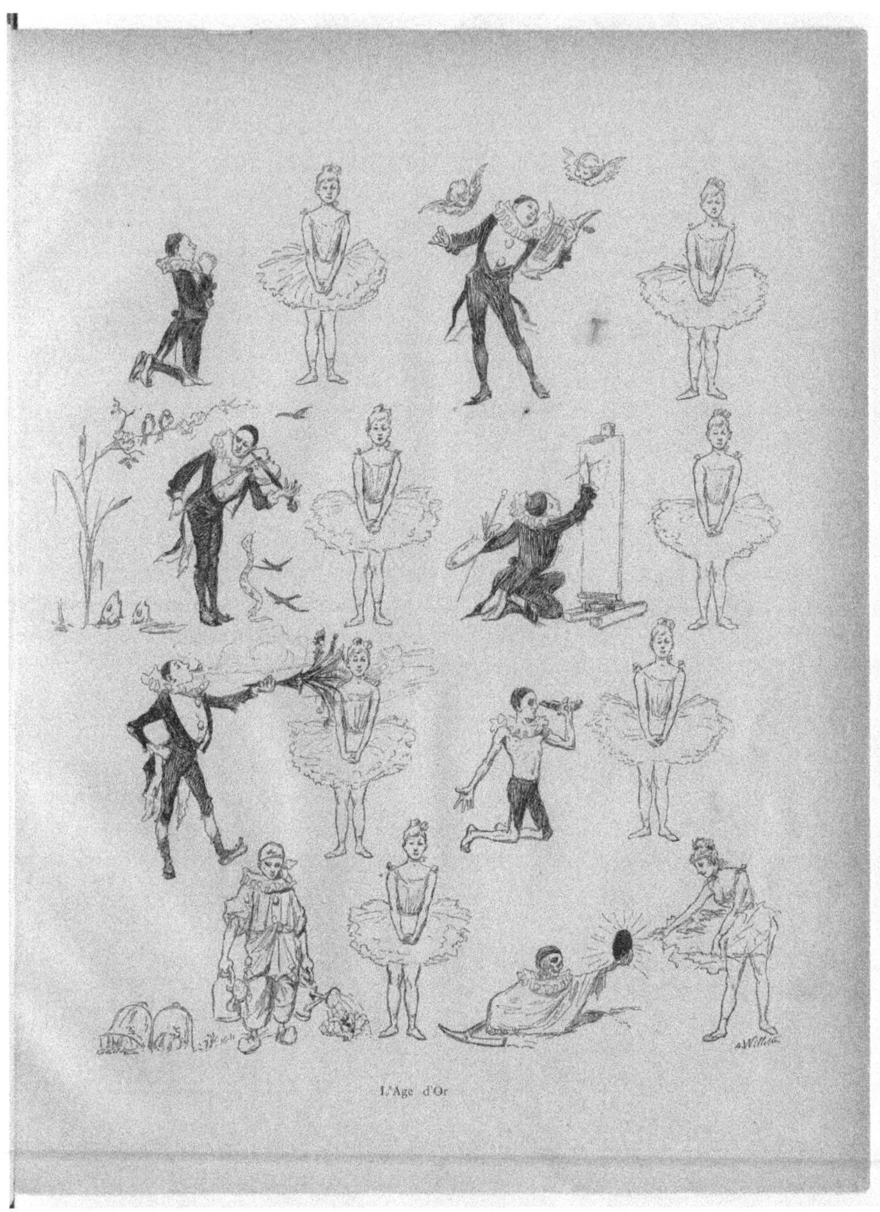

4.15   Adolphe Willette, *L'âge d'or*, from *Le Pierrot*, 10 August 1888. Lithograph. Source: Bibliothèque Nationale de France, Paris. FOL-LC 13–348 ©BNF.

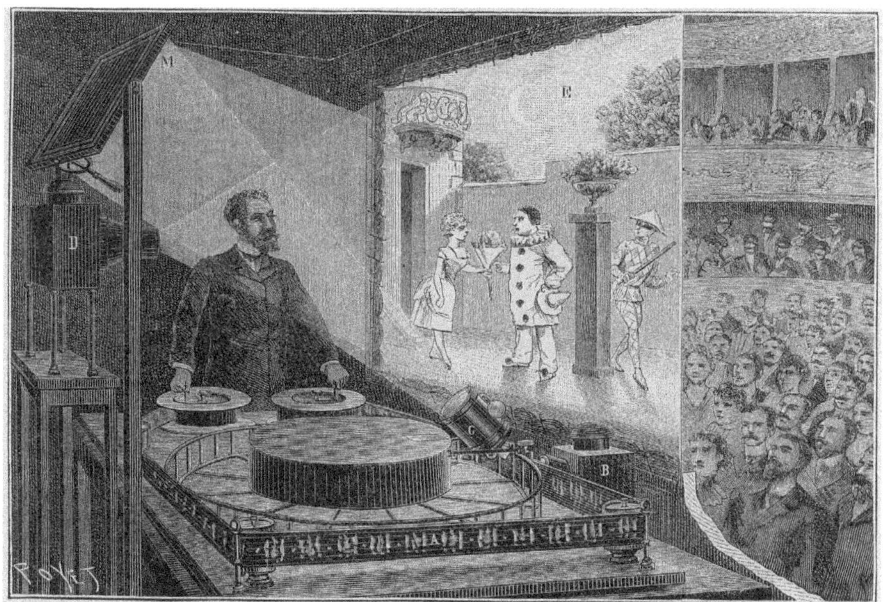

4.16   Louis Poyet after Gaston Tissandier, *Le Théâtre Optique de M. Reynaud* in
La Nature, no. 999, 23 July 1892. Wood engraving. Source: Bibliothèque Nationale de
France, Paris. 4-R-45 ©BNF.

Chéret's mature aesthetic, exemplified by the poster for the luminous
pantomimes, recalls the spectral ballet of the original phantasmagoria, now
saturated with colour and displayed on the boulevard. Affixed in large frames
to the façade of the Musée Grévin on the Boulevard Montmartre, the posters
also recalled the old *parades*. While dispensing with the physical bodies of
the performers, the posters enacted a 'performative enunciation' destined to
attract the attention of the passerby.[83] Other posters were even more explicit
about their role as virtual *parades*. For example, Henri-Gabriel Ibels's advertisement for a dealer in posters (a poster for posters), showed Pierrot and
other Italian masks performing a *parade* on a trestle-stage.[84] Chéret's formula
attested to the continuing allure of the floating figure, whose buoyancy
expressed a delightful immunity to the determining effects of environment. As
Jean Starobinski has suggested, the acrobatic lightness of the *fin-de-siècle* clown
represented metaphysical freedom.[85] Yet this visual language, when used as a
marketing technique, was also run through with the dreamlike characteristics
of the world of goods.

Responses to the incredible density of advertising posters rippled through
literature and social debates.[86] Posters were glued to the walls of houses and
plastered on the Morris columns on the pavement; many of these posters
advertised theatrical spectacles and music hall performances.[87] While progres-
sive authors like Roger Marx praised the 'open air museum' enabled by posters,

other critics bemoaned the vulgarity of the 'crying' poster – the term used was *criard*.[88] In this account, the urban crier has been replaced by the poster, although the crier had already been replaced by the *cris de Paris* as a transformation of the market into a theatrical repertoire. What remains consistent, however, is the marketplace as a stage for theatrical address. Chéret was frequently compared to rococo artists, including Boucher, Fragonard, and Watteau. His poster style was thought to access 'French gaiety', 'a national tradition of public festivity and humor', as exemplified by the *fête galante*.[89] As an explicit medium of marketing, however, the advertising poster reflected the way that this festive mode had already been linked to the activities of the market. As Marcus Verhagen has shown, the poster transformed the streets of Paris into a perpetual carnival, attended by Pierrots and *chérettes*. Yet this was carnival 'as a moment of intensified trade', a *fête marchande* rather than a Rabelaisian world upside down.[90]

Pierrot in early cinema

As an advertisement for the luminous pantomime, Chéret's weightless figures expressed the state to which Reynaud's rather wooden figures aspired. Like many a *parade*, the posters both distilled and exceeded what happened inside the theatre. Nevertheless, Reynaud's simple and sweet narratives, as well as his use of a scrolling, semi-transparent band, would anticipate the content as well as the mechanism of early cinema. Without pretensions to high culture, at least during its first decade, early cinema prospered as a fairground attraction. Not only were short films screened widely at carnivals, but early films themselves, like sideshows, were brief, arresting, comic spectacles. It is no surprise then to find Pierrot a favourite figure in the 'cinema of attractions', a mode characterised by exhibitionism and *Schaulust*.[91]

Pierrot starred in simple little films by the Lumière brothers like *Pierrot and the fly* (*Pierrot et la mouche*) of 1898, in which Pierrot appears against a black cloth and dozes, only to be awoken by a fly, which he struggles to swat.[92] With a very simple décor, sometimes consisting of only a dark fabric backdrop, these films resembled the *mise-en-scène* of the fairground *parade*. Pierrot was also well suited to early forms of filmed theatre that relied upon the familiar characters of the Comédie Italienne. In 1898, the Société Lumière produced several films featuring Pierrot, Colombine, and Arlequin jumping in and out of windows and beating each other up.[93] These films used a fixed camera, pointed at a décor structured exactly like a stage set, with houses on either side of the stage functioning as wings and determining the edges of the frame. The address of these early films was theatrical. As critics like Tom Gunning and Jean Mitry have argued, early cinema 'faced' the viewer, frankly presenting itself to be looked at.[94] The theatrical address of early cinema offered a bridge from the old, familiar medium to a new one. The frontality of the theatrical *mise-en-scène* suggested an image that appeared for the viewer, rather than one that exceeded the viewer in its superior capacity for movement and vision. The silly tricks and little acrobatic performances put on by the Pierrots of early cinema, like the plate-spinning Pierrot in a short film of 1899, *Assiette tournante*, were reassuring in both their familiarity and their theatrical address.[95]

Pierrot appeared in many early films that made use of one of the first kinds of cinematic 'special effects', the 'trick' (*truc*), a technique borrowed from the tricked décors of the nineteenth-century pantomime.[96] The cinematic *truc* was a simple device that relied on the fact that many early films had a fixed camera angle throughout. This allowed the camera to be stopped, a broom substituted for Arlequin, and filming resumed.[97] The resulting reel would show a broom suddenly transformed into Arlequin. The master of the tricked film, Georges Méliès, claimed that he constructed his films entirely around the *trucs*. Once the tricks were chosen, he then determined 'what era would be best to costume my characters', and finally, both in choice and importance, what narrative strand or *fil* would string the tricks together.[98] This technique recalls Champfleury's experience as an 'author' at the Funambules. Summoned to pen a narrative, or so he thinks, he finds himself playing with little bits of cardboard, tied together with string, to design a series of *trucs*. The tricked genre tends to neglect character development, hence its choice of easily recognisable, predetermined masks, like Pierrot, for its characters. Méliès frequently featured Pierrots in his films.[99]

The technique of the *truc* suggests the extent to which the early cinematic image was subject to manipulation and fragmentation.[100] Another early *truc* involved cutting bits of filmstrip and pasting them together in order, for example, to create the appearance of a painting coming to life. In the Pathé film *La folie de Pierrot* (1906), an artistically inclined Pierrot is subject to numerous apparitions within his apartment.[101] Colombine's head appears in place of a sculpted portrait bust and laughs at him, while a blank canvas is transformed into a little film within a film, showing a re-enactment of Gérôme's hugely popular *Duel after the Masked Ball*, the tableau in which Pierrot falls to Arlequin's sword. As Pierrot angrily gouges out the stretched canvas, a mannequin wearing a Swiss Guard's costume transforms into Arlequin. Each of these tricks would have involved the delicate cutting and pasting of bits of film, as well as the earlier 'tricked' technique of stopping and restarting the camera. These antics also recall the gag at the seventeenth-century Comédie Italienne, when Colombine stuck her head through the full-length, life-size portrait of Arlequin. This treatment of a painting as in effect a costume was echoed in the production of costume prints themselves, in which an artist mixed and matched a stock repertoire of facial features and social, professional, and national costumes to assemble a 'complete' figure. Similarly, early practitioners of cinema, by altering and trimming the image, performed the fungibility of the visible world as a clothed surface. While these kinds of practice may not have led to broader reflections on the apparitional character of the social front, they suggested a willingness to conceive of the filmed image as a manipulable surface, where appearance could be freely recostumed.

The narrative of optical devices and early cinema that I have traced is a familiar one. Less familiar is the way that Pierrot's history is woven through it.

There is much more to say about 'primitive cinema' and its use of the Italian masks. I have limited my own account to a few, very cursory observations about the way that early cinema returned to the territory of the *fête marchande*, which is also Pierrot's domain. In 1855, the Tournachons' 'Pierrots' cast the character as the front man of their photographs, while also introducing viewers to the spectacle of a single figure, at full length, in multiple 'frames', presented as a series. In the context of mid-century photographic culture, the series cast Pierrot onto the marketplace for celebrity while promoting photography as a medium of celebrity. Pierrot's appearance in the photographs recalled both the figural repertoire and the composition of many magic lantern slides, which presented a figure against an empty ground, which was then projected onto a fabric backdrop. The allusion to the magic lantern slide drew attention to the phantasmagoric qualities of the marketplace, which Nadar had already realised were ideally suited to the promotion of celebrity as a person and a chimaera. The apparitional character of the celebrity was also key to imagining figural animation as taking place in a state of groundlessness. It was Pierrot, as a figure always, already, groundless; always, already, turned towards the marketplace; who enabled the extraordinary multivalence of these photographs. The Pierrot that was sealed in the photographs would enjoy the same mobile existence that had characterised the eighteenth-century Pierrot. In this guise, he did what he had always done – he played the front man and stood at the threshold of the marketplace. From the Universal Exposition he moved to the boulevard and then back again to the fairground, where he fronted early cinema. Yet nearly a century after the Tournachons loosed Pierrot from the Funambules, the character would find himself returned, once again, to this milieu. In the two-part film, *Children of Paradise* (1945), Pierrot's efforts to experience artistic apotheosis as weightlessness would be countered by another version of the revenant – the ghost of an old-clothes seller.

Notes

1   Nikolaus Pevsner, *A History of Building Types* (London: Thames and Hudson, 1976), p. 246.

2   Raymond Isay, *Panorama des Expositions Universelles*, 8th edn (Paris: Gallimard, 1937), p. 23. For a general introduction to the nineteenth-century French universal exhibitions, see also Pascal Ory, *Les Expositions Universelles de Paris: panorama raisonné* (Paris: Éditions Ramsay, 1982).

3   For an important analysis of this display as announcing the de-politicisation of art, see Patricia Mainardi, 'The political origins of modernism', *Art Journal* 45:1 (1985), 11–17. See also her book-length study, Patricia Mainardi, *Art and Politics of the Second Empire: The Universal Expositions of 1855 and 1867* (New Haven, CT and London: Yale University Press, 1987).

4   Rosalind H. Williams, *Dream Worlds: Mass Consumption in Late Nineteenth-Century France* (Berkeley: University of California Press, 1982), pp. 59, 66.

5   This is the argument of Thomas Crow, *Painters and Public Life in Eighteenth-Century Paris* (New Haven, CT: Yale University Press, 1985). However, Crow is

careful to maintain that the public for painting was in large part a construction of the critics.

6 *Exposition Universelle de 1855, rapports du jury mixte international publiés sous la direction de S.A.I. le Prince Napoléon, président de la commission impériale* (Paris: Imprimerie impériale, 1856), pp. 1233–41. The official report of the jury emphasised photography's transformation from scientific curiosity to useful tool.

7 For critical accounts of the photographic display at the Exposition, see André Rouillé, 'La photographie Française à L'Exposition Universelle de 1855', *Le Mouvement Social* 131 (1985), 87–103. See also Hélène Bocard, *Les critiques des expositions de photographie à Paris sous le Second Empire* (Paris: Mémoire de D.E.A., Université Paris Sorbonne, Paris IV, 1995).

8 See *Exposition Universelle de 1855, rapports du jury*, p. 1236.

9 On photography's role as a helpmate to industry, particularly the dissemination of models for the decorative arts, see Elizabeth Anne McCauley, *Industrial Madness: Commercial Photography in Paris 1848–1871* (New Haven, CT: Yale University Press, 1994), pp. 233–64.

10 Nadar, *Quand j'étais photographe* (1900; Paris: Actes Sud, 1998), p. 103. Nadar commented on the public's delight in being able to see, up close, the images of celebrities that they had only seen from afar.

11 Ernest Lacan, *Esquisses photographiques à propos de l'Exposition Universelle et de la Guerre d'Orient* (Paris: Grassart, A. Gaudin et frère, 1856), p. 129.

12 The number eight is given by Paul Périer, *Compte rendu de l'exposition universelle de 1855* (Paris: Mallet-Bachelier, 1855), p. 49. This publication consists of articles that Périer had previously published in the bulletin of the Société Française de Photographie.

13 For example, Janin's biography was heavily illustrated. See Nye's publications for the best (and most accurately labelled) period illustrations, in particular Edward Nye, 'Portraits of Deburau in Janin's *Deburau, l'histoire du théâtre à quatre sous*', *L'Esprit Créateur* 59:1 (2019), 66–81.

14 Philippe Willems, 'Between panoramic and sequential: Nadar and the serial image', *Nineteenth-century Art Worldwide* 11:3 (2012), www.19thc-artworldwide.org/autumn12/willems-nadar-and-the-serial-image, accessed 28 April 2023.

15 Jean Adhémar, 'Propositions pour une thématique des portraits photographiques par Nadar', *Gazette des Beaux-Arts* 107:128 (1986), 157–62, here p. 159.

16 Maria Morris Hambourg, *Nadar: Les années créatrices* (Paris: Réunion des Musées Nationaux, 1995), p. 20. Hambourg's catalogue provides a useful chronology of Nadar's life.

17 Adhémar suggests that Nadar had indeed begun to use Adrien for this purpose in 1854. Adhémar, 'Propositions', 158.

18 On the Panthéon see Kathrin Yacavone, 'George Sand and Nadar: portraiture between lithography, sculpture, and photography', *L'Esprit Créateur* 59:1 (2019), 111–27, here pp. 112–16. See also Hambourg, *Nadar*, pp. 21–3.

19 See Willems' exemplary exploration of the tension in Nadar's work between the panoramic and the sequential: Willems, 'Between panoramic and sequential'.

20 On the *portrait charge* see Judith Wechsler, *A Human Comedy: Physiognomy and Caricature in Nineteenth Century Paris* (Chicago: University of Chicago Press, 1982), pp. 76–9, 137–9.

21 Gautier, 'Panthéon Nadar', *La Presse*, 21 March 1854, 2: '[u]ne immense lithographie se prélasse aux vitres de tous les marchands de gravures'. On other forms of literary publicity, as well as the *Panthéon* more generally, see also Adeline Wrona,

'Des Panthéons à vendre: le portrait d'homme de lettres, entre réclame et biographie', *Romantisme* 155 (2012), 37–50.

22 George Sand, 'Deburau' (February 1846), in *Questions d'art et de littérature* (Paris: C. Lévy, 1878), pp. 215–22, here p. 221. Sand only recounts the fall through the trap, not the ensuing death, but this story would be amplified in other accounts. These kinds of story, in which an artist died for the sake of his craft, having exposed himself to risk on stage, were popular. The beloved Arlequin of the seventeenth-century Comédie Italienne, Dominique, was supposed to have died because he caught cold while performing for hours before an insatiable Louis XIV.

23 Sand, 'Deburau', p. 219.

24 Maurice Sand wrote of Charles: 'le fils de Deburau est peut-être le plus joli et le plus élégant Pierrot qui ait existé. C'est par la souplesse, la grâce et la fantaisie charmante, qu'il s'est acquis, à bon droit, une grande vogue'. Sand cited in Louis Péricaud, *Le Théâtre des Funambules, ses mimes, ses acteurs et ses pantomimes, depuis sa fondation jusqu'à sa démolition* (Paris: Léon Sapin, 1897), p. 406.

25 On Charles and Paul see Péricaud, *Le Théâtre des Funambules*; and Tristan Rémy, *Jean-Gaspard Deburau* (Paris: L'Arche, 1954), pp. 172–5 for a comparison of the styles of Paul and Baptiste. The Department of Arts du Spectacle at the Bibliothèque Nationale de France conserves numerous pamphlets relating the life stories of Paul and Charles in the Collection Rondel – these are often included as clippings in albums without date or the name of the author: for example, J.V., *Notice biographique sur M. Paul le Grand, successeur de Deburau au théâtre des Funambules, par l'auteur de Pierrot Marié* (Paris: Gallet, 1847) and *Biographie de Charles Deburau, fils* (Paris: Dechaume, n.d.).

26 *Pierrot ministre* (Paris: Gallet 1848). Nadar also wrote another pantomime, after the photographs were exhibited, entitled *Pierrot boursier* (1856).

27 On photography's efforts to rival painting 'by composing fictions that introduced the idea of time, narration, sentiment, and even the ideal', see Françoise Heilbrun, *La photographie au Musée d'Orsay* (Paris: Flammarion, 2008), p. 174.

28 Rosalind Krauss, 'Tracing Nadar', *October* 5 (1978), 29–47. Krauss argues that in this series the arts of mime and photography double one another as arts of non-verbal imitation.

29 For example see Périer, *Compte rendu*, pp. 1–13.

30 Périer, *Compte rendu*, p. 49; Lacan, *Esquisses photographiques*, p. 129.

31 On this distinction, and the influence upon photography of its status as a retail medium, see Jillian Lerner, 'Nadar's signatures: caricature, self-portrait, publicity', *History of Photography* 41:2 (2017), 108–25, here p. 125.

32 Périer, *Compte rendu*, p. 57: 'frappé.

33 Lacan, *Esquisses photographiques*, p. 141.

34 On Susse as a retail outfit, see Nicholas Green, *The Spectacle of Nature: Landscape and Bourgeois Culture in Nineteenth Century France* (Manchester University Press, 1990), p. 26.

35 Lacan, *Esquisses photographiques*, p. 141.

36 Périer, *Compte rendu*, p. 2.

37 Ferdinand de Lasteyrie, 'Exposition Universelle: photographie', *Le Siècle*, 25 October 1855, 3.

38 Disdéri cited in Bocard, *Les critiques des expositions de photographie*, p. 27.

39 Lacan, *Esquisses photographiques*, pp. 52–3.

40 On the Diorama see Heinz Buddemeier, *Panorama, Diorama, Photographie* (Munich: W. Fink, 1970), pp. 26–39.

41 Jules Janin, 'Le daguérotype' [*sic*], *L'Artiste*, ser. 2, 2:11 (1839), 145–8; Jules Janin, 'La description du daguérotype', *L'Artiste*, ser. 2, 3:17 (1839), 277–83; Jules Janin, 'Le daguérotype: nouvelle exercise', *L'Artiste*, ser. 2, 4:1 (1839), 1–3. On Janin's contribution to the early aesthetic discourse of photography, see Stephen Pinson, 'Trompe l'œil: photography's illusion reconsidered', *Nineteenth-Century Art Worldwide* 1:1 (2002), www.19thc-artworldwide.org/spring02/195-trompe-loe il-photographys-illusion-reconsidered, accessed 28 April 2023.

42 See Eugène de Mirecourt, *Jules Janin* (Paris: G. Havard, 1857), p. 77 for a description of Janin performing as a Pierrot in his *feuilleton* for the *Journal des Débats*. See also the anonymous critic, who weaves a depiction of Janin as performing the *parade* on the *tréteaux* into his obituary for Deburau: 'Oraison funèbre', *Silhouette*, 12 July 1846, cited in Péricaud, *Le Théâtre des Funambules*, p. 291.

43 Janin, 'Le daguérotype: nouvelle exercise', p. 2: 'le pinceau invisible de la reine Mab, la reine des fées'. In another article, Janin also suggests that one could mistake the photographic plate, with its extraordinary detail, for having been made by the 'breath of some inspired fairy' ('*le souffle de quelque fée inspirée*'): Janin, 'La description du daguérotype', p. 279.

44 Philippe Hamon, 'Introduction. Littérature et réclame: le cru et le cri', *Romantisme* 155 (2012), 3–10.

45 Lerner, 'Nadar's signatures', pp. 110–18.

46 The play, performed at the Théâtre du Palais Royal, was a vaudeville about the making of the caricatures, featuring the 'Binette', a helpful, *fée*-like character who arises from a box of discarded caricatures. Clairville, Cordier and Commerson, *Les Binettes Contemporaines, revue en trois actes et sept tableaux* (Paris: Beck, 1855). On the making of the *Binettes* see also Loie Chotard, *Nadar: caricatures, photographies* (Paris: Maison de Balzac, 1990), pp. 87–9.

47 Roger Greaves, *Nadar ou le Paradoxe vital* (Paris: Flammarion, 1980), p. 52.

48 On this intimate studio practice and its resulting portraits, see my article, Marika Takanishi Knowles, 'Lost ground: the performance of Pierrot in Nadar and Adrien Tournachon's photographs of Charles Deburau', *Oxford Art Journal* 38:3 (2015), 365–86, here pp. 384–6. See also McCauley, *Industrial Madness*, pp. 118–41.

49 See Perry's analysis of two surviving albums, in which *cartes-de-visite* are mixed with other media, including printed reproductions of paintings: Lara Perry, 'The *carte de visite* in the 1860s and the Serial dynamic of photographic likeness', *Art History* 35:4 (2012), 728–49.

50 Elizabeth Anne McCauley, *A.A.E. Disdéri and the Carte de Visite Portrait Photograph* (New Haven, CT: Yale University Press, 1985), p. 62.

51 At the Bibliothèque Nationale de France, see the Nadar studio catalogues, which were likely used both as documentation for the studio and also as repertoires for clients: *Album de reference de l'atelier Nadar*, vol. 14, NA-237 (7)-FT 4 and *Album de reference de l'atelier Nadar*, vol. 65, NA-238 (51)-FT 4.

52 On the official rhetoric surrounding the exhibition, see Anne Green, 'France exposed: *Madame Bovary* and the Exposition Universelle', *Modern Language Review* 99:4 (2004), 915–23, here pp. 916–19.

53 For a crucial account of the nineteenth-century French expositions as aesthetic frames, see Philippe Hamon, *Expositions: Littérature et Architecture au XIXe siècle* (Paris: José Corti, 1989), p. 15: 'd'un bric-à-brac et d'une organisation', 'lieu d'un

divertissement', 'l'exposition d'un savoir', 'exemplaire', 'provisoire, démontable et transitoire'.

54 Hamon, *Expositions*, p. 14: 'un monde réductible à un grand magasin bien organisé'.

55 On foreign visitors as objects of curiosity at the Exposition, see Green, 'France exposed', p. 919.

56 Lerner calls this repertoire an 'image bank': Lerner, 'Nadar's signatures', p. 123.

57 Margaret Cohen, 'Walter Benjamin's phantasmagoria', *New German Critique* 48 (1989), 87–107, here p. 105. See also Gyorgy Markus, 'Walter Benjamin or: the commodity as phantasmagoria', *New German Critique* 83 (2001), 3–42. On commodity fetishism and the Universal Expositions, see Williams, *Dream Worlds*, pp. 58–106.

58 Walter Benjamin, 'Paris, capitale du XIXeme siècle, exposé', in Walter Benjamin, *Gesammelte Schriften* (Frankfurt am Main: Suhrkamp Verlag, 1991), 1:60.

59 Laurent Mannoni and Donata Pesenti Campagnoni, *Lanterne magique et film peint: 400 ans de cinéma* (Paris: La Cinémathèque française, 2009), pp. 132–40.

60 See the 'Lanterna Magica' collection of the Cinémathèque Française, PLM-00604–068, 'Bonsoir'.

61 Cohen, 'Walter Benjamin's phantasmagoria', 92.

62 On Robertson's phantasmagoria and Benjamin's comparison, see Tom Gunning, 'Illusions past and future: the phantasmagoria and its specters', presentation at the University of Chicago, 2004, available at www.mediaarthistory.org/.

63 On this glass, and the exhibition's 'emergent image world of commercial display', see the excellent article: Katie Hornstein, 'The Saint-Gobain *grande glace*: transparency and display culture at the Exposition Universelle of 1855', *Oxford Art Journal* 44: 3 (2021), 399–417.

64 Benjamin, 'Paris, capitale du XIXeme siècle', 1:60: 'ces fantasmagories du marché, où les hommes n'apparaissent que sous des aspects typiques'.

65 Mannoni, *Lanterne magique*, p. 206.

66 Terry Castle, 'Phantasmagoria: spectral technology and the metaphorics of modern reverie', *Critical Inquiry* 15:1 (1988), 26–61. Comparisons were also made between mental images and bas-relief sculpture, another medium that presented figures against a bare ground: Emmelyn Butterfield-Rosen, *Modern Art and the Remaking of Human Disposition* (Chicago: University of Chicago Press, 2021), pp. 200–04. Butterfield-Rosen persuasively demonstrates a link between the theories of the art historian Emmanuel Löwy on the characteristics of memory images and proto-cinematic technologies like Reynaud's luminous pantomimes (on Reynaud see below).

67 Janin, 'La description du daguérotype', p. 279: *'aussitôt pris, aussitôt pendu'*.

68 For a recent, richly illustrated introduction to the efflorescence of visual forms leading to the birth of cinema, see Dominique Païni, Paul Perrin, and Marie Robert (eds), *Enfin le cinéma: arts, images et spectacles en France (1833–1907)* (Paris: Réunion des Musées Nationaux, 2021).

69 Mariel Oberthür, *Le Chat Noir 1881–1897* (Paris: Les Dossiers du Musée d'Orsay, Éditions de la Réunion des musées nationaux, 1992), pp. 40–51.

70 For a description of the shadow plays and Salis's style as a *bonimenteur*, see Maurice Donnay, *Autour du Chat Noir* (1926; Paris: Bernard Grasset, 1966), pp. 31–5.

71 Oberthür, *Le Chat Noir*, p. 36. On Willette as the Chat Noir, see also Mary Shaw and Philip Dennis Cate, *The Spirit of Montmartre: Cabarets, Humor, and the Avant-Garde* (New Brunswick, NJ: Rutgers University Press, 1996), pp. 34–8.

72 Elena Cueto-Asin, 'The Chat Noir's Théâtre d'Ombres: shadow plays and the recuperation of public space', in Gabriel P. Weisberg (ed.), *Montmartre and the Making of Mass Culture* (New Brunswick, NJ: Rutgers University Press, 2001), pp. 223–46.

73 On the vogue for the 'primitive' silhouette in *fin-de-siècle* artistic circles, and the belief that the silhouette expressed the essence of character, see Nancy Forgione, '"The shadow only": shadow and silhouette in late-nineteenth century Paris', *Art Bulletin* 81:3 (1999), 490–512.

74 See the cover of *Le Pierrot*, 2:13 (1889).

75 The decorations of this tavern are known as black and white photographs, conserved at the Musée Carnavalet, in Paris. CARPHTOP4478–4480.

76 Adolphe Willette, *Pierrot pendu*, 1894. Lithograph, 46.5 × 29.1 cm. In *L'album originale*, Metropolitan Museum of Art, New York. Acc. 22.82.1–60.

77 See for example the page illustrating 'Satan, ou le pacte infernal' in the *Musée Philipon*, 23 (1843), 184. Paris: Bibliothèque nationale de France, TF-619-4.

78 On the way that these devices relied upon the recently theorised 'persistence of vision' in order to create the illusion of movement, see Jonathan Crary, *Techniques of the Observer: On Vision and Modernity in the Nineteenth Century* (Cambridge, MA: MIT Press, 1990), pp. 104–12.

79 Dominique Auzel, *Émile Reynaud et l'image s'anima* (Paris: Editions Dumay, 1992), pp. 28–38.

80 Auzel, *Émile Reynaud*, pp. 43–8. See also Mannoni, *Lanterne magique et film peint*, pp. 249–53. Reynaud also marketed and sold by mail miniature praxinoscope theatres, which came with a wide selection of décors and several bands featuring serial images of a figure.

81 Reynaud's drawings for *Pauvre Pierrot* are conserved at the Archives françaises du film, Centre national du cinéma et de l'image animée (CNC), at Bois d'Arcy. A filmed and abbreviated reconstruction of the pantomime, restored by Julien Pappé, which also features reconstructed sound – piano music and singing accompanied Reynaud's performances – can also be seen at the CNC. On the tense relationship between the Musée Grévin, which thought of itself as a wax-museum newspaper, and Émile Reynaud, see Vanessa Schwartz, *Spectacular Realities: Early Mass Culture in Fin-de-Siècle Paris* (Berkeley: University of California Press, 1998), pp. 177–90.

82 On Chéret see the excellent recent catalogue: Réjane Bargiel and Ségolène Le Men, *La Belle Époque de Jules Chéret: De l'affiche au décor* (Paris: Les Arts Décoratifs/ Bibliothèque nationale de France, 2010).

83 Ségolène Le Men, 'L'œuvre de Chéret en résonance', in Bargiel and Le Men (eds), *La Belle Époque de Jules Chéret*, pp. 51–75, here p. 63.

84 This poster was drawn to my attention by Marcus Verhagen, 'The poster in *fin-de-siècle* Paris: "that mobile and degenerate art"', in Leo Charney and Vanessa R. Schwartz (eds), *Cinema and the Invention of Modern Life* (Berkeley: University of California Press, 1995), pp. 103–29, here pp. 113–14.

85 For an interpretation of the clown's acrobatic lightness as metaphysical freedom, see Jean Starobinski, *Portrait de l'artiste en saltimbanque* (Geneva: Albert Skira, 1970), pp. 27–41.

86 Philippe Hamon has suggested that the omnipresence of the poster was yet another form of 'exhibition', a symptom of the same structural turn towards spectacle and flatness (*platitude*) that lay at the heart of the Universal Expositions: Hamon, *Expositions*, pp. 125–35.

87 On advertising and the Morris column (wide, short columns placed in the street for mounting advertising posters), see H. Hazel Hahn, *Scenes of Parisian Modernity: Culture and Consumption in the Nineteenth Century* (New York: Palgrave Macmillan, 2009), pp. 143–60, 183–204.

88 Noriko Yoshida, 'Jules Chéret et la critique d'art de Roger Marx à Gustave Kahn', in Bargiel and Le Men (eds), *La Belle Époque de Jules Chéret*, pp. 109–19, here p. 114: 'musée en plein vent'.

89 Verhagen, 'The poster in *fin-de-siècle* Paris', p. 111.

90 Verhagen, 'The poster in *fin-de-siècle* Paris', p. 121.

91 On the cinema of attractions see Tom Gunning, 'The cinema of attractions: early cinema, its spectator and the avant garde', in Thomas Elsaesser (ed.), *Early Cinema: Space Frame Narrative* (London: British Film Institute, 1990), pp. 56–62. See also Tom Gunning, '"Now you see it, now you don't": the temporality of the cinema of attractions', *The Velvet Light Trap* 32 (1993), 3–12.

92 Lumière et ses fils, *Pierrot et la mouche*, 1898, 46 seconds, CNC. (The CNC does not use catalogue numbers; I offer here the information that can be found in the catalogue of the CNC archives.)

93 Société Lumière et ses Fils, *Sérénade de Pierrot*, 1898, 54 seconds, CNC; Société Lumière et ses Fils, *Pierrot surpris*, 1898, 29 seconds, CNC.

94 Tom Gunning, '"Primitive" cinema: a frame-up? Or the trick's on us', in Elsaesser (ed.), *Early Cinema*, pp. 95–103, here pp. 99–101; Jean Mitry, 'Le montage dans les films de Méliès', in Madeleine Malthête-Méliès (ed.), *Méliès et la naissance du spectacle cinématographique* (Paris: Klincksieck, 1984), pp. 149–55, here p. 150–51.

95 Auguste Baron, *Assiette tournante*, 1899, 8 seconds, CNC.

96 The Lumières, despite their reputation for verism, made plenty of tricked films featuring Pierrot. See Lumière et ses Fils, *Pierrot et le fantôme*, 1898, 54 seconds, CNC; Société Lumière et ses Fils, *Pierrot et la flûte enchantée*, 1903, 1 minute 42 seconds, CNC.

97 Mitry, 'Le montage dans les films de Méliès', p. 150.

98 Méliès cited in André Gaudreault, 'Théâtralité et narrativité dans l'œuvre de Georges Méliès', in Malthête-Méliès (ed.), *Méliès et la naissance du spectacle cinémato-graphique*, pp. 199–219, here p. 211: 'je cherchais quelle époque serait la meilleure pour habiller mes personnages'.

99 See, for example, Georges Méliès, *Au clair de la Lune ou Pierrot Malheureux*, 1904, 3 minutes; Georges Méliès, *Le Cauchemar*, 1896, 1 minute 7 seconds; Georges Méliès, *La lune à un mètre (The Astronomer's Dream)*, 1898, 3 minutes, 11 seconds. *La lune à un mètre* features childish Pierrots, reminiscent of Willette's baby Pierrots, tumbling out of the mouth of the Moon.

100 On the 'spliced' and fragmentary nature of the early cinematic image, see Tom Gunning, '"Primitive" cinema', p. 150.

101 Pathé Frères, *La folie de Pierrot*, 1906, 3 minutes 17 seconds, CNC. On this film and other early narrative shorts featuring Pierrot, see Barthélémy Amengual, 'D'un Pierrot à l'autre', in Pierre Guibbert (ed.), *Les Premiers Ans du Cinéma Français* (Perpignan: Institut Jean Vigo, 1985), pp. 147–9.

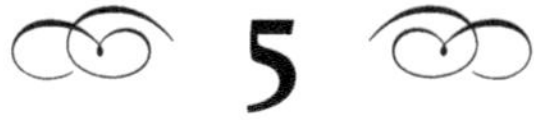

Old clothes and the dreams
of the artist

On 9 March 1945, *Children of Paradise (Les enfants du paradis)* premiered at the Palais Chaillot in Paris. In this two-part backstage drama, directed by Marcel Carné to a script by Jacques Prévert, Baptiste Deburau and other (male) celebrities of Romantic Paris are reincarnated, their characters animated by a shared love for a fictional woman, Garance, daughter of a laundress from Ménilmontant.[1] The Théâtre des Funambules is recreated in exquisite detail, from its smoky auditorium to its wings crowded with set-pieces and costumes, and the pantomimes that were played on its stage. The Boulevard du Temple is also restaged, built from scratch at a studio in Nice and densely populated with *parades*, sideshow tents, tightrope walkers, and hundreds of extras clothed in period costume.[2] Played by the celebrated actor Jean-Louis Barrault, who had trained as a mime, Pierrot returns to the ground – the Funambules and the Boulevard du Temple – which Nadar's photographs had excluded. In this chapter, I analyse the film's representation of the relationship between Pierrot and the marketplace. I suggest that the film's cultural politics reflect the advent of conservative, anti-Semitic ideologies, which advanced an association between Jewishness and market practices perceived as exploitative and 'un-French'. In the representations discussed here, Pierrot's relationship to the market is replaced by a rhetoric of popular 'simplicity' and French 'classicism'. I say that the film 'reflects' conservative cultural politics because, ultimately, I do not think that the film endorses any one of these dispositions, or tones. Even so, the film is played on the strings of an instrument tuned within the tense atmosphere of the Occupation, which held a particularly tight grip on the world of French film.

Occupied cinema

The premiere of *Children of Paradise* was marketed as a great cultural event, which would celebrate the liberation of France from German occupation and demonstrate the resilience of French culture and artistry. However, the film was very much a product of the Occupation, in terms of the financing that made its gargantuan production possible and in its visual style and choice of a historical subject. When the German army invaded France in 1940, the country was split into two zones, with the Nazis occupying Paris and the north-west of the country (the occupied zone), and the south-eastern part of the country under the Vichy regime led by Pétain. The Nazis quickly established their own film studio in Paris, Continental, which took over the studios, distribution networks, and cinemas of several Jewish business owners.[3] All other film-making was submitted to the control of the Comité d'Organisation de l'Industrie Cinématographique (COIC), which worked closely with the occupiers and abided by their rules regarding appropriate content – no reference to the occupiers would be made – and personnel – no Jews would be allowed to work in the film industry.[4] Ironically, Nazi regulation proved instrumental in restoring the functionality of the French film industry, which had been on the verge of financial ruin.[5] Many film personnel left France for Hollywood, refusing to work with the Germans in any way, whether at Continental or with the 'independent' production companies that were in fact subject to Nazi control.

Carné was one of the only giants of the 1930s French 'classical' cinema to remain in France. He defended this controversial decision by arguing that he stayed in order to defend and to preserve French spirit and tradition.[6] It has been noted that Carné and his close collaborator Jacques Prévert, who wrote the screenplay for *Children of Paradise* and many of Carné's best films, worked *en clandestine* with the set designer Alexandre Trauner and the composer Joseph Kosma, both of whom were Jewish and therefore in hiding. *Children of Paradise* was produced by André Paulvé, who funded it with an Italian partner, Scalera.[7] When Italy surrendered to the Allies in the autumn of 1943, production was briefly halted, as Italy was no longer an ally of Germany. Paulvé fell under suspicion of having Jewish ancestors; responsibility for the film was taken over by the production company Pathé.

The weight of history

Undoubtedly, the film has a story. In previous chapters, stories unfolded around and from Pierrot, in the space between the work and the viewer, or in the movement of Pierrot from one ground or one medium to another. Yet there was no sustained narrative internal to the work itself. *Children of Paradise*, however, has many different stories, which are bound up with one another in complex ways.[8] The film's Pierrot has two primary narrative strands: the evolution of Baptiste's commanding artistry in the role of Pierrot, and Baptiste's love for Garance, the working-class heroine who earns her living as an artist's model and a performer in various Boulevard spectacles. In the film's opening sequence, Baptiste, performing in the *parade* for the Funambules (see Figure 0.3), sees Garance in the audience. In a reversal of the traditional relationship, a performer fixates on a member of the audience: Baptiste immediately falls in love. Meanwhile, his improvised performance, inspired by Garance, is a huge success; Baptiste is given a chance to play the role of Pierrot on the theatre's main (interior) stage.

Baptiste struggles to separate the ideal of love from its physical realisation. Although he runs into Garance that same evening at the cabaret, and even takes her back to his boarding house, he resists consummating the relationship. Lonely and bored, Garance falls into the arms of Frédérick Lemaître, a bold, extroverted actor, who has recently taken a job at the Funambules and a room in the same boarding house. Lemaître, like Baptiste, is based on a legendary actor; one of the many roles for which the historical Lemaître was famous was that of a ragpicker. The relationship of convenience between Frédérick and Garance horrifies and devastates Baptiste. Meanwhile, Garance has been implicated in a criminal plot orchestrated by the dandy-poet Lacenaire (another historical person). Garance then disappears with a wealthy noble, the Comte de Montray. This concludes the film's first hundred minutes.

At the beginning of the film's second *époque*, Garance returns to Paris and finds that Baptiste has married the daughter of the Funambules' manager, Nathalie. Baptiste and Nathalie have a child. In Garance's absence, both Baptiste and Frédérick have become theatrical celebrities, Baptiste as Pierrot and Frédérick as the star of melodramas, comedies, and eventually *Othello*, which he performs in blackface. In Garance's absence, Baptiste has allowed the tentacles of his milieu, the administrative structure of his artistry, to subsume him. The film's final scene makes this very clear. Baptiste has spent the night with Garance, but in the morning she leaves him. It is Carnival and the Boulevard is packed with people. Baptiste chases Garance into the crowd, but cannot catch her. Instead, he is caught up in a stampede of revellers, many of whom are dressed as Pierrot. The shots cut between Baptiste attempting to push his way out of the sea of Pierrots and Garance alone in her carriage. As he tries to reach her, Baptiste is chased by Jericho, an old-clothes seller who supplies the costumes for the pantomimes as well as the clothing and household goods of the actors. As they jostle in the crush of the crowd, Jericho literally holds back Baptiste, grabbing his arm, leading Baptiste to cry 'let me go, let me go!' (*'laisse-moi, laisse-moi!'*). Originally, Prévert had wanted Baptiste to kill Jericho during this scene, an allusion to the fact that Deburau had been tried for killing a man who was harassing him on the street. In the final version, however, Baptiste is too fixated on Garance to turn his full wrath upon Jericho. Garance's carriage spirits her away and the camera pans out above the crowd, eventually losing Baptiste. A curtain falls over the frame; the film ends.

In this long film, most of the characters end up alone, a refrain that is repeated in the film's poetic dialogue by Garance and the old-clothes seller, Jericho, about whom I will have much more to say. 'I am all alone' (*'je suis toute seule'*), Garance tells Baptiste's little son, when he visits her in her private box at the Funambules (*loge*). The final shot of Garance confirms this loneliness, showing her isolated in her plush carriage, a stark contrast to the mêlée of the Boulevard outside. In her white satin gown, set against the dark velvet cushions of the carriage, she has become Nadar's original Pierrot, a white figure against a dark ground (Figure 5.1). The loneliness of the characters is all the more striking because, with a few exceptions, they are utterly surrounded by things. The décor of the film is ornate; many of the camera angles are designed so as to crowd the frame with objects, figures, and texture.

The film-makers lovingly staged this décor, building the set of the Boulevard in a studio in Nice, using period prints from the Musée Carnavalet to create both the Boulevard and the interiors. From the *coulisses* of the Funambules to the boarding house of Madame Hermine, where most of the characters live, the décor manifests a *horror vacui*. The boarding house, decorated within an inch of its shabby life with striped wallpaper, cheap lithographs, fringed lampshades, and paisley bedspreads, wraps its inhabitants in a stifling embrace. The film's opening and closing sequences show the Boulevard teeming with people and spectacles. Tightrope walkers (*funambules*) teeter above the crowds, *paillasses* performing the *parade* populate the façades of theatres, café terraces overflow with customers. No patch of space is without its *figurant*, its body in motion. Backstage at the Funambules, actors and extras are in constant movement, presenting a mobile tapestry of spangles, feathered headdresses, striped tights, silk wings, and a range of papier-mâché set-pieces, including a cactus, a Madonna, trees, a miniature fleet of ships, and a grandfather clock (Figure 5.2). The

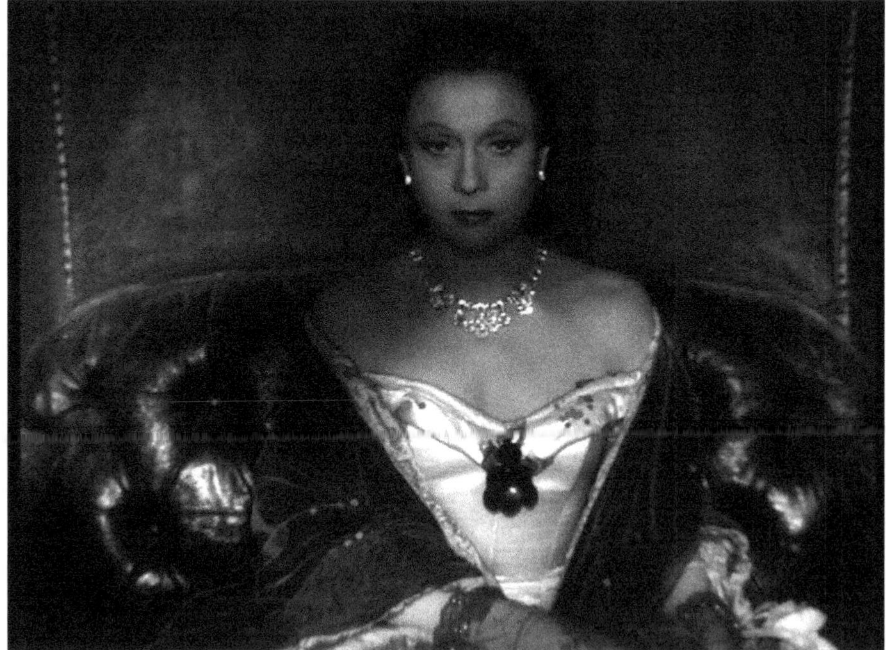

5.1   Marcel Carné (dir.), *Garance alone in her carriage during carnival*, 1945. Source: Pathé.

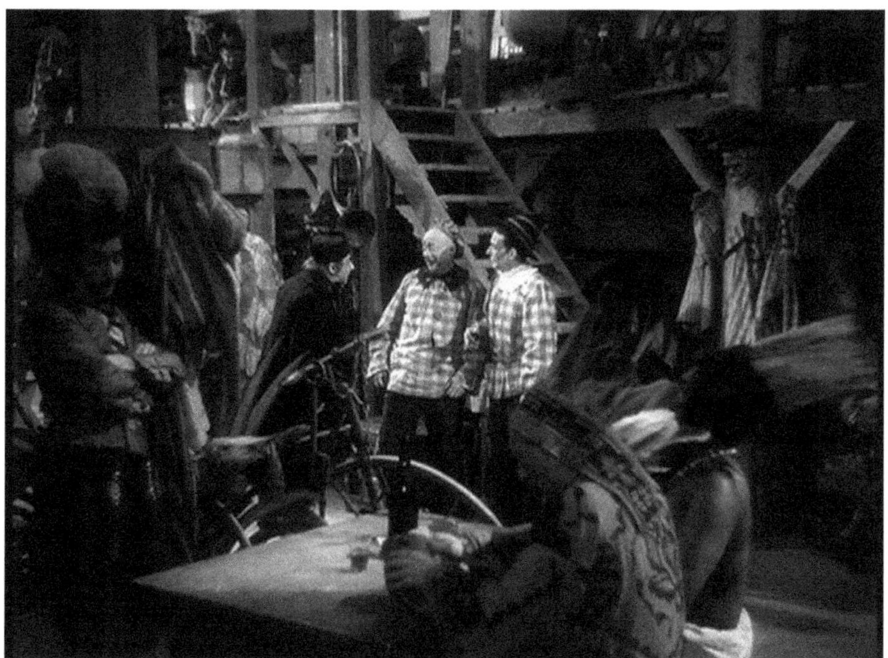

5.2   Marcel Carné (dir.), *Backstage at the Théâtre des Funambules*, 1945. Source: Pathé.

camera angles minimise depth to maximise the riot of texture. In the actors' dressing rooms, costumes and props hang from the walls; even the folding screen, behind which Garance changes, is papered with a *découpage* of figures cut from fashion plates (Figure 5.3). The spectacular décor creates a distraction that would smother lesser actors. Yet these actors are all intense physical presences, directed skilfully by Carné and granted poetic, even ponderous dialogue by Prévert.

In its richness, the décor increasingly becomes an additional character whose presence alters the fate of other characters. For the viewer, the décor grounds the protagonists within 1830s Romantic Paris. For the characters themselves, the environment determines their options, but to different degrees. Baptiste suffers the most acutely in this regard. When he tries to explain to Garance the sublime nature of his love for her, he refers to the character of the Moon: 'it is my country, the Moon'. Unmoored amongst his contemporaries, he has been told that his dreams are impossible, 'but why impossible, because I dream of them, these things!' Early in the film, we are introduced to Nathalie, a young actress and daughter of the manager of the Funambules, who is deeply in love with Baptiste. She wants to marry and to settle down, to have children who will become actors at the Funambules, furthering the ties between the family and the theatre. Towards Nathalie, Baptiste feels kindly indifference. In Garance, he identifies an ideal, a love

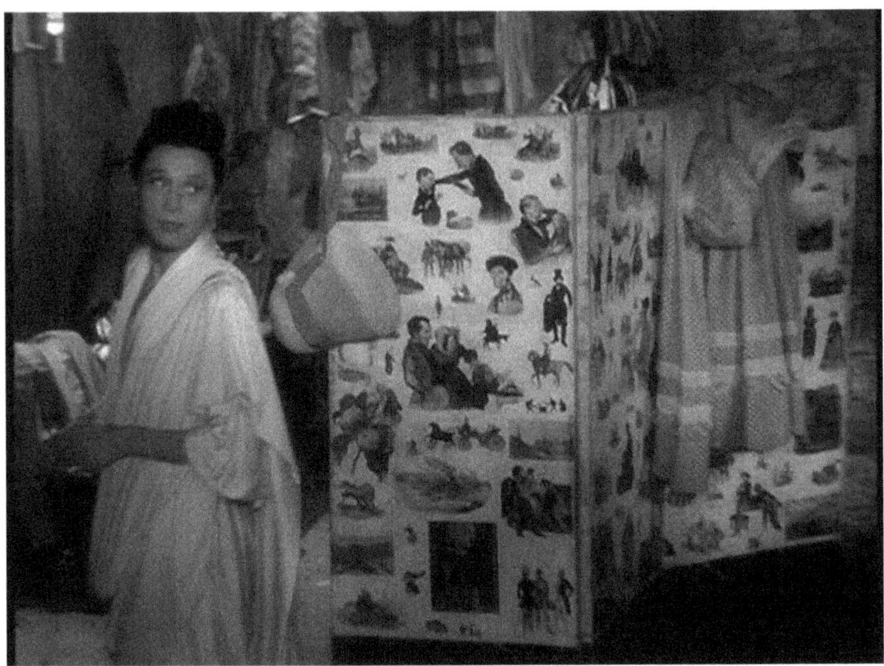

5.3   Marcel Carné (dir.), *Garance in her dressing room, wearing her statue costume*, 1945. Source: Pathé.

that is nocturnal and cerebral – a love that is lunar. Garance in fact seems much earthier. She is named for a flower, not a star, but Baptiste sees what he chooses. Garance is at home in Madame Hermine's boarding house, amid the cluttered décor to which she adds her own dress and stockings, hung to dry on a line outside her window (Figure 5.4). In pursuit of his ideal of love, however, Baptiste must escape this environment. This is apparent in the final sequence, when he chases Garance through the crush of the crowd on the Boulevard.[9] This is probably the film's most famous scene, commented on by almost all the contemporary critics, a self-conscious *tour-de-force* in which the screen is filled entirely by bodies clad in white fabric. White confetti, streamers, and ribbons litter the shots, which are cropped to show only the busts of the participants, with the camera raised so that the legs and feet of the revellers are invisible (Figure 5.5). Architectural, structural markers disappear, replaced by fabric and pale faces, some of which are painted white. Baptiste loses his footing; we see not his body, but only his torso, as he is borne along in the sea of Pierrots. In this stampede, he no longer appears to touch the ground, nor is there any ground to be touched (Figure 5.6).

During this scene, Jericho, the old-clothes seller, restrains Baptiste. Indeed, Jericho is allied with Nathalie in his effort to bind Baptiste to the prosaic and the everyday. Throughout the film, Jericho is the viewer's guide to the mêlée of the

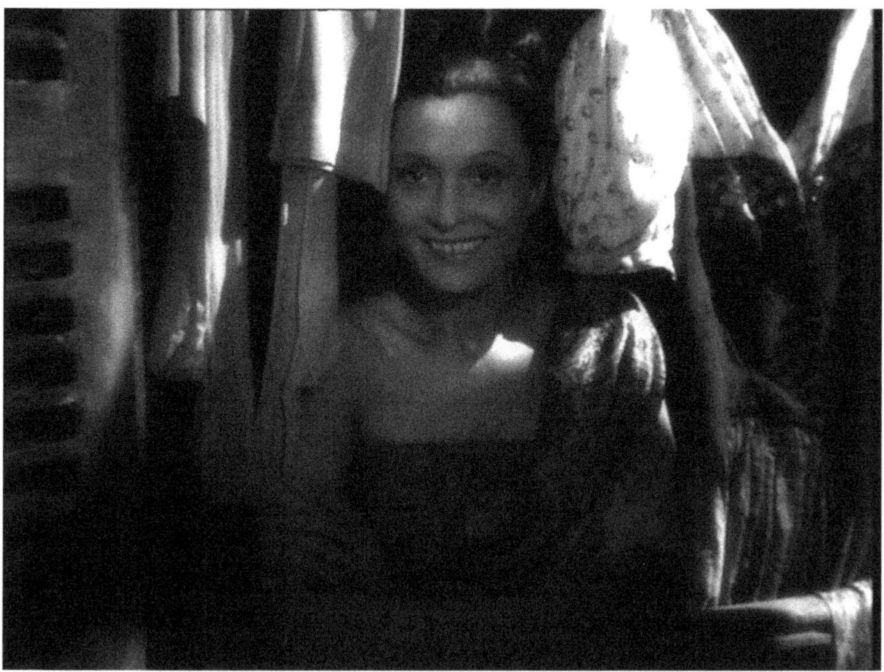

5.4   Marcel Carné (dir.), *Garance at her boarding-house window, surrounded by her drying clothes*, 1945. Source: Pathé.

Boulevard. His trumpet and cry – *chand d'habits!* – open the film, as the viewer follows him down a set of steps into the crowd on the Boulevard. (This makes *marchand* the first word in the film.) Soon after, Jericho appears backstage at the Funambules (Figure 5.7). He wears a striped scarf and shirt, a waistcoat in need of patching, and carries a load of cutlery, *épaulettes*, old clothes, and the brass trumpet with which he accompanies his cry. He offers the besotted Nathalie a second-hand wedding gown, reminding her to buy her silverware from him when she finally marries Baptiste. As this exchange indicates, Jericho sells props and costumes to the Funambules. He sells much of the same merchandise to the actors, to clothe themselves and furnish their actual homes. Madame Hermine, no doubt, has purchased most of her boarding house's well-worn décor from Jericho. In this regard, the film's décor is an accurate reflection of an environment furnished by the locales that Janin describes in his tribute to 'Pierrot-peuple': pawnshops, the second-hand linen market at the Place de Grève, the quays of the Seine, and makeshift stalls (*échoppes*).[10] Jericho and other old-clothes sellers would also have been the source of the costumes worn by the carnival revellers in the final scene. The fact that Jericho sells costumes may be one of the reasons that Baptiste despises him, because the old-clothes seller makes artistic vocation into a matter of what costume is available at what time. Frédérick, in his first appearance at the Funambules, climbs eagerly into a

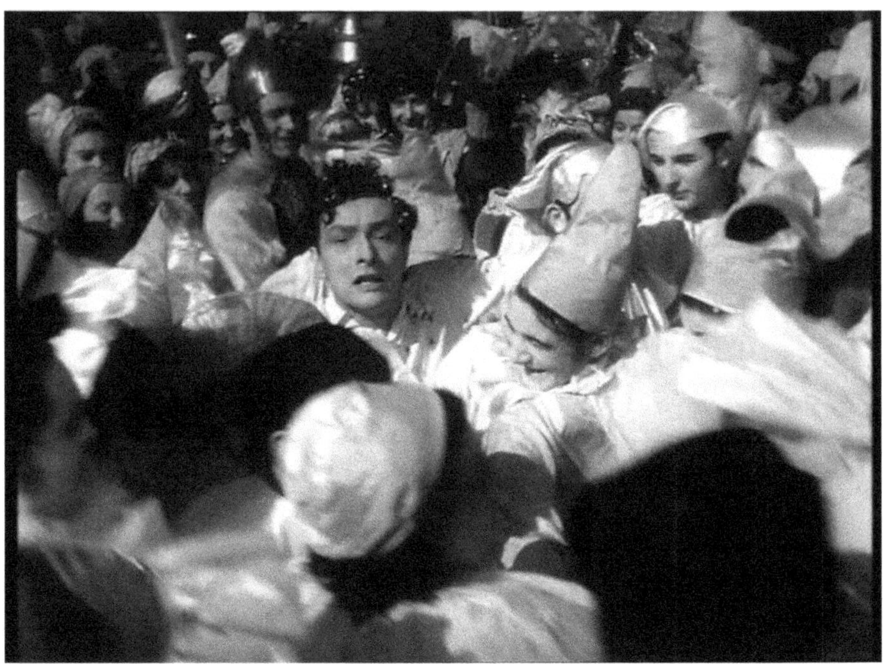

5.5   Marcel Carné (dir.), *Baptiste struggling through a crowd of carnival revellers as he tries to reach Garance*, 1945. Source: Pathé.

lion costume, a sign of his opportunism, whereas Baptiste's commitment is to the role as more than skin- (or fabric-)deep.

The conflict between Baptiste and Jericho is further highlighted in the pantomime staged in the film's second half. This pantomime is none other than *Marchand d'habits*, the scenario invented by Gautier in 1842, in which Pierrot kills an old-clothes seller to steal the costume of a nobleman. Pierrot uses the clothing to gain the favours of the beautiful Countess Musidora, but the ghost of the old-clothes seller haunts Pierrot ceaselessly. Since its premiere in 1842, this pantomime had been revived at major Parisian venues dozens of times. It had become a rite of passage, in a sense, for any mime looking to attempt the role of Pierrot. Both of the pantomimes staged by the film, one of which is performed in each *époque*, re-enact the actors' offstage drama. In *Marchand d'habits*, the Countess is Garance, who has become polished and elegant because of her association with the Comte de Montray. Pierrot's demise at the end of *Marchand d'habits*, when he and the old-clothes seller tumble together into hell, anticipates Baptiste's final scene, as he tries to shake off Jericho while drowning in a sea of carnival costumes.

Most of the characters have an aversion to Jericho, but Baptiste is extreme in his dislike, quivering with distaste whenever Jericho approaches. No reason for the extent of Baptiste's revulsion is ever given. It may have to do with the

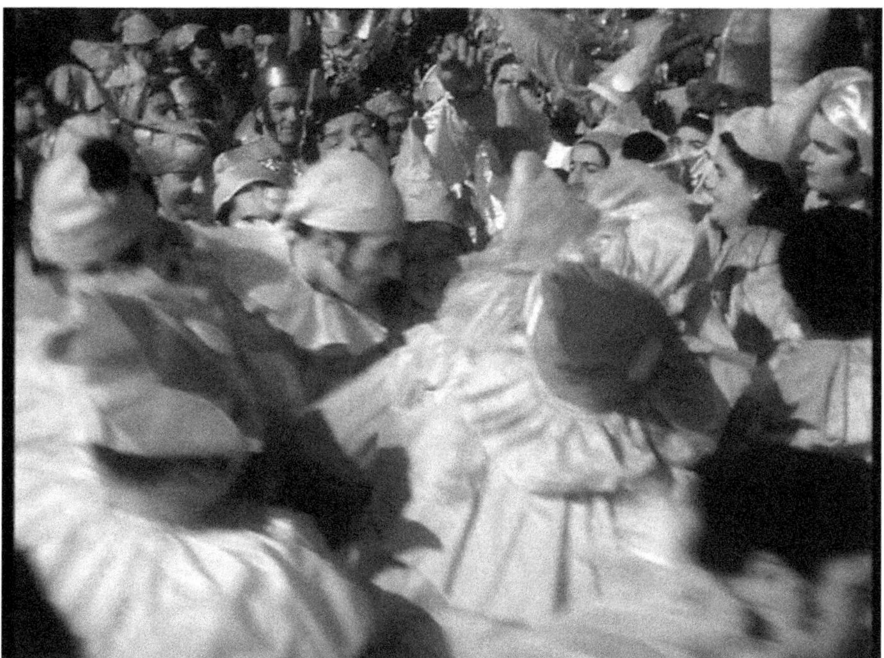

5.6   Marcel Carné (dir.), *Baptiste's struggle to reach Garance continues, as he is pushed nearly out of the frame by carnival revellers dressed as Pierrots*, 1945. Source: Pathé.

way that Jericho represents the world of things that will not let Baptiste go. Jericho's merchandise builds the home that Baptiste shares with Nathalie, the home that prevents him from escaping with Garance. Yet Baptiste's hostility also offers a clue to the film's allegorical stakes. Because the constraints of the Occupation meant that films could not directly address the current situation in the country, many films were understood to do so allegorically.[11] Certainly, this is how Carné and Prévert hoped the films they made during the Occupation would be understood. Numerous allegorical readings of *Children of Paradise* have been offered.[12] Frequently, critics have suggested that Garance represents France, a nation once joyous, carefree, and loving, which has been frozen into apparent submission by the Occupation.[13] Garance's enduring love for Baptiste (despite her association with other men) represents the French appreciation of popular artistry and creative genius.

In offering my own allegorical reading of the film, I want to focus on the enmity between Baptiste and Jericho. Geneviève Sellier suggests that Jericho represents the negative effects of the Occupation itself, which had turned the occupied against one another, engendering cruelty, paranoia, and bitterness.[14] Lacenaire accuses Jericho of being a snitch, a serious charge in the era of Occupation, when people were pressured to denounce their neighbours as Jews or as members of the resistance. I want to press further on Jericho's

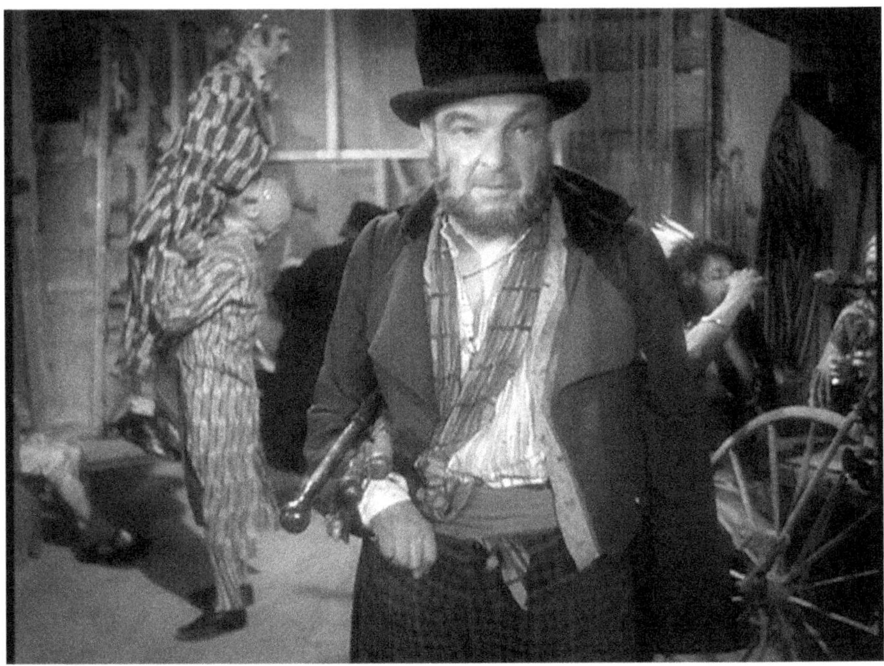

5.7   Marcel Carné (dir.), *Jericho, played by Pierre Renoir, backstage, with a collection of canes beneath his arm, and wearing the old-clothes seller's trademark shabby top-hat, 1945.* Source: Pathé.

Semitic associations, as well as on the connection that can be drawn between Jericho as a figure of Jewishness and a recasting of the values associated with the marketplace.[15] Over the course of the nineteenth century, the type of the old-clothes seller had increasingly acquired Semitic associations in France (the type had long had these associations in British and Germanic imagery).[16] Jericho incarnates the themes and myths of French anti-Semitism, as they had developed over the course of the previous century, peaking at moments like the Dreyfus affair, but steadily simmering up to and through the Second World War and the German Occupation. Originally, Jericho's role was written for Robert Le Vigan, who was associated with the film until late 1943. Le Vigan was a well-known anti-Semite and would have been aware of the Semitic associations of the old-clothes seller.[17] As the German position weakened, the actor fled France; the role was given to Pierre Renoir. The pitting of Pierrot against an anti-Semitic type is not as surprising as it might first appear. In fact, since the *fin-de-siècle*, a number of influential artists and actors had brought Pierrot into the fold of cultural conservatism, nationalism, and anti-Semitism. By taking the time to evaluate these deeply conservative versions of Pierrot, we can understand what was at stake in this showdown between Pierrot and the old-clothes seller. To trace the origins of Pierrot's conservatism, I must also evaluate, finally, Pierrot's whiteness, which accrued additional meaning in the context of racist and xenophobic cultural discourse.

Pierrot's whiteness

Gautier's scenario for *Marchand d'habits* explicitly elaborates the 'whiteness' of Pierrot prior to his encounter with the old-clothes seller:

> Pierrot who walks through the street in his white tunic, his white trousers, his face whitened with flour, preoccupied with vague desires, is this not the symbol of the human soul still innocent and white, tormented by infinite aspirations towards superior regions?[18]

In ceding to temptation, both the temptation of the old-clothes seller's merchandise and the temptation to kill in order to obtain the merchandise, Pierrot's soul will leave innocence and whiteness behind. Gautier's language here relies on the rhetorical opposition of whiteness and blackness.[19] This was a longstanding binary, forged in cultural representations that consistently associated goodness and purity with whiteness and evil and dirt with blackness.[20] This opposition is crucial to conservative approaches to Pierrot, which share an effort to 'protect' Pierrot's whiteness. In this section, I want to briefly explore the opposition between whiteness and blackness as it unfolds in Pierrot's eighteenth- and early nineteenth-century career.

As he appeared in the repertoire of the Comédie Italienne, Pierrot wore a costume that was all white in colour, an unusual choice in an era when uniformly white garments were associated exclusively with underclothes (*linge*).[21] The whiteness of the costume was noticeable on the stage, because it was so plain. All the other characters wore dark colours: Arlequin's motley was of red, yellow, green, and brown, the Doctor's cloak was black wool. In the eighteenth century, white was not particularly associated with virginity. Brides did not wear white. The Virgin Mary tended to wear blue. The flag of the French monarchy featured a white ground. 'Blanc' was used to mean 'blank' in reference to paper or paper documents, and to the centre of a target. Carthusian monks wore white habits. Indeed, one of the most celebrated works of seventeenth-century French art, Eustache Le Sueur's Saint Bruno series, depicted the founder of the Carthusian order and his followers in their white habits. 'Blanc' also referred to the makeup with which courtiers whitened their faces. I am inclined to believe that the initial associations of Pierrot's costume were those of the blank. He represented a kind of unmarked primacy, a simplicity that reflected his naïveté and lack of sophistication. He was the proverbial blank slate, the foil or target for the activities of other characters.

Over the course of the eighteenth century, the invention of systems of racial categorisation caused whiteness to acquire more problematic associations. Increasingly, attention was drawn to differences in human skin colours, which were then used to develop theories of racial difference.[22] As France established colonies in the Caribbean, such ideologies became ever more necessary in order to justify the enslavement of the Africans who laboured on the planta-tions there.[23] To characterise the enslaved as 'Black' was to associate their char-acters with an existing repertoire of negative values. Many eighteenth-century commentators aligned aesthetic preferences with moral judgement, arguing that the 'beauty' of fair skin reflected moral superiority of character.[24] These pseudo-scientific racial theories allowed visual art to play an important role in the performance of racial difference through contrasts in colour, as in the pair-ing of an aristocratic woman with an enslaved child.[25] During the nineteenth century, France's invasion and occupation of significant territories in north Africa (Morocco, Tunisia, Algeria) encouraged the continued elaboration of whiteness and blackness as categories of moral difference that could also be mapped onto racial difference.

In one of the more explicitly racialising elements of costume in the Comédie Italienne, Pierrot's foil, Arlequin, wore a black or dark brown leather mask.[26] When the play was set in an 'exotic' locale, Arlequin often took on the role of the racial other, playing a Native American, or '*iriquois*'; or a Moorish prince. In the nineteenth-century pantomimes, Pierrot increasingly became the victim of 'dark' tyrants in pantomimes that took him to Spain, Algeria, Morocco, North America, South America, and China. These pantomimes reflected the popular Orientalisms that circulated in the wake of French military engagement in north Africa. Pierrot often appears as the valet to a French or English officer in a colonial army. Sent to eradicate 'despotism', Pierrot and his master are constantly under threat. Tyrants want to keep him as a pet, yet Pierrot still manages to lend a hand to the women imprisoned in the harem. In these pantomimes, Pierrot is not the instigator of these colonial missions, but a servant reluctantly following his employer. Indeed, he often liberates if he can, because he wants others to share his freedom, because he does not understand the worldly reasons for maintaining people and nations in subjection. This is not in the slightest to suggest that Pierrot was an anti-colonial hero. Quite the contrary, he was an alibi, a vision of whiteness as comic innocence, a cover for whiteness as a justification for oppression.

A fascinating illustration of the binary of white and black in the reception of Pierrot is in fact Janin's first *feuilleton* devoted to Deburau, published in November 1830. Janin begins his review at the Théâtre Français, the heir of the Comédie-Française, where he reviews a four act drama in free verse, *Le nègre*, by Ozanneaux. *Le nègre* tells the story of an enslaved man whose son, who is also enslaved, is in love with a white woman.[27] Eventually, the son kills himself; the father, desolate, seeks vengeance. The enslaved characters would have been played by white actors wearing makeup in a range of shades of black, brown, and copper. In *Le nègre*, the curtain rises upon a tableau juxtaposing the whiteness of the young female heroine, Marie, with a troop of adoring slaves. Janin is sceptical of the heroine's 'extreme whiteness', given the tropical climate – a standard concern regarding French colonists, whose whiteness was said to be compromised by the brutal circumstances and hot climates in which they lived.[28] The play's final tableau repeats this contrast of whiteness and Blackness, with the enslaved father clutching Marie at the edge of a cliff, threatening to hurl them both into the abyss. In the end he kills only himself.

Janin takes no stand on the condition of the enslaved, although the play seems to have expressed mild anti-slavery sentiments with a healthy dose of paternalism. Instead, Janin complains about the play's excessive verbiage, the extensive monologues and harangues that interrupt the predictable action. Two pages into the three-page *feuilleton*, however, the critic pivots dramatically, dismissing *Le nègre* and declaring that the only true actor in Paris is 'Deburau, the Gille of the Funambules'. I have discussed this article at length in Chapter 3, in particular Janin's creation of an aesthetic of joyful, chaotic bric-à-brac linked to the character of the 'people'. For the critic, the Funambules and Deburau are naïve, joyous, and French, whereas the Théâtre Français has lost its truthfulness and its naturalness to empty verbiage. All Deburau needs is a simple tunic, 'a bit of flour' to whiten his face, a few candles, and 'two out-of-tune violins'.[29] It is difficult to know what to make of this fascinating coincidence, which may in fact be just that: Janin disliked a play he saw at the Théâtre Français and decided to talk about something else. It must be acknowledged that he does not use 'white' to characterise Pierrot in the text that follows, although he does mention the 'flour' that Deburau used to whiten his face. It was only later in the nineteenth century that Deburau's type of pantomime would be referred to as 'white pantomime' (*pantomime blanche*). What is significant, however, is the fact that Janin's aesthetic judgement also falls along racial lines; the bad play has a Black hero and the good pantomime a white one. Turning performatively from Black play to white play, Janin reinforces the colourist binary and its associated values.

A similar binary is presented in *Children of Paradise*, not only between Jericho and Baptiste, but between Baptiste and Frédérick Lemaître. Although briefly rivals in love, these two performers get on well in the film, frequently declaring their admiration for the other's artistry. Yet it is clear that Frédérick's artistry is of a distinct character. As Baptiste's father remarks with the greatest scorn, Frédérick is an 'actor', not a mime. Frédérick's gift is deeply verbal. While performing at the Funambules, he longs to present the plays of Shakespeare. At the end of the film, he gets his wish and stars in *Othello*. The premiere of this play is a set-piece in the film's dénouement, with all the major characters meeting in the green room after the performance. Frédérick greets his admirers still wearing the costume, including blackface, in which he played his role on stage. This is Frédérick's crowning achievement, because he has finally become Baptiste's equal, but in his own genre. As Baptiste has appeared in whiteface since his first performance in the film, Frédérick, finally, appears in the mask that is appropriate to an actor whose brilliance derives from the written word. Baptiste is the blank page; Frédérick is writing, ink. (In at least one pantomime at the Funambules, Pierrot falls into a giant ink bottle and is dyed black.) Frédérick is a sympathetic and charming character, who at times utterly steals the show, but he is not the film's hero. That status belongs solely to Baptiste, whose whiteness is ever more affirmed by Frédérick's performance as Othello. Frédérick's apotheosis as an actor requires him not only to don blackface but to perform an English play. As a result, the association is sealed between Baptiste, whiteness, and Frenchness.

French anti-Semitisms and the rhetoric of old clothes

While Gautier repeatedly emphasises 'whiteness' in his scenario for *Marchand d'habits*, he eschews more specific allusions to race. When *Marchand d'habits* was revived, however, in the late nineteenth century, the Semitic associations of the old-clothes seller would have been palpable.[30] These associations reflected the acceleration and intensification of French anti-Semitism.[31] The events of *circa* 1870 – the defeat at the hands of the Germans in the Franco-Prussian War, the abdication of Napoléon III and the end of the Second Empire, the carnage of the Paris Commune – conspired to make the young Third Republic ripe ground for ideologies of conservative nationalism. The French were humiliated. Rebuilding a new sense of the nation required a scapegoat. It was easy to associate Jews with the problems accompanying post-Revolutionary modernity, because it was only during the Revolution, in 1791, that the French government had 'emancipated' Jews, granting them the same civil rights as Christians.[32] While the population of Jews remained tiny (although much larger than the population of the formerly enslaved), during the nineteenth century Jews were visible for the first time on French economic and cultural stages, where they quickly rose to prominence.[33] Myths of the greedy Jewish capitalist, preying upon Aryan workers, offered an outlet for frustration. The first widely read work of popular French anti-Semitism was Édouard Drumont's *La France juive* (1886). Drumont (1844–1917) transformed anti-Semitism into a powerful and all-encompassing discourse, which explained a host of the French nation's ills.[34] Drumont's claims would be elaborated by other authors, each of whom took a slightly different slant on the topic, including Maurice Barrès (1862–1923) and the leader of the royalist group Action Française, Charles Maurras (1868–1952).[35] Against a description of Semitic culture as nomadic, capitalist, and cosmopolitan, these authors erected Frenchness as rooted in the land, in the monarchy, in tradition.

In *La France juive* Drumont claimed that Jews and capitalist exploitation (of non-Jews) were inseparable.[36] Drumont also believed that Jews were the cause of the degenerate state of the French aristocracy, whose weaknesses for fashion, art, and gambling had been cunningly exploited by Jews.[37] In his view, Jews had also been responsible for the Revolution of 1789, a 'conspiracy' launched in order to weaken the nobility and to open markets to newly emancipated Jewish financiers.[38] Financial speculation as an engine of wealth was represented as the opposite of agricultural work, the true source of French prosperity. Drumont followed popular contemporary racial theory in insisting upon the opposition between 'Semite' and 'Aryan'.[39] For Drumont, 'the semite is mercantilist, venal, intriguing, subtle, crafty; the Aryan is an enthusiast, heroic, chivalric, disinterested, frank, confiding to the point of naïveté'.[40] Proof of this distinction, he claimed, lay in the number of Jews who worked as *brocanteurs* and *marchands d'habits*, flooding the marketplace with fakes, 'false *bibelots*, pastiched canvases', silver masquerading as copper, 'fake Sèvres and Meissen figurines'.[41] Drumont's argument was about more than populating the second-hand marketplace with Jewish agents; it insisted on the particular character of Jewish work. Like the merchant mercers of the eighteenth century, Jews, for Drumont, were 'sellers of everything, makers of nothing' in a culture that associated making, craftsmanship, and origins with the Aryan.[42] Moreover, Jewish merchants, since they made nothing themselves, preyed upon Aryan producers, buying the objects of Aryan labour cheaply and selling them dearly, after a few feats of marketing and publicity, another parasitical enterprise. How could the Aryan, 'child of the heavens unceasingly preoccupied with superior aspirations', compete?[43]

Drumont's characterisation of the Aryan is strikingly close to Gautier's description of Pierrot, clothed in white, aspiring to higher things. In *Marchand d'habits*, as it is performed in the second half of *Children*, Pierrot sees the Countess in her fine gown, attending a ball with other elegant people. He tries to follow her but is refused entry by two guards. At first, he curls up sadly in the street outside the ball, morosely examining the fabric of his own garment. This gesture recalls one of Pierrot's lines from the repertoire of the old Comédie Italienne: that it is hard to attract women with only a suit of canvas to wear. Then the old-clothes seller enters, bearing his mobile *étalage*, a cross of wood upon which garments are displayed. With jackets and trousers dangling from his rack, the old-clothes seller cries the vacancy of the signs that he carries, marketing their availability to be worn by anyone. Pierrot, whose dreams are bigger than his empty pockets, cannot resist this call. To read this pantomime in the light projected from Drumont's anti-Semitism, had the old-clothes seller never appeared, Pierrot would have never sought to disguise himself. He would have remained 'white'. In the 1880s and 1890s, Adolphe Willette would make this aspirational Pierrot, who falls victim to greedy capitalists, into the kernel of his anti-Semitic project.

Adolphe Willette

The connection between Pierrot and Aryanism was made painfully explicit by the painter and illustrator Adolphe Willette (1857–1926).[44] I do not wish to dwell at length on Willette, but his career demonstrates the ease with which Pierrot became an emblem of conservative cultural politics. In addition to dressing as Pierrot and referring to himself as 'Willette called Pierrot' on his identity card, Willette wrote pantomimes featuring Pierrot and was portrayed as Pierrot in a series of artist portraits by Marcellin Desboutin, exhibited at the Salon of the Société Nationale des Beaux-Arts in 1896. His most copious production, however, was his *oeuvre* of lithographic illustrations for journals *Le chat noir*, *Le courrier français*, and his own journal, *Le Pierrot*. In 1889, Willette ran for the Legislative Assembly as a '*Candidat Antisémite*'.[45] On his candidate's poster, which he signed 'A. Willette, Directeur du *Pierrot*', he presented a slew of text bashing Jews as a 'different race and enemy of our race'.[46] Willette also worked as an illustrator for *La libre parole*, an anti-Semitic organ run by Drumont. The illustrator espoused a stew of fashionable *fin-de-siècle* conservatism, combining anti-capitalism and anti-Semitism with a fondness for both the rococo and mediaevalism. Willette's Pierrot, who we have already encountered as a silhouette in the Shadow Theatre, was a dysfunctional dreamer poet: pale because he was hungry and maligned, unfit for the cut-throat capitalism of modern life. *Ad nauseam*, Willette depicted Pierrot as the victim of Jewish capitalists and Jewish artists, such as Sarah Bernhardt who had played Pierrot in the pantomime *Pierrot assassin* in 1883.[47] In a stained-glass window, *The Triumph of the Golden Calf*, that Willette designed for Rodolphe Salis's Chat Noir cabaret, he depicted Pierrot's decapitated head, with his own features, handed to an allegorical figure of Power, alongside Fortune as the 'golden calf of Israel'.[48] The choice of mediaevalising stained glass reflected anti-Semitic ideologies that sought to return to the Christian, agrarian era, represented as prior to the invasion of Jewish, capitalist influence.[49] In an interview for the collection *Mimes et Pierrots* (1889), Willette told the author Paul Hugounet that his Pierrot, 'perpetually simple and saintedly naïve', is the '*Goym* unceasingly duped by Semites or by all those who carry in a Christian body a Jewish soul'.[50] Hugounet followed with his own commentary, describing the Parisian stock market as a 'temple to the cult of gold raised by Jewish finance', in the shadow of which roams Pierrot, 'this hero of dreams who doesn't have in his pocket even the five *sols* of Isaac Laquedem'.[51]

Interestingly, Willette styled his Pierrot two different ways, as Pierrot *noir*, who wore a black tuxedo and Pierrot *blanc*, in the typical flowing tunic and wide-legged trousers. Although the symbolic difference between the two is not entirely clear, Willette explained in a letter to Théodore de Banville that Pierrot *noir* signified the character's 'mourning for his lost illusions and his mistreated, assassinated youth'.[52] It is Pierrot *noir* who features more frequently in Willette's *histoires sans paroles*, the little stories that he told by serially representing Pierrot engaged in various physical shenanigans, little vignettes arranged in a grid, like the one in which Pierrot *noir* and Sarah Bernhardt perform a bizarre series of duels, ending with Pierrot trapping Bernhardt in a coffin. Willette's Pierrot *blanc* is the dreamier of the two, who often appears with a large patch on the knee of his trousers, who is well fed and physically substantial, as opposed to the calligraphic emaciation of Pierrot *noir*. For Willette, Pierrot *noir* represents the modern, fallen state of Pierrot, the condition in which he dwells in the *beau monde* of the Third Republic, doing his best to keep up, but inevitably falling into the traps – women, gambling, and drink – that capitalist society sets for him. This is Pierrot as Drumont's poor Aryan, whose delicate and naïve longing for fine things makes him the victim of the endless scheming that Drumont attributed to Jews.

Children of Paradise betrays none of Willette's outright anti-Semitism. Nor are there any greedy capitalists amongst the film's repertoire of characters, although it certainly would have been possible to lend these features to Garance's wealthy protector, the Comte de Montray. Yet the film's representation of Pierrot–Baptiste as a dreamy artist can certainly be traced to Willette's interpretation of the type. Onstage, Baptiste is Pierrot *blanc*, silly and foolish. Offstage, Baptiste is a version of Pierrot *noir* in his neat suits, wearing the costume of modernity but always standing a little apart. Most importantly, Baptiste's attitude towards love and dreams, which he places under the sign of the Moon (another emblem of whiteness), reflects the characteristics of Willette's Pierrot. This opposition, between an ethereal temperament as a sign of the artist, and materialist greed as a sign of the capitalist, is not present in earlier versions of Pierrot. Baptiste Deburau's Pierrot was not an artist; he was *peuple*, frantic and acquisitive. Gautier's Pierrot, in the original *Marchand d'habits*, is a social climber, not an artist. The film, by conjoining the onstage Pierrot with the offstage Baptiste, allows the narrative of artistic aspiration to be projected onto the stage character, casting Pierrot's desire for fine clothes as the artist's quest for beauty. Now, to threaten Pierrot is to threaten a particular conception of the artist as dreamer.

White pantomime

The other major alliance between Pierrot and whiteness that should be considered in relationship to *Children of Paradise* lies in the career of the mime Séverin (1863–1930), who was a regular on Parisian stages from 1896 to the late 1920s. After a lull in the early years of the Third Republic, the *fin-de-siècle* saw a revival of the pantomime and a proliferation of different Pierrot interpreters, including Willette, Raoul de Najac, Rouffe, and Séverin.[53] It was in this context that Pierrot, and the pantomime, began to be vaunted as both 'classical' and essentially 'French'. Conscious that English pantomime, represented in France by the hugely popular Hanlon Lee brothers, cultivated a style of frenetic, 'epileptic' movements, French artists and amateurs suggested as a counterpoint a French style of *pantomime blanche*.[54] Favouring expressive gesture and physiognomic expressivity over acrobatics and grotesque grimace, the *pantomime blanche* based itself loosely on an idea of Deburau's style of pantomime, which was cast as the French heir to both the *commedia dell'arte* and the Greco-Roman mimes of antiquity.

Since the Franco-Prussian war, numerous varieties of neo-classicism had swept through French culture. Classicism proved a highly 'elastic' concept, appropriated by factions on both the right and the left, who ascribed to it different meanings.[55] Only in some forms, and with particular fervour during the First World War, was classicism explicitly associated with the Greco-Roman tradition.[56] In other iterations, being 'classic' meant a return to French origins, which were conceived alternately as lying in the Celts, the land, mediaeval France, or the France of Louis XIV.[57] For those classicists who followed the influential writings of Maurice Barrès, classicism and nationalism were inseparable; to be classical was to be French and thus even a Romantic artist like Delacroix could be considered a classical exemplar.[58] The *commedia* characters, who had long featured on French stages, were the popular avatars of this kind of Franco-Latin classicism, depicted as such by André Derain and Pablo Picasso.[59] Another feature of the nostalgic, classicising rhetoric of this period was the fetishising of 'simplicity', 'clarity', and 'harmony', which were cast as distinctively French values. This 'simplicity' was often attached to a rhetoric of the popular and the pleasures of the 'people'. André Antoine, writing about Séverin in 1920, lamented the scarcity of pantomime in Paris, but referred to its preservation in the Latinate Midi, from Naples to Marseille, where 'these naïve and light spectacles still inspire popular theatres with joy'. Naïve, light – these are other terms for simplicity and clarity, all of which belong to the cultural spectrum of whiteness and Frenchness.[60]

Séverin's career spanned this cultural moment, in which he flourished as the most 'classical' of Pierrots. Trained in Marseille by Rouffe, another famous Pierrot who had created an 'academy' for training mimes, Séverin debuted in Paris in 1896 in Catulle Mendes's adaptation of *Chand d'habits* (this alteration to the title *Marchand d'habits* was intended to express the old-clothes seller's abbreviation of his characteristic cry). This production opened at the Grand-Guignol but quickly moved to the larger Folies-Bergère. *Chand d'habits* was revived three times in the following years: once in 1906, and then in 1920 and 1921. Séverin, despite his increasing age, continued to play Pierrot. Throughout his career, the mime styled himself as '*l'homme blanc*', the title of his autobiography published in 1929. Critics associated Séverin's whiteness with nobility, tradition, and classicism – his face was like the 'mask of Roman emperors' – and clarity (*clarté, netteté*).[61] In 1920, reviewing *Chand d'habits*, Marc Henry repeatedly praised the legibility of Séverin's expressive arc: 'one sees sentiments born, developing, and disperse on this pale face ... The entire genesis of the crime appears on this white face. It is truly beautiful, of a great art.'[62] Whiteness, beauty, and emotional lucidity are here associated, against which Henry juxtaposes the 'violently coloured composition of Farina',[63] the mime who played the old-clothes seller (Farina also played Pierrot in other productions). In 1925, Gustave Fréjaville connected Séverin's 'whitened face' to 'classical mimes' and praised the way that 'on this white mask, as if on a screen of a miraculous sensibility, emotions and thoughts come to be inscribed in neat and fugitive traces ...'[64] Embedded in this language is not only the implicit value placed upon lightness and clarity, but an older association between white skin and emotional legibility, as opposed to the inexpressive muteness attributed to Black skin.[65] In this opposition, legibility is valued as the reflection of a superior mental function, a complex inner life that cannot help but manifest itself on the skin, whereas the silence of Black skin suggests an absence of thought, providing yet another justification for enslavement. This rhetoric of clarity and white lightness, extremely widespread in the critical response to Séverin, culminated in the laudatory reviews of his autobiography, *L'homme blanc*.[66]

On the final page of this memoir, Séverin concludes: 'the Blacks (*les noirs*) have taken the place of the White man in the taste of the public ...'[67] Séverin was likely referring to the vogue for performers of African descent in Paris, a trend initiated when Josephine Baker appeared in 1925 in *La revue nègre* at the Théâtre des Champs-Elysées, the stage where Séverin had performed in 1921 in *Chand d'habits*. The *succès de scandale* of the *La revue nègre* led to Baker's employment at the Folies-Bergère, another theatre that had once staged *Chand d'habits*.[68] Séverin's complaint drew the expected equivalence between race, colour, and morals, suggesting that the inclination for Black performers would muddy the 'clarity' or 'cleanness' (*clarté, netteté*) of the classical pantomime. In 1929, in their reviews of Séverin's autobiography, the critics took up Séverin's complaint. Agreeing that 'blackness abounds' on the French theatrical scene, H. Espian praised Séverin, by contrast, as a master of 'the completely classical tradition'.[69] André Antoine, recalling Deburau as the ancestor of Séverin, wrote that 'the white face of Pierrot became the striking mirror of the soul of the character and [Deburau] learned to write on this white page ...'[70] Séverin's career and its critical reception affirmed the association between whiteness, Pierrot, and a tradition of classical, French pantomime.

There is certainly an effort, in *Children of Paradise*, to cast the Boulevard du Temple during the 1830s as a form of French 'classicism', in the sense of an era of particularly French creativity, the impetus for which could be traced to the desires of *le peuple*. To Frédérick, Baptiste explains his affinity for his audience of *pauvres gens*: 'I am like them. I love them. I recognise their life is very small, but their dreams are big.'[71] It is not the low price of the tickets but love that brings the people to the Funambules. Both Nathalie and Garance tell Baptiste that 'loving is simple' (Nathalie), 'it is so simple, love' (Garance). When the mime continues to press Garance with the gravity of his love, she responds with a smile: 'I am not what you dreamed. You must understand me. I am simple, so simple.' This simplicity also extends to the lives of the people, as Garance describes the lives of the working-class neighbourhood, Ménilmontant, in which she grew up: 'people sleep and wake', 'it's not much' ('*c'est peu de chose*'), but they are happy. Some of this jolly simplicity is represented in the first of the two pantomimes performed in the film, in which Pierrot seeks the love of a beautiful white statue – Garance draped in silky white and holding a lyre (Figure 5.8) – while disdaining the affections of a pretty laundress played by Nathalie. The aesthetic of the stage décor trades the elaborate sets of the *féerie* for a few painted flats, an unsophisticated presentation that recalls the rural, village milieu evoked by Champfleury (Figure 5.9). Nathalie as the happy laundress who needs *peu de chose* to sing as she works is an allusion to Garance's origins, but masks the urban slum with the screen of the pastoral. The transformation of Garance into a statue suggests that Baptiste, at least, wants to perform an affinity between antiquity and the popular – simple draperies, simple lives. The linens that her mother laundered become classical draperies. With Baptiste, the film seeks to return to the kind of performance that Séverin's were meant to recall: simple, light performances, without the 'colourful' hoopla of the music halls.

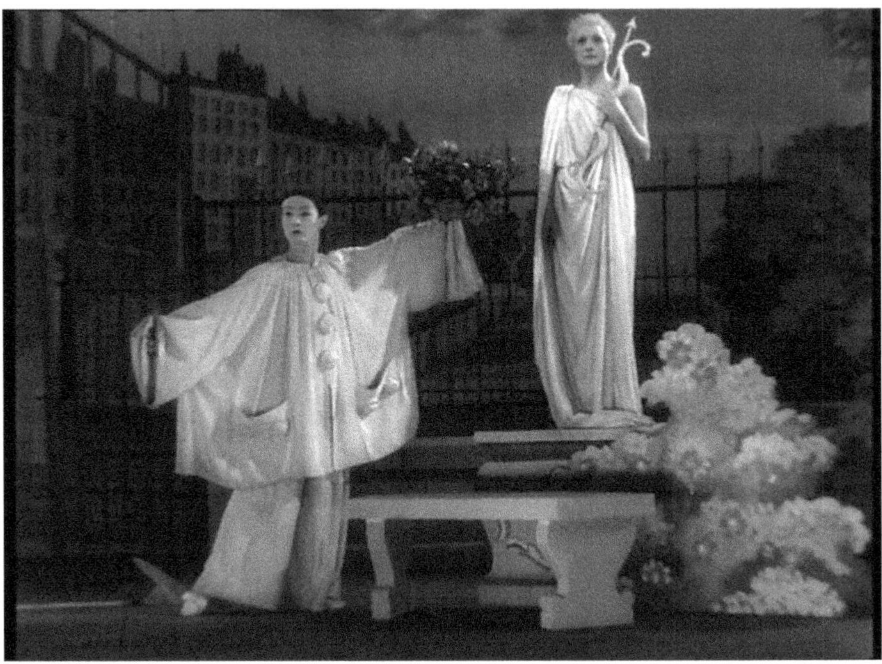

5.8   Marcel Carné (dir.), *Garance in white drapery as a statue, to whom Baptiste dressed as Pierrot appeals*, 1945. Source: Pathé.

Old clothes and the shadow world

The importance of *Chand d'habits* to Séverin's repertoire draws us back to the world of old things.[72] The language of bric-à-brac and curiosity tended to be playful, light, and expansive. Yet clothing was a different kind of second-hand thing, in part because of its closeness to the body, as well as the ghostly appearance it produced when displayed for sale, hanging from a peg or a hook without a body inside it.[73] In their account of Renaissance clothing, Jones and Stallybrass emphasise the way that garments passed between wearers had an empowering effect, vesting the new wearer with the garment's symbolic, identificatory power.[74] The situation in the eighteenth and nineteenth centuries was somewhat different. More clothes were available (although still very few clothes in comparison to the present day). As a result, second-hand clothes tended to circulate further from their original wearers, losing their vesting power along the way. It was difficult to feel that in donning a second-hand coat one was becoming the garment's original wearer, if that wearer was utterly unknown. Mercier, whose poetics of second-hand artworks I discussed in Chapter 3, was considerably more circumspect when it came to old clothes. He seemed to admire the second-hand clothing sellers on the Quai de la Mégisserie, who had hung a pair of trousers as a sign, but he did not have the same goodwill towards the *fripiers* in the Carrousel du Louvre, this neighbourhood where Clément

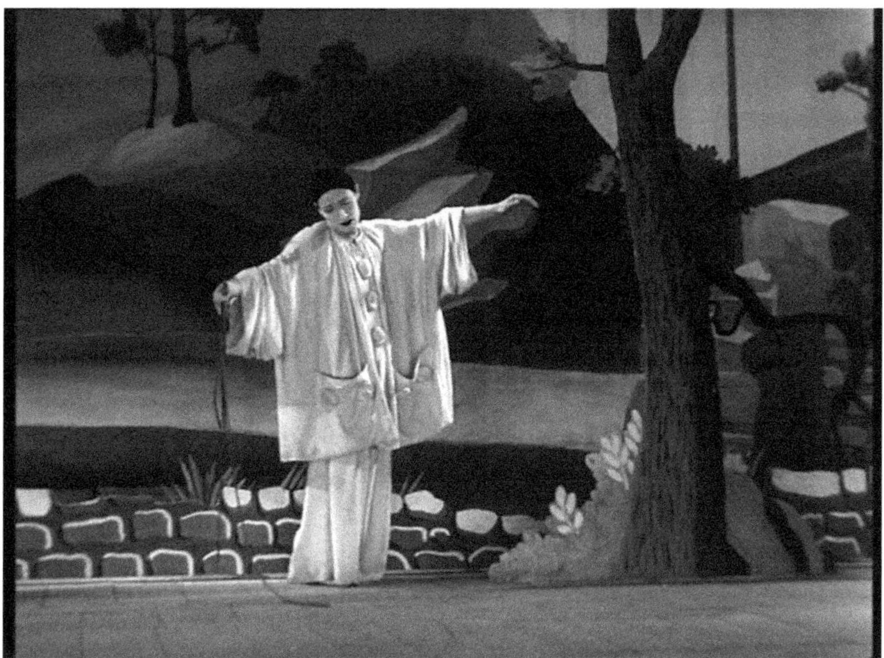

5.9　Marcel Carné (dir.), *The rural décor for the pantomime performed in the first époque,* 1945 Source: Pathé.

de Ris located Denon's discovery of Watteau's Pierrot, used as a sign outside a bric-à-brac shop.[75] This fascinating neighbourhood sold a bit of everything, from living birds, to drawings and prints, lemonade, and cups of *café au lait*, to antiques and old clothes. Mercier opens his description of this quarter with a contrast, between 'this superb colonnade that all foreigners admire' and 'a bunch of old clothes, which, suspended from strings, turning in the wind, form a hideous display'.[76] This 'dirty and indecent' frippery is not only a hideous stain on the façade of the Louvre, it is a vector of disease.[77] Mercier claims that 'contagious miasmas' have been left in the cloth by previous wearers; the worker who buys the garment receives the disease 'by contact with the cloth'.[78] Yet the clients of these shops, too poor to do any better, continue to buy these sources of 'hidden poisons', which *fripiers* have harvested from the unwashed bodies of the dead.[79] Its contact with the popular body makes the old garment a threatening second-hand object. This is not patina but plain old dirt.

In the nineteenth century, the heart of the old-clothes market lay in the Temple, in a series of covered markets, and in particular the Rotunda of the Temple.[80] Marc Fournier's description in *La grande ville* (1843) represents the interior of this market as an 'inextricable labyrinth', where bony hands extend from the darkness and grasp the arms of potential customers, pulling them into stalls, where clothes are hung from wooden boards.[81] Old clothes, in quantity and hung up like ghosts, threaten to engulf those who come too close. Yet Fournier also recognises the festive aspects of the market, the quaintness of which recalled the markets of old Paris. He describes the picturesque disorder of theatrical costumes and the 'exhilarating wardrobe of carnival, the black velvet mask, the domino',[82] as well as feathers, flowers, lace: 'it is a disorder relieved by a bizarre *cachet*, of singular aspect and allure'.[83] An alert visitor may catch sight of a famous courtesan or actress, who has dropped into the market looking for a last-minute addition to her evening *toilette*. Meanwhile, in the square outside the market, in front of the Rotunda, the mob of old-clothes sellers, their shoulders hunched under their wares, sell their inventory to *fripiers* and trade with other old-clothes sellers. This was the 'stock market' of old clothes, where daily prices for trousers, shirts, and overcoats were set, where old-clothes sellers speculated in the stocks of garments. Great fortunes could be made, Fournier suggests, citing the owner of a magnificent *hôtel particulier* in the Faubourg Saint Germain, Maître Pautrel, a Norman who came to Paris to repair faience and to 'speculate in the stocks of trousers'.[84] Writing in 1843, Fournier claims that most old-clothes sellers are from Normandy. He does not mention Jewishness. Yet the association between speculation and old clothes lays out the path by which this type would gradually come to be associated with Jews, who would be depicted as deriving their wealth from speculation, which is to say at the expense of others and without making anything themselves.

Unsurprisingly, in addition to the centrality of *Marchand d'habits* to the film's plot, clothes and costume play an important role in *Children of Paradise*. Costumes function both as décor – draped and hung everywhere in the actors' dressing rooms – and as surfaces taken on and off by the characters. To get a job at the Funambules, Frédérick grabs a discarded lion costume and puts it on: 'let me just enter into the skin of my character'. In the next scene, Nathalie is seen backstage, holding a wedding dress against her body and admiring herself in the mirror. Garance frequently takes her clothes on and off. Her first night at the boarding house, she hangs her wet dress outside her window. It functions like a sign, alerting Frédérick to her presence and her availability. She appears in the window in response to his call; her head is framed by her stockings on one side and her dress on the other (Figure 5.4). When Garance is first approached by the Comte de Montray, she goes behind her dressing screen and throws off the toga, which she has worn in her role as a sculpture that comes to life (Figure 5.3). She puts on her dress while discussing with the Comte the possibility that she will change roles yet again, to become his mistress. Indeed, the *loge* witnesses many of the film's crucial encounters, a reflection of its importance (as dressing room, as box for spectators, and as boutique at the fair) in the spatial dynamics of the marketplace. In this waiting room for those about to tread the boards of the marketplace, costumes are put on and off, purchased, and assessed.

Given the importance of costumes to the film's theatrical world, it can be difficult to understand Baptiste's dislike for Jericho. Yet this has to do with the way that Baptiste's relationship to his role differs from that of the other characters. In fact, it is in this regard that Baptiste truly is *tout simple*, because

Pierrot is Baptiste's one and only role and therefore not so much a role as a destiny. All traces of the arbitrary are erased from Baptiste's relationship to Pierrot. This role is no random assemblage of bits and parts, but a classical whole, draped in a garment of uniform whiteness, a garment that is not so much a covering as an emanation of the spirit of Pierrot. For Baptiste, Jericho 'pollutes' the relationship of an actor to a role, which should be a matter of nature rather than costume.

Flea market filmmakers

In the anti-Semitic imaginary, the old-clothes seller was joined by a considerably more powerful figure, the Jewish financier or capitalist. This type appears frequently in nineteenth-century French literature, from the Baron de Nucingen of Balzac's *Splendeurs et Misères des Courtisanes* (1844), via Gundermann and Busch in Zola's *L'argent* (1891), to the Baron de Rozenfeld in Victor Joze's novel, *La reine de joie* (1892), for which Toulouse Lautrec made a publicity poster that indulged in anti-Semitic visual stereotyping.[85] Despite the gulf between the itinerant old-clothes seller and the capitalist in his gilded palace, anti-Semitic rhetoric sought to represent the two types as essentially the same, as 'sellers of everything and makers of nothing'. This was the case in a virulent tract, *Les Tribus du Cinéma et du Théâtre*, published by Lucien Rebatet in 1941. A well-known royalist and anti-Semite, who had written the film reviews for *Action Française* during the 1930s, Rebatet had welcomed the Nazi Occupation and the purging of Jews from French society.[86] Rebatet's pamphlet is a notorious document in histories of the Occupation and film industry, yet what has not been sufficiently analysed is the association he made, following Drumont, between Jewish participation in the French film industry and the resale tactics of *brocanteurs* and *fripiers*.[87] Rebatet argued that Jews, only interested in making money, contribute nothing in the way of artistic intelligence or artisanal skill to the film industry. Rather, they package and resell what others (Aryans, presumably), have made.[88] As a result, cinema becomes not an art, but a 'boutique'.[89] Like Drumont, Rebatet depicted Aryan artists (like the Lumière brothers) as helpless dreamers, creators who had no sense for business.[90] He went beyond metaphor to claim that many of the most successful Jews in the American film industry – Marcus Loew, Adolphe Zukor, William Fox, and Carl Laemmle – had in fact worked as *brocanteurs* or *fripiers* prior to coming to Hollywood, in the 'obscure ghettos of Eastern Europe or the most sordid alleys of Whitechapel'.[91]

Rebatet had very specific remarks to make on Carné, which elaborated upon his reactions to Carné's films throughout the 1930s, films made in the style known as Poetic Realism. Collaborations between Carné and Prévert like *Quai des Brumes* (1938) and *Le Jour se Lève* (1938) were largely responsible for creating and perfecting this style, which sets its stories in the milieu of the working classes and features shadowy, expressionist cinematography. The central story tends to be that of a love affair between a beautiful young woman and a well-meaning but compromised and doomed male hero. Additional interest is created by the presence of charismatic secondary characters drawn from the repertoire of the *physiognomies*: prostitutes, vaudeville performers, petty criminals, kindly restaurateurs. The 'poetic' aspect of these productions was the result of stylised set design, lighting, and cinematography – many of which were the work of German *émigré* film personnel – as well as Prévert's melancholy dialogue. Rebatet, as well as other conservative critics, found this all extremely *noir*. (Poetic Realism was an important influence upon American *film noir* of the 1940s and 1950s, created by teams of film-makers who had passed through Paris on their way to Hollywood.) Rebatet believed that the subjects and milieus of Poetic Realism were vicious, repugnant, nihilist, and sordid. Moreover, he found that these films reflected the 'destructive' point of view of their Jewish backers, and were intended to demoralise the French, to depict them as 'almost animal' and without 'will'.[92] For Rebatet, Carné, a gentile, represented 'jewed talent' (*talent enjuivé*).[93]

There is no doubt that Carné and Prévert would have read Rebatet's publication. Certainly, the anti-Semitic actor Robert Le Vigan, originally slated to play Jericho, would have been familiar with the text. Perhaps the name 'Jericho' even came from Rebatet's description of Jewish film personnel migrating to Hollywood and England 'proceeded by renown more discordant than the trumpets of Jericho'.[94] While another film made by Carné and Prévert during the Occupation, *Les Visiteurs du Soir* (1943), is remarkably 'white' in its tonalities – the film is set in a white fortress and the protagonists end up as two white statues – *Children of Paradise* returns to the historical origins of the popular milieus depicted in Poetic Realism. This was an expedient choice. During the Occupation, the Nazi administration strongly discouraged film-makers from choosing the contemporary settings of *Quai des Brumes* and *Le Jour se Lève*, and both films had been banned at the start of the Occupation because of their 'degenerate' qualities. The choice of the Boulevard du Temple allowed Carné and Prévert to approach, as nearly as possible, the social milieus of their earlier films, while also constructing a paean to French culture during the heyday of Romanticism.

It seems highly unlikely that Carné and Prévert wanted to denounce the Jewish influence on French films, although pitting the historical French Pierrot against an old-clothes seller would certainly have been one way to do that. No matter what any of the film's makers intended, however, this opposition is at the heart of the film. Jericho opens and closes the film; in the final scene Jericho prevents the hero from reaching the woman he loves. Given that both Carné and Prévert, as well as their collaborators, would have known Rebatet's text, then it must at least be assumed that the film-makers would have been aware that the film's central conflict would resonate within a set of characterisations being used by anti-Semitic, pro-German critics. However, the film is an entity complex enough to refuse to take sides. Baptiste's story is one of many stories, each of which advances a different interpretation of artistry. Except for one night, Baptiste and Garance are never able to come together, because Baptiste cannot understand the simplicity of which Garance speaks. Baptiste is a dreamer, but Garance, the truer emissary of the popular, is a realist.

The film as a whole has none of the 'clarity' that characterises the classical pantomime. While Baptiste feels oppressed, the film itself delights in the crowding of its shots and the *bibelot*-ifying of its décor. Upon launching the project, Carné went immediately to Paris, where he raided the prints department at the Musée Carnavalet, seeking nineteenth-century images of the Boulevard du Temple and period interiors. This 'second-degree' naturalism was intended to inspire recognition of the mythic image of the period, an image that was cluttered, full of bric-à-brac, infused with the poetics of the second-hand. When she delivers the line 'je suis toute seule' Garance's face is covered by a marvellous spangled, black-net veil, which leaves only her eyes visible; her head is silhouetted by the lattice-work wall of the private box at the Funambules (Figure 5.10). This shot suggests that despite her mournful proclamation, Garance is far from alone, because she is embedded in a web of costume. When she says 'c'est tout simple, l'amour' she has just wrapped her naked body in the paisley bedspread of her furnished room at the lodging house. Décor has become a mock-classical toga. There is no way that Baptiste can accept this declaration of simplicity, from a woman who has just donned the very sticky old fabric that he is attempting to flee. Baptiste loves the people, but he does not love their things, or their clothes.

I do not think that *Children of Paradise* is a fascist film. It is characterised by layers and multiplicity; it is multi-vocal.[95] Yet in this very dense allegorical text,

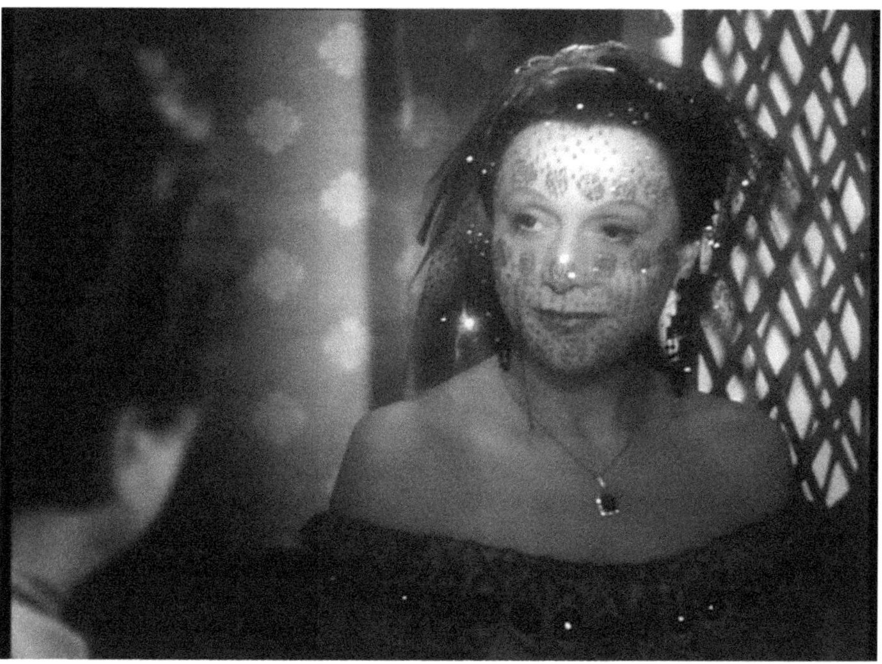

5.10   Marcel Carné (dir.), *Garance veiled*, 1945 Source: Pathé.

certain fascist aesthetics and cultural associations coalesce around the figure of Pierrot, his whiteness, and his struggle to distinguish himself. However, the film does not let a single kind of whiteness overwhelm it. Indeed, the final sequence on the Boulevard transforms the white clarity of the filmed pantomimes into white confusion, proof that what is white does not have to be lucid. Nor do I think that Pierrot's whiteness, in the film, is intended to be a secret text, a coded endorsement of conservative cultural politics. As the complex product of many different contributors at many different stages of the process, from Le Vigan who is not even in the final film, to Barrault, to Carné, Prévert, Kosma, and Trauner, it would be very difficult for the film to have a consistent, hidden meaning. Yet most of the team would have been aware that they were trading, deliberately, in the realm of myth, myths of the past and of the popular. Even if Jericho is maligned by the film's other characters, he does, ultimately get his way, when he pulls Baptiste back into the mêlée of carnival. There will be no fascist apotheosis for Baptiste; he will never become those airborne, floating bodies of the first minutes of Leni Riefenstahl's *Triumph of the Will* (1935).

The film marks an increasing tension between a vision of art as the product of dreams and the marketplace conceived as purely venal. Since his inception, Pierrot was tied to the marketplace, as the stage where he appeared, and as the world that his 'cry' addressed. Dreaming was not absent from this world, but it was understood as one of the tools and the media of a repertoire responsive to the marketplace and the desires that unfolded in it, like Pierrot's dream of ribbons. Baptiste is always asking others to believe in his dreams, but he dreams of ascending to a realm from which the market's things have been banished. Janin and Champfleury had envisioned the popular milieu as packed with shabby, yet characterful old things, which had arrived at their destination thanks to clever marketplace practitioners, like the *gamin* who started a business selling old neckties. For the critics who lauded Séverin's *pantomime blanche*, however, the popular world was minimalist, whitewashed, and bathed in the light of the 'south', as in the light of Greece and Italy. The film juxtaposes these two aesthetics, posing the happy and generative clutter of the offstage world with the uncompromising simplicity of a stage dominated by an actor who has merged utterly with his mask. Pierrot finds himself once again on the threshold, living in the bric-à-brac world but longing for a home that is as bare, and as white, as the Moon.

Notes

1 For an introduction to the film see Jill Forbes, *Les Enfants du Paradis* (London: British Film Institute, 1997). See also Geneviève Sellier, *Les Enfants du Paradis (Marcel Carné Jacques Prévert)* (Paris: Armand Colin, 1992). For the film's script, see Marcel Carné and Jacques Prévert, *Les Enfants du Paradis* (Paris: Balland, 1974).

2 For the drawings on which the sets were based see Alexandre Trauner, *Alexandre Trauner, Décors de cinéma, entretiens avec Jean-Pierre Berthomé* (Paris: Jade-Flammarion, 1988).

3 On the cinema of the Occupation, see Evelyn Ehrlich, *Cinema of Paradox: French Filmmaking under the German Occupation* (New York: Columbia University Press, 1985); Alan Williams, *Republic of Images: A History of French Filmmaking* (Cambridge, MA: Harvard University Press, 1992), pp. 245–71.

4 A detailed source on the mechanisms of organisation of the film industry during the Occupation is Colin Crisp, *Classic French Cinema 1930–1960* (Bloomington: Indiana University Press, 1993), pp. 43–57.

5 This argument is made by numerous scholars: Crisp, *Classic French Cinema*, pp. 50–55 (Crisp also points out the importance of a closed market, from which American films were forbidden); Williams, *Republic of Images*, pp. 248–53.

6 Edward Baron Turk, *Child of Paradise: Marcel Carné and the Golden Age of French Cinema* (Cambridge, MA: Harvard University Press, 1989), pp. 182–3.

7 For a detailed account of the film's financing and the politics of its production, see Jean-Pierre Berthomé and Guillaume Vernet, 'Des parents italiens pour *les Enfants du Paradis*', *1895, revue d'histoire du cinéma* 67 (2012), 32–61.

8 Turk has offered a useful discussion of the mechanisms of fragmentation and narrative incompletion in the film. See Turk, *Child of Paradise*, pp. 231–5.

9 On the idealisation of Garance as well as other psycho-sexual tensions in the film and their relationship to Occupation cinema, see Geneviève Sellier, 'Les Enfants du paradis dans le cinéma de l'Occupation', *1895, revue d'histoire du cinéma* 22 (1997), 55–66.

10 Jules Janin, 'Théâtre Français: première représentation du *Nègre*, drame en quatre actes et en vers libres, par M. Ozanneaux', *Journal des débats*, 1 November 1830, 1–3, here p. 3.

11 Williams, *Republic of Images*, pp. 266–7.

12 Dudley Andrew identifies multiple allegorical registers in the film, including an allegory of Poetic Realism itself, the genre of filmmaking in which Carné and Prévert worked together during the 1930s, producing classics like *Quai des Brumes* (1938) and *Le Jour se Lève* (1939): Dudley Andrew, *Mists of Regret: Culture and Sensibility in Classic French Film* (Princeton, NJ: Princeton University Press, 1995), pp. 319–32.

13 Andrew, *Mists of Regret*, p. 324; Sellier, *Les Enfants du Paradis*, pp. 61–3.

14 Sellier, 'Les Enfants du paradis', p. 65.

15 Sellier is the only author to mention it, and she does so decisively, if briefly: Sellier, *Les Enfants du Paradis*, p. 54.

16 Antoine Compagnon, *Les chiffonniers de Paris* (Paris: Gallimard, 2017), p. 296. On Jewish old-clothes sellers in eighteenth-century and nineteenth-century Britain, see Betty Naggar, 'Old-clothes men: 18th and 19th centuries', *Jewish Historical Studies* 31 (1988–90), 171–91.

17 Turk, *Child of Paradise*, p. 226.

18 Théophile Gautier, 'Shakespeare aux Funambules', in *L'art moderne* (Paris: Michel Lévy, 1856), pp. 167–79, here p. 177: 'Pierrot qui se promène dans la rue avec sa casaque blanche, son pantalon blanc, son visage enfariné, préoccupé de vagues désirs, n'est-ce pas la symbolization de l'âme humaine encore innocente et blanche, tourmentée d'aspirations infinies vers les regions supérieures?'

19 The pathbreaking work on whiteness in this vein is Richard Dyer, *White* (New York: Routledge, 1997). Dyer's work is primarily concerned with twentieth-century America and film, yet it nevertheless has proven useful as a framework for the analysis of other cultures. A useful bibliographic introduction to whiteness and the multiple fields (anthropology, sociology, political science, literary studies) in which

it has been studied is Steve Garner, *Whiteness: An Introduction* (London: Routledge, 2007).

20 This vital argument is made by Morrison in reference to American literature: Toni Morrison, *Playing in the Dark: Whiteness and the Literary Imagination* (Cambridge, MA: Harvard University Press, 1992), pp. 32–5. For an excellent discussion of whiteness as a value in nineteenth-century French art, see Katherine Brion, 'Courbet's *The Bathers* and the "Hottentot Venus": destabilizing whiteness in the mid-nineteenth-century nude', *Word & Image* 35:1 (2019), 12–32.

21 On associations of whiteness in eighteenth-century France, see Marika Takanishi Knowles, 'Making whiteness: art, luxury, and race in eighteenth-century France', in 'Race', ed. Stephanie O'Rourke and Susannah Blair, special issue, *Journal18* 13 (2022), www.journal18.org/6214, accessed 28 April 2023.

22 François Bernier's *Nouvelle division de la terre* (1684) was an instrumental text in the association of skin color and race. See Pierre H. Boulle, 'François Bernier and the origins of the modern concept of race', in Sue Peabody and Tyler Stovall (eds), *The Color of Liberty: Histories of Race in France* (Durham, NC: Duke University Press, 2003), pp. 11–41. The theories of the Comte de Buffon were also influential. Buffon argued that that white skin was nature's most perfect creation; non-white skin represented a degradation, usually attributed to climate, of this original state: Tzvetan Todorov, *On Human Diversity: Nationalism, Racism and Exoticism in French Thought*, trans. Catherine Porter (Cambridge, MA: Harvard University Press, 1993), pp. 96–105. On Buffon see also Sue Peabody, *'There are no slaves in France': The Political Culture of Race and Slavery in the Ancien Régime* (Oxford: Oxford University Press, 1997), pp. 61–6. Other philosophers, like Voltaire and the Abbé Raynal, floated the idea that different skin colours marked different species: see William B. Cohen, *The French Encounter with Africans: White Responses to Blacks, 1530–1880* (1980; Bloomington: Indiana University Press, 2003), pp. 84–6. 'Race' as a means of distinguishing between the hereditary features of different humans was already a familiar concept to the French, used to argue that the nobility possessed distinct, and superior, 'bloodlines' from non-nobles. The classic study on the understanding of race as a form of noble lineage in the French context is the thesis of Arlette Jouanna, *L'idée de race en France au XVIe siècle et au début du XVIIe siècle (1498–1614)* (Paris: Honoré Champion, 1976).

23 On the 'rigidification of French racial ideology' in the second half of the eighteenth century see Peabody, *'There are no slaves in France'*, p. 68. On the emergence of ideologies of whiteness and race in the French colonies, which made their way back to the metropole, see Elsa Dorlin, *La matrice de la race: généalogie sexuelle et colonial de la Nation française* (2006; Paris: La Découverte, 2009), pp. 193–203.

24 David Bindman, *From Ape to Apollo: Aesthetics and the Idea of Race in the 18th Century* (Ithaca, NY: Cornell University Press, 2002), pp. 11–21.

25 Anne Lafont, 'How skin color became a racial marker: art historical perspectives on race', *Eighteenth-Century Studies* 51:1 (2017), 89–113. Mechthild Fend has also drawn important connections between skin color, 'pigmentation', and visual art: see Mechthild Fend, 'Flesh-tones, skin colour and the eighteenth-century colour print', in Felix Ensslin and Charlotte Klink (eds), *Aesthetics of the Flesh* (Berlin: Sternberg Press, 2014), pp. 211–32. Finally, see Angela Rosenthal, 'Visceral culture: blushing and the legibility of whiteness in eighteenth-century British portraiture', *Art History* 27:4 (2004), 563–92.

26 For a discussion of Arlequin's mask in Watteau's work, see Aaron Wile, 'Blackface in Watteau's *The Italian Comedians?*' National Gallery of Art Blog, 5 August 2021,

www.nga.gov/blog/blackface-in-watteaus-italian-comedians.html, accessed 28 April 2023.

27 A handful of plays about Black individuals were performed at French theatres during the Revolution and the early nineteenth century. *Ourika* had been adapted by four different troupes: Sylvie Chalaye, 'Un théâtre en noir et blanc pour défendre les couleurs de la liberté', in Martial Poirson (ed.), *Le Théâtre sous la Révolution: politique du répertoire (1789–1799)* (Paris: Desjonquères, 2008), pp. 297–313.

28 Yvonne Fabella, 'Redeeming the "character of the Creoles": whiteness, gender and creolization in pre-revolutionary Saint Domingue', *Journal of Historical Sociology* 23:1 (2010), 40–72.

29 Janin, 'Le Théâtre Français', p. 3: 'un peu de farine sur la figure', 'deux violons faux'.

30 Sander Gilman has shown that Jews were often described as 'Black' in nineteenth-century European accounts. While this usually referred to the association of Jews with dirt and illness, some authors did claim that Jews had 'African' features: Sander Gilman, *The Jew's Body* (New York: Routledge, 1991), pp. 172–7.

31 There is a large literature on French anti-Semitisms, which will be cited below. Some helpful overviews include Pierre Birnbaum, *Un mythe politique: la 'République juive', de Léon Blum à Mendès France* (Paris: Gallimard, 1988); Pierre Birnbaum, *'La France aux Français': Histoire des haines nationalistes* (Paris: Seuil, 1993); David Carroll, *French Literary Fascism: Nationalism, Anti-Semitism, and the Ideology of Culture* (Princeton, NJ: Princeton University Press, 1995).

32 Michel Winock, *La France et les Juifs, de 1789 à nos jours* (Paris: Éditions du Seuil, 2004), pp. 11–27.

33 Winock, *La France et les Juifs*, pp. 29–49. See also Maurice Samuels, *The Right to Difference: French Universalism and the Jews* (Chicago: University of Chicago Press, 2016), pp. 50–55.

34 On the influence of this publication as the 'departure point' for modern French anti-Semitism, see Gérard Noiriel, *Immigration, antisémitisme et racisme en France (XIXe–XXe siècle). Discours publics, humiliations privées* (Paris: Fayard, 2007), pp. 208–33.

35 For overviews of the work of each of these authors, see Carroll, *French Literary Fascism*.

36 Michel Winock, *Édouard Drumont et Cie: antisémitisme et fascisme en France* (Paris: Éditions du Seuil, 1982), pp. 25–58.

37 This is the primary refrain of Chapter 5 of *La France juive*: Édouard Drumont, 'Paris juif et la société Française', in *La France juive*, ed. Alain Soral (Paris: Les InfréKentables, 2013), pp. 393–528. On the importance of Drumont to the anti-republican, nationalist movements in *fin-de-siècle* and early twentieth-century France, see Birnbaum, *'La France aux Français'*, pp. 103–14.

38 Christian Delacampagne, *Une histoire du racisme, des origines à nos jours* (Paris: Librairie Générale Française, 2000), p. 196.

39 Aryanism is a highly complex term. Originally used to refer to the belief, based upon linguistic evidence, that white Europeans originated in India, it eventually came to refer to white Europeans more broadly, as a separate and superior race. On Aryanism, one of the early proponents of which was Jules Michelet, see Claude Liauzu, *Race et civilisation: l'autre dans la culture occidentale, anthologie historique* (Paris: Syros/Alternatives, 1992), pp. 173–5, 226–34; Léon Poliakov, *The Aryan Myth: A History of Racist and Nationalist Ideas in Europe*, trans. Edmund Howard (London: Sussex University Press, 1971), pp. 17–36, 215–54.

40 Drumont, *La France juive*, p. 19: 'le Sémite est mercantile, cupide, intrigant, subtil, rusé; l'Aryen est enthousiaste, héroïque, chevaleresque, désintéressé, franc, confiant jusqu'à la naïveté'.

41 Drumont, *La France juive*, p. 436: 'de faux bibelots, des toiles pastichées', 'fausse figurines de Sèvres et de Saxe'.

42 This insistence on the Jewish identity as mercantile middlemen, as go-betweens rather than farmers or craftspeople, was present in much of the French anti-Semitic rhetoric that preceded Drumont. See Winock, *La France et les Juifs*, pp. 40–7.

43 Drumont, *La France juive*, p. 19: 'fils du ciel sans cesse préoccupé d'aspirations supérieures'.

44 A recent and comprehensive source on Willette is *Adolphe Willette 1857–1926* (Paris: Lienart éditions, 2014).

45 For a discussion of this episode, which is rather apologetic, see Philip Dennis Cate, 'Le côté sombre de Willette: mort et antisémite', in *Adolphe Willette 1857–1926*, pp. 170–77.

46 *Affiche pour les élections législatives du 22 septembre 1889*, in *Adolphe Willette 1857–1926*, p. 179: 'une race différente et ennemie de la nôtre'.

47 See *Le chat noir* (6 May 1882). On Bernhardt and anti-Semitism in nineteenth-century France, see the essays by Sander Gilman, 'Salome, syphilis, Sarah Bernhardt, and the modern Jewess', pp. 97–120, and Carol Ockman, 'When is a Jewish star just a star? Interpreting images of Sarah Bernhardt', pp. 121–39, in Linda Nochlin and Tamar Garb (eds), *The Jew in the Text: Modernity and the Construction of Identity* (London: Thames and Hudson, 1995).

48 Mariel Oberthür, *Le Chat Noir 1881–1897* (Paris: Éditions de la Réunion des musées nationaux, 1992), pp. 5–16 on the décor of the cabaret, pp. 36–9 on Willette's contributions to the décor.

49 Laura Morowitz, 'Anti-Semitism, medievalism and the art of the *fin-de-siècle*', *Oxford Art Journal* 20:1 (1997), 35–49.

50 Paul Hugounet, *Mimes et Pierrots: notes et documents inédits pour servir à l'histoire de la pantomime* (Paris: Librairie Fischbacher, 1889), p. 212: 'perpétuellement simple et saintement naïf', 'le *Goym* sans cesse dupé par les Sémites ou par tous ceux qui portent en corps chrétien une âme juive'.

51 Hugounet, *Mimes et Pierrots*, p. 213: 'temple élevé par la finance juive au culte d'or', 'ce héros du rêve qui n'a pas même dans sa poche les cinq sols d'Isaac Laquedem'.

52 Adolphe Willette, 'A Théodore de Banville', *Le Pierrot* 3:1, 20 March 1891, 2: '[Pierrot] portait le deuil de ses illusions et de sa jeunesse maltraitée, assassinée'.

53 On this period, see the excellent study by Ariane Martinez, *La pantomime: théâtre en mineur, 1880–1945* (Paris: Presses Sorbonne Nouvelle, 2008).

54 Martinez, *La pantomime*, p. 24.

55 On the 'elastic' nature of *fin-de-siècle* and early twentieth-century classicism, see Neil McWilliam, 'Action Française, classicism, and the dilemmas of traditionalism in France, 1900–1914', in 'Nationalism and French Visual Culture, 1870–1914', special issue, *Studies in the History of Art* 69 (2005), 268–91, here p. 270. McWilliam's work has emphasised the varieties of neo-classicism amidst conservative cultural theorists and historians of art. See also Neil McWilliam, 'Towards a new French renaissance: memory, tradition and cultural conservatism in France before the First World War', *Art History* 40:4 (2017), 724–43.

56 Kenneth Silver, *Esprit de Corps: The Art of the Parisian Avant-Garde and the First World War, 1914–1925* (Princeton, NJ: Princeton University Press, 1989), pp. 89–105.

57 See Romy Golan's work on the French obsession between the wars with the 'naturalistic' and mediaevalism. Golan argues that the French, wary of Italy's fascism, had moved decisively away from Italianate neo-classicism by the 1930s: Romy Golan, *Modernity and Nostalgia: Art and Politics in France Between the Wars* (New Haven, CT: Yale University Press, 1995), pp. 9, 28.

58 David Cottington, *Cubism in the Shadow of War: The Avant-Garde and Politics in Paris 1905–1914* (New Haven, CT: Yale University Press, 1998), pp. 60–67.

59 Silver, *Esprit de Corps*, pp. 126–30.

60 André Antoine (23 February 1920): 'ces spectacles naïfs et légers font encore la joie des salles populaires'. BNF, Collection Rondel, RO 11382.

61 Francisque Sarcey, *Le Temps* (18 May 1896), cited in the program for *Chand d'habits* performed at the Folies-Bergère in 1896. BNF, Collection Rondel, RO 11378: 'le masque des empereurs romains'.

62 Marc Henry, 'Une soirée au music-hall', *Europe nouvelle*, 28 February 1920, n.p.: 'on voit sur cette face pâle naître, se développer puis se disperser les sentiments ... Toute la génese du crime apparaît sur la figure blanche. C'est vraiment beau, d'un très grand art.' BNF, Collection Rondel, 8 RO 11631.

63 Henry, 'Une soirée au music-hall': 'la composition violemment colorée de Farina'.

64 Gustave Fréjaville, 'Chronique de la semaine, à l'empire – le mime Séverin dans *Marotte d'artiste*', *Comoedia*, 3 September 1925, BNF, Collection Rondel, 8 RO 11631: 'face blanchie', 'mimes classiques', 'sur ce masque blanc, comme sur un écran d'une sensibilité miraculeuse, les sentiments et les pensées viennent s'inscrire en traits nets et fugitifs ...'

65 Rosenthal, 'Visceral culture', p. 575.

66 Fernand Gregh, 'Chand d'habits', *Comoedia*, 10 March 1921; Jane Catulle-Mendes, 'Chand d'habits', *La Presse*, 10 March 1921; René Widner, 'La renaissance de la pantomime', 29 February 1920, BNF, Collection Rondel, 8 RO 11382; Henri Béraud, 'Les grands artistes: Séverin', 4 February 1920, BNF, Collection Rondel, 8 RO 11382. As is the case for the last two sources, not all the clippings in the Collection Rondel are clearly labelled. I have not been able to determine the name of the journal in these cases.

67 Séverin, *L'homme blanc, souvenirs d'un Pierrot*, intro. and notes Gustave Fréjaville (Paris: Librairie Plon, 1929), p. 300: 'les noirs ont pris la place de l'Homme blanc dans le goût du public'.

68 On the popularity of *'ballets nègre'* at the music hall, see Sylvie Chalaye, *Du Noir au nègre: l'image du Noir au théâtre de Marguerite de Navarre à Jean Genet, 1550–1960* (Paris: L'Harmattan, 1998), pp. 279–84.

69 H. Espian, 'Les Souvenirs d'un Pierrot', *Echo*, 29 July 1929: 'le noir abonde', 'la tradition toute classique'. BNF, Collection Rondel, 8 RO 11633.

70 Gerard d'Houville, 'L'homme blanc', *Figaro*, 28 July 1929; André Antoine, 'Homme blanc, souvenirs d'un Pierrot, par le mime Séverin', *Information*, 28 July 1929: 'le visage blanc du Pierrot devenait le miroir saississant de l'âme du personnage et il apprit a écrire sur cette page blanche [...]'. BNF, Collection Rondel, 8 RO 11633.

71 'Je suis comme eux, je les aime, je reconnais leur vie est toute petite, mais ils ont grand rêves'. Carné and Prévert, *Les Enfants du Paradis*.

72 *Chand d'habits* was also the pantomime chosen by the actor, director, and filmmaker Sacha Guitry to open his play *Deburau*, a light drama written in rhyming

free verse about Deburau's fictional love affair with the heroine of Dumas' *La dame aux camélias*. The play was premiered in 1918 and relaunched in 1926 at the newly restored Théâtre Sarah Bernhardt. See the *recueil* with press clippings, BNF, Collection Rondel, 8-RF-61594. Undoubtedly, Guitry's *Deburau* was an important influence for *Les Enfants du Paradis*, in that it showed Baptiste Deburau both on and off stage, masked and unmasked.

73 On the phenomenon of second-hand clothing and its uncanny aspect in nineteenth-century English literature, see Catherine Waters, *Commodity Culture in Dickens's Household Words: The Social Life of Goods* (Aldershot: Ashgate, 2008), pp. 141–56.

74 Ann Rosalind Jones and Peter Stallybrass, *Renaissance Clothing and the Materials of Memory* (Cambridge: Cambridge University Press, 2000).

75 Louis-Sébastien Mercier, *Tableau de Paris*, ed. Jean-Claude Bonnet (Paris: Mercure de France, 1994), 1:711–15.

76 Mercier, *Tableau de Paris*, 1:711–12: 'cette superbe colonnade que tout étranger admire', 'beaucoup de vieilles hardes, qui, suspendues à ficelles, et tournant au vent, forment un étalage hideux'.

77 Mercier, *Tableau de Paris*, 1:712: 'sale et indécent'.

78 Mercier, *Tableau de Paris*, 1:713: 'les miasmes contagieux', 'par le contact de l'étoffe'.

79 Mercier, *Tableau de Paris*, 1:714: 'des poisons cachés'.

80 On the second-hand clothing trade in nineteenth-century Paris, see Philippe Perrot, *Les dessus et les dessous de la bourgeoisie, une histoire du vêtement au XIXe siècle* (Paris: Fayard, 1981), pp. 78–92.

81 Marc Fournier, 'La Rotonde du Temple', in Paul de Kock (ed.), *La grande ville: nouveau tableau de Paris, comique, critique et philosophique* (Paris: Au Bureau Central des Publications Nouvelles, 1843), 2:39–56, here 2:43: 'labyrinth inextricable'.

82 Fournier, 'La Rotonde', 2:45: 'la garde-robe exhilarante du carnaval, le loup de velours noir, le domino'.

83 Fournier, 'La Rotonde', 2:45: 'c'est un désordre relevé d'un cachet bizarre, singulier d'aspect et d'allure'.

84 Fournier, 'La Rotonde', 2:48: 'spéculer sur les fonds de culottes'.

85 Gale B. Murray, 'Toulouse Lautrec's illustrations for Victor Joze and Georges Clemenceau and their relationship to French anti-Semitism of the 1890s', in Nochlin and Garb, *The Jew in the Text*, pp. 56–82. For a dated, but still useful evaluation of Zola's depiction of Jewish characters in *L'argent*, see Richard B. Grant, 'The Jewish question in Zola's *L'Argent*', *Proceedings of the Modern Language Association* 70:5 (1955), 955–67.

86 On Rebatet's prewar film criticism, in which many of the ideas of *Les tribus* are developed, see Christopher Faulkner, 'Theory and practice of film reviewing in France in the 1930s: eyes right (Lucien Rebatet and Action Française 1936–1939)', *French Cultural Studies* 3 (1992), 133–55. On Rebatet's fascist tendencies more generally and his response to the Occupation, see Robert Belot, 'Lucien Rebatet, de l'intellectuel fasciste', *Esprit* 201:5 (1994), 65–94. On Rebatet's fascist radio broadcasts during the Second World War, see Alice Kaplan, *Reproductions of Banality: Fascism, Literature, and French Intellectual Life* (Minneapolis: University of Minnesota Press, 1986), pp. 125–41.

87 Lucien Rebatet, *Les tribus du cinéma et du théâtre* (Paris: Nouvelles Éditions Françaises, 1941).

88 Rebatet, *Les tribus*, pp. 10–12.

89 Rebatet, *Les tribus*, p. 12.
90 In 1913 Léon Daudet, one of the leaders of Action Française, made the same comparison regarding Jewish participation in the theatre business: Léon Daudet, 'Le Trucquage du Théâtre Juif', *Action Française*, 5 September 1913: '[le juif] fait des pièces comme il fait de la brocante, en rapetassant les idées d'autrui, en combinant, dans le sucré ou dans le salé, des 'arlequins' à la mode du jour ...'
91 Rebatet, *Les tribus*, p. 11: 'ghettos obscurs de l'Europe orientale ou des impasses les plus sordides de Whitechapel'.
92 Rebatet, *Les tribus*, p. 87: 'destructive', 'presque animale', 'volonté'. On Rebatet's interest in fascist concepts of will, some of which were represented in *Triumph of the Will* (1935, dir. Leni Riefenstahl), see Belot, 'Lucien Rebatet', pp. 89–90.
93 Rebatet, *Les tribus*, p. 86.
94 Rebatet, *Les tribus*, pp. 50–1: 'ces Juifs précédés d'une renommée plus fracassante que toutes les trompettes de Jéricho'.
95 On the single 'overvoice' of fascist cinema, see Kaplan, *Reproductions of Banality*, p. 153.

Conclusion

Over the course of this study, Pierrot has functioned most meaningfully in works of art that enable him to act as a front, presenting his vast surface to the viewer as a blank to be inscribed or projected upon. He has functioned most practically as a figure that lends himself to being cut out and placed elsewhere, whether literally cut out with scissors or excerpted by the mind of an artist or viewer who can either reiterate him in a new artwork or hang him on the wall of the mind. What I have tried to show is that these practices of use and re-use are not unrelated to Pierrot's affective charge. Many viewers perceive Watteau's *Pierrot* as sad, funny, or mildly embarrassing. Personally, I find Pierrot to be all of these things at once. He is pathetic, but he is also brave. None of these perceptions are right or wrong, although they may well be anachronistic. What is of significance, however, is the fact that these projections of feeling are made possible by the way Watteau presents Pierrot, and the way that Watteau presents Pierrot is indebted to the theatricality of the early eighteenth-century marketplace. Emotional states cast onto Pierrot's receptive surface are a result of the way that the marketplace sets things forth to be judged. As post-Romantics, however, we are less likely to assess Pierrot's worth than to feel something about him. Or rather, assessment of worth and the experience of feeling have become fully intertwined.

I will go so far as to say that I do think that Watteau recognised in Pierrot a vision of what it means to address a public of strangers, which was what Watteau was expected to do as an artist, particularly as the kind of artist who might have his work sold in a place like Gersaint's shop. (What is more, it was Watteau's own painting that imagined Gersaint's shop as a place where paintings were displayed as if decorating a theatrical set, when in fact the shopfront itself was narrow and closed to the street.) Watteau's drawings, turned fervently inward towards the artist as their privileged interlocutor, suggest that he preferred not to make this address. Jullienne would have to wait until the painter was dead and do it for him, by designing the *Figures of different characters* as an instrument of both hagiography and marketing.

Watteau's Pierrot addresses the marketplace in a manner that is simultaneously open and opaque. He is without excitement, but he does not appear to resist the obligation to stand forth. Again, his frankness with regards to what he is doing – presenting himself to the viewer who will assess him – makes explicit the underlying address of the theatrical artwork. While Diderot believed that theatrical art prevented reflection on and contemplation of the depicted subject, this was because Diderot did not want to think about art as an object in the world. He primarily wanted to think about the world *in* the artwork. What I have tried to show is that there are ways to think about art as an object in the world that do not necessarily have to do with either histories of pricing or even materiality. Instead, I have tried to think about how works of art have given Pierrot a place in the world.

Furthermore, and this is what I have hoped to add to an understanding of theatricality as an artistic mode, Pierrot's address is formed within the marketplace as a theatrical venture. The marketplace was theatrical because it was liminal, a space distinguished from the everyday, where participants stepped into a role, exploiting artifice to elevate the value of goods or to bend the terms of a deal. Mandeville's adept salesman awaits his customer at the door of the shop and then, once the customer has crossed the threshold, slips behind the counter. Gleefully, the salesman throws off one role for another, accessing the marketplace as a locale of intoxicating transformations. With less bravura but with considerably more bluntness, Pierrot also marks the threshold, assuming his role as the herm of the marketplace. The herm was a stone sculpture, half-man, half pillar, used to mark boundaries; herms were used widely in seventeenth- and eighteenth-century French garden design and featured heavily in the gardens of Versailles.[1] In the ancient world, the herm stood over the marketplace as an agent of Hermes, patron of artisans and traders as well as of fleet-footed movement. The herm established the marketplace as a boundary, the threshold across which exchanges were made.[2] In Watteau's large painting, a herm stands in the trees behind Pierrot. It faces inwards, looking across the painting rather than out of it. Like Pierrot, the herm is immobile and expressionless, a columnar presence placed at distance from the characters harrassing the donkey in the ditch. Watteau encloses the classical prototype within the woodland background, while drawing Pierrot forward. The herm is nude; Pierrot is clothed, because the new marketplace sells garments as the medium of personality. Pierrot is Watteau's herm, who appears throughout the painter's *oeuvre* as the sign of art's obligatory address, which is both art's vulnerability and the core of its sociability.

Earthy – in Molière's play Pierrot was occupied in throwing clods of dirt at a friend when he saw Don Juan drowning – Pierrot nevertheless is constantly in motion throughout this study. Throughout the eighteenth century he is constantly being moved by others, by artists and collectors and viewers. Eventually, movement becomes a property of his figure, as he scampers and vaults through Willette's stories without words, as he somersaults on the stage of the Funambules in *Children of Paradise*. From dirt to the Moon, Pierrot will enact with his own figure the mobility to which others had subjected him. For a long time, however, Pierrot's immobility maintained the address of his figure as a presentation of a surface. In Watteau's work, in the rococo, and in Manet's painting, Pierrot is a creature of surface. By staying still, and facing forward, Pierrot's figure expressed its commitment to the art of being a surface, to the surface as the threshold of appearance. He was all front. *Children of Paradise* does its best to contest this front, by providing a back story – the life of the actor. Yet the film also indulges in the world of surfaces that has characterised this study. There are costumes everywhere, which are put on and put off. Its characters wear the recognisable masks of the *physiognomies*: the dandy, the thief, the actor, the *grisette–lorette–courtesan*, the old-clothes seller, the poet. For some characters, like the Comte de Montray, the front is all there is. Garance is also all front, but in a more complex way. She assumes different female fronts throughout the film, from the *grisette* of the boulevards, daughter of a singing laundress, to the pampered courtesan. Baptiste tries to access her love as a form of essence, but Garance refuses and returns to the world of masks, which is where she first found Pierrot. The film offers two visions of creativity. One of these forms of creativity muddles through a richly textured object world and uses these objects to construct fronts, as Garance does when she transforms the paisley bedspread into a toga or gazes at Frédérick through the spangled veil. The other arises as a perfect whole whose artistry is a matter of the mind.

The marketplace is present in these visions of creativity as a residue of things. For the artist in the medium of bric-à-brac, the marketplace is a source of materials and a model for practice. In this study, I have considered the marketplace both as a social frame and as a material practice. From Watteau's *oeuvre*, where Pierrot's figure announces the conditions of the marketplace encounter, I moved to the rococo, where Pierrot's recurrence becomes an effect of marketplace practices of re-use and assembly. Manet's painting *The Old Musician* offers a merger of sorts, by considering the marketplace as a visual field, where people and things wait to be chosen. Manet reads fatigue as well as a certain brutality in the mobility of objects in the marketplace; he imagines his types as weary from long journeys. Nevertheless, rather than patronise them, he gives his figures a gritty flippancy. In the Tournachons' photographs, Pierrot is cleaned up for sale. Displayed at the Universal Exposition, Pierrot performed his readiness for the marketplace in the form of the dreamworld – the human mind as a phantasmagoria of commerce. In *Children of Paradise*, Baptiste equates artistry with the weightlessness of a figure projected from a magic lantern. This is simplicity, to Baptiste. This is love. Yet what the film finally confirms is that Baptiste is not Pierrot. I would agree. As a front man, Pierrot is always just Pierrot. His back stories can differ. There was a model, after all, for Watteau's *Pierrot*, a young man with dark, thick brows and dark eyes above full cheeks and a small chin. But this is not Pierrot's face, really, because Pierrot does not have a single face but rather many surfaces, many fronts, some of which take the character of faces, as in Watteau's drawing (Plate 11).

My final Pierrot does not have a face at all. This is Eugène Atget's photograph of a headless mannequin outside a shop on the Avenue des Gobelins (Figure 6.1). Atget was a favorite of the Surrealists, artists who regarded the world of goods as a world of dreams. The mannequin wears white trousers and a loose white shirt. These are probably pyjamas sold by a shop whose

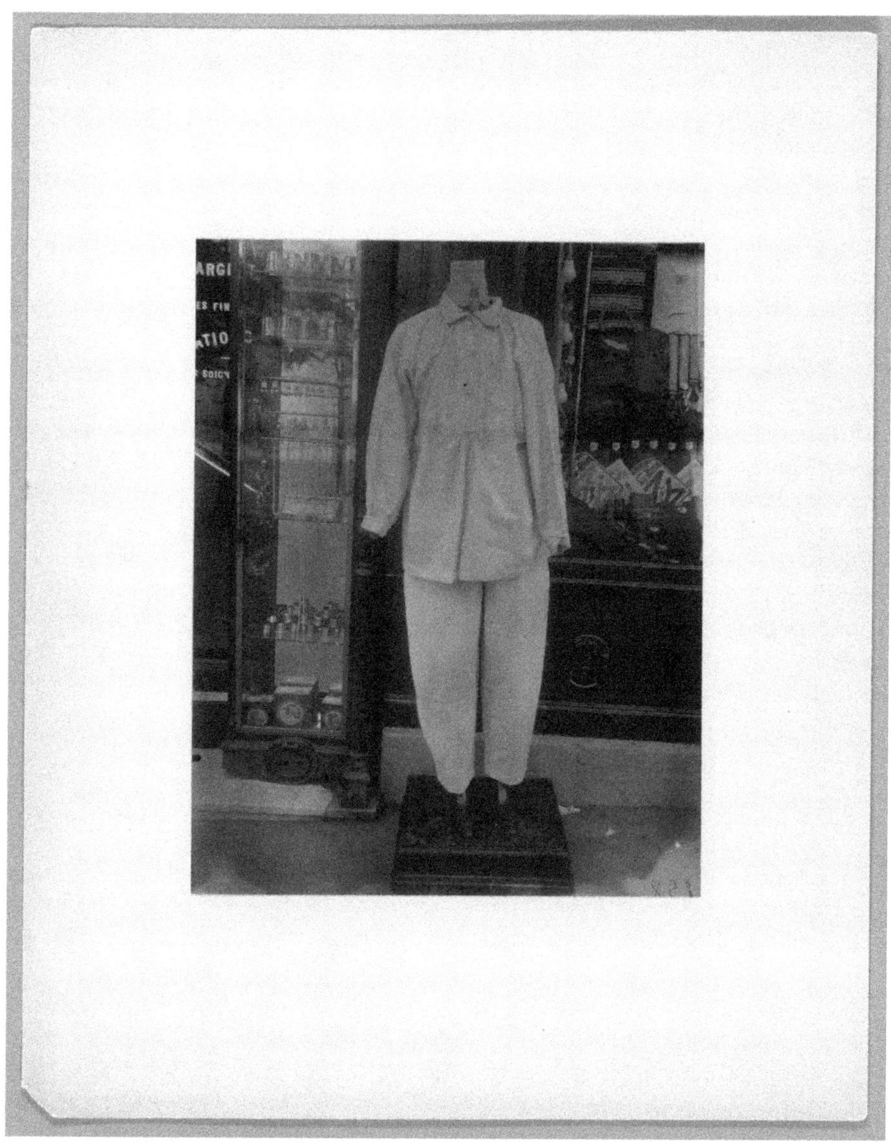

6.1   Eugène Atget, *Avenue des Gobelins*, 1927. Silver-gelatin print from a glass negative, 36.8 × 28.6 cm. Source: Metropolitan Museum of Art, New York. 1994.271 ©The Metropolitan Museum of Art, Dist. RMN-Grand Palais/image of the MMA.

vitrine, stocked with braces and garters, is visible behind the mannequin. The mannequin addresses the passerby with a show of vacancy. If seen out of the corner of the eye, outside the shop, perhaps it would appear to be nothing special (indeed, Pierrot was nothing special, before Watteau, and later Denon, stopped to look). Yet the photograph stills the mannequin's address, frames it, and points it at the viewer. For a long time, I wondered what this figure shared with Pierrot, apart from mere morphology in the matter of white pyjamas. It haunted me. I forgot the other parts of the photograph and the central figure, this wrinkly suit, dwelt in my mind. It hung around. Which is what Pierrot does – he hangs around. What I realised, however, and what I have tried to show in this book, is that this suit of linen (Pierrot's *habit de toile*) hangs around because it is on a mannequin outside a shop, in the marketplace, which it addresses. This book has sought to understand why that realisation matters. It matters not because art is a commodity among others, but because the marketplace is a way of being and a way of seeing and a way of encountering other people. To follow Pierrot is to follow the changing nature of this encounter, as the distance enacted through the counter as a form of retail architecture becomes the weightlessness of a figure projected by light, as old clothes become new ones, and new clothes old.

Pierrot's dream of ribbons is a dream of foldable, transformative surfaces, which can be worn, removed, and replaced. It is a dream of embellishment, of decoration and supplement. Modelled at the theatre, slipping easily into the marketplace, it is also a dream of visual art as a surface with the power to constitute personality. Visual art gives Pierrot his most lasting, most haunting, costume. With a bit of luck, no one must wear their first costume forever. Those who have worn Pierrot's costume may trade up. But Pierrot persists, as long as there is someone to pick up his clothes and hang them outside a shop, as long as there are artists to lend him ribbons.

Notes

1 Betsy Rosasco, 'The herms of Versailles in the 1680s', *Princeton University Library Chronicle* 76:1–2 (2015), 145–75.
2 See Agnew's discussion of the herm as the 'threshold' of the marketplace in Jean-Christophe Agnew, *Worlds Apart: The Market and the Theater in Anglo-American Thought, 1550–1750* (Cambridge: Cambridge University Press, 1986), pp. 17–23.

Bibliography

Abélès, Luce, ed. *Champfleury: L'art pour le peuple*. Paris: Réunion des Musées Nationaux, 1990.

Adams, Steven. '"Noising things abroad": art, commodity, and commerce in post-Revolutionary Paris.' *Nineteenth-Century Art Worldwide* 12:2 (2013), www.19thc-art worldwide.org/autumn13/adams-on-art-commodity-and-commerce-in-post-revolu tionary-paris, accessed 28 April 2023.

Adhémar, Hélène. *Watteau: sa vie, son œuvre*. Paris: Éditions Pierre Tisné, 1950.

Adhémar, Hélène. 'Watteau, les romans et l'imagerie de son temps.' *Gazette des Beaux-Arts* 90 (1977), 165–72.

Adhémar, Jean. 'Propositions pour une thématique des portraits photographiques par Nadar.' *Gazette des Beaux-Arts* 107:128 (1986), 157–62.

Agnew, Jean-Christophe. *Worlds Apart: The Market and the Theater in Anglo-American Thought, 1550–1750*. Cambridge: Cambridge University Press, 1986.

A.J., 'Collections de curiosités et d'objets d'art: Cabinets de MM. Denon, Sauvageot et de Guignes', *L'Artiste*, ser. 1, 9:12 (1835), 141–3.

Altmann, Lothar. *Die Figuren des F.A. Bustelli*. Munich: Scaneg, 1993.

Amengual, Barthélémy. 'D'un Pierrot à l'autre.' In Pierre Guibbert, ed. *Les Premiers Ans du Cinéma Français*, pp. 147–9. Perpignan: Institut Jean Vigo, 1985.

Anderson, George K. *The Legend of the Wandering Jew*. Providence, RI: Brown University Press, 1965.

André, Louis. *Machines à Papier en France 1789–1860*. Paris: Éditions de l'école des hautes études en sciences sociales, 1996.

Andrew, Dudley. *Mists of Regret: Culture and Sensibility in Classic French Film*. Princeton, NJ: Princeton University Press, 1995.

Andrews, Richard. *The Commedia dell'Arte of Flaminio Scala: a translation and analysis of 30 scenarios*. Lanham, MD: Scarecrow Press, 2008.

Attinger, Gustave. *L'esprit de la commedia dell'arte dans le théâtre français*. Paris: Librairie théâtrale, 1950.

Auzel, Dominique. *Émile Reynaud et l'image s'anima*. Paris: Editions Dumay, 1992.

Baetjer, Katherine. *Watteau, Music, and Theater*. New York: Metropolitan Museum of Art, 2009.

Bailey, Colin. 'Toute seule elle peut remplir et satisfaire l'attention: the early appreciation and marketing of Watteau's drawings, with an introduction to the collection of modern French drawings during the reign of Louis XV.' In Alan Wintermute, ed. *Watteau and his World: French Drawing from 1700–1750*, pp. 68–92. London: Merrell Holberton, 1999.

Bakhtin, Mikhail. *Rabelais and His World*. Trans. Hélène Iswolsky. Bloomington: Indiana University Press, 2009.

Barish, Jonas. 'Exhibitionism and the antitheatrical prejudice.' *ELH* 36:1 (1969), 1–29.

Barish, Jonas. *The Antitheatrical Prejudice*. Berkeley: University of California Press, 1981.

Bargiel, Réjane and Ségolène Le Men. *La Belle Époque de Jules Chéret: De l'affiche au décor*. Paris: Les Arts Décoratifs/Bibliothèque nationale de France, 2010.

Bastian, Jacques. *Strasbourg: Faïences et porcelaines, 1721–1784*. 2 vols. Strasbourg: Éditions M.A.J.B., 2002.

Bastian, Jacques and Marie-Alice Bastian. *Faïences de Strasbourg: Manufacture Hannong*. Riggisberg: Abegg-Stiftung, 2013.

Baticle, Jeannine. 'Pierrot, Gilles, et les autres.' In François Moureau and Morgan Grasselli, eds. *Antoine Watteau (1684–1721): le peintre, son temps et sa légende*, pp. 37–41. Paris: Clairefontaine, 1987.

Baudelaire, Charles. *Oeuvres complètes*. Edited by Claude Pichois. 2 vols. Paris: Gallimard, 1975.

Bauer, Hermann. *Rocaille: Zur Herkunft und Zum Wesen einer Ornament-Motivs*. Berlin: Walter de Gruyter, 1962.

Bauer, Hermann. *Rokokomalerei: Sechs Studien*. Mittenwald: Mäander Kunstverlag, 1980.

Bédard, Jean-François. 'Prints by Gabriel Huquier after Oppenord's Decorated "Ripa".' *Print Quarterly* 29:1 (2012), 37–43.

Belot, Robert. 'Lucien Rebatet, de l'intellectuel fasciste.' *Esprit* 201:5 (1994), 65–94.

Bénichou, Paul. *L'école du désenchantement: Sainte Beuve, Nodier, Nerval, Gautier*. Paris: Gallimard, 1992.

Benjamin, Walter. *Charles Baudelaire: A Lyric Poet in the Era of High Capitalism*. Trans. Harry Zohn. London: Verso, 1973.

Benjamin, Walter. *Das Passagen-Werk*. Edited by Rolf Tiedemann. 2 vols. Frankfurt am Main: Suhrkamp Verlag, 1982.

Benjamin, Walter. 'Paris, capitale du XIXeme siècle, exposé.' In Rolf Tiedemann and Hermann Schweppenhäuser (eds), *Gesammelte Schriften*, vol. 1 edited by Rolf Tiedemann, pp. 60–77. Frankfurt am Main: Suhrkamp Verlag, 1991.

Bernardin, Napoléon-Maurice. *La Comédie Italienne en France et les théâtres de la foire et du boulevard (1570–1791)*. Paris: Éditions de la 'Revue bleue', 1902.

Bernstein, Robin. 'Toward the integration of theater history and affect studies: shame and the Rude Mech's *The Method Gun*.' *Theater Journal* 64:2 (2012), 213–30.

Berthomé, Jean-Pierre and Guillaume Vernet. 'Des parents italiens pour *les Enfants du Paradis*.' *1895, revue d'histoire du cinéma* 67 (2012), 32–61.

Beurdeley, Michel. *La France à l'encan, 1789–1799: exode des objets d'art sous la Révolution*. Paris: Librairie Jules Tallandier, 1981.

Bielecki, Emma. '"Un artiste en matière de chiffons": the rag-picker as a figure for the artist in Champfleury's *La Mascarade de la vie Parisienne*.' *Nineteenth-century French Studies* 37:3–4 (2009), 262–75.

Bindman, David. *From Ape to Apollo: Aesthetics and the Idea of Race in the 18th Century*. Ithaca, NY: Cornell University Press, 2002.

Birnbaum, Pierre. *Un mythe politique, la 'République juive': de Léon Blum à Mendès France.* Paris: Gallimard, 1988.

Birnbaum, Pierre. *'La France aux Français': Histoire des haines nationalistes.* Paris: Seuil, 1993.

Blanc, Charles. *Le trésor de la curiosité.* 2 vols. Paris: Jules Renouard, 1857.

Bocard, Hélène. *Les critiques des expositions de photographie à Paris sous le Second Empire.* Paris: Mémoire de D.E.A., Université Paris Sorbonne, Paris IV, 1995.

Boindin, Nicolas. *Lettres historiques à Mr D*** sur la nouvelle Comédie italienne, 3eme lettre.* Paris: The Author, 1717.

Bonnaffé, Edmond. *Le commerce de la curiosité.* Paris: Honoré Champion, 1895.

Bonnet, Jean-Claude. 'Mercier et l'art du recyclage.' *Revue d'histoire littéraire de la France* 118:3 (2018), 517–22.

Bornecque, Jacques-Henry. *Lumières sur les fêtes galantes de Paul Verlaine: avec le texte critique des Fêtes galantes.* Paris: Nizet, 1959.

Boulle, Pierre H. 'François Bernier and the origins of the modern concept of race.' In Sue Peabody and Tyler Stovall, eds. *The Color of Liberty: Histories of Race in France,* pp. 11–41. Durham, NC: Duke University Press, 2003.

Bourget, Ernest. *Physiologie du gamin de Paris, galopin industriel.* Paris: J. Laisne, 1842.

Bouvier, Émile. *La bataille réaliste.* Geneva: Slatkine Reprints, 1973.

Brady, Patrick. 'Rococo and neo-classicism.' *Studi Francesi* 22 (1964), 34–49.

Bratton, Jacky. *New Readings in Theatre History.* Cambridge: Cambridge University Press, 2003.

Bretonne, Rétif de la. *Les nuits de Paris.* Edited by Michel Delon. Paris: Gallimard, 1986.

Bridgeman, Jane. 'The origins of dress history and Cesare Vecellio's "pourtraits of attire".' *Costume* 44 (2010), 37–45.

Brion, Katherine. 'Courbet's *The Bathers* and the "Hottentot Venus": destabilising whiteness in the mid-nineteenth-century nude.' *Word & Image* 35:1 (2019), 12–32.

Brown, Marilyn. 'Manet's "Old Musician": portrait of a gypsy and naturalist allegory.' *Studies in the History of Art* 8 (1978), 77–87.

Brown, Marilyn. *The Gamin de Paris in Nineteenth-Century Visual Culture: Delacroix, Hugo, and the French Social Imaginary.* New York: Routledge, 2017.

Bruand, Yves. 'Un grand collectionneur, marchand et graveur du XVIIIe siècle, Gabriel Huquier, 1695–1772.' *Gazette des Beaux Arts* (July–September 1950), 99–114.

Buddemeier, Heinz. *Panorama, Diorama, Photographie.* Munich: W. Fink, 1970.

Burke, Peter. *The Fabrication of Louis XIV.* New Haven, CT: Yale University Press, 1992.

Burke, Peter. 'Performing history: the importance of occasions.' *Rethinking History* 9:1 (2005), 35–52.

Burns, Elizabeth. *Theatricality: A study of convention in the theatre and in social life.* London: Longman, 1972.

Butterfield-Rosen, Emmelyn. *Modern Art & the Remaking of Human Disposition.* Chicago: University of Chicago Press, 2021.

Çakmak, Gülru. 'Jean-Léon Gérôme: the innovative years (1851–1859).' PhD dissertation, Johns Hopkins University, 2010.

Çakmak, Gülru. *Jean-Léon Gérôme and the crisis of history painting in the 1850s.* Liverpool: Liverpool University Press, 2017.

Camp, Pannill. *The First Frame: Theatre Space in Enlightenment France.* Cambridge: Cambridge University Press, 2014.

Carlson, Marvin. 'The resistance to theatricality.' *SubStance* 31:2–3 (2002), 238–50.

Carné, Marcel and Jacques Prévert. *Les Enfants du Paradis.* Paris: Balland, 1974.

Carroll, David. *French Literary Fascism: Nationalism, Anti-Semitism, and the Ideology of Culture*. Princeton, NJ: Princeton University Press, 1995.

Cassidy-Geiger, Maureen, ed. *Fragile Diplomacy: Meissen Porcelain for European Courts ca. 1710–63*. New York: Bard Graduate Center and Yale University Press, 2007.

Castle, Terry. 'Phantasmagoria: spectral technology and the metaphorics of modern reverie.' *Critical Inquiry* 15:1 (1988), 26–61.

Cate, Philip Dennis. 'Le côté sombre de Willette: mort et antisémite.' In *Adolphe Willette 1857–1926*. Exhibition catalogue, pp. 170–77. Paris: Lienart éditions, 2014.

Chalaye, Sylvie. *Du Noir au nègre: l'image du Noir au théâtre de Marguerite de Navarre à Jean Genet, 1550–1960*. Paris: L'Harmattan, 1998.

Chalaye, Sylvie. 'Un théâtre en noir et blanc pour défendre les couleurs de la liberté.' In Martial Poirson, ed. *Le Théâtre sous la Révolution: politique du répertoire (1789–1799)*, pp. 297–313. Paris: Desjonquères, 2008.

Champfleury. *Les aventures de mademoiselle Mariette*. 3rd edn. Paris: Michel Lévy, 1857.

Champfleury. *Souvenirs des Funambules*. Paris: Michel Lévy frères, 1859.

Champfleury. 'L'oncle Topino, *La mascarade de la vie parisienne*.' *L'opinion nationale*, 16 September 1859, 1–3.

Champfleury. 'L'oncle Topino (Suite), *La mascarade de la vie parisienne*.' *L'opinion nationale*, 17 September 1859, 1–3.

Champfleury. *L'hôtel des commissaires-priseurs*. Paris: E. Dentu, 1867.

Champfleury. *Histoire de l'imagerie populaire*. Paris: E. Dentu, 1869.

Chastel, André. 'Les temps modernes: masque, mascarade, mascaron.' In *Le Masque*. Exhibition catalogue, pp. 87–93. Paris: Musée Guimet, Éditions des Musées Nationaux, 1959.

Chastel, André. *La grottesque*. Paris: Le Promeneur, 1988.

Chatelain, Jean. *Dominique Vivant Denon et le Louvre de Napoléon*. Paris: Librairie Académique Perrin, 1973.

Chotard, Loïc. *Nadar: caricatures, photographies*. Paris: Maison de Balzac, 1990.

Christout, Marie-Françoise. 'La féerie Romantique au théâtre: de la *Sylphide* (1832) à *La Biche au bois* (1845), chorégraphies, décors, trucs et machines.' *Romantisme* 12:38 (1982), 77–86.

Clairville, Cordier and Commerson. *Les Binettes Contemporaines, revue en trois actes et sept tableaux*. Paris: Beck, 1855.

Clark, T.J. *The Painting of Modern Life: Paris in the Art of Manet and his Followers*. Revised edn. Princeton, NJ: Princeton University Press, 1999.

Clarkson, Leslie. 'The linen industry in early modern Europe.' In David Jenkins, ed. *The Cambridge History of Western Textiles*, vol. 1, pp. 472–92. Cambridge: Cambridge University Press, 2003.

Clément de Ris, Louis. *Les Amateurs d'autrefois*. Paris: E. Plon et Cie, 1877.

Coffin, Sarah D., ed. *Rococo: The Continuing Curve 1730–2008*. New York: Smithsonian Cooper-Hewitt National Design Museum, 2008.

Cohen, Margaret. 'Walter Benjamin's phantasmagoria.' *New German Critique* 48 (1989), 87–107.

Cohen, Margaret. 'Panoramic literature and the invention of everyday genres.' In Leo Charney and Vanessa R. Schwartz, eds. *Cinema and the Invention of Modern Life*, pp. 227–52. Berkeley: University of California Press, 1995.

Cohen, Sarah. 'Body as "character" in early eighteenth-century French art and performance.' *Art Bulletin* 78:3 (1996), 454–66.

Cohen, Sarah R. *Art, Dance, and the Body in French Culture of the Ancien Régime*. Cambridge: Cambridge University Press, 2000.

Cohen, William B. *The French Encounter with Africans: White Responses to Blacks, 1530–1880*. 1980; Bloomington: Indiana University Press, 2003.

Compagnon, Antoine. *Les chiffonniers de Paris*. Paris: Gallimard, 2017.

Conlin, Jonathan. 'Vauxhall on the boulevard: pleasure gardens in London and Paris, 1764–1784.' *Urban History* 35:1 (May 2008), 24–47.

Coquery, Natacha. 'The language of success: marketing and distributing semi-luxury goods in eighteenth-century Paris.' *Journal of Design History* 17:1 (2004), 71–89.

Coquery, Natacha. 'The social circulation of luxury and second-hand goods in eighteenth-century Parisian shops.' In Ariane Fennetaux, Amelie Junqua and Sophie Vasset, eds. *The Afterlife of Used Things: Recycling in the Eighteenth Century*, pp. 13–24. New York: Routledge, 2014.

Coquery, Natacha. 'Luxury goods beyond boundaries: the Parisian market during the Terror.' In Johanna Ilmakunnas and Jon Stobart, eds. *A Taste for Luxury in Early Modern Europe: Display, Acquisition and Boundaries*, pp. 283–302. London: Bloomsbury Academic, 2017.

Cottington, David. *Cubism in the Shadow of War: The Avant-Garde and Politics in Paris 1905–1914*. New Haven, CT: Yale University Press, 1998.

Crary, Jonathan. *Techniques of the Observer: On Vision and Modernity in the Nineteenth Century*. Cambridge, MA: MIT Press, 1990.

Crisp, Colin. *Classic French Cinema 1930–1960*. Bloomington: Indiana University Press, 1993.

Crow, Thomas. *Painters and Public Life in Eighteenth-Century Paris*. New Haven, CT: Yale University Press, 1985.

Crowston, Clare Haru. *Fabricating Women: The Seamstresses of Old Regime France, 1675–1791*. Durham, NC: Duke University Press, 2001.

Crowston, Clare Haru. *Credit, Fashion, Sex: Economies of Regard in Old Regime France*. Durham, NC: Duke University Press, 2013.

Cueto-Asin, Elena. 'The Chat Noir's Théâtre d'Ombres: shadow plays and the recuperation of public space.' In Gabriel P. Weisberg, ed. *Montmartre and the Making of Mass Culture*, pp. 223–46. New Brunswick, NJ: Rutgers University Press, 2001.

Cugy, Pascale. *La Dynastie Bonnart: Peintres, Graveurs, et Marchands de Modes à Paris sous l'Ancien Régime*. Rennes: Presses Universitaires de Rennes, 2017.

Dacier, Émile and Albert Vuaflart. *Jean de Jullienne et les graveurs de Watteau au XVIIIe siècle*, 4 vols. Paris: Les Auteurs, 1921–9.

Daudet, Léon. 'Le trucquage du théâtre juif.' *Action Française*, 5 September 1913.

Davidson, Gail S. 'Ornament of bizarre imagination: rococo prints and drawings from Cooper-Hewitt's Léon Decloux Collection.' In Sarah D. Coffin, ed. *Rococo: The Continuing Curve*, pp. 40–71. New York: Smithsonian Cooper-Hewitt National Design Museum, 2008.

Davis, Tracy C. 'Nineteenth-century repertoire.' *Nineteenth Century Theatre and Film* 36:2 (2009), 6–28.

[Deburau, Charles]. *Biographie de Charles Deburau, fils*. Paris: Dechaume, n.d.

Delacampagne, Christian. *Une histoire du racisme, des origines à nos jours*. Paris: Librairie Générale Française, 2000.

Demoriane, H. 'Le *Gilles* de Watteau.' *Connaissance des Arts* 270 (1974), 34–5.

De Piles, Roger. *L'Idée du peintre parfait*. 1699; Paris: Gallimard, 1993.

Descat, Sophie. 'La boutique magnifiée: commerce de détail et embellissement à Paris et à Londres dans la seconde moitié du XVIIIe siècle.' *Histoire urbaine* 2:6 (2002), 69–86.

Deshairs, Léon. 'Les arabesques de Watteau.' In *Mélanges offerts à M. Henry Lemonnier*, pp. 287–300. Paris: Champion, 1913.

Diderot, Denis. *Salons*. Edited by Michel Delon. Paris: Gallimard, 2008.

Diderot, Denis and Jean le Rond d'Alembert, eds. *Encyclopédie, ou dictionnaire raisonné des sciences, des arts et des métiers, etc.* Edited by Robert Morrissey and Glen Roe. University of Chicago: ARTFL Encyclopédie Project. http://encyclopedie.uchicago.edu/, accessed 28 April 2023.

Donnay, Maurice. *Autour du Chat Noir*. 1926; Paris: Bernard Grasset, 1966.

Dorlin, Elsa. *La matrice de la race: généalogie sexuelle et colonial de la Nation française*. 2006; Paris: La Découverte, 2009.

Drumont, Édouard. *La France juive*. Edited by Alain Soral. Paris: Les InfréKentables, 2013.

Duchon, Nicole. *Tendre porcelaine de Mennecy Villeroy*. Mennecy: Maury Imprimeur, 2016.

Duncan, Carol. *The Pursuit of Pleasure: The Rococo Revival in French Romantic Art*. New York: Garland Publishing, 1976.

Dupuy, Marie-Anne, ed. *Dominique-Vivant Denon: l'œil de Napoléon*. Paris: Réunion des Musées nationaux, 1999.

Dupuy, Marie-Anne, ed. *Vivant Denon, directeur des musées sous le Consulat et l'Empire: correspondance 1802–1815*. Paris: Réunion des musées nationaux, 1999.

Dyer, Richard. *White*. New York: Routledge, 1997.

Ehrlich, Evelyn. *Cinema of Paradox: French Filmmaking under the German Occupation*. New York: Columbia University Press, 1985.

Eidelberg, Martin. *Watteau's Drawings: Their Use and Significance*. New York: Garland Publishing, 1977.

Eidelberg, Martin. 'Gabriel Huquier – friend or foe of Watteau?' *The Print Collector's Newsletter* 15 (1984), 157–64.

Eidelberg, Martin. 'Huquier in the guise of Watteau.' *On Paper* 1 (1996), 28–32.

Eidelberg, Martin. 'Reconsidering Watteau's *Enseigne de Gersaint*.' http://watteauandhiscircle.org/Gersaint.htm, accessed 28 April 2023.

Elsaesser, Thomas, ed. *Early Cinema: Space Frame Narrative*. London: British Film Institute, 1990.

Emelina, Jean. *Les valets et les servantes dans le théâtre comique en France de 1610 à 1700*. Grenoble: Presses Universitaires de Grenoble, 1975.

Eriksen, Svend and Geoffrey de Bellaigue. *Sèvres Porcelain: Vincennes and Sèvres 1740–1800*. London: Faber and Faber, 1987.

Exposition Universelle de 1855, rapports du jury mixte international publiés sous la direction de S.A.I. le Prince Napoléon, président de la commission impériale. Paris: Imprimerie impériale, 1856.

Fabella, Yvonne. 'Redeeming the "character of the Creoles": whiteness, gender and creolization in pre-revolutionary Saint Domingue.' *Journal of Historical Sociology* 23:1 (2010), 40–72.

Fairchilds, Cissie. *Domestic Enemies: Servants & Their Masters in Old Regime France*. Baltimore, MD: Johns Hopkins University Press, 1984.

Fairchilds, Cissie. 'The production and marketing of populuxe goods in eighteenth-century Paris.' In John Brewer and Roy Porter, eds. *Consumption and the World of Goods*, pp. 228–48. London: Routledge, 1993.

Faulkner, Christopher. 'Theory and practice of film reviewing in France in the 1930s: eyes right (Lucien Rebatet and Action Française 1936–1939).' *French Cultural Studies* 3 (1992), 133–5.

Faÿ-Hallé, Antoinette et al. *Faïences françaises, XVIe–XVIIIe siècles.* Paris: Éditions de la Réunion des Musées Nationaux, 1980.

Featherstone, Mike. 'Perspectives on consumer culture.' *Sociology* 24:1 (1990), 5–22.

Fend, Mechthild. 'Flesh-tones, skin colour and the eighteenth-century colour print.' In Felix Ensslin and Charlotte Klink, eds. *Aesthetics of the Flesh*, pp. 211–32. Berlin: Sternberg Press, 2014.

Féral, Josette. 'Performance and theatricality: the subject demystified.' Trans. Terese Lyons. *Modern Drama* 25:1 (1982), 170–81.

Fischer-Lichte, Erika. 'Introduction: theatricality, a key concept in theatre and cultural studies.' *Theatre Research International* 20:2 (1995), 85–9.

Fischer-Lichte, Erika. 'From *theatrum mundi* to theatricality.' In Elena Penskaya and Joachim Küpper, eds. *Theater as Metaphor*, pp. 253–63. Berlin: De Gruyter, 2019.

Folie du Jour, ou la promenade à la Foire Saint-Germain. Paris: Valade, 1770.

Forbes, Jill. *Les Enfants du Paradis.* London: British Film Institute, 1997.

Forgione, Nancy. '"The shadow only": shadow and silhouette in late-nineteenth century Paris.' *Art Bulletin* 81:3 (1999), 490–512.

Forray-Carlier, Anne. *Les Boiseries du Musée Carnavalet.* Dordan: Vial, 2010.

Fournel, Victor. *Les spectacles populaires et les artistes des rues.* Paris: E. Dentu, 1863.

Fournier, Édouard. *Histoire des enseignes de Paris.* Paris: Libraire de la Société des Gens de Lettres, 1884.

Fournier, Marc. 'La Rotonde du Temple.' In Paul de Kock, ed. *La grande ville: nouveau tableau de Paris, comique, critique et philosophique*, vol. 2, pp. 39–56. Paris: au Bureau Central des Publications Nouvelles, 1843.

Fried, Michael. 'Art and objecthood.' *Artforum* 5:10 (1967), 12–23.

Fried, Michael. *Absorption and Theatricality: Painting and Beholder in the Age of Diderot.* Chicago: University of Chicago Press, 1980.

Fried, Michael. *Manet's Modernism, or, The Face of Painting in the 1860s.* Chicago: University of Chicago Press, 1996.

Fritz, Gérard. *L'idée de peuple en France du XVIIe au XIXe siècle.* Strasbourg: Presses Universitaires de Strasbourg, 1988.

Frühes Meissener Porzellan: Kostbarkeiten aus deutschen Privatsammlungen. Exhibition catalogue. Munich: Hirmer Verlag, 1997.

Fuhring, Peter. 'The print privilege in eighteenth century France – I.' *Print Quarterly* 2:3 (1985), 175–93.

Fuhring, Peter. 'The print privilege in eighteenth century France – II.' *Print Quarterly* 3:1 (1986), 19–33.

Fuhring, Peter. 'Juste-Aurèle Meissonnier and his patrons.' In Sarah D. Coffin, ed. *Rococo: The Continuing Curve*, pp. 22–39. New York: Smithsonian Cooper-Hewitt National Design Museum, 2008.

Gallo, Daniela, ed. *Les vies de Dominique-Vivant Denon: actes du colloque organisé au Musée du Louvre.* Paris: la Documentation française, 2001.

Gambelli, Delia, ed. *Arlecchino a Parigi.* 3 vols. Rome: Bulzoni, 1993–7.

Garavini, Fausta, ed. *Lettres à Bettine.* Arles: Actes Sud, 1999.

Garner, Steve. *Whiteness: An Introduction.* London: Routledge, 2007.

Gaudreault, André. 'Théâtralité et narrativité dans l'œuvre de Georges Méliès.' In

Madeleine Malthête-Méliès, ed. *Méliès et la naissance du spectacle cinématographique*, pp. 199–219. Paris: Klincksieck, 1984.

Gaudriault, Raymond. *Répertoire de la gravure de mode française des origines à 1815*. Nantes: Promodis, 1988.

Gautier, Théophile. *L'art moderne*. Paris: Michel Lévy, 1856.

Gautier, Théophile. *Poésies Complètes*. Paris: Charpentier, 1858.

Gautier, Théophile. *L'art moderne*. 1856; edited by Corinne Bayle and Olivier Schefer. Lyon: Fage éditions, 2011.

Gherardi, Evariste. *Le théâtre italien de Gherardi ou le recueil général de toutes les comédies et scènes françoises jouées par les comédiens italiens du roi, pendant tout le temps qu'ils ont été au service de sa Majesté*. 6 vols. Amsterdam: Chez Adrian Braakman, 1701.

Gilman, Sander. *The Jew's Body*. New York: Routledge, 1991.

Gilman, Sander. 'Salome, syphilis, Sarah Bernhardt, and the modern Jewess.' In Nochlin, Linda and Tamar Garb, eds. *The Jew in the Text: Modernity and the Construction of Identity*, pp. 97–120. London: Thames and Hudson, 1995.

Girard, Marie-Hélène. 'Denon et la notion de monument.' In Francis Claudon and Bernard Bailly, eds. *Vivant Denon: colloque de Chalon-sur-Saône, 14 et 15 Mai 1999*, pp. 35–50. Chalon-sur-Saône: Université pour tous de Bourgogne, 1998.

Glorieux, Guillaume. *À l'enseigne de Gersaint: Edme-François Gersaint, Marchand d'Art sur le Pont Notre-Dame (1694–1750)*. Paris: Champ Vallon, 2002.

Glorieux, Guillaume. 'Pierre Sirois (1665–1726): le premier marchand de Watteau.' In Jeremy Warren and Adriana Turpin, eds. *Auctions, Agents and Dealers: The Mechanisms of the Art Market 1660–1830*, pp. 87–98. Oxford: The Wallace Collection, 2007.

Goby, Émile. *Pantomimes de Gaspard et Charles Deburau*. Paris: E. Dentu, 1889.

Goffman, Erving. *The Presentation of the Self in Everyday Life*. Reprint. Edinburgh: University of Edinburgh Press, 1958.

Golan, Romy. *Modernity and Nostalgia: Art and Politics in France Between the Wars*. New Haven, CT: Yale University Press, 1995.

Grant, Richard B. 'The Jewish question in Zola's *L'Argent*.' *Publications of the Modern Language Association* 70:5 (1955), 955–67.

Grasselli, Margaret Morgan, Pierre Rosenberg and Nicole Parmantier. *Watteau: 1684–1721*. Exhibition catalogue. Paris: Éditions de la Réunion des musées nationaux, 1984.

Greaves, Roger. *Nadar ou le Paradoxe vital*. Paris: Flammarion, 1980.

Green, Anne. 'France exposed: *Madame Bovary* and the Exposition Universelle.' *Modern Language Review* 99:4 (2004), 915–23.

Green, Nicholas. *The Spectacle of Nature: Landscape and Bourgeois Culture in Nineteenth Century France*. Manchester: Manchester University Press, 1990.

Groshens, Marie-Claude. 'La pratique théâtrale foraine: contribution à l'étude de la fête marchande.' *Ethnologie française* 17 (1987), 53–8.

Gueullette, J.-E. *Thomas-Simon Gueullette: un magistrat du 18e Siècle, ami des lettres, du théâtre et des plaisirs*. Paris: Librairie E. Droz, 1938.

Gueullette, Thomas Simon. *Théâtre des boulevards, ou recueil des parades*. 3 vols. Paris: A. Mahon de l'imprimerie de Gilles Langlois, 1756.

Guichard, Charlotte. *Les Amateurs d'art à Paris au XVIIIe siècle*. Seyssel: Champ Vallon, 2008.

Guichard, Charlotte. 'Le marché au coeur de l'invention muséale? Jean-Baptiste-Pierre Lebrun au Louvre (1792–1802).' *Revue de synthèse* 132:6:1 (2011), 93–117.

Gunning, Tom. 'The cinema of attractions: early cinema, its spectator and the avant garde.' In Thomas Elsaesser, ed. *Early Cinema: Space Frame Narrative*, pp. 56–62. London: British Film Institute, 1990.

Gunning, Tom. '"Primitive" cinema: a frame-up? Or the trick's on us.' In ibid., pp. 95–103. London: British Film Institute, 1990.

Gunning, Tom. '"Now you see it, now you don't": the temporality of the cinema of attractions.' *The Velvet Light Trap* 32 (1993), 3–12.

Gunning, Tom. 'Illusions past and future: the phantasmagoria and its specters.' Presentation at the University of Chicago, 2004, available at www.mediaarthistory. org/refresh/Programmatic%20key%20texts/pdfs/Gunning.pdf, accessed 23 May 2023.

Gwilt, Joanna. *Vincennes and Early Sèvres Porcelain from the Belvedere Collection*. London: V&A Publishing, 2014.

Habermas, Jürgen. *The Structural Transformation of the Public Sphere: An Inquiry into a Category of Bourgeois Society*. 1962; trans. Thomas Burger and Frederick Lawrence. Cambridge, MA: MIT Press, 1991.

Hahn, H. Hazel. *Scenes of Parisian Modernity: Culture and Consumption in the Nineteenth Century*. New York: Palgrave Macmillan, 2009.

Hale, J.R. *Artists and Warfare in the Renaissance*. New Haven, CT: Yale University Press, 1990.

Hambourg, Maria Morris. *Nadar: Les années créatrices*. Paris: Réunion des Musées Nationaux, 1995.

Hamon, Philippe. *Expositions: littérature et architecture au XIXe siècle*. Paris: José Corti, 1989.

Hamon, Philippe. *Imageries: littérature et image au XIXe siècle*. Revised edn. Paris: José Corti, 2001.

Hamon, Philippe. 'Introduction. Littérature et réclame: le cru et le cri.' *Romantisme* 155 (2012), 3–10.

Hanson, Anne Coffin. 'Manet's subject matter and a source of popular imagery.' *Art Institute of Chicago Museum Studies* 3 (1968), 63–80.

Hanson, Anne Coffin. 'Popular imagery and the work of Édouard Manet'. In Ulrich Finke, ed. *French 19th Century Painting and Literature, with Special Reference to the Relevance of Literary Subject-Matter to French Painting*, pp. 133–63. Manchester: Manchester University Press, 1972.

Harmand, C. *Manuel de l'amateur des arts dans Paris pour 1824*. Paris, 1824.

Haug, Wolfgang Fritz. *Critique of Commodity Aesthetics*. 1971; trans. Robert Bock. Cambridge: Polity Press, 1986.

Hautecoeur, Louis. 'De l'échoppe aux grands magasins.' *La Revue de Paris* 7 (1933), 811–41.

Hédouin, Pierre. 'Watteau III.' *L'Artiste*, ser. 4, 5:5 (1845), 78–80.

Heilbrun, Françoise. *La photographie au Musée d'Orsay*. Paris: Flammarion, 2008.

Hellman, Mimi. 'The nature of artifice: French porcelain flowers and the rhetoric of the garnish.' In Alden Cavanaugh and Michael Yonan, eds. *The Cultural Aesthetics of Eighteenth-Century Porcelain*, pp. 39–64. Farnham: Ashgate, 2010.

Heulhard, Arthur. *La Foire Saint-Laurent: Son Histoire et Ses Spectacles*. Paris: Alphonse Lemerre, 1878.

Hille, Christiane. 'Albrecht Dürer and the tailoring of the human form.' *RES: Anthropology and Aesthetics* 73/74:1 (2020), 10–22.

Honig, Elizabeth Anne. *Painting and the Market in Early Modern Antwerp*. New Haven, CT: Yale University Press, 1998.

Hornstein, Katie. 'The Saint-Gobain *grande glace*: transparency and display culture at the Exposition Universelle of 1855.' *Oxford Art Journal* 44:3 (2021), 399–417.

Hugounet, Paul. *Mimes et Pierrots: notes et documents inédits pour servir à l'histoire de la pantomime*. Paris: Librairie Fischbacher, 1889.

Isay, Raymond. *Panorama des Expositions Universelles*, 8th edn. Paris: Gallimard, 1937.

Isherwood, Robert M. 'Entertainment in the Parisian fairs in eighteenth-century Paris.' *The Journal of Modern History* 53:1 (1981), 24–48.

Janin, Jules. 'Théâtre Français: première représentation du *Nègre*, drame en quatre actes et en vers libres, par M. Ozanneaux.' *Journal des débats*, 1 November 1830, 1–3.

Janin, Jules. 'Les petits métiers.' In *Paris, ou le livre des cent-et-uns*, 15 vols; Vol. 4. Paris: L'advocat, 1832.

Janin, Jules. *Deburau, l'histoire du théâtre à quatre sous*. Paris: C. Gosselin, 1832.

Janin, Jules. 'Le daguérotype.' *L'Artiste*, ser. 2, 2:11 (1839), 145–8.

Janin, Jules. 'La description du daguérotype.' *L'Artiste*, ser. 2, 3:17 (1839), 277–83.

Janin, Jules. 'Le daguérotype: nouvelle exercise.' *L'Artiste*, ser. 2, 4:1 (1839), 1–3.

Jasinski, René. *Les années romantiques de Théophile Gautier*. Paris: Librairie Vuibert, 1929.

Jones, Ann Rosalind and Peter Stallybrass. *The Politics and Poetics of Transgression*. Ithaca, NY: Cornell University Press, 1986.

Jones, Ann Rosalind and Peter Stallybrass. *Renaissance Clothing and the Materials of Memory*. Cambridge: Cambridge University Press, 2000.

Jones, Jennifer Michelle. *Sexing 'La Mode': Gender, Fashion and Commercial Culture in Old Regime France*. Oxford: Berg, 2004.

Jones, Louisa E. *Sad Clowns and Pale Pierrots: Literature and the popular comic arts in 19th-century France*. Lexington, KY: French Forum Press, 1984.

Jouanna, Arlette. *L'idée de race en France au XVIe siècle et au début du XVIIe siècle (1498–1614)*. Paris: Honoré Champion, 1976.

Kaplan, Alice. *Reproductions of Banality: Fascism, Literature, and French Intellectual Life*. Minneapolis: University of Minnesota Press, 1986.

Kilian, Jennifer M. *The Paintings of Karel Du Jardin, 1626–1678, Catalogue Raisonné*. Amsterdam: John Benjamins Publishing Company, 2005.

Kimball, Fiske. *The Creation of the Rococo Decorative Style*. 1943; New York: Dover Publications, 1980.

Kirchner, Thomas. *Le héros épique: Peinture d'histoire et politique artistique dans la France du XVIIe siècle*. Trans. Aude Virey-Wallon and Jean-Léon Muller. Paris: Éditions de la Maison des sciences de l'homme, 2008.

Kisluk-Grosheide, Daniëlle. 'The reign of *magots* and pagods.' *Metropolitan Museum Journal* 37 (2002), 177–97.

Knowles, Marika Takanishi. 'Pierrot's costume: theater, curiosity, and the subject of art in France, 1665–1860.' PhD dissertation, Yale University, 2013.

Knowles, Marika Takanishi. 'The microcosm as interior in Théophile Gautier's "Marilhat".' In Anca I. Lasc, ed. *Visualizing the Nineteenth-Century Home: Modern Art and the Decorative Impulse*, pp. 3–18. New York: Routledge, 2016.

Knowles, Marika Takanishi. 'Lost ground: the performance of Pierrot in Nadar and Adrien Tournachon's photographs of Charles Deburau.' *Oxford Art Journal* 38:3 (2015), 365–86.

Knowles, Marika Takanishi. 'Affect, citation, and rapt looking in Manet's *The Old Musician*.' *Word & Image* 34:2 (2018), 111–25.

Knowles, Marika Takanishi. *Realism and Role-Play: The Human Figure in French Art from Callot to the Brothers Le Nain*. Newark, DE: University of Delaware Press, 2020.

Knowles, Marika Takanishi. 'Time-chaste damsels: Ingres, Nerval, and *Sylvie*.' *RES: Anthropology and Aesthetics* 73/74 (2020), 140–54.

Knowles, Marika Takanishi. 'Making whiteness: art, luxury, and race in eighteenth-century France.' In 'Race', edited by Stephanie O'Rourke and Susannah Blair, special issue, *Journal18* 13 (2022), www.journal18.org/6214, accessed 28 April 2023.

Knowles, Marika Takanishi and Christopher Wood. 'Editorial: *La parade*.' *RES: Anthropology and Aesthetics* 73/74:1 (2020), 1–9.

Krauss, Rosalind. 'Tracing Nadar.' *October* 5 (1978), 29–47.

La Font de Saint-Yenne, Étienne. *Reflexions sur quelques causes de l'état présent de la peinture en France, avec un examen des principaux ouvrages exposés au Louvre le mois d'Août 1746.* The Hague: Jean Neaulme, 1747.

La Bruyère, Jean de. *Les caractères ou les moeurs de ce siècle.* 1691; edited by Robert Pignarre. Paris: Garnier-Flammarion, 1965.

Lacan, Ernest. *Esquisses photographiques à propos de l'Exposition Universelle et de la Guerre d'Orient.* Paris: Grassart, A. Gaudin et frère, 1856.

Lafont, Anne. 'How skin color became a racial marker: art historical perspectives on race.' *Eighteenth-Century Studies* 51:1 (2017), 89–113.

Lajer-Burcharth, Ewa. 'Modernity and the condition of disguise: Manet's *Absinthe Drinker*.' *Art Journal* 45:1 (1985), 18–26.

Lane, Arthur. *English Porcelain Figures of the Eighteenth Century.* London: Faber and Faber, 1961.

Laporte, Véronique. 'Dans les coulisses de la séduction. Les divertissements à la foire Saint-Germain-des-Prés, Paris, 18e siècle.' MA thesis, Université de Sherbrooke, 2005.

Lasteyrie, Ferdinand de. 'Exposition Universelle: photographie.' *Le Siècle*, 25 October 1855.

Laufer, Roger. *Style rococo, style des lumières.* Paris: José Corti, 1963.

Leca, Benedict. 'An art book and its viewers: the "Recueil Crozat" and the uses of reproductive engraving.' *Eighteenth-Century Studies* 38:4 (2005), 623–49.

Le Duc, Geneviève. *Porcelaine tendre de Chantilly au XVIIIe siècle.* Paris: Hazan, 1996.

Legrand, Marc-Antoine. *La Foire Saint-Laurent.* Paris: P. Ribou, 1709.

Leiris, Alain de. 'Manet, Guéroult and Chrysippos.' *The Art Bulletin* 46:3 (1964), 401–4.

Lelièvre, Pierre. *Vivant Denon: homme des lumières, 'Ministre des arts' de Napoléon.* With the collaboration of Madeleine Barbin. Paris: Picard, 1993.

Le Men, Ségolène. 'L'œuvre de Chéret en résonance.' In Réjane Bargiel and Ségolène Le Men, eds. *La Belle Époque de Jules Chéret: De l'affiche au décor*, pp. 51–75. Paris: Les Arts Décoratifs/Bibliothèque nationale de France, 2010.

Le Men, Ségolène. 'Chiffonniers de papier.' *Revue d'histoire littéraire de la France* 118:3 (2018), 559–70.

Le Men, Ségolène. 'Le portrait du collectionneur en chiffonnier, vu par Champfleury (1859).' In Jacques Guillerme, ed. *Les collections: fables et programmes*, pp. 275–82. Seyssel: Champ Vallon, 1993.

Lerner, Jillian Taylor. 'The French profiled by themselves: social typologies, advertising posters, and the illustration of consumer lifestyles.' *Grey Room* 27 (2007), 6–35.

Lerner, Jillian. 'Nadar's signatures: caricature, self-portrait, publicity.' *History of Photography* 41:2 (2017), 108–25.

Lesage, Alain-René and Jacques Philippe d'Orneval. *Le theatre de la foire, ou l'opéra comique.* 9 vols. Paris, 1721–37.

Lethuillier, Jean-Pierre. 'Plumes et rubans à la Cour et sur le théâtre de Molière.' In Carine Barbafieri and Alain Montandon, eds. *Sociopoétique du textile à l'âge classique:*

du vêtement et de sa représentation à la poétique du texte, pp. 279–302. Paris: Hermann, 2015.

Liauzu, Claude. *Race et civilisation: l'autre dans la culture occidentale, anthologie historique*. Paris: Syros/Alternatives, 1992.

L'incendie de la Foire Saint Germain et sa nouvelle reconstruction, poëme en quatre chants. Paris: Langlois, 1764.

Mainardi, Patricia. 'The political origins of modernism.' *Art Journal* 45:1 (1985), 11–17.

Mainardi, Patricia. *Art and Politics of the Second Empire: The Universal Expositions of 1855 and 1867*. New Haven, CT and London: Yale University Press, 1987.

Mainzler, Joseph. 'Le marchand d'habits.' In *Les Français peints par eux-mêmes. Encyclopédie morale du dix-neuvième siècle*, 5:250–6. Paris: L. Curmer, 1841.

Mannoni, Laurent and Donata Pesenti Campagnoni. *Lanterne magique et film peint: 400 ans de cinéma*. Paris: La Cinémathèque française, 2009.

Mariette, Pierre-Jean. 'Lettre sur Leonard de Vinci, peintre florentin, à Monsieur le C[omte] de C[aylus].' In *Recueil de Testes de caractere et de charges dessinées par Leonard de Vinci Florentin et gravées par M. le C. de Caylus*, pp. 1–22. Paris: J. Mariette, 1730.

Markus, Gyorgy. 'Walter Benjamin or: the commodity as phantasmagoria.' *New German Critique* 83 (2001), 3–42.

Martin, Roxane. *La féerie romantique sur les scènes parisiennes, 1791–1864*. Paris: Honoré Champion, 2007.

Martinez, Ariane. *La pantomime: théâtre en mineur, 1880–1945*. Paris: Presses Sorbonne Nouvelle, 2008.

Maternati-Baldouy, Danielle et al. *La faïence de Marseille au XVIIIe siècle: La manufacture de la Veuve Perrin*. Marseille: Musées de Marseille/Editions Agep, 1990.

Maza, Sarah C. *Servants and Masters in Eighteenth-Century France: The Uses of Loyalty*. Princeton, NJ: Princeton University Press, 1983.

McCauley, Elizabeth Anne. *A.A.E. Disdéri and the Carte de Visite Portrait Photograph*. New Haven, CT: Yale University Press, 1985.

McCauley, Elizabeth Anne. *Industrial Madness: Commercial Photography in Paris 1848–1871*. New Haven, CT: Yale University Press, 1994.

McClellan, Andrew. *Inventing the Louvre: Art, Politics, and the Origins of the Modern Museum in Eighteenth-Century Paris*. Cambridge: Cambridge University Press, 1994.

McClellan, Andrew. 'Watteau's dealer: Gersaint and the marketing of art in eighteenth-century Paris.' *Art Bulletin* 78:3 (1996), 439–53.

McCracken, Grant. *Culture and Consumption: New Approaches to the Symbolic Character of Consumer Goods and Activities*. Bloomington: Indiana University Press, 1988.

McKendrick, Neil, John Brewer and J.H. Plumb. *The Birth of a Consumer Society: The Commercialization of Eighteenth-Century England*. London: Hutchinson, 1983.

McTighe, Sheila. 'Perfect deformity, ideal beauty, and the *imaginaire* of work: the reception of Annibale Carracci's "Arti di Bologna" in 1646.' *Oxford Art Journal* 16:1 (1993), 75–91.

McTighe, Sheila. 'Foods and the body in Italian genre paintings, about 1580: Campi, Passarotti, Carracci.' *Art Bulletin* 86:2 (2004), 301–23.

McWilliam, Neil. 'Action Française, classicism, and the dilemmas of traditionalism in France, 1900–1914.' In 'Nationalism and French Visual Culture, 1870–1914', special issue, *Studies in the History of Art* 69 (2005), 268–91.

McWilliam, Neil. 'Towards a new French renaissance: memory, tradition and cultural conservatism in France before the First World War.' *Art History* 40:4 (2017), 724–43.

Mercier, Louis-Sébastien. *Tableau de Paris*. 2 vols. Edited by Jean-Claude Bonnet. Paris: Mercure de France, 1994.

Mercier, Louis-Sébastien. 'Sur le dépôt des Petits-Augustins, dit le Musée des Monuments français'. *Journal de Paris*, 2 October 1797, 42–3.

Michel, Christian. *Le 'célèbre' Watteau*. Geneva: Droz, 2008.

Michel, Christian. '*Le goût contre le caprice*: Les enjeux des débats sur l'ornement au milieu du XVIIe siècle.' In *Histoires d'ornement: Actes du colloque de l'Académie de France à Rome, 27–28 Juin 1996*, pp. 203–14. Paris: Klincksieck, 2000.

Michel, Christian. 'Le goût pour le dessin en France au XVIIe et XVIIIe siècle: de l'utilisation à l'étude désintéressé.' *Revue de l'art* 143 (2004), 27–34.

Michel, Patrick. *Le commerce du tableau à Paris dans la seconde moitié du XVIIIe siècle.* Villeneuve d'Ascq: Presses Universitaires du Septentrion, 2007.

Michel, Patrick. *Peinture et plaisir: les goûts picturaux des collectionneurs parisiens au XVIIIe siècle.* Rennes: Presses Universitaires de Rennes, 2010.

Milliot, Vincent. 'La ville au miroir des métiers. Représentations du monde du travail et imaginaires de la ville (XVIe et XVIIIe siècle).' In Claude Petitfrère, ed. *Images et imaginaires dans la ville à l'époque moderne*, pp. 181–204. Tours: Presses universitaires François-Rabelais, 1998.

Milliot, Vincent. *Les Cris de Paris ou le peuple travesti: Les représentations des petits métiers parisiens XVIe–XVIIIe siècles.* Paris: Publications de la Sorbonne, 2014.

Mirecourt, Eugène de. *Jules Janin.* Paris: G. Havard, 1857.

Mitry, Jean. 'Le montage dans les films de Méliès.' In Madeleine Malthête-Méliès, ed. *Méliès et la naissance du spectacle cinématographique*, pp. 149–55. Paris: Klincksieck, 1984.

Molière, *Dom Juan ou le Festin de Pierre.* In *Théâtre complet.* Edited by Robert Jouanny, vol. 1, pp. 707–76. Paris: Garnier Frères, 1960.

Morowitz, Laura. 'Anti-Semitism, medievalism and the art of the *fin-de-siècle*.' *Oxford Art Journal* 20:1 (1997), 35–49.

Morrison, Toni. *Playing in the Dark: Whiteness and the Literary Imagination.* Cambridge, MA: Harvard University Press, 1992.

Moureau, François. *Le goût italien dans la France rocaille: théâtre, musique, peinture.* Paris: Presses de l'université Paris-Sorbonne, 2011.

Moureau, François and Margaret Morgan Grasselli, eds. *Antoine Watteau (1684–1721): le peintre, son temps et sa légende.* Paris: Clairefontaine, 1987.

Moynet, M.J. *L'envers du théâtre: machines et décorations.* Paris: Hachette, 1873.

Moynet, Georges. *La machinerie théâtrale: trucs et décors.* Paris: Librairie Illustrée, 1893.

Murray, Gale B. 'Toulouse Lautrec's illustrations for Victor Joze and Georges Clemenceau and their relationship to French anti-Semitism of the 1890s.' In Linda Nochlin and Tamar Garb, eds. *The Jew in the Text: Modernity and the Construction of Identity*, pp. 56–82. London: Thames and Hudson, 1995.

Nadar, *Quand j'étais photographe.* 1900. Paris: Actes Sud, 1998.

Naggar, Betty. 'Old-clothes men: 18th and 19th centuries.' *Jewish Historical Studies* 31 (1988–90), 171–91.

Nemeitz, J.C. *Séjour de Paris, c'est à dire, instructions fidèles pour les voyageurs de condition.* 2 vols. Leyden: Jean van Abcoude, 1727.

Nerval, Gérard de. *Petits châteaux de Bohême.* Paris: Eugène Didier, 1853.

Nesci, Catherine. *Le flâneur et les flâneuses: les femmes et la ville à l'époque romantique.* Grenoble: Université Stendhal, 2007.

Nochlin, Linda. 'Gustave Courbet's meeting: a portrait of the artist as a Wandering Jew.' *The Art Bulletin* 49:3 (1967), 209–22.

Nochlin, Linda and Tamar Garb, eds. *The Jew in the Text: Modernity and the Construction of Identity*. London: Thames and Hudson, 1995.

Noiriel, Gérard. *Immigration, antisémitisme et racisme en France (XIXe–XXe siècle). Discours publics, humiliations privées*. Paris: Fayard, 2007.

Nye, Edward. 'Jean-Gaspard Deburau: romantic Pierrot.' *New Theatre Quarterly* 30:2 (2014), 107–19.

Nye, Edward. 'The pantomime repertoire of the Théâtre des Funambules.' *Nineteenth Century Theatre and Film* 43:1 (2016), 3–20.

Nye, Edward. 'The romantic myth of Jean-Gaspard Deburau.' *Nineteenth-Century French Studies* 44:1–2 (2016), 46–64.

Nye, Edward. 'Portraits of Deburau in Janin's *Deburau, l'histoire du théâtre à quatre sous*.' *L'Esprit Créateur* 59:1 (2019), 66–81.

Oberthür, Mariel. *Le Chat Noir 1881–1897*. Paris: Éditions de la Réunion des musées nationaux, 1992.

Ockman, Carol. 'When is a Jewish star just a star? Interpreting images of Sarah Bernhardt.' In Linda Nochlin and Tamar Garb, eds. *The Jew in the Text: Modernity and the Construction of Identity*, pp. 121–39. London: Thames and Hudson, 1995.

Ory, Pascal. *Les Expositions Universelles de Paris: panorama raisonné*. Paris: Éditions Ramsay, 1982.

Païni, Dominique, Paul Perrin, and Marie Robert, eds. *Enfin le cinéma: arts, images et spectacles en France (1833–1907)*. Paris: Réunion des Musées Nationaux, 2021.

Palacio, Jean de. *Pierrot fin-de-siècle: ou, les métamorphoses d'un masque*. Paris: Séguier, 1990.

Panofsky, Dora. '*Gilles* or Pierrot? Iconographic notes on Watteau.' *Gazette des Beaux-Arts* 39 (1952), 319–40.

Panofsky, Erwin. '*Et in arcadia ego*: on the conception of transience in Poussin and Watteau.' In R. Klibansky and H.J. Paton, eds. *Philosophy and History: The Ernst Cassirer Festschrift*, pp. 223–54. New York: Harper & Row, 1936.

Panzanelli, Roberta and Monica Preti-Hamard, eds. *La circulation des oeuvres d'art 1789–1848*. Rennes and Los Angeles: Universitaires de Rennes and Getty Research Institute, 2007.

Pappas, Sara. 'The lessons of Champfleury.' *Nineteenth-Century French Studies* 42:1–2 (2013–14), 51–73.

Pardailhé-Galabrun, Annik. *La naissance de l'intime: 3000 foyers Parisiens XVIIe–XVIIIe siècles*. Paris: Presses Universitaires de France, 1988.

Parfaict, Claude and François Parfaict. *Mémoires pour servir à l'histoire des spectacles de la foire, par un acteur forain*. 2 vols. Paris: Briasson, 1743.

Parfaict, Claude and François Parfaict. *Histoire de l'ancien théâtre italien depuis son origine en France, jusquà sa suppression en l'Année 1697*. Paris: Chez Lambert, 1753.

Parmal, Pamela A. 'Fashion and the growing importance of the *marchande des modes* in mid-eighteenth-century France.' *Costume* 31:1 (1997), 68–77.

Peabody, Sue. *'There are no slaves in France': The Political Culture of Race and Slavery in the Ancien Régime*. Oxford: Oxford University Press, 1997.

Pearson, Tony. 'Evreinov and Pirandello: twin apostles of theatricality.' *Theatre Research International* 12:2 (1987), 147–67.

Péricaud, Louis. *Le Théâtre des Funambules, ses mimes, ses acteurs et ses pantomimes, depuis sa fondation, jusqu'à sa démolition*. Paris: Léon Sapin, 1897.

Périer, Paul. *Compte rendu de l'exposition universelle de 1855*. Paris: Mallet-Bachelier, 1855.

Pérignon, A.N. *Description des objets d'arts qui composent le cabinet de feu m. le baron V. Denon*. Paris: Hippolyte Tilliard, 1826.

Peronnet, Benjamin. 'Denon, collectionneur typique ou atypique?' In Daniela Gallo (ed.), *Les vies de Dominique-Vivant Denon: actes du colloque organisé au Musée du Louvre*, pp. 741–59. Paris: la Documentation française, 2001.

Perrot, Philippe. *Les dessus et les dessous de la bourgeoisie, une histoire du vêtement au XIXe siècle*. Paris: Fayard, 1981.

Perry, Lara. 'The *carte de visite* in the 1860s and the serial dynamic of photographic likeness.' *Art History* 35:4 (2012), 728–49.

Pevsner, Nikolaus. *A History of Building Types*. London: Thames and Hudson, 1976.

Pichois, Claude and Jacques Dupont, eds. *L'atelier de Baudelaire: Les Fleurs du Mal, édition diplomatique*. 2 vols. Paris: Honoré Champion, 2005.

Pinson, Stephen. '*Trompe l'œil*: photography's illusion reconsidered.' *Nineteenth-Century Art Worldwide* 1:1 (2002), www.19thc-artworldwide.org/spring02/195-trompe-loe il-photographys-illusion-reconsidered, accessed 28 April 2023.

Plax, Julie Ann. *Watteau and the Cultural Politics of Eighteenth-Century France*. Cambridge: Cambridge University Press, 2000.

Poliakov, Léon. *The Aryan Myth: A History of Racist and Nationalist Ideas in Europe*. Trans. Edmund Howard. London: Sussex University Press, 1971.

Pomian, Krzysztof. 'Marchands, connaisseurs, curieux à Paris au XVIIIe siècle.' *Revue de l'art* 43 (1979), 23–36.

Posner, Donald. 'Another look at Watteau's *Gilles*.' *Apollo* 117 (February 1983), 97–9.

Postles, Dave. 'The market place as space in early modern England.' *Social History* 29:2 (2004), 41–58.

Pougetoux, Alain. 'Le directeur et l'impératrice.' In Daniela Gallo (ed.), *Les vies de Dominique-Vivant Denon: actes du colloque organisé au Musée du Louvre*, pp. 105–17. Paris: la Documentation française, 2001.

Pucci, Suzanne R. 'Watteau and theater: movable fetes.' In Mary Sheriff, ed. *Antoine Watteau: Perspectives on the Artist and the Culture of His Time*, pp. 106–22. Newark, DE: University of Delaware Press, 2006.

Pullins, David. 'Techniques of the body: viewing the arts and *métiers* of France from the workshop of Nicolas I and Nicolas II de Larmessin.' *Oxford Art Journal* 37:2 (2014), 135–55.

Quinn, Michael. 'Concepts of theatricality in contemporary art history.' *Theatre Research International* 20:2 (1995), 106–13.

Radisich, Paula. 'The *cris de Paris* in the LACMA Recueil des Modes.' In Kathryn Norberg and Sandra Rosenbaum, eds. *Fashion in the Age of Louis XIV: Interpreting the Art of Elegance*, pp. 55–71. Lubbock: Texas Tech University Press, 2014.

Ratcliffe, Barrie M. 'Perceptions and realities of the urban margin: the rag pickers of Paris in the first half of the nineteenth century.' *Canadian Journal of History* 27 (1992), 197–233.

Ravel, Jeffrey S. 'Trois images de l'expulsion des comédiens Italiens en 1697.' *Littératures classiques*, 82 (2013), 51–60.

Rebatet, Lucien. *Les tribus du cinéma et du théâtre*. Paris: Nouvelles Éditions Françaises, 1941.

Reff, Theodore. 'On "Manet's sources".' *Artforum* 8:1 (1969), 40–48.

Reiffenberg, Frédéric Auguste Ferdinand Thomas de. *Souvenirs d'un pélerinage en l'honneur de Schiller* (Bussels and Leipzig: C. Muquardt, 1839).

Rémy, Tristan. *Jean-Gaspard Deburau*. Paris: L'Arche, 1954.

Rieger, Dietmar. '"Ce qu'on voit dans les rues de Paris": marginalités sociales et regards bourgeois.' *Romantisme* 59 (1988), 19–29.

Roche, Daniel. *The People of Paris: An Essay in Popular Culture in the 18th Century*. Trans. Marie Evans and Gwynne Lewis. New York: Berg, 1987.

Roche, Daniel. *La culture des apparences: une histoire du vêtement XVIIe–XVIIIe siècle*. Paris: Fayard, 1989.

Roche, Daniel. *France in the Enlightenment*. Trans. Arthur Goldhammer. Cambridge, MA: Harvard University Press, 1998.

Roland Michel, Marianne. 'L'ornement rocaille: quelques questions.' *Revue de l'art* (1982), 66–75.

Roland Michel, Marianne. *Lajoue et l'art Rocaille*. Neuilly-sur-Seine: Arthena, 1984.

Roland Michel, Marianne. *Watteau: An Artist of the Eighteenth Century*. Trans. Richard Wrigley. London: Trefoil Books, 1984.

Roland Michel, Marianne. 'Watteau et les *Figures de différents caractères*.' In Moureau and Morgan Grasselli, eds. *Antoine Watteau (1684–1721): le peintre, son temps et sa légende*, pp. 117–27. Paris: Clairefontaine, 1987.

Rosasco, Betsy. 'The herms of Versailles in the 1680s.' *Princeton University Library Chronicle* 76:1–2 (2015), 145–75.

Rosenberg, Pierre. 'Watteau: le recueil de Valenciennes.' *La Revue du Louvre* 415 (1986), 286–9.

Rosenberg, Pierre and Louis-Antoine Prat. *Antoine Watteau 1684–1721: Catalogue raisonné des dessins*, 3 vols. Milan: Leonardo Arte, 1996.

Rosenthal, Angela. 'Visceral culture: blushing and the legibility of whiteness in eighteenth-century British portraiture.' *Art History* 27:4 (2004), 563–92.

Rosenthal, Margaret F. and Ann Rosalind Jones. *The Clothing of the Renaissance World: Europe, Asia, Africa, the Americas: Cesare Vecellio's Habiti Antichi et Moderni*. London: Thames & Hudson, 2008.

Rouillé, André. 'La photographie Française à L'Exposition Universelle de 1855.' *Le Mouvement Social* 131 (1985), 87–103.

Roulland, Léon. 'La Foire Saint-Germain sous les règnes de Charles IX, de Henri III et de Henri IV.' *Mémoires de la société de l'histoire de Paris et de l'Ile-de-France* 3 (1877), 192–218.

Sabattier, Jacqueline. *Figaro et son maître: les domestiques au XVIIIe siècle*. Paris: Perrin, 1984.

Sahut, Marie-Catherine and Florence Raymond. *Antoine Watteau et L'Art de l'Estampe*. Paris: Musée du Louvre, 2010.

Saisselin, Rémy G. 'The rococo as a dream of happiness.' *Journal of Aesthetics and Art Criticism* 19:2 (1960), 145–52.

Saisselin, Rémy G. *Le bourgeois et le bibelot*. Trans. Jacqueline Degueret. Paris: Albin Michel, 1990.

Samuels, Maurice. *The Right to Difference: French Universalism and the Jews*. Chicago: University of Chicago Press, 2016.

Sand, George. 'Deburau'. In *Questions d'art et de littérature*, pp. 215–22. Paris: C. Lévy, 1878.

Sargentson, Carolyn. *Merchants and Luxury Markets: the marchands merciers of eighteenth-century Paris*. London: Victoria and Albert Museum, 1996.

Sargentson, Carolyn. 'The manufacture and marketing of luxury goods: the *marchands merciers* of late 17th- and 18th-century Paris.' In Robert Fox and Anthony Turner, eds. *Luxury Trades and Consumerism in Ancien Régime Paris*, pp. 99–137. Aldershot: Ashgate, 1998.

Scarron, Paul. 'La Foire Saint-Germain.' In *La ville de Paris en vers burlesques*, pp. 86–99. Troyes: Jean Oudot, 1705.

Schechner, Richard. *Performance Theory*. Revised edn. New York: Routledge, 1988.

Schnapper, Antoine. *Curieux du Grand Siècle: Collections et collectionneurs dans la France du XVIIe siècle*. 1994. Paris: Flammarion, 2005.

Schneider, Marlen. *Belle comme Vénus: le portrait historié entre Grand siècle et Lumières*. Trans. Aude Virey-Wallon. 2015; Paris: Deutsches Forum für Kunstgeschichte, 2020.

Schwartz, Vanessa. *Spectacular Realities: Early Mass Culture in Fin-de-Siècle Paris*. Berkeley: University of California Press, 1998.

Scott, Katie. *The Rococo Interior: Decoration and Social Spaces in Early Eighteenth-century Paris*. New Haven, CT: Yale University Press, 1995.

Scott, Katie. 'Playing games with otherness: Watteau's Chinese cabinet at the Château de la Muette.' *Journal of the Warburg and Courtauld Institutes* 66 (2003), 189–248.

Scott, Katie. 'Edme Bouchardon's "Cris de Paris": crying food in early modern Paris.' *Word and Image* 29:1 (2013), 59–91.

Sellier, Geneviève. *Les Enfants du Paradis (Marcel Carné Jacques Prévert)*. Paris: Armand Colin, 1992.

Sellier, Geneviève. '*Les Enfants du paradis* dans le cinéma de l'Occupation.' *1895, revue d'histoire du cinéma* 22 (1997), 55–66.

Sennett, Richard. *The Fall of Public Man*. 1974; New York: W.W. Norton & Company, 1992.

Séverin. *L'homme blanc, souvenirs d'un Pierrot*. Introduction and notes by Gustave Fréjaville. Paris: Librairie Plon, 1929.

Shaw, Mary and Philip Dennis Cate. *The Spirit of Montmartre: Cabarets, Humor, and the Avant-Garde*. New Brunswick, NJ: Rutgers University Press, 1996.

Shovlin, John. 'The cultural politics of luxury in eighteenth-century France.' *French Historical Studies* 23:4 (2000), 577–606.

Sieburth, Richard. 'Une idéologie du lisible: le phénomène des physiologies.' *Romantisme* 47 (1985), 39–60.

Silver, Kenneth. *Esprit de Corps: The Art of the Parisian Avant-Garde and the First World War, 1914–1925*. Princeton, NJ: Princeton University Press, 1989.

Silverman, Kaja. *The Threshold of the Visible World*. New York: Routledge, 1996.

Simmel, Georg. *The Philosophy of Money*. Edited by David Frisby and trans. Tom Bottomore, David Frisby and Kaethe Mengelberg. New York: Routledge, 1990.

Slater, Don. *Consumer Culture and Modernity*. Cambridge: Polity Press, 1997.

Smentek, Kristel. 'Entrepreneurial art history: Pierre-Jean Mariette and the *Recueil d'estampes* in eighteenth-century Europe.' In Cordélia Hattori, Estelle Leutrat and Véronique Meyer, eds. *À l'origine du livre d'art: Les recueils d'estampes comme entreprise éditoriale en Europe (XVIe–XVIIIe siècles)*, pp. 131–9. Milan: Silvana Editoriale, 2010.

Smyth, Patricia. 'Theatricality, Michael Fried and nineteenth-century art and theater.' *Performance Research* 24:4 (2019), 5–9.

Solomon-Godeau, Abigail. 'The other side of Venus: the visual economy of feminine display.' In Victoria de Grazia and Ellen Furlough, ed. *The Sex of Things: Gender and Consumption in Historical Perspective*, pp. 113–50. Berkeley: University of California Press, 1996.

Sprigath, Gabriele. 'Sur le vandalisme révolutionnaire (1792–1794).' *Annales historiques de la Révolution française* 52:242 (1980), 528–31.

Stammers, Tom. *The Purchase of the Past: Collecting Culture in post-Revolutionary Paris, c1790–1890.* Cambridge: Cambridge University Press, 2020.

Stammers, Tom. 'Scavenging rococo: *trouvailles, bibelots* and counter-revolution.' In Katie Scott and Melissa Hyde, eds. *Rococo Echo: Art, Theory and Historiography from Cochin to Coppola,* pp. 71–85. Oxford: Oxford Studies in the Enlightenment, 2015.

Stammers, Tom. 'The bric-à-brac of the *ancien régime*: collecting and cultural history in post-Revolutionary France.' *French History* 22:3 (2008), 295–315.

Starobinski, Jean. *L'Invention de la liberté 1700–1789.* Geneva: Albert Skira, 1964.

Starobinski, Jean. *Portrait de l'artiste en saltimbanque.* Geneva: Albert Skira, 1970.

Steindl, Barbara. 'La documentation graphique sur la collection de Vivant Denon et *Les Monuments des Arts du Dessin.*' In Daniela Gallo (ed.), *Les vies de Dominique-Vivant Denon: actes du colloque organisé au Musée du Louvre,* pp. 771–807. Paris: la Documentation française, 2001.

Storey, Robert. *Pierrot: A Critical History of a Mask.* Princeton, NJ: Princeton University Press, 1978.

Storey, Robert. *Pierrots on the Stage of Desire: Nineteenth-century French Literary Artists and the Comic Pantomime.* Princeton, NJ: Princeton University Press, 1985.

Sund, Judy. 'Why so sad? Watteau's Pierrots.' *Art Bulletin* 98:3 (2016), 321–47.

Szanto, Mickaël. 'Les frères Le Nain à l'heure du marché de l'art; l'invention de la noble "gueuserie".' In Nicolas Milovanovic and Luc Piralla-Heng Vong, eds. *Le Mystère Le Nain,* pp. 33–41. Lens: Musée du Louvre-Lens, 2017.

Thompson, Patrice. 'Essai d'analyse des conditions du spectacle dans le Panorama et le Diorama.' *Romantisme* 38 (1982), 47–64.

Tillerot, Isabelle. *Jean de Jullienne et les collectionneurs de son temps: un regard singulier sur le tableau.* Paris: Editions de la Maison des sciences de l'homme, 2010.

Tillerot, Isabelle. 'Graver les dessins de Watteau au XVIIe siècle.' In Emmanuelle Delapierre and Sophie Raux, eds. *Quand la gravure fait illusion: Autour de Watteau et Boucher, Le Dessin Gravé au XVIIIe siècle,* pp. 27–31. Valenciennes: Musée des Beaux-Arts, 2006.

Tillier, Bertrand. 'Jules Janin, chiffonnier, antiquaire et naturaliste de Paris.' *Revue d'histoire littéraire de la France* 118:3 (2018), 599–610.

Todorov, Tzvetan. *On Human Diversity: Nationalism, Racism and Exoticism in French Thought.* Trans. Catherine Porter. Cambridge, MA: Harvard University Press, 1993.

Trauner, Alexandre. *Alexandre Trauner, Décors de cinéma, entretiens avec Jean-Pierre Berthomé.* Paris: Jade-Flammarion, 1988.

Turk, Edward Baron. *Child of Paradise: Marcel Carné and the Golden Age of French Cinema.* Cambridge, MA: Harvard University Press, 1989.

Turner, Victor. *From Ritual to Theater: The Human Seriousness of Play.* New York: Performing Arts Journal Publications, 1982.

Turner, Victor and Edith Turner. 'Performing ethnography.' *Drama Review* 26:2 (1982), 33–50.

Tynna, J. de la. *Almanach du Commerce de Paris, des Départements de l'Empire Français, et des Principales Villes du Monde.* Paris, L'an VII – 1808.

V., J. *Notice biographique sur M. Paul le Grand, successeur de Deburau au théâtre des Funambules, par l'auteur de Pierrot Marié.* Paris: Gallet, 1847.

Vaillancourt, Daniel. 'Le spectacle du lieu public: éléments d'esthétique urbaine.' In Marie-France Wagner and Claire Le Brun-Gouanvic, eds. *Les arts du spectacle dans la ville (1404–1721)*, pp. 205–36. Paris: H. Champion, 2001.

Verhagen, Marcus. 'The poster in *fin-de-siècle* Paris: "that mobile and degenerate art".' In Leo Charney and Vanessa R. Schwartz, eds. *Cinema and the Invention of Modern Life*, pp. 103–29. Berkeley: University of California Press, 1995.

Verlet, Pierre. 'Le commerce des objets d'art et les marchands merciers: à Paris au XVIIIe siècle.' *Annales, Histoire, Science Sociales* 13:1 (1958), 10–29.

Vidal, Mary. *Watteau's Painted Conversations, Art, Literature, and Talk in Seventeenth and Eighteenth Century France*. New Haven, CT: Yale University Press, 1992.

Vinck, Carl de. *Place du Carrousel*. Paris: Société d'Iconographie Parisienne, 1931.

Vouilloux, Bernard. 'Champfleury, ou l'écrivain-collectionneur en chiffonnier.' *Revue d'histoire littéraire de la France* 118:3 (2018), 623–36.

Waters, Catherine. *Commodity Culture in Dickens's Household Words: The Social Life of Goods*. Aldershot: Ashgate, 2008.

Walsh, Claire. 'Shop design and the display of goods in eighteenth-century London.' *Journal of Design History* 8:3 (1995), 157–76.

Wechsler, Judith. *A Human Comedy: Physiognomy and Caricature in Nineteenth Century Paris*. Chicago: University of Chicago Press, 1982.

Weigert, Roger-Armand. 'Sur les Larmessin et les costumes grotesques.' *Nouvelles de l'estampe* 2 (1969), 67–75.

Welch, Evelyn S. *Shopping in the Renaissance: Consumer Cultures in Italy, 1400–1600*. New Haven, CT: Yale University Press, 2005.

Wicky, Éricka and Kathrin Yacavone. 'Introduction: *portraitomanie* and intermediality in nineteenth-century France.' *L'Esprit Créateur* 59:1 (2019), 1–11.

Wile, Aaron. 'Watteau, reverie, and selfhood.' *Art Bulletin* 96:3 (2014), 319–37.

Wile, Aaron. 'Blackface in Watteau's *The Italian Comedians*?' National Gallery of Art Blog, 5 August 2021, www.nga.gov/blog/blackface-in-watteaus-italian-comedians. html, accessed 28 April 2023.

Willems, Philippe. 'Between panoramic and sequential: Nadar and the serial image.' *Nineteenth-century Art Worldwide* 11:3 (2012), www.19thc-artworldwide.org/autumn 12/willems-nadar-and-the-serial-image, accessed 28 April 2023.

[Willette, Adolphe]. *Adolphe Willette 1857–1926*. Exhibition catalogue. Paris: Lienart éditions, 2014.

Williams, Alan. *Republic of Images: A History of French Filmmaking*. Cambridge, MA: Harvard University Press, 1992.

Williams, Rosalind H. *Dream Worlds: Mass Consumption in Late Nineteenth-Century France*. Berkeley: University of California Press, 1982.

Williamson, Elaine. 'A *vraie–fausse* statue of William the Conqueror: representation and mis-representation of Anglo-French History.' *Franco-British Studies* 19 (1995), 21–5.

Wilson, Bronwen. 'Reproducing the contours of Venetian identity in sixteenth-century costume books.' *Studies in Iconography* 25 (2004), 221–74.

Wilson-Bareau, Juliet. 'Manet and Spain.' In Gary Tinterow and Genevieve Lacambre, eds. *Manet/Velazquez: The French Taste for Spanish Painting*, pp. 203–51. New York: The Metropolitan Museum of Art, 2003.

Winock, Michel. *Édouard Drumont et Cie: antisémitisme et fascisme en France*. Paris: Éditions du Seuil, 1982.

Winock, Michel. *La France et les Juifs, de 1789 à nos jours*. Paris: Éditions du Seuil, 2004.

Wintermute, Alan. 'Le pèlerinage à Watteau: an introduction to the drawings of Watteau and his circle.' In Alan Wintermute, ed. *Watteau and his World: French Drawing from 1700–1750*, pp. 8–49. London: Merrell Holberton, 1999.

Wisner, David A. 'Jean Naigeon at the Dépôt de Nesle.' *Journal of the History of Collections* 8:2 (1996), 155–65.

Wrigley, Richard. 'Between the street and the salon: Parisian shop signs and the spaces of professionalism in the eighteenth and early nineteenth centuries.' *Oxford Art Journal* 21:1 (1998), 45–67.

Wrona, Adeline. 'Des Panthéons à vendre: le portrait d'homme de lettres, entre réclame et biographie.' *Romantisme* 155 (2012), 37–50.

Wyngaard, Amy. 'Switching codes: class, clothing, and cultural change in the works of Marivaux and Watteau.' *Eighteenth-Century Studies* 33:4 (2000), 523–41.

Yacavone, Kathrin. 'George Sand and Nadar: portraiture between lithography, sculpture, and photography.' *L'Esprit Créateur* 59:1 (2019), 111–27.

Yates, Frances. *The Art of Memory*. London: Penguin, 1966.

Yoshida, Noriko. 'Jules Chéret et la critique d'art de Roger Marx à Gustave Kahn.' In Réjane Bargiel and Ségolène Le Men, eds. *La Belle Époque de Jules Chéret: De l'affiche au décor*, pp. 109–19. Paris: Les Arts Décoratifs/Bibliothèque nationale de France, 2010.

Index

Titles of artworks and literary works are under the names of artists and authors. Figures are indicated by page numbers in italics. Plates are indicated by pl. followed by the plate number.

Nadar (*cont.*)
  in dispute with Champfleury 117–18
  exhibition at Universal Exposition 137,
    140
  full-length figures, use of 152
  Gérôme's painting based on Pierrot
    photograph by 10–11
  hot air balloon, photographs taken
    from 152, 164
  influence of 13
  Invitation to a 'Feste Champestre' 152,
    153
  *Lanterne magique des auteurs et
    journalistes* 142, 143, 150, 160
  Panthéon 142–4, 144, 151, 165
  Paul Legrand 154–6, 156, 158
  Pierrot at 'Feste Champestre' 152, 153
  Pierrot ministre 145
  'Pierrot' photographs of Charles
    Deburau 10, 14, 109, 137–8, 140–1,
    145–61, 146–8, 162–4, 170, 212, pl.14
  as theatrical producer 151
Nanteuil, Célestin 107
Napoléon Bonaparte 14, 102
Napoléon III 138, 190
La Nature 165, 167
Nazi occupation of France 13, 15, 177–8,
  185–6, 199–200, 201–2
Nemeitz, J.C. 26, 27
Nerval, Gérard de 106–8, 111, 126, 142
  Petits châteaux de Bohême 108
Nesci, Catherine 126
Nodier, Charles 111

old-clothes sellers 1, 8, 15, 86, 99–100,
  116, 121–7, 124, 136n.133, 190–1,
  196–9
  see also *Children of Paradise* for
    character Jericho; Gautier,
    Théophile, for *Marchand d'habits*;
    ragpickers
Orientalism 107, 188
ornament prints 78–81, *80*, 84, 85,
  94nn.54–5, 95n.59
  see also cartouches
ornemantistes 65, 75, 77, 91n.6
Othello (play) 179, 189–90
Oudry, Jean-Baptiste 72
Ozanneaux: *Le nègre* 188–9

painting exhibitions as part of Parisian
  public life 139
Palacio, Jean de 13
Palais Royal 28, 30, 36
Panofsky, Dora 37
Panofsky, Erwin 21
panoramic literature/vision 99–100,
  115–16, 118, 120, 121, 126, 127
Panthéon Nadar 142–4, 144, 151, 165
pantomime
  fair theatres using 23
  luminous pantomime 164–5, 167, 168
  Orientalism reflected in 188
  revival in late 1890s 193
  in Théâtre des Funambules 109, 112,
    114
  truc from, used in early cinema 169
  'white pantomime' 189, 193–5, 202
  see also Comédie Italienne; Pierrot;
    specific actors who play Pierrot
parades (promotional skits performed
  outside theatres)
  on Boulevard du Temple in mid-1800s
    109
  in *Children of Paradise* (film) 8, 11, 177,
    178, 180
  at country homes 57n.17, 100
  early films as 168
  ecce homo motif and 38
  Janin's newspaper columns as 150
  as marketing approach 33
  as methodology 8–11
  painters' signs as 51–2
  Pierrot (Gilles) appearing in 8–12,
    9–11, 23–5, 54, 103, 167
  promotional posters as 165–8
  Tournachons' photographs of Pierrot
    as 149, 154
Parfaict brothers 51
Parisian fairs 13–14, 20–1, 22–8, 33
  see also Foire Saint Germain
Pathé 169, 178
Paulvé, André 178
Périer, Paul 149, 171n.12
personality 5–6, 55, 214
le peuple 111, 115, 133n.80, 189, 193, 195,
  201
Peyrotte, Alexis: *Acanthus leaf design* 79,
  80

EU authorised representative for GPSR:
Easy Access System Europe, Mustamäe tee 50,
10621 Tallinn, Estonia
gpsr.requests@easproject.com

www.ingramcontent.com/pod-product-compliance
Ingram Content Group UK Ltd.
Pitfield, Milton Keynes, MK11 3LW, UK
UKHW062135150726
7214IPUK00024B/418